**Series
Dräger
Foundation**

**FUTURE
FUTURE
FUTURE**

Volume 14

edited by
Paul Kirchhof
Donald P. Kommers

responsible: Sonja Lahnstein-Kandel

Germany
and Its Basic Law

Past, Present and Future –
A German-American Symposium

Nomos Verlagsgesellschaft
Baden-Baden

Die Deutsche Bibliothek – CIP-Einheitsaufnahme

Germany and Its Basic Law: Past, Present and Future; A German-American Symposium / ed. by Paul Kirchhof; Donald P. Kommers. – 1. Aufl. – Baden-Baden: Nomos Verl.-Ges., 1993
  (Zukunft; Vol. 14)
  ISBN 3-7890-2696-4
NE: Kirchhof, Paul [Hrsg.]; GT

1. Auflage 1993
© Nomos Verlagsgesellschaft, Baden-Baden 1993. Printed in Germany.
Alle Rechte, auch die des Nachdrucks von Auszügen, der photomechanischen Wiedergabe und der Übersetzung, bei der Dräger Stiftung.

Table of Contents

List of Abbreviations   9

Preface   11

Introduction   13

Part 1:
An Assessment of the Basic Law and its Political
Practice   15

Klaus Stern
General Assessment of the Basic Law - A German View   17

W. Cole Durham
General Assessment of the Basic Law - An American View   37

Donald P. Kommers
Comments on Part 1   65

Part 2:
Federalism   69

Peter Lerche
Principles of German Federalism   71

Arthur B. Gunlicks
Principles of American Federalism   91

Francis X. Beytagh, Jr.
Comments on Part 2   117

Part 3:
Representative Democracy   119

Helmut Steinberger
Political Representation in Germany   121

Walter F. Murphy
Excluding Political Parties: Problems for Democratic and Constitutional Theory   173

Donald P. Kommers
Comments on Part 3   207

Part 4:
Basic Rights and Liberties   211

Kurt Sontheimer
Principles of Human Dignity in the Federal Republic   213

John B. Attanasio
Personal Freedoms and Economic Liberties:
American Judicial Policy   221

Fritz Ossenbühl
Economic and Occupational Rights   251

Mary Ann Glendon
Comments on Part 4   283

Part 5:
The Basic Law and the Economic System   289

Horst Siebert
Principles of the Economic System in the Federal Republic – An
Economist's View   291

Reiner Schmidt
Principles of the Economic System in the Federal Republic of
Germany – A Legal View   311

Christopher S. Allen
Principles of the Economic System – An American View   339

Ellen Kennedy
Comments on Part 5   355

Part 6:
Special Contributions   363

Rudolf Dolzer
The Path to German Unity: The Constitutional, Legal and International Framework   365

Roman Herzog
The Separation and Concentration of Power in the Basic Law   391

Annemarie Renger
The Role of the Plebiscite in Representative Democracy   403

Warren E. Burger
200 Years of American Constitutionalism   407

William Rehnquist
Constitutional Courts – Comparative Remarks   411

Summary   413

Appendix   417

The Authors   419

Index   427

List of Abbreviations

FAZ	Frankfurter Allgemeine Zeitung (newspaper)
FRG	Federal Republic of Germany
AnwBl.	Anwaltsblatt
AöR	Archiv des öffentlichen Rechts
BGB	Bürgerliches Gesetzbuch
BTDrucks.	Drucksachen des Deutschen Bundestages
BVerfGE	Entscheidungen des Bundesverfassungsgerichts
BVerfGG	Gesetz über das Bundesverfassungsgericht
BVerwGE	Entscheidungen des Bundesverwaltungsgerichts
BWahlG	Bundeswahlgesetz
DJZ	Deutsche Juristenzeitung
DÖV	Die öffentliche Verwaltung
DRiG	Deutsches Richtergesetz
DRiZ	Deutsche Richterzeitung
DRZ	Deutsche Rechts-Zeitschrift
DStZ	Deutsche Steuer-Zeitung
DUZ	Deutsche Universitäts-Zeitung
DVBl.	Deutsches Verwaltungsblatt
EuGH	Gerichtshof der Europäischen Gemeinschaften
EuGRZ	Europäische Grundrechte-Zeitschrift
MDR	Monatsschrift für Deutsches Recht
Jura	Juristische Ausbildung
JuS	Juristische Schulung
JW	Juristische Wochenschrift
JZ	Juristenzeitung
HDSW	Erwin v. Beckerath u. a. (Hg.), Handwörterbuch
HdWW	Willi Albers, Karl Erich Born u. a. (Hg.), Handwörterbuch der Wirtschaftswissenschaft, erster Band 1977, zweiter Band 1980, dritter Band 1981, vierter Band 1978, fünfter Band 1980, sechster Band 1981, siebter Band 1977, achter Band 1980, neunter Band 1982
JA	Juristische Arbeitsblätter
JöR	Jahrbuch des öffentlichen Rechts
NJW	Neue Juristische Wochenschrift
NVwZ	Neue Zeitschrift für Verwaltungsrecht
RGBl.	Reichsgesetzblatt
SJZ	Schweizerische Juristen-Zeitung
StGB	Strafgesetzbuch
VVDStRL	Veröffentlichungen der Vereinigung der Deutschen Staatsrechtslehrer
ZRP	Zeitschrift für Rechtspolitik
ZaöRV	Zeitschrift für ausländisches öffentliches Recht und Völkerrecht
ZBR	Zeitschrift für Beamtenrecht

Preface

In the interest of international understanding, the Dräger Foundation has been sponsoring for almost two decades now various programs, conferences, symposia and publications in the areas of social and economic policy. One of its main purposes in this regard, beyond the level of officialdom, is to contribute to the strengthening of German-American relations.

In addition to a joint project with the Minda de Gunzburg Center for European Studies at Harvard University, we wanted to plan a special event in 1989 to commemorate the 40th anniversary of the Basic Law as well as the 200th anniversary of the United States Constitution. With this in mind, the Foundation - again in cooperation with an American academic institution - the American Institute for Contemporary German Studies at Johns Hopkins University, Baltimore-Washington, D.C. - organized a German-American conference on a variety of constitutional issues of concern to both coutries.

The centerpiece of the conference was the German Basic Law. Questions dealing with representative democracy, federalism, principles of economic order and political practice, viewed from German and American perspectives, highlighted the conference. An interdisciplinary group of distinguished scholars, joined by high-ranking persons in government and the judiciary took part in an intensive three-day exchange of ideas. In addition to Klaus Kinkel, state secretary in the Ministry of Justice - later Federal Minister of Justice and currently Germany's Foreign Minister - and the then Vice-President of the German Bundestag, Annemarie Renger, the participants included Professor Roman Herzog, President of the Federal Constitutional Court, William H. Rehnquist, Chief Justice of the United States, and his immediate predecessor as Chief Justice, Warren E. Burger.

The substantially revised papers of the German and American contributors who participated in the conference are included in this publication. During the preparation and organization of the conference, when the Dräger Foundation was simultaneously organizing a ground-breaking conference on East-West relations, no one had any idea of the significance that the year 1989 would have for the issues taken up by the conference as a result of the historic political changes that occurred before the end of the year and in the following years.

The fact that this German-American conference, held on the occasion of the 40th anniversary of the Basic law, took place at the threshold of the democratic revolution in the former GDR, hardly diminishes the topicality of the present publication. Already at the time of the conference, the question of the possible unification of Germany did not pass unmentioned – almost to the surprise of the participants. The Basic Law is at the center of public attention, not only with reference to German unity but also because it serves as a possible model for constitution-makers in various eastern European nations. The Dräger Foundation hopes and trusts that this book will be a learned and informative contribution to an understanding of this foundational document.

It is therefore a pleasure and an honor to be able to offer this book to a wider public audience in both German and English editions.

We wish to thank the two conference chairmen, Professor Donald P. Kommers, University of Notre Dame, and Professor Paul Kirchhof, Justice of the Federal Constitutional Court, for their efforts in soliciting and editing the conference papers. Needless to say, we are also grateful to all the authors of the essays and commentaries included in this publication. Finally, we extend our thanks to the Director of the American Institute for Contemporary German Studies of Johns Hopkins University, Mr. Gerald Livingston, and his staff for their dedication and cooperation in organizing the conference.

Dräger-Stiftung

Dieter Feddersen
Member of the Board

Sonja Lahnstein-Kandel
Director

Introduction

On the occasion of the 40th anniversay of the Basic Law, the Dräger Foundation, in cooperation with the American Institute for Contemporary German Studies, sponsored a German-American conference that took place in Washington, D.C. during October 23-25, 1989. The conference focused mainly on the respective German and American experiences with federalism and representative democracy, the common commitment of our two countries to fundamental rights, particularly personal and economic freedoms, the constitutional basis of our economic systems, and the issue of insuring the continued legitimacy of the Basic and its openness to a united Germany.

The principles of federalism, democracy, and the rule of law are widely recognized today as the basis of solid transatlantic relationships. These common values no longer need to be expressly invoked in our daily economic and technical exchanges nor in our cooperative entreprenurial and economic activity. They have become the working assumptions of constitutional life in both countries. However, since the state is always being called upon to take on new tasks and must deal with the legal relations between states in the face of changing circumstances, it will always be necessary to ensure that our constitutions remain open to new developments while being able to regulate their flow and to shape the future.

The constitution does not stand as an immovable object in the stream of change; rather, it stabilizes and directs change in a legally binding way. The constitution is like a tree in the storm of time, whose roots are firmly planted in a given place and preserved by its cultural environment; whose trunk visibly expands with the years and thus provides orientation to those who live under it; whose branches are flexible enough to withstand wind and weather without losing their firm attachment and proximity to the trunk; whose leaves are renewed every year in such a way as to restore the tree to the fullness of the preceeding Fall.

Perhaps we are at the threshold of a new era: the leaves are falling and many constitutional institutions and principles are in need of renewal, but the structures of the Basic Law must be secured. This Washington symposium has dealt with the question of the Basic Law's stability and flexibility over the last 40 years and its openness to the demands of the future in five stages. First, we have examined the enduring principles and fixed foundation of the Basic Law, now emphatically confirmed by German reunification. Second, we have considered the federal systems of both states along with the differences to be found in their functions and powers. Third, we have looked at representative democracy, an idea more than 2000 years old – it is the legitimating basis of the constitution, organs of the state and their decision-making procedures – but which in practice has had the capacity to transform itself in legal thought. Fourth, we have underscored the obvious importance of basic rights that the constitution grants to individual persons and citizens, above all their dignity and freedom as individuals, but also their freedom of action in the community, particularly their occupational and economic activity. Finally, the conference concerned itself with the impact of the constitution on the economic system, a particularly important area of constitutional law and reality in terms of the cooperation between our two counties.

Our two day journey through the Basic Law has given us many new insights into the constitution, not because we have been exposed to the variety and richness of the constitutional state as a whole, but rather because we have visited important institutions and have been guided by experts who live in these institutions and who have formed and given them shape. We have been in the company of builders and architects who manifest different styles of leadership, but who represent that same basic understanding of how to build a state. The reports included in this volume offer a comprehensive overview of as well as a backward glance at our Washington symyposium. Like a photo album it includes only shapshots but nevertheless rather clearly sets forth the ideas, concerns, and main arguments of the symposium.

With the publication of these proceedings, we hope to make sure that the core ideas of our constitution – seen from both German and American perspective – will deepen and appreciation of our state and force the constitutional state, with is solidity and reliability, deeper into the consciousness of the community of states.

The Editors

Part 1:
An Assessment of the Basic Law and its Political
Practice

Klaus Stern

General Assessment of the Basic Law – A German View

I. *Introduction*

We are gathered here at this German-American Conference to commemorate the 40th anniversary of the Federal Republic of Germany. Our distinguished conference chairmen have asked me to offer a general assessment of the Basic Law from a German point of view. I could not undertake this task without saying at least a few words about America's involvement in its creation. My American audience and friends should also regard this as a word of thanks from a German for all that the United States of America has given to the German people.

If it is true that Germans made major contributions towards the creation of the American federal state, it is just as true that the American people repaid their debt at the end of the Second World War, in particular to a defeated Germany, initially through the Marshall Plan, then through the guarantees of the North Atlantic Treaty, and finally - and most significantly – through the reorganization of the western zones of occupation and the creation within these zones of a freely elected government. The Basic Law of the Federal Republic of Germany would probably not have come about if America's policy toward Germany had not taken a new turn in the summer of 1946, a change documented mainly in the Stuttgart speech of the American foreign minister, James F. Byrnes. The idea of a new German federal constitution was born at that time.[1] However, a hard struggle was yet to occur between the three allied powers, not to mention the arguments that took place between Germans and the military governors, before the Parliamentary Council could meet in Bonn on September 1, 1948.[2]

The Parliamentary Council, convened to create the constitution, was not elected directly by the people. Instead, the popularly elected parliaments of the western occupied zones elected the members of the Parliamentary Council. Good reasons led the minister-presidents of the West German

Länder to their indirect basis of legitimacy in order to point out that a decision of the whole German people cannot be anticipated in this way.

Irrespective of the Allied conditions set down in the so-called Frankfurt Documents, all members of the Parliamentary Council, perhaps with the exception of two members of the Communist party, had a clear idea of the basic principles of this constitution. There was no doubt, as there had been after the 1919 Weimar National Assembly, about the kind of government they would produce. It would not follow the model based on government by commissars.[3] The western liberal, democratic constitutional states were the uncontested models. The ideas of American and Western European constitutional government shaped the political and legal ideas of the 70 men and women who produced the Basic Law in Bonn in just under 9 months.

The remarks of the Herrenchiemsee committee of experts – that is, the committee which paved the way to the Parliamentary Council – were entirely out of place. The views of Jefferson and Hamilton in creating the Constitution of the United States of America, said the committee, are »today for us at best of literary interest, but politically lacking in vitality.«[4] Precisely the opposite is true: The views of Jefferson and Hamilton were objectively significant and politically relevant to the Council.

In the last 200 years, liberal democracy and constitutionalism, shaped as they have been by the notion of basic rights, have become the main pillars of many states and the central ingredients of present German-American political and legal thinking. The Basic Law has been heavily influenced by the guiding ideas of the American Declaration of Independence of 1776, the American Federal Constitution of 1787, and the Bill of Rights in 1789.[5] With good reason we endeavored to use these principles as basic blocks in building a solid community of nations, even if we know that existing political systems contradict these principles.

The Basic Law of the Federal Republic of Germany has taken these basic constitutional principles and made them the pillars of the German state reorganized in freedom. Substantial parts of the American and German constitutions were constructed along the same lines. Let me describe these features as they appear in the Basic Law, a constitution which in turn has recently served as the model for several other European constitutions, such as those of Spain, Greece and Portugal. In view of the special lectures we will hear on German reunification and European integration, federalism, political representation, basic rights, and the economic system, I shall restrict myself to a discussion of the Basic Law's general features, although there will be some overlap in subject matter.

I want to turn my attention, first, to the importance of the Basic Law *as a constitution* and the constitutional jurisprudence that undergirds and supports it, for it is here that German and American constitutional thinking have the most in common. Second, I want to discuss the Basic Law's commitment to a democratic and social constitutional state, including its establishment of a *party* democracy, especially since certain divergencies between the right to establish laws and political reality have become apparent in this area, which are certainly not restricted to the Federal Republic of Germany. Third, I will try to assess the significance of basic rights which in truth constitute the centerpiece of constitutionalism in the Federal Republic of Germany. Finally, I will end with an overall assessment of the Basic Law.

II. *The Constitution and Constitutional Jurisprudence*

1. In their original deliberations, the creators of the Basic Law were confronted in many respects with the inescapable facts of Germany's past and of the German present embedded in international politics. Historical experience and the present situation therefore substantially determined the shape of the new constitution. In spite of the destruction and crimes of the Hitler regime - none of which could be glossed over - the German people were looking to the future. They set out to draft a constitution which would avoid the deficiencies of earlier constitutions and create a government based on human dignity and human rights - that is, a constitution that would create a basic liberal and democratic system, a socially oriented constitution, and a federal state which would recognize German unity and the importance of European integration, and with which all Germans could identify. If these goals were to be realized, the constitution could not be, first and foremost, a political document of a mere programmatic nature. Rather, its status and normative character would have to be upgraded. It would have to become a legal constitution in the strict sense, legitimized by the ultimate source of state power, namely the people.[6]

The division of Germany presented the first dilemma. The preamble and Articles 23, 116, and 146 have, in my opinion, furnished a good solution. The Basic Law would be a constitution having all the attributes generally attached to post-18th century constitutions while simultaneously underscoring its non-finality and the fact that it would be created by only a part of the German people. Thus the Basic Law would not be approved in a popular referendum, but this has been offset by a sort of plebiscite through a number of general elections since 1949, the results of which always came out impressively in favor of the established constitutional parties.[7]

2. Although the Basic Law has been amended 35 times in the last 40 years, it does not represent a typically unstable constitution. Although set up as a »transitional state« for a reunified Germany, it was nevertheless designed from the outset as a genuine constitution, to bring about as it were a »perfect provisional solution« (B. Freudenfeld) for a divided nation. Conditions laid down by the allies did result in certain deficiencies in the Basic Law with respect to military and emergency situations. These deficiencies, however, were finally corrected in 1954-56 and 1968, resulting in a »constitution made whole.«[8] Only the budgetary and financial provisions of the Basic Law underwent further substantial changes, in 1967 and 1969. In general, other changes in the distribution of governmental authority did not affect the essential core of the Constitution.[9]
Things would have been different if certain suggestions of the Bundestag's Constitutional Reform Inquiry Commission of the 70's and the blue-chip commission on »government objectives and legislative tasks« of the early 80's had been accepted.[10] However, there is no longer any thought of implementing their suggestions except perhaps for the inclusion in the Basic Law of environmental protection as a state objective.[11] And so, the number of constitutional amendments made since 1949 does not permit an adverse judgment on the quality or durability of the constitution. Its basic principles and structural decisions have survived unchanged, and they have proven successful.

3. Following the American constitutional tradition, the Basic Law provided from the very beginning a state system subject to law. The Constitution was adopted as a law of paramount obligation to which all other law was – and is – subordinate. It has perhaps become more than anywhere else *the* legal rule of legal rules, and reference to it is deemed good style in politics. (As an aside, the fact that this is sometimes too much of a good thing is illustrated in the witty remark that one becomes »a little expert« on the Constitution if he or she proves that a certain rule contradicts the Basic Law and a »great expert« if he or she shows that it cannot be implemented because it contravenes »the eternity clause« of Art. 79, par. 3, of the Basic Law). As »fundamental law« it lays down the organizational structure of the

state, sets the limits of state power, guarantees the fundamental rights of individuals and citizens, and, finally, sets forth certain state objectives.

Article 20, par. 3, of the Basic Law requires that legislation conform to the constitutional order as well. Moreover, Art. 1, par. 3, of the Basic Law emphasizes that basic rights are binding upon the legislature as directly valid law. »Soft law,« however it is defined, is in principle outside of the Basic Law.[12] In this manner, the constitution takes on central significance for the legal system as a whole. State power may only be exercised in conformity with the Constitution.

The Basic Law, then, lays claim to a comprehensive validity, for it directly shapes the political and social life of the community, a feature that is new to German constitutionalism. Confidence in German constitutional law remains unshaken after 40 years of the Basic Law. Therefore, in whatever light the 40th anniversary is viewed, this German constitution has been celebrated as a stroke of luck for German history.[13] It must be added, however, that the actual litmus test has not yet been applied because there have been no real constitutional crises. The Federal Constitutional Court has settled the few major cases of conflict with prudence and skill, and the state has not languished against the backdrop of Germany's highly developed constitutional consciousness.[14]

4.   In speaking of the Federal Constitutional Court, I refer to the institution which has breathed the most life into the letter of our constitutional law - that is, the tribunal entrusted with the resolution of constitutional disputes. Viewed by the Basic Law as »a guardian of the constitution,« it has performed an enormous task of interpretation in its 38 years of operation. There are almost 80 volumes of official judgments together with preliminary rulings and memorandum decisions handed down by the various three-judge committees - they are now called »chambers« - as provided by § 93a of the Law on the Federal Constitutional Court. One would think that all areas of constitutional law would have been adjudicated by now. Yet Roman Herzog (current President of the Federal Constitutional Court) has discovered some »blank spots on the map of constitutional adjudication.«[15] We shall not be concerned with that here nor with the multiplicity of declarations coming out of Karlsruhe, but rather with the key function that constitutional jurisprudence usually assumes in the process of constitutional interpretation and the improvement of constitutional law.

At this point, it is unnecessary to consider Charles E. Hughes's observation that »The Constitution is what the judges say it is,«[16] an exaggeration to be sure but nonetheless essentially regarded as true even in the Federal

Republic of Germany. Let me put it another way: the authority of the Federal Constitutional Court and the constitutional courts of the Länder is such that their judgments are observed in areas of law and politics well beyond what is required by the legally binding force of § 31 of the law on the Federal Constitutional Court, even if on occasion experts and politicians sharply criticize their judgments.[17] However, we do not have a government of judges.[18] What has evolved is that which was expressed by the Parliamentary Council and which could also be said about the Supreme Court of the United States of America: »The foundation of the state is at stake here: Law is either recognized as the basis of human society and enforced with the necessary guarantees for its implementation, or political expediency will rule the day, leading once again to the dangerous fundamentalist dogmas of the past where law is reduced simply to what benefits the people or the government or the state.«[19]

In this light, constitutional jurisdiction in the Federal Republic of Germany embraces a wide area of competence, including the review of laws in terms of their constitutionality and the constitutional complaints of ordinary citizens. The Constitutional Court's competence to hear disputes between branches and levels of government, to supervise legal rules, to ban political parties, to hear election disputes, and to pass on constitutional complaints has resulted in an extensive constitutional jurisprudence unparalleled throughout the world.

In practice, this extensive jurisdiction means that any constitutional matter may be brought before the Court in any form. Ordinary citizens especially have come to rely on the Court for the vindication of their rights. Despite procedural barriers and a variety of brakes developed by the Court, the ordinary citizens do not usually consider their cases fully resolved until a decision comes down from the Constitutional Court. Just under two percent of all constitutional complaints have been successful, yet the Court has an impressive record in monitoring basic rights, a process that has had an obvious effect on political figures. Karlsruhe is taken into account in all legislative procedures; even *obiter dicta* are taken seriously and often weighed very carefully. Occasionally, this results in sharp conflicts between the Court and the legislature, as the decisions on abortion and on the right to informational self-determination have shown.[20]

Yet the Federal Constitutional Court has by and large exercised restraint towards the legislature. The dogmatic basis of this restraint - one that also prevails in American constitutional law - is the Court's tendency to construe laws consistent with the constitution as opposed to declaring them unconstitutional.[21] In the case of Germany, especially when called upon to

22

adjudicate equal protection claims, the Court follows the practice of holding a statute unconstitutional but not null and void, while simultaneously appealing to the legislature to remove the offending classification.[22] In this way, the Court manages to walk the narrow tightrope between politics and judicial control.[23]

III. *Constitutional State, Welfare State and Parliamentary Democracy*

Articles 20 and 28 of the Basic Law define and constitute the Federal Republic of Germany as a social constitutional state and as a (parliamentary) democracy. The party-state nature of German democracy has been manifested less through the incorporation of political parties into the Basic Law, as provided by Article 21, than through their actual and constantly growing role. Together with the founders' decision in favor of a republic and a federal state, the growth and maturity of the party system has helped to shape the states's structure. Article 79, par. 3, of the Basic Law lays down the governing principles of the constitutional order and even limits the extent of constitutional change. Just as 70 years ago the Weimar Constitution declared an end to the Empire in favor of the Republican State form, the Basic Law not only encompasses the concept of the Federal State, but also establishes the constitutional state, the welfare state, and democracy as the essential ingredients of the existing state structure.

1.   The concept of the legal, as opposed to the power, state is a product of a specifically German etymology virtually 200 years old. Its content is familiar in Europe and in America, even if under different names. The Basic Law associates it with the guarantee of basic rights, in particular the rights of freedom and equality, as well as the principle of political cooperation, division of power, the rule of law, judicial independence, and a system of compensation with justly acquired rights in the event of state interference or misconduct, the result being a state based on the principles of proportionality, justice, and legal certainty. Constitutionalism means not only a formal constitution in which law governs, but also a material constitution which incorporates substantive values and insures their protection in law. All of this is undisputed in theory and substantiated by a wealth of literature and jurisprudence.[24]

23

Nevertheless, three months ago a high German judge, the presiding judge of the Federal Administrative Court in Berlin, read an anniversary paper entitled, »The 40 Year-Old Constitutional State Under the Basic Law: More Shadow than Light?« Citing numerous examples of dangers to constitutionalism, he was extremely critical of the modern state.[25] He concluded that »even a well-meaning observer must worry about how the constitutional state appears in many respects today. ...«[26] Is there in fact a gap between constitutional theory and the reality of the constitutional state?

Constitutional deficiencies are unavoidable. The *res publica* will always need to be improved in the light of the constitutional ideal. This is also true of the Federal Republic of Germany and its Basic Law, of which so much is expected by government bodies and citizens, and in which material constitutionality is also »an idealistic concept of fundamental importance to German constitutional development.«[27] Constitutionalism is a principle of the highest rank, especially in Germany where it was trampled underfoot in a frightening way between 1933 and 1945. It places great demands on politics and people in the community, demands which neither has always been able to meet. Three fundamental dangers to the principle of constitutionalism have become apparent in recent times, giving cause for the warning, »*Videant consules, ne quid res publica detrimenti capiat.*«

a)   Constitutionalism becomes problematic when, owing to the abundance of legal rules, the law is no longer recognizable. This is not only a matter of law as such, but in particular a matter of the quality and quantity of laws.[28] The law, about which much both good and bad has been written over the centuries, and the method of passing laws must be reconsidered. At some point everyone has been victimized by the flood of laws: citizens, entrepreneurs, parliament, executive authorities, and the courts. At the same time, however, the latter have also caused the hypertrophy of legislation. To safeguard the constitutional state, one must probe the depths of various areas of law and remove the excesses so that law becomes stable, reliable and calculable again. This is certainly easier said than done, yet it must be done if, for example, tax law or social law are not to become completely obscure. These observations lead to the central question of what the law can actually achieve, which has yet to be answered.

b)   The abundance and complexity of laws inevitably leads to weaknesses and deficiencies in their application. Often mentioned examples are the areas of environmental[29] and tax law.[30] Problems associated with environmental law, for example, will not be solved by including environmental

24

protection as a state objective in the constitution, but rather through the convincing interpretation of applicable law. In tax law, on the other hand, no one, whether revenue officer, tax attorney, expert, or ordinary citizen, is in a position to enforce tax justice. Here is a legal emergency which, as the voluntary financing of political parties has shown, casts doubt on and causes one to despair of the constitutional state.[31] Judicial clarification is usually lengthy[32] and often only partially removes legal deficiencies; sometimes it even creates new problems.

c) Unclear laws cast doubt on the obedience and loyalty of citizens towards law. They burden the courts if the citizen begins fighting for his rights or if at best they lead to »limited infringements of the rules« or at worst to what is called in veiled language »civil disobedience,«[33] a presumed right to resist decisions by democratic majorities.[34] Obedience to the law is a fundamental obligation in a constitutional state,[35] and the constitutional state has many built-in safeguards to accomplish this. Behind what is euphemistically called a »limited infringement of the rules,« there lies in reality a »decline in legal consciousness« caused by the »general loss of authority of the law«, which is a fundamental challenge to the constitutional state.[36] The authority of the law will be restored more easily if citizens are made aware of the fact that for the government also loyalty to the law is to be preferred to its breach.

What explains these current challenges to the constitutional state? They might be associated with the increasing absence of ethical thinking in law.[37] In the absence of a legal consciousness rooted in respect for law and the constitution – the two requirements for peace – and in the absence of recognizing the State's monopoly of force, the constitutional state is in a precarious position.

2. In the case of the constitutional state, the Basic Law was able to continue a long tradition. The constitutional declaration in favor of the social welfare state is a somewhat new approach, equivalent to some extent to the notions of »general welfare« or »public welfare« which appeared in state constitutions before 1946. This does not mean that earlier states had no social awareness; social thinking and action were extremely widespread in Prussia. However, the Basic Law's social welfare proclamation initially presented the interpreters of the constitution with the puzzle as to whether or not it was to be understood as binding constitutional law, especially since the history of its origins yielded virtually no clues.[38] Nowadays, a welfare state objective is familiar to many constitutions,[39] even if it is not expressly

written into the text of the constitution, and in practice social welfare has become a basic plan of liberal democratic states. In Europe, as the preamble and Article 2 of the European Economic Community Treaty shows, the idea of social welfare has had a powerful impact on the development of the European Communities.

Still, after 40 years, the concept is not as sharply defined as the constitutional state. The term »social« can be interpreted in many ways. For this reason, the welfare state principle of the Basic Law poses the »danger of politically opportunistic claims«[40] justifying all possible demands on the state and bringing about a questionable »attitude of demanding« and a »mentality of avoiding responsibility« on the part of the individual or of whole groups.[41]

Despite numerous scholarly efforts to clarify the meaning of the welfare state principle, a convincing material definition has not yet been formulated. Agreement exists only in the most general sense of being oriented towards social justice, social security and a fair and just social and economic system. Nevertheless, this is little more than a guideline or directive which the legislative body must define more precisely.[42] The welfare state clause is constitutional law's way of responding to questions posed by a pluralistic, industrially organized mass society based on a division of labor.[43]

Hence, the social welfare state principle acts as an open-ended concept subject to almost any varying interpretation. The Länder constitutions define basic social rights in abundance, but in the final analysis this is unfruitful because their realization comes up against virtually insurmountable legal problems. The Federal Constitutional Court has declared that as a declaratory proposition of the Basic Law, it sets »the state a task but does not describe how this task should be achieved.«[44] The social state principle is directed mainly at the legislator who must have political leeway in shaping the meaning of »social.« For the executive and judicial branches, the social welfare principle is primarily a guideline for interpreting the application of laws. The constitutional state aims simply to guarantee freedom with security. In the last four decades, the Federal Republic of Germany has fulfilled this great normative claim.

3. The Weimar Republic's Constitution provided for referenda and plebiscites (Articles 73 and 76), together with the direct election of the Reich president (Article 41).[45] The Basic Law, by contrast, opted for a strictly parliamentary democracy. Unlike the majority of Länder constitutions, forms of direct democracy were not instituted at the federal level

(except in the case of regional reorganization as provided by Article 29 of the Basic Law), a consequence of the Weimar and the National Socialist experiences. In the final analysis, therefore, the people influence public policy only through elections, and they have often been called upon to vote at the federal, state and local level and, since 1984, even at the European level. Herein lies a certain »mediafication« of the people, which has promoted the strength of the parties and has given unimagined influence to the media, particularly television, bringing the term »telecracy« into common usage.

In 1974, on the occasion of the 25th anniversary of the Basic Law, H.P. Ipsen wrote that »the democratic principle is being challenged from a variety of directions.«[46] This was in the heyday of efforts at democratization in such areas of society as the economy, university, school, and other training and educational establishments, and of the demand for reorganization of the system of representation by imperative mandates, for reinforcement of the power of association, in particular that of unions, and for the institutionalization of social power in economic and social councils in addition to parliaments. Fifteen years later, in 1989, hardly any attention is being paid to the principle of democracy in most situations. Is it therefore in the best of health?

The worries of that time cannot be swept aside lightly. They have left their mark on our institutions but have not turned them upside down, as many had hoped. Their efficiency, however, has certainly not been improved. No economic and social councils were established[47] and parliaments have remained the sole elected representative bodies. Democratic legitimation rightly remained the right of the people and not that of any haphazardly created portion of the people,[48] but the dangers for parliamentary democracy today threaten from elsewhere.

a) The Constitutional Reform Inquiry Commission of the German Bundestag, established in 1971 to reassess the Basic Law – its membership consisted of seven members of the Bundestag, seven representatives appointed by the Länder, and seven independent experts – clearly rejected proposals in favor of referenda, plebiscites or the popular election of the Federal President.[49] Recently, and in particular with respect to so-called existential matters, there have been greater demands for direct popular decision-making.[50] Indeed, the argument goes, popular decision making is included in the concept of »voting« within the meaning of Article 20, par. 2, of the Basic Law.[51] In this context, there is repeated reference to the maturing process, which the people of the Federal Republic of Germany have experienced and which has supposedly made obsolete the »prudery of the Basic Law vis-a-vis direct democratic elements.«[52]

The reference to democratic maturing may be true, but the disadvantages of incorporating plebiscitarian components into the system of representation outweigh the advantages. The reasons for the inquiry commission's vote of rejection are still valid today: referenda neither strengthen nor satisfy the parliamentary system. They may, on the contrary, trigger greater polarization. Furthermore, such decisions by the people could only be corrected by another referendum which, in fast-moving times, would inevitably lead to considerable difficulty. If in 1973, at the peak of the oil crisis, there had been a referendum on the use of nuclear power, large numbers would definitely have voted in favor.[53]

b) The call for direct material decision-making power of the people is a sign of the people's dissatisfaction with their parliamentary representatives. In recent times, lack of enthusiasm and fading loyalty towards the established political parties – parties which have alternately held power since 1949 – have increased sharply. In a commemorative paper, Paul Kirchhof, writing about political parties said, in very measured language, that by bolstering the financial strength and independence of other parties, in terms both of their organization and personnel, the state seems to have contributed, at least to some extent, to a growing alienation from the nation and the electorate.[54]

The Vice-President of the Federal Constitutional Court expressed himself more clearly at the Cologne International Symposium on the 40th anniversary of the Basic Law.[55] In reality, the uneasiness of the citizen is demonstrated particularly in the number of nonvoters or protest voters who turned first to »left wing« and then to »right wing« parties. These parties see themselves primarily as movements, concentrating as they do on single issues or a partial political program.

It is undeniable that today the parties of the political center are declining in their standing and ability to handle problems. The number of political parties, which at first continuously declined, will, if appearances do not deceive, increase again. All parties, large or small, whether represented in parliament or not, obtain free television and broadcasting time,[56] and their election campaign costs are reimbursed if they win at least 0.5% of second ballot votes (see § 18 of the Law on Political Parties). If they win seats in parliament, they are certain to be awarded a number of offices and financially secure posts. If political parties were once the »partie honteuse« (G.

28

Radbruch) of German constitutional law, they now dominate parliament and government and share power in the fields of administration and jurisprudence, and particularly in the electronic media, since it has not been possible to keep these domains free of party-oriented actions.[57]

It is certainly true that no useful alternative to party democracy exists in Germany or elsewhere. Changes in the law can only partially compensate for the public's loss of confidence in political parties.[58] What is needed is more democracy within the parties, restraint in their appropriation of funds, reduction of office patronage, and more time devoted to the concerns of the citizen than to themselves. The stability of the parliamentary system of government gained through the constitution must not be put at risk politically. No democratic system is immune to »separating power from the welfare of the people and the marshalling of that power in the self-interest of its holders.«[59]

IV. The Influence of Basic Rights

Constitutionally, the social welfare state and democracy have retained a strong inner strength by virtue of the decision of the Parliamentary Council to incorporate »basic rights« into the Basic Law. These rights appear in Section 1 of the Constitution. This placement of basic rights at the forefront of the Constitution was deliberate, differing as it does from their placement in the Frankfurt Constitution of 1849 and the Weimar Constitution. In fact, basic rights have achieved an undisputed leading position in constitutional law and constitutional reality, a point in need of emphasis in any general assessment of the Basic Law. The constitutional norms guaranteeing basic rights in Articles 1 to 19 and 101 to 104 of the Basic Law have had effects on the government and society of the Federal Republic, the results of which the founders of the constitution could not have imagined in their wildest dreams. If the Virginia Bill of Rights and the French Declaration des Droits de l'Homme et du Citoyen acted as an impetus for many states of the old and new world, then the basic rights of the Bonn Basic Law have made it possible to bring the free part of Germany back into the community of democratic states and internally to form a state system in which people are guaranteed freedom, equality of rights, guarantees of justice, and participation in the development of the political consensus.

The most important elements of the Parliamentary Council's concept of basic rights were: (1) a commitment to the value of human dignity and guarantees of inalienable and inviolable human rights (Article 1, pars. 1 and 2) including those »traditional« rights of the individual; (2) the direct, binding effect of basic rights upon legislators (Article 1, par. 3); (3) the capacity of individuals to enforce their rights in courts of law (Article 19, par. 4, and, since 1969, Article 93, par. 1); (4) the prohibition on any interference with the essence of a basic right (Article 19, par. 2); and (5) the limits imposed on legislative interference with basic rights. The Chairman of the Parliamentary Council's main committee, Professor Dr. Carlo Schmid, explained early on that »basic rights must govern the Basic Law.«[60]

Like few other sections of the Basic Law, the bill of rights has, in the course of our constitutional development, entitled us today to speak of a constitutional state governed by basic rights and of a rights-oriented constitutionalism.[61] The Virginia Bill of Rights was once described as the »basis and foundation of government.« We can also now say that this has been achieved under the Basic Law. Basic rights have become the centerpiece of the system of community life in the Federal Republic of Germany.

1. This elevation of basic rights is due not only to the work of the scholarly academic community, but overwhelmingly to the jurisprudence of the Federal Constitutional Court. As early as the 1950s, the Court attached increasing importance to basic rights norms, which today are described in terms such as their »multifunctionality,« »multidimensionality« or »multilayering.«[62] It is not possible at this point to detail the complex dogmatic constructions which are associated with these norms. This much, however, may be said: in addition to those traditional subjective rights that protect individuals against state intervention, they embrace other important dimensions of rights best described in terms of their capacity to promote the *effective* exercise of basic rights and thus to reinforce the validity of such rights. In concrete terms, this means that basic rights may simultaneously embody:
- the guarantee of certain institutions, such as marriage and the family or private ownership;
- the radiating effect of constitutional values on the legal system as a whole, in particular their indirect application to private law;
- the state's obligation to protect certain legal goods, particularly the life and health of persons;
- organizational and procedural rules with respect to such matters as the structure and organization of the judiciary, administrative procedure, the universities, and the broadcast media.

2. In principle, these concepts are acknowledged in legal scholarship and judicial decisions, even though much of the detail is still controversial.[63] Particularly controversial is the extent to which individual rights can be derived from the practical substance of basic rights, particularly if they are directed against the legislator. In this respect, the Federal Constitutional Court has not yet found a standard approach.[64] It is obvious that this question will have an explosive effect in view of the latest developments in natural science, medicine and engineering. Examples are biotechnology and the nuclear industry.[65] How much security may or must the state guarantee to its citizens?[66] This question is likely to be a major rights problem in Europe and North America in the 1990's.

V. *General Assessment*

Let me conclude: it is an undisputed fact that the Basic Law is a successful constitution of the post-war period. This was certainly not its condition at the beginning; its creators gave birth to it within the framework of a defeated, divided, and economically devastated country. Its citizens had to contend with the worries and needs of everyday struggle, which were only somewhat alleviated by the recent currency reform.

Outwardly the product of a history too little determined by Germans, the Basic Law has nevertheless evolved into a genuine German constitution, the constitution of a German partial state which has already outlasted the constitution of the first German republic. What was started and failed in the Paulskirche in 1848-49 – the attempt of the Frankfurt Parliament to combine constitutionalism, individual rights, and national unity – was achieved in 1949 with the establishment of a liberal, democratic political system. The goal of the preamble »to accomplish the unity and freedom of Germany in free self-determination« was finally realized in 1990. Internally, a constitution was created which restricts governmental omnipotence, ensures the personal and political freedom of the individual, is committed to social justice, and gives the market economy a normative framework in which achievement is rewarded. In the genealogy of constitutions, the Basic Law is part of the common European-Atlantic inheritance with a wealth of intellectual, legal and political ideas with many roots.[67] The constitutional agreement struck in 1949 remains intact to the present day, though not without intermittent trouble. Nevertheless, the Basic Law has yet to weather real storms. Its judicial armory of protection is adequate, but the political force to use it must not weaken, particularly if threatened from within. A constitution of freedom must guard against losing the willingness to defend itself against the enemies of freedom.[68]

On balance, the results of the Basic Law after 40 years of experience are positive. It is the most liberal constitution that Germans have ever had. Not all the credit goes to the German people. The international East-West conflict, which brought the West closer than ever under American leadership, is partly responsible for the durability of German constitutionalism. This must never be forgotten, and those who did not experience the fateful years of Germany should be continually vigilant.

One notable aspect of the Basic Law is its commitment to internationalism, especially European Union, a far-sighted feature of its preamble and Article 24. It was thus possible tó harmonize the European Communities and the North Atlantic Treaty Organization with national constitutional law even if the consequence was a loss of sovereignty.[69] The march towards a strengthened European (political) union fostered by the Single European Act of 1986 – one that goes beyond economic union – however it is organized, will not change the fact that the Basic Law imposes a responsibility on Germans who now enjoy freedom in self-determination.[70] If Germans are to be faithful to the Basic Law and its grand purposes, they must meet the challenge of the future by using every opportunity available to them to embed Germany in a larger context of freedom and international cooperation.[71] The circle is completed at this point: the constitution of Germany was neither in past centuries nor in the four decades which we have reviewed here a problem for Germans alone. Even in the future, the unity of Germany in freedom requires the assistance of the friends we have made in the course of the young history of the Federal Republic of Germany.

Notes:

1 The Germans of course had their own plans for a constitution. See K. Stern, Staatsrecht der Bundesrepublik Deutschland, III/1, 1988, § 60 I 1. General Lucius D. Clay was alleged to have remarked, »Every leading German has a constitution in his pocket.« Quoted in J. v. Wagner, Der Parlamentarische Rat, 1948-1949, Akten und Protokolle, 1, 1975, p. XXVIII.
2 For further details see K. Kröger, NJW 1989, 1318; R. Morsey, DÖV 1989, 471; R. Mussgnug, HdbStR, I, 1987, § 6; R. Morsey-K. Repgen (eds.), Christen und Grundgesetz (1989).

3   As F. Naumann noted in the constitutional committee of the Weimar National
    Assembly: »The political question for us today is whether we will be dragged into
    the Russian Soviet-type constitutional framework or whether we will adopt the
    Western European-American model.« (Protokoll des Verfassungsausschusses,
    Aktenstück No. 391, p. 180).
4   Der Parlamentarische Rat, 1948-1949, 2, 1981, p. 73. see also B. Pieroth, NJW
    1989, 1333.
5   Cf. K. Stern, Grundideen europäisch-amerikanischer Verfassungsstaatlichkeit
    1984; H. Steinberger, 200 Jahre amerikanische Bundesverfassung 1987; W.
    Brugger, Grundrechte und Verfassungsgerichtsbarkeit in den Vereinigten
    Staaten von Amerika 1987.
6   As to the meaning of the Constitution, see K. Stern, Staatsrecht, I, 2nd ed.,
    1984, §§ 3 and 4; and J. Isensee and P. Kirchhof, HdbStR, I, 1987, §§ 13 and
    19.
7   R. Mussgnug, supra note 2 at § 6 Rdnrn. 100.
8   D. Grimm, NJW 1989, 1307; G. Robbers, NJW 1989, 1324 et seq.
9   Cf. H. Hofmann, HdbStR, I, 1987, § 7.
10 See the Final Report of the Enquete Commission on Constitutional Reform, Zur
    Sache 3/76 and 2/77 and the Bericht der Sachverständigenkommission
    »Staatszielbestimmungen – Gesetzgebungsaufträge« (Bundesminister des Innern
    und der Justiz 1983). See also D. Grimm, NJW 1989, 1305 and G. Robbers,
    NJW 1989, 1325.
11 See K. Stern, NWVBl. 1988, 1.
12 These parallel legal categories in international law. See F. Ermacora, Festschrift
    für W. Geiger, 1989, p. 145 et seq.
13 See especially the speeches of Federal President R. v. Weizsäcker, Bundestag
    President R. Süssmuth and Bundesrat President B. Engholm (Bulletin des
    Presse- und Informationsamtes der Bundesregierung, No. 51, p. 445 et seq. as
    well as D. Grimm, NJW 1989, 1305; B. Diestelkamp, NJW 1989, 1312; K.
    Kröger, NJW 1989, 1318; G. Robbers, NJW 1989, 1325; P. Kirchhof, JZ 1989,
    453; W.-R. Schenke, JZ 1989, 653; A. v. Mutius, 40 Jahre Grundgesetz –
    Erfahrungen und Perspektiven (Magistrat der Stadt Eckernförde, 1989).
14 See in this regard K. Stern, Festschrift der Rechtswissenschaftlichen Fakultät
    zur 600-Jahr-Feier der Universität zu Köln 1988, 845 (862 et seq.); see also K.
    Stern, NWVBl 1990, 1.
15 Festschrift K. Doehring, 1989, p. 323.
16 C.E. Hughes, Addresses, 1908, p. 139.
17 See, e.g., the quotations in K. Schlaich, Das Bundesverfassungsgericht, 1985, p.
    218.
18 Excessively harsh is the criticism in B.-O. Bryde, Verfassungsentwicklung,
    1982, p. 300.
19 A. Süsterhenn, Parlamentarischer Rat, Plenum, Stenographische Berichte, 25.
    See also the proclamation, which the resistance fighters planned to sign in case
    the attack on Hitler's life on July 20, 1944, would have succeeded: »Our first task
    is to reestablish the unimpaired majesty of the law . . . No human society can
    exist without law; no one, not even those who fail to honor the law can do
    without it.« (Beck-Goerdeler in W. v. Schramm (ed.), Gemeinschaftsdokumente
    für den Frieden, 1965, p. 233.

20 Cf. BVerfGE 39, 1 and 65, 1. With regard to the various judicial opinions on the constitutionality of abortion see D.G. Morris, 11 Hastings International and Comparative Law Review 159 (1988).

21 Cf. BVerfGE 2, 266 (282); 32, 373 (383); 51, 304 (323); 54, 251 (275); 64, 229 (242); 75, 201 (217); and 77, 263 (271). This point is made especially clear when the Federal Constitutional Court declares a law unconstitutional. »An interpretation in conformity with the Constitution ... is not possible.« See BVerfGE 71, 81 (105). See also BVerfGE 78, 58 (75).

22 Cf. BVerfGE 50, 290 (335); 56, 54 (78); 59, 119 (127); 65, 1 (56); 68, 155 (175); 73, 118 (181); and BVerfGE, NJW 1982, 869 (870).

23 Cf. K. Stern, Staatsrecht, III/1 1988, § 73 IV 3, 4; G. Püttner, Festschrift zum 125 jährigen Bestehen der Juristischen Gesellschaft zu Berlin, 1984, p. 573 *et seq.*

24 Cf. K. Stern, Staatsrecht, I, (2nd ed.), 1984, § 24. See also Ph. Kunig, Das Rechsstaatsprinzip 1986; E. Schmidt-Assmann, HdbStR, I (1987), § 24.

25 H. Sendler, DÖV 1989, 482. See also NJW 1989, 1761 and G. Püttner, DÖV 1989, 137. See also Ipsen, Starck, and Bachof.

26 See Sendler, ibid., at 487.

27 U. Scheuner in E. Forsthoff, Rechtsstaatlichkeit und Sozialstaatlichkeit 1968, p. 463.

28 Cf. K. Stern, Mehr Recht durch weniger Gesetze? in Rechtstatsachenforschung (Bundesministerium der Justiz, 1987), p. 15 *et seq.*

29 Cf. H. Hofmann in Die Zukunftsgestalten, 28 der Veröffentlichungen der Walter-Raymond-Stiftung, 1989, p. 37.

30 See Tipke-Lang, Steuerrecht (12th ed.), 1989, §§ 2 and 3. With regard to the necessity, basis, and suggestions for tax simplification see Karl-Bräuer-Institut des Bundes der Steuerzahler, 60 (1986).

31 J. Isensee, NJW 1985, 1007; W. Hill, Recht und Politik, 1984, 37; and Felix, MDR 1985, 457. See also H. O. Mühlleisen (ed.), Das Geld der Parteien, Parteienfinanzierung zwischen staatspolitischer Notwendigkeit und Kriminalität, 1986; H.G. Horlemann, DStZ 1988, 116; and W. Jakob (ed.), Die Förderung politischer Parteien über Spendensammelvereine, 1986.

32 For a discussion of related problems see P. Kirchhof, Festschrift K. Doehring, 1989, p. 439 *et seq.*

33 See especially P. Glotz (ed.) Ziviler Ungehorsam im Rechtsstaat, 1983; R. Wassermann, Rechtsstaat ohne Rechtsbewusstsein?, 1988; H. Klages (Wandlungen im Verhältnis der Bürger zum Staat 1988, p. 17.

34 On the significance of the right to resistance laid down in Art. 20, par. 4, of the Basic Law, see K. Stern, Staatsrecht, II, 1980, § 57; with regard to the right of resistance generally see D. Delwing, Schweizerische Juristenzeitung 1986, p. 289.

35 Cf. K. Stern, Festschrift K. Doehring 1989, p. 969 *et seq.*

36 For recent examples see J. Burmeister, Gedächtnisschrift W. Geck, 1989, p. 98.

37 F. Bydlinski, Fundamentale Rechtsgrundsätze, 1988, p. VII and H. Schambeck, Ethik und Staat 1986.

38 Cf. K. Stern, Staatsrecht, I, (2nd ed.), 1984, § 21 I 2 a, b.

39 See H.F. Zacher, HdbStR, I, 1987, § 25 Rdnr. 17.

40 E. Benda, HdbVerfR. 1983, p. 523.
41 K. Doehring, Gedächtnisschrift W. Geck 1989, 141 (150); J. Burmeister, *supra* note (36) at 102; H. Hofmann, Die Zukunftsgestalten, 28 der Veröffentlichungen der Walter-Raymond-Stiftung 1989, p. 32.
42 See K. Stern,»Sozialstaat,« Evangelisches Staatslexikon (3rd ed.), 1987, 3269; F.H. Schnapp, Sozialstaatlichkeit und soziale Grundrechte in der Bundesrepublik Deutschland in Politik und Kultur, 6 (1988), 22.
43 See P. Badura, *supra* note 42 at 492.
44 BVerfGE 59, 231 (263).
45 See W. Frotscher, DVBl 1989, 541.
46 DOV 1974, 289.
47 See K. Stern, JöR n. F. 25 (1976), p. 103.
48 See NW VerfGH, DVBl 1981, 216 (217). Another current development is aimed not at splintering the people electorally but rather at increasing the number of foreigners eligible to vote. See in this connection BVerfGE 83, 37 and 60 *et seq.*
49 Beratungen und Empfehlungen zur Verfassungsreform (I) in Zur Sache 3/76, p. 55; but see P. Krause, HdbStR, II, 1988, p. 313.
50 See the collective petition of around 100,000 citizens, Verh. des Deutschen Bundestages, 11 WP. 77. Sitzung am 5.5.1988, Sten. Ber., Vol. 144, p. 5251 *et seq.* and BT-Drucks. 11/2117.
51 See E. Stein, AK-GG, 2nd ed., 1989, Art. 20, pars. 1-3 II, Rdnrn. 39 *et seq.*
52 H. H. von Arnim, DOV 1985, 593 (603).
53 See the statements of legislators on the occasion of the passage of the Emergency Energy Law of 9.11.1973. (BT-Sten. Ber., 7. WP. p. 3833 *et seq.).* See also K. Stern, Energierecht im Widerstreit zwischen Bundes- und Landeskompetenz (Bochumer Beiträge zum Berg- und Energierecht, 1988).
54 P. Kirchhof, JZ 1989, 453 (457).
55 See the reports of H. Krüger, DÖV 1989, 768 *et seq.;* H. Siekmann, DVBl 1989, 866 *et seq.;* Chr. Pielow, NWVBl. 1989, Heft 10, p. IV. The reports and the discussions were published in 1990. See also K. Stern (ed.), 40 Jahre Grundgesetz: Bewährung und internationale Ausstrahlung, 1990.
56 Private broadcasters are opposed to these statutory requirements.
57 In 1985 the Association of German Public Law Teachers dealt with the topic, »Parteienstaatlichkeit Krisensymptome des demokratischen Verfassungsstaats?« See VVDStRL, Heft 44, 1986, p. 1 *et seq.* The crisis highlighted in the reports by M. Stolleis, H. Schäffer and R. A. Rhinow has intensified in the last four years.
58 It is difficult to regulate political parties by rules of law in the light of their internal dynamics. The regulation of party finances and legislative allowances have made this indisputably clear. See H.H. von Arnim, ZRP 1989, 257 *et seq.*
59 J. Isensee, HdbStR, III, 1988, § 57 Rdnr. 9.
60 Sten. Ber. des Plenums, p. 14.
61 See K. Stern, Staatsrecht, III/1, 1988, § 61 and 72 I 2.
62 *Ibid.*, § 61 IV 2 and E. Klein, NJW 1989, 1633 *et seq.*
63 K. Stern, *supra* note (6) at § 69. See also R. Alexy, Theorie der Grundrechte, 1985; G. Lübbe-Wolff, Die Grundrechte als Eingriffsabwehrrechte, 1988.
64 See also K. Stern, *supra* note 6, at § 69 VI 3.

65 See R. Lukes and R. Scholz, Rechtsfragen der Gentechnik, 1986; Chr. Enders in Mellinghoff-Trute (ed.), Die Leistungsfähigkeit des Rechts, 1988, p. 157 *et seq.;* P. Kirchhof, NVwZ 1988, 97 *et seq.;* R. Breuer, NVwZ 1988, 104; Chr. Rabben, Rechsprobleme der atomaren Entsorgung, 1988; K.-R. Luchow, Nukleare Brennstoffkreisel im Spiegel des Atomrechts 1988; N. Pelzer, Friedliche Kernenergienutzung und Staatsgrenzen in Mitteleuropa, 1987; D. Giesen, JZ 1989, 369 *et seq.* See also the reports of J. Ipsen, D. Murswiek and B. Schlink given at the 1989 meeting of public law teachers in VVDStRL, Heft 49, 1990, p. 1 *et seq.*

66 See J. Isensee, Das Grundrecht auf Sicherheit, 1983; D. Murswiek, Die Staatliche Verantwortung für die Risiken der Technik, 1985; and G. Robbers, Sicherheit als Menschenrecht, 1987).

67 See K. Stern, Grundideen europäisch-amerikanischer Verfassungsstaatlichkeit, 1984.

68 On the protection of the constitution see K. Stern, Staatsrecht, I, 2nd ed., 1984, § 6.

69 On the law of the European Communities see BVerfGE 37, 271; 52, 167; 73, 339; and 75, 223. With regard to NATO see BVerfGE 68, 1 and E. Klein, NJW 1989, 1633 et seq.; see generally K. Stern, Staatsrecht, III/1, 1988, § 62 III 9 b.

70 See E. Klein, Festschrift K. Doehring, 1989, p. 459 *et seq.*

71 See K. Stern, NWVBl. 1990, 1 *et seq.*

W. Cole Durham

General Assessment of the Basic Law – An American View

I. *Introduction*

Looking back over the past century, one cannot help being struck by the contrast of the periods following the two world wars. Where World War I seemed to mark the final sunset on a vanishing world order – the final severing of twentieth century life from a disappearing form of social life – the aftermath of World War II was a time of reconstruction. The harsh reparations required by the victors following World War I were supplanted by the Marshall Plan payments after World War II. The economic devastation of inflation and world depression in the twenties and thirties contrasts with the economic miracle of the fifties and sixties. Gleaming through everything else, at least in the West, was the emergence of a new constitutional order, symbolized perhaps most visibly by the West German Basic Law.

The »most visibly« in the prior sentence is an important caveat, because we can be blinded by the drama of high constitutional moments such as May 23, 1949, when the Basic Law was adopted. In many respects, the aftermath of World War II witnessed the emergence of a new constitutional order not only in West Germany, but throughout the West, including the United States. To be sure, the new constitutional order had its roots in Weimar and the New Deal, in the philosophy of nineteenth century liberalism, in the Enlightenment and the 18th Century revolutions, and in such towering figures as Locke and in Kant. It was heavily influenced at certain moments by the tensions of the cold war. In different countries, the constitutional fabric was woven from the threads of divergent histories and traditions. But fundamentally, constitutionalism had to confront the realities of a transformed social setting. Technological change, enhanced communication and modes of transportation, extended life expectancy, mass markets and mass politics – all of these factors and many others combined to make the setting after World War II much more complex and interdependent.

Post-World War II constitutionalism reflects not only the nature of the social world to which modern constitutional law must be applied, but perhaps even more significantly, the size and nature of the state that it constrains. *Sozialstaatlichkeit* has become an established ideal, to a greater or lesser extent, in most western countries. The liberal night-watchman state has been supplanted by what has been variously called the affirmative state, the performance state, the welfare state, or the regulatory state. A fourth branch of government – administrative bureaucracy – has grown up to handle the growing number of tasks assigned to government each year.

These complexities are treated in much greater detail in the Basic Law, but they are of course not unknown in the constitutional law of the United States. Because of the Delphic character of so many of the phrases of the constitutional text and the difficulty of the amendment process in the United States, it has been necessary to deal with such matters primarily through case law rather than by explicit constitutional revision. Yet the fundamental shift in the character of constitutionalism is evident in both countries. A new genre of constitutionalism has come of age, reflecting the heightened complexity of society and the broadened sphere of the state.

In what follows, I will explore several aspects of the German and American versions of late 20th Century constitutionalism. In Section II, I describe major features of this phenomenon. I use examples drawn from the church-state area in part because of their intrinsic fascination, and in part to avoid overlaps with treatment of similar themes in other papers. I am convinced, however, that the changes identified sweep across all of contemporary constitutional law, and my sense is that the other papers published in this volume support this thesis. In Section III, I argue that within the general setting of post-World War II constitutionalism, the German and American approaches to constitutional law embody competing visions of freedom. Finally, in Section IV, I reflect more generally on the nature of interactions between the constitutional cultures of the Federal Republic and the United States. German influence on American constitutional law has often been most significant, though not always fully obvious, at the level of theory, and it is perhaps at this level rather than at the level of concrete institutions and rules that one can continue to expect the most significant interactions of our legal cultures. In all of this, my aim is not so much to analyze developments in detail as to sketch the contours of a framework within which general patterns of commonality and contrast in the Federal Republic and the United States can be assessed.

II. Basic Features of the New Constitutionalism

Ideas of religious liberty and church-state arrangements are among the oldest features of constitutionalism. It was the birth of religious pluralism at the time of the reformation that ultimately pressed societies throughout the western world toward pluralistic, open and tolerant societies. The course of development in this regard has been marked by much travail and little alacrity, but religious liberty is now an axiomatic feature of constitutionalism. At first blush, it might seem that the sheer age of conceptions of religious liberty would make them unlikely candidates for a study of the new constitutionalism. But in fact, it is precisely in viewing the way that an old liberty has been actualized since World War II that one sees the characteristic marks of the new order.

Because religious liberty has been a key constitutional value since the adoption of the first amendment and before, we tend to forget how much of the American constitutional law in this area has been worked out since World War II. In fact, with a few notable exceptions,[1] virtually all of the Supreme Court decisions interpreting the religion clause of the first amendment have been decided since 1939. The explanation for this is straightforward: it was not until 1940 that the Supreme Court expressly held that the free exercise clause was applicable to the states as a result of incorporation in fourteenth amendment due process.[2] The establishment clause incorporation was not officially recognized until 1947.[3] Thus, the bulk of case law construing the United States religion clauses is not appreciably older than the Basic Law.[4]

What is true for the religion clauses is true for many other strands of our constitutional jurisprudence: many of the main features of contemporary American constitutionalism are not much older than the Basic Law. The rise of the new equal protection, with its strict scrutiny of suspect classifications and legislation that trenches on fundamental interests, is clearly a post-1950 phenomenon, as is the constitutionalization of criminal procedure. The expansion of the commerce clause as a basis for federal legislation commenced slightly earlier during the New Deal era, and has become a key constituent of post-World War II constitutionalism in the United States. Doctrines such as freedom of speech[5] and just compensation for takings of property have undergone fundamental revision. Finally, the emergence of deferential patterns of review with respect to social welfare, economic and regulatory legislation has operated as a kind of back-handed acknowledgement of the value of *Sozialstaatlichkeit*.

In the constitutional setting that existed prior to World War II, the federal government was a creature of genuinely limited powers, and the likelihood that it would trench on the religious or other liberties of an individual or group was quite remote. In the area of religious liberty, this is evidenced as much as anything else by the paucity of case law. The regulatory reach of federal legislation had not begun to expand, so there were few areas in which churches would feel the burdens of regulation. Welfare programs such as the Social Security system were in their infant stages. Federal aid to education had not begun. In general, Jefferson's »wall of separation« between church and state was not a hotly contested barrier. It was more like an isolated stone fence located on essentially vacant ground separating the domains of two land owners whose residences were in fact sufficiently separated that they seldom visited each other.

A.   The Federalization of Rights

Since World War II, four fundamental trends have combined to transform the bucolic image suggested by Jefferson's »wall of separation« metaphor: the federalization, the subjectification, and the judicialization of rights, and the growth of the state. The first of these, the federalization of rights, has already been implicitly mentioned. With the incorporation of the first amendment into fourteenth amendment due process, all state action encroaching on religious domain became subject to review under federal constitutional principles. Because federal constitutional issues can be raised in any court at any level in the United States (and need not be referred to a federal constitutional court, as in West Germany), the principles invoked in church-state disputes even in state courts came to be primarily the federal constitutional principles. The fact that the various states had their own constitutional regimes with respect to religious liberty and separation of church and state was largely forgotten, at least until recently,[6] because of the easy availability of federal remedies. Again, this change is evident in many areas. The constitutionalization of criminal procedure is one of the more obvious examples.

B.   The Subjectification of Rights

The idea of »subjectification of rights« needs some clarification. What I intend by this notion may be more readily apparent to German than Amer-

40

ican readers,[7] since Germans use the notion of subjective rights to distinguish claims an individual subject makes against the state (or others) from objective right (which refers to the legal order as a whole). By subjectification I do not mean the relativizing of rights – the notion that in a pluralistic society, rights are »subjective« in the sense that there is no objective measure of what the substantive content of rights is. Rather, what I have in mind is the rise of individual rights consciousness and the notion that the boundaries of liberty are staked out in terms of vindication of the rights of individual subjects.

The triumph of the subjectification of rights is evident at a superficial level in a rather trivial contrast in the structure of the United States Constitution and the Basic Law. The latter was drafted in a period when the focus on personal rights had become primary, and this fact is emphasized by the fact that the *Grundrechte* – the fundamental rights – are positioned at the beginning of the Basic Law. In contrast, the American Bill of Rights comes after (and was adopted after) the United States Constitution. There was considerable doubt and controversy at the time our Bill of Rights was proposed about whether it was necessary to spell out individual rights against a state with sharply limited powers. Primary protection of liberty was thought to be amply embodied in the articles that described the frame of government and enumerated (and thereby limited) the powers of the federal regime. Whatever the early American constitutional theory had been, however, it was clear by the 1940's that the key focus in protecting liberty was on protecting individual rights, and that emphasis has continued ever since.

The subjectification of rights is a key ongoing feature of our constitutional culture. Stated differently, one of the distinctive marks of post-World War II constitutional law is the shift from what could be called an »absence of power« perspective to a »rights« perspective. Instead of striving to protect liberty by showing there is an absence of power or authority for the challenged state action, litigants and courts focus on whether the threatened or injured individual has a constitutionally cognizable right. The most dramatic task of constitutional law is to spell out those rights and their limits.

This shift in constitutional law is well known and well-documented. In the church-state area it is probably most visible in free exercise cases. Today we tend to read the small number of pre-1940 free exercise decisions from the vantage point of the rights perspective. Thus, *Reynolds v. United States*,[8] the leading Mormon polygamy case, is seen primarily as the unsuccessful effort of an unpopular religious group to vindicate its free exercise rights. Interestingly, when *Reynolds* is read closely, it contains very little talk about rights, and the analysis is structured primarily in terms of appropriate spheres of power: the individual has full freedom of belief, but once belief reaches outward into action, the state is authorized to exercise its powers to protect traditional moral values. As in the *Slaughter-House Cases*[9] and *Munn v. Illinois*,[10] decided about the same time, the court was very hesitant to recognize any right that required striking down a state statute. Unlike contemporary free exercise cases, the *Reynolds* decision does not invoke a »balancing« test – the favorite intellectual construct in contemporary American constitutional law for analyzing claims about rights.

The contemporary approach is to assess first whether state action imposes a significant coercive burden on religion, and then whether there is a compelling state interest which cannot be achieved in some less burdensome way. The issue is no longer whether there is a sufficient basis for state action (because ample grounds for state action are now always available), but (to provide a few examples) whether a state's interest in mandatory education overrides the religiously-based interest of Amish parents in keeping their children out of public schools after the eighth grade (no),[11] or whether the military's interest in having a defined uniform outweighed the interest of an Orthodox Jewish officer in wearing a yamulke with his uniform (unbelievably, yes).[12] There is not time to expand on these and other examples. The point is that there has been a fundamental shift of emphasis in free exercise cases between the time of the *Reynolds* decision and the present. I do not wish to make too much of this point, since *Reynolds* was decided at a time when the Supreme Court was gradually moving toward the articulation of various rights.

Subjectification is perhaps less obvious in the establishment clause context, in part no doubt because that clause addresses the structural relationship between church and state and was originally designed, like other structural features of the American constitution, to foster individual liberty indirectly by setting limits to institutional power. That is, the establishment clause clearly stems from the era of »absence of power« analysis. Nonetheless, there is a drift toward subjectification. Rules regarding standing, despite recent tightening,[13] suggest that any taxpayer has a right to challenge an establishment violation.[14] Opponents of parochiaid, school prayer, bible reading, moments of silence, creation science, and so forth, all proceed to litigation as though their rights were being violated. And the tripartite *Lemon* test for establishment violations,[15] with its attention not only to state action that advances religion, but also to state action that inhibits religion, suggests that any departure from state neutrality toward religion may violate religious liberty rights.

The Basic Law's approach to church-state issues is arguably more subjectified in that it has no real corollary to the American establishment clause. Its requirement that »[t]here shall be no state church«[16] has never been construed in the expansive manner of the establishment clause to forbid anything which remotely smacks of state aid to or favoring of religion. This is mainly because the whole tenor of the church-state scheme in West Germany is more cooperationist than separationist, but it is nonetheless noteworthy that the Basic Law approaches religious liberty issues essentially from a rights perspective. One of the major puzzles of the early Hesse school prayer case,[17] which followed *Engel v. Vitale*[18] in holding school prayer unconstitutional, was how the court had extracted this establishment clause-type conclusion from a constitutional scheme lacking an establishment clause. When the issue ultimately reached the Constitutional Court, the justices in Karlsruhe were unable to perform the legal alchemy that the judges in Hesse had performed, and they accordingly adopted a more tolerant attitude toward school prayer.[19]

C.   *The Judicialization of Rights*

The subjectification of the constitutional law is directly linked to its judicialization. The pressure to provide precise answers to questions about the boundaries of individual rights calls almost inevitably for judicial solutions. But there is an even stronger tie. By the end of World War II, humanity had learned some indelible lessons about the need to find effective constraints for governmental abuse of power. Despite the risks of government by judges, felt most deeply within the civilian tradition, the post-World War II era has witnessed a pronounced convergence toward reliance on the »least dangerous branch« to control such abuses through judicial review.[20] The proliferation of constitutional courts and the growing reliance on judicial review to vindicate rights in a subjectified legal order – reflected in Germany by the establishment of the Constitutional Court and its burgeoning workload – is another hallmark of the new constitutionalism.

In a sense, the judicialization of constitutional law is an outgrowth of guilt – a recognition of things gone awry, and a symbolic (and hopefully effective) commitment to remedy past wrongs and make certain they do not recur. That is certainly a major theme of the Basic Law, and a major justification for the existence of the Constitutional Court. But note that it is also true of the United States in the post-war era. America had no holocaust, but it had a history of racism that courts began to dismantle beginning in the 1950's. The risk that minorities, whether racial or religious, will not be adequately protected by typical majoritarian processes is one of the strongest justifications for judicial review. The heightened pluralism of the late twentieth century means that more and more of us are part of some minority or other, and in any event, the need to protect pluralism from insensitive majoritarianism has reinforced the need for the judicialization of rights.

D. The Growth of the Affirmative State

The fourth factor that has transformed constitutionalism has been the growth of the state itself. To revert to the »wall of separation« metaphor, the old agrarian estates separated by an isolated wall have been subdivided, and buildings have been packed into all available space, leaving no open spaces, set backs, or side yards. There is no longer a sanitized boundary between public and private realms. In fact, the expansion of the state has gone further: the state is a pervasive matrix within which private enclaves seek to flourish. We are increasingly dependent on the state for everything from physical infrastructure such as roads, sewer, and water to social safety net institutions such as social security, medical care, unemployment coverage, and the like.

In many ways, the other three transformations in constitutional law are merely a result of the growth of the state. Federalization is merely one manifestation of the growth. Subjectification was a necessary response once state expansion occurred. As the state becomes pervasive, there is no residual buffer zone between the domain of individual rights and the domain of state power. The state seems to occupy all available space unless it is expressly excluded by individual rights. And in a state characterized by massive expansion of executive, legislative and administrative power, the »least dangerous branch« must expand if it is to be an effective counterweight.

One of the hazards of life in the expanded state is that traditional rights must be construed with sensitivity and creativity if they are to be protected from erosion by the growth of the state. For example, wooden reading of the establishment clause to exclude religious influence from any domain occupied by the state can result in a situation in which growth of the state presses religion into an excessively narrow corner - a result quite inconsistent with fundamental religious liberty concerns. This has been a concern in a variety of establishment clause cases, such as those involving whether religious groups should have »equal access« to public college or high school facilities as compared with that provided to other secular organizations, or those involving questions of the permissibility of religious exemptions to labor law regulations. I mention this problem because it seems representative of the larger issue the American and German systems have faced in connection with the new constitutionalism: how to reinterpret classical liberal values in the altered context of the affirmative state. This is a recurrent theme of the new constitutionalism, and strikes me as an area in which we have much to learn from each other.

III. *German and American Constitutionalism as Alternative Visions of Freedom in the Affirmative State*

A. *The Contrast of Facilitative and Privatizing Models of Freedom*

The features of the new constitutionalism I have identified - undoubtedly not an exclusive list - are obviously shared characteristics of the German and American systems. Yet there can be no doubt that German and American constitutionalism reflect fundamentally different visions of the ideal of freedom. Within each system, traditions of liberty are woven from a variety of different and often conflicting threads, but the dialectic of competing views in each system revolves around a different center of gravity.

1. *The German Facilitative Model*

The German approach is fundamentally more sympathetic to a conception in which the state plays a role in facilitating the actualization of freedom. Rather than being the key power that needs to be constrained if liberty is to be preserved, the state is seen as the vehicle for achieving freedom. This tradition, which I shall refer to as »facilitative freedom,« has deep roots in the German past,[21] and is manifested in a wide variety of current constitutional doctrines. It is a tradition in which freedom tends to be seen not as the polar opposite of community, but as a value that must be achieved in synthesis with community.[22] In this setting, it is natural for the state to assume a more affirmative role in actualizing specific constitutional rights.[23] The claims of *Sozialstaatlichkeit* and economic and social rights dovetail

45

more easily with this view of freedom than with the American counterpart. The »New Property« of Charles Reich[24] and minimum welfare notions of Frank Michelman,[25] trendy suggestions of the sixties that never took hold in the United States, might well have found a home in the German system.[26]

In a deep sense, the German system of facilitative freedom has strong affinities with Kant. The notion of dignity embodied in Article 1 of the Basic Law has roots in Kantian ethics.[27] Similarly, the tendency to think of constitutional law as embodying an objective ordering of fundamental values is consistent with the deontological cast of Kant's thought about the nature of republican institutions. Anti-utilitarian instincts in German adjudication also harmonize with the Kantian heritage. In contrast to Locke, Kant's derivation of private property and other institutions of freedom starts with a world of community, and asks how private holdings are individuated out of the common pool.[28] More generally, Kant thought of justice as »the aggregate of those conditions under which the will of one person can be conjoined with the will of another in accordance with a universal law of freedom.«[29] This approach, while making freedom and dignity central, connects them to concerns about a community of free persons. The effect of the social compact is for man to abandon the »wild, lawless freedom« of the Hobbesian state of nature »in order to find his whole freedom again undiminished in a lawful dependency, that is, in a juridical state of society.«[30] Genuine autonomy in this system will harmonize with reason and universalizable values; arbitrary private choice is mere heteronomy of the will.

2. The American Privatizing Model

In contrast, the American scheme, which I shall refer to as »privatized freedom,« remains deeply Lockean. The private sector is the domain of freedom. The state is a creature of delegated powers. Expanding the public sector means contracting the private sector, and thus, the liberty of individuals. That government which governs best is accordingly that which governs least. In the zero-sum ledgers of liberty, every affirmative obligation assumed by the state is offset by a reduction of liberty somewhere in the system. *Sozialstaatlichkeit* is hazardous to the health of privatized freedom. Property is acquired by mixing one's labor with portions of the material world sufficiently small that one can manage them. The only communitarian caveat is that »as much and as good« must be left over for others, and one shouldn't waste. But the world is large and relatively empty, and leaves plenty of room for individual initiative. Claims that there is something called rational autonomy, in which the claims of true morality come into

46

harmony with rational freedom, are illusory. There is nothing but the »wild and lawless« freedom of the state of nature, and claims to the contrary are nothing but disguised assertions of authority, which are even worse than heteronomy of the will, since they represent domination by others, not merely by one's preferences.

B. *The Example of the School Prayer Cases*

A few examples will suffice to show the residual hold of these basic orientations toward freedom. Consider first the contrasting treatment of the school prayer issue in the United States and the Federal Republic. In *Engel v. Vitale*,[31] the Supreme Court held that daily recitation of a non-sectarian prayer in public schools violated the establishment clause. The fact that participation in the prayer was not coerced and students who objected to the prayer could absent themselves from the classroom during the prayer was deemed irrelevant. Public controversy surrounding this issue has continued, and there was talk during the Reagan years of a constitutional amendment on this issue. A Louisiana statute which left school prayer to the voluntary actions of teachers was struck down on the grounds that a state employee (the teacher) was still sponsoring the prayer.[32] More recently, in *Wallace v. Jaffree*, the court considered an Alabama statute which authorized teachers to announce a moment of silence to be »observed for meditation or voluntary prayer.« In reviewing the legislative history of the statute, the Court found that the purpose of the statute was to endorse school prayer, and accordingly held the statute unconstitutional. Many believe that the Court might sustain a moment of silence statute adopted with less transparent motivation as a reasonable symbolic accommodation of the interests of believers.

While some of the early cases dealing with the school prayer issue in Germany reached similar results,[33] the outcome in the Constitutional Court was quite different. In the key decision on this issue, the Constitutional Court commenced its analysis by noting that parents have the right and duty under Article 6 of the Basic Law to raise their children according to their own beliefs.[34] From the beginning then, the Court takes into account the relationship of religious liberty to family values. The Court next pointed out that the question of school prayer must be analyzed in connection with school type.[35] This is an inquiry quite foreign to American constitutional law, since German constitutional law allows the Länder to elect to have confessional schools. The problem in the cases consolidated before the

Constitutional Court was that the students were attending secular community schools. The question was whether every aspect of the curriculum (except the religious instruction mandated by Article 7(3) of the Basic Law – again, a notable departure from American patterns) must be stripped of all matters of religious belief or world view. The very setting within which the analysis unfolds recognizes several respects in which religion can play a much stronger role in German schools.

The Court acknowledged that the school prayer was in effect sponsored by school,[36] but stated that »the role of the state is limited to providing an organizational framework within which school prayer requested by parents or students can occur.«[37] The Court held that so long as the rights of those with divergent beliefs are not injured, allowing a religious element within public schools falls within the range of choice the state has in choosing how to structure its schools. In the Court's view, Article 4 of the Basic Law protects not only the right to believe, but the right to confess that belief in public.

The Court next examined whether school prayer violated the rights of those who objected to the practice. The crucial issue here involved the relationship of positive confessional freedom (the freedom to confess one's belief) and negative confessional freedom (the freedom to avoid disclosing one's beliefs). In 1965, a Hesse court had held that since negative confessional freedom was an absolute right, but positive confessional freedom was necessarily limited, since it might impact on others, the negative confessional freedom of those opposing school prayer took precedence over the positive freedom of those desiring to participate in such exercises. The Constitutional Court rejected this analysis, reasoning that a reasonable accommodation of the the two competing interests could be found. Those not wishing to participate could be allowed to leave the room, or to simply remain at their seats and not participate. The Court acknowledged that this might put particular pressure on some children, and could in the worst case result in discrimination or ostracism. On the other hand, the court noted that the experience might provide the teacher with an excellent opportunity to teach the importance of tolerance and mutual respect.[38]

Like its American counterpart, the German school prayer decision is a lengthy and closely reasoned opinion. The decision clearly emanates from a very different church-state tradition than that which led to the decisions in *Engel* and *Jaffree*. The German tradition tends to think of church and state as joint bearers of the public order. This goes back to medieval theory, according to which the »two powers« – church and state – were joint bearers of the larger religious-metaphysical community of Christendom.[39] The influence of this idea is also evident in the so-called »coordination theory,« which dominated German thought on church-state problems well into the twentieth century.[40] According to this theory, church and state are institutions of equal rank, whose disputes and joint endeavors can be regulated only by mutual agreement through church contracts or concordats.[41] Despite the eventual demise of the »coordination theory«[42] and the steady liberalization of church-state relations in recent years, the notion that religion is an integral element of the public realm remains. The public corporation status of major denominations and the taxing power associated with this status are merely outer reminders of a deeper phenomenon.[43] The more tolerant attitude toward school prayer is a corollary. The state is a vehicle for actualizing religious liberty.

The American approach, with its much more stringent separationism, is a manifestation of American affinity for Lockean notions. Locke's *Letter Concerning Toleration* argued that state intervention in matters of conscience is futile because salvation cannot be compelled[44] and that a policy of toleration is more likely to breed social peace than an effort to eliminate sources of heterogeneity by persecuting dissenters.[45] These notions are consistent with the characteristic tendency in the American tradition to confine religion exclusively to the realm of private activity. The fact that there is no public solution to the problem of salvation is taken to imply that there is no public justification for state involvement in religious affairs. And the effort to handle the problem of religious divisiveness by tolerating diversity instead of by homogenizing religious views is essentially an effort to defuse and depoliticize religious issues – to confine them to the private sector by preventing them from emerging as matters of public concern. The Lockean cast of American thought has consistently reinforced the tendency to conceptualize the boundary between church and state in terms of the boundary between public and private. Public schools are accordingly off limits for school prayer.

C. *Freedom of Speech, State Action, and Drittwirkung*

A second area in which one sees the contrast between facilitative and privatizing freedom involves freedom of speech. More precisely, the contrast is implicit in differential approaches to thinking about the interaction of freedom of speech with other private law rights such as libel or slander. American law analyzes these issues using the doctrine of state action;

German law uses the subtly different notion of *mittelbare Drittwirkung* (indirect third party effect of constitutional norms). For the sake of brevity, I will not attempt to analyze these rather complex doctrines here. Let me simply quote some of the conclusions in the excellent recent article on this topic by Peter Quint.[46] Professor Quint maintains that »German and American doctrines appear to reflect fundamentally differing views about the nature of the distinction between the public and private realms.«[47] The American state action approach makes a sharp dichotomy between state and private action, and only the state is bound by free speech and other constitutional constraints.[48] This is a doubly Lockean notion. First, it reflects the Lockean pattern of conceptualizing liberty in terms of the public/private divide. And second, it views the constraints as fundamentally a limitation on government.

In contrast, the German approach is to assume that the private law norms continue to govern the relation between third parties, but that constitutional values have an indirect impact on their relationship, because the private law norms must be construed to give effect to fundamental constitutional norms. Thus, constitutional values have an indirect effect on third parties (*mittelbare Drittwirkung*). According to Professor Quint, this

> German view is skeptical of the position that the fundamental law should apply only to the »public« realm, even assuming that such a realm can be clearly delineated. The German doctrine rests on the position that certain constitutional values are so fundamental – for a decent life for all – that those values should permeate state and society, wherever the line between the two (if any) is to be drawn. This position may seem paradoxical in light of the clear traditional distinction between public and private law in German theory, but the doctrine that constitutional values should »influence« even private law indicates that, when constitutional values are at issue, the distinction between public and private realms cannot be absolute.[49]

Constitutional norms feed into and are actualized through private law. They reflect an objective public order that must be affirmatively actualized. In this respect,

> the German and American treatment of the impact of constitutional values on the private realm reflect the more fundamental fact that American constitutional theory generally excludes constitutional provisions that impose affirmative obligations on the government to act in society, whereas the German system acknowledges certain affirmative constitutional requirements of social welfare and also certain requirements that

50

the government act affirmatively to impose certain burdens on individuals.[50]

Facilitative freedom is evident here in the notion that the state must not only refrain from violating certain constitutional norms; it must actively participate in their actualization in the private order.

D.   *The Abortion Cases*

A third area in which the contrast is evident is in the abortion area. Here again, I will try to avoid going into excessive detail, since several extended comparative analyses of the cases and the issues are available.[51] However, particularly on the German side, some review of the 1975 decision is necessary to highlight the features of the case in which one sees the traces of the German approach to freedom. The abortion cases constitute two of the most dramatic cases of the past two decades not only because of the heated moral controversies they involve, but because they pose some of the deepest questions about the nature and legitimacy of judicial review in the age of the new constitutionalism. Several things about these cases are noteworthy.

Looking first at *Roe v. Wade*,[52] it seems to fit squarely within the tradition of privatizing freedom. To be sure, the older Lockean conceptualization drawing heavily on property models is transmuted into the more contemporary privacy analysis, which arguably meshes more neatly with post-World War II styles of constitutionalism. The idea of privacy is necessarily more hazy at its edges, is more highly subjectivized than property notions, and almost inevitably entails interest balancing. But at core the decision is one that reasons from the identification of liberty with the private sphere. In the court's view, reproductive choices are among the most private of all decisions, and therefore they should be almost totally free of state intervention. The model of autonomy at play is clearly the more Lockean autonomy of arbitrary choice. During the first trimester, the abortion choice is to be totally unfettered, regardless of the reason for the abortion. Subsequent abortion decisions have made it clear that measures that might impact on the rationality and considered nature of the abortion choice such as informed consent, counseling, or waiting period requirements constituted impermissible state regulation.[53]

The West German approach is quite different. Starting from an analysis of Article 2, Paragraph 2 of the Basic Law, which provides that »[e]veryone has the right to life and bodily integrity,« the court concluded, on the basis of legislative history that referenced the particularly high value placed on human life in reaction to the Nazi experience, that »everyone« included »every life-possessing human individual« and not merely every »finished« person.[54] Having concluded that fetuses deserve legal protection, the Constitutional Court went on to analyze the level of protection that needed to be provided. The starting point of this analysis involves one of the most striking features of West German constitutional jurisprudence: the commitment to the notion that the Basic Law embodies and reflects an »objective order of values« (*objektive Wertordnung*) involving not only defensive rights against the state (*Abwehrrechte*) but a positive obligation incumbent on the state to see that the values are actualized. Because the right to life constitutes a preeminent value within the general constitutional scheme, the state obligation to protect developing life not only barred direct state action which might infringe on fetal rights; it also implied a duty for the state to protect fetuses from illegal abortions, and – most controversially – to protect the fetus from its own mother.[55]

The Court acknowledged that denial of the right to obtain an abortion could result in significant restrictions on the »free unfolding« of the mother's personality (also guaranteed by Article 2 of the Basic Law), but held that in the absence of extenuating circumstances, the fetal right to life outweighed the maternal interest in personal autonomy. According to Article 2, the right to »free unfolding of the personality« extends »only so far as the rights of others are not injured and the constitutional order and moral law are not infringed.«[56] The mother's rights are thus limited by the rights of the fetus, and in balancing the law, the Court found that the interests of the fetus generally deserve greater protection. The special relationship of the mother to the developing child, far from constituting an excuse for abortion, casts a special responsibility upon her to protect the fetus.[57] Moreover, in the abortion context, the values at stake are the life of the fetus on the one hand and, for the most part, merely the freedom of the mother on the other. Hence, the Court concluded, because protection of life takes priority over protecting freedom, when viewed from the perspective of respecting human dignity, the rights of the fetus must be preferred to those of the mother throughout the pregnancy.[58] Making the woman's right to self-determination the central issue in the analysis was inconsistent, at least in the majority's view, with the German constitutional scheme.[59] From its perspective, the central norms to be inferred from the Basic Law were the presumptive duty of the expectant mother to carry a pregnancy to term, and the obligation resting on the state to make it clear that abortion is fundamentally wrongful (*Unrecht*), and to avoid conveying the impression that the decision to terminate a preg-

52

nancy is merely a matter of personal discretion on a par with the decision to seek medical assistance in curing an illness.[60]

The court recognized that precisely how fetal life was to be protected was a matter for the legislative branch, but a *Roe v. Wade*-type solution which would leave the abortion choice solely to the discretion of the woman in the first trimester was constitutionally unacceptable, because it would mean there were gaps in the state's condemnation of abortion. The Court recognized broad extenuating circumstances under which carrying the pregnancy to term could not fairly be expected of the woman, but in the absence of any of the »indications,« the state was obligated to maintain a stance of disapproval toward abortion. In the absence of effective alternatives to criminal liability for purposes of protecting incipient life, criminal sanctions had to be maintained.[61] The dissenters contended that the »time-phase« solution was within legislative prerogative, since the legislature could reasonably believe that decriminalizing abortion during the first trimester on the condition of participation in counseling might result in a larger number of women obtaining counseling and being persuaded not to obtain an abortion. The majority rejected that view in a ringing denunciation of the utilitarian notion that constitutionally mandated protection of individual life may be compromised in order to achieve the otherwise laudable aim of saving other lives.[62] The Court repeatedly stressed the constitutional obligation to provide individual protection for every separate, concrete life, and seemed to find an affront to human dignity in the mere process of attempting to compare the constitutional merits of legislative approaches to the abortion problem by estimating which program (criminal deterrence or counseling) would save the most lives.[63]

The contrast with *Roe v. Wade* is remarkable on several fronts. First, while the Court acknowledged the autonomy interest of the mother, and gave that autonomy fairly wide play by recognizing a fairly broad range of circumstances under which exercise of that autonomy in favor of abortion might be constitutionally permissible,[64] it seems clear that this is not the autonomy of arbitrary choice, but the more Kantian rational autonomy. In the Court's view, counseling needed to be oriented toward persuading a woman not to have an abortion.[65] The abortion choice is not to be made in accordance with arbitrary preference, but in accordance with moral duty to the unborn child and due regard for the objective order of values embodied in the Basic Law. The issue is not whether the woman has a right of privacy that insulates her choice from state intervention, but the scope of the state's obligation to actualize the interactive freedom of both the woman and the fetus. And while the counterpoised interests and rights have to be weighed in some sense, they are not to be balanced in a utilitarian manner that pits life against life.

Examples could be multiplied, but what emerges is a fairly sharp contrast between two fundamental models of constitutionalism: a facilitative vision in which the state is affirmatively committed to serving as a vehicle for actualizing freedom, and a privatizing vision, which has ultimately chosen to be deferential to the expansion of the affirmative state, but which continues to conceptualize such expansion as a potential threat to liberty.

IV. *The Significance of Foreign Theory in the Molding of Constitutional Traditions*

A. *The Structure of Interactional Influences*

The unfolding of a constitutional tradition obviously occurs against the backdrop of an exceedingly complex social, economic, political, historical, philosophical and cultural setting, and differences between traditions inevitably reflect these background contrasts. At the same time, constitutional traditions do not develop in hermetically sealed national compartments. Reciprocal influences between differing cultures are constantly felt. Borrowings occur at numerous levels. Wording in one constitution may be borrowed in another; ideas about key rights may be shared; new developments in one system may be the impulse for change in another; doctrine and theory worked out in one system may enrich the thinking in another; and so on. Significantly, cultural interaction affecting law may occur in contexts that go far beyond what appears to be explicitly legal. For example, theories of literary criticism worked out in one country may percolate into literary circles in another country and then spill over into legal theory. Technological innovation in one country (e.g., television, computers, telecommunications) may so alter modes of social life that new areas of law emerge or old areas need to be adapted (e.g., media law, *Datenschutz*).

Intercultural transmission occurs at different rates in different areas. The result is that different elements in the total constellation of ideas, values, attitudes and socio-economic infrastructure that constitute a mode of social life take on different weights and meanings. Similar ideas may have different cultural resonances. The idea of dignity, for example, has somewhat different connotations in German and American culture. In the

United States, dignity is linked to self-reliance. Without trivializing the idea, what comes to mind here when one speaks of dignity is a worker living at the poverty line who is unwilling to accept welfare or charity. To treat the elderly with dignity means to give them help and respect, but in ways that would not undercut their sense of self-reliance. In Germany, the notion of dignity has closer ties to duty – to the grandeur of the »moral law within« as envisioned by Kant's moral philosophy. To take a more concrete example, discussion of the right to life in the American abortion cases does not evoke instant memories of atrocities from the Nazi era the way it did in the German abortion opinion.

Against such differing and ever-shifting constellations of social consciousness, similar acts may take on differing meanings. Thus against the historical background of the *Kulturkampf* of the Bismarck era and the *Kirchenkampf* of the Hitler period, cutting off state aid to schools could not help but appear as a repetition of prior acts of religious persecution. The framers of the Basic Law thus allowed long-standing patterns of support for religious schools and religious instruction to continue. In the United States, in contrast, where separation of church and state has great symbolic significance as the embodiment of religious liberty, aid to parochial education and religious exercises such as prayer, bible reading, or even a moment of silence have been held unconstitutional.

B. *The Rhetorical Model: Intercultural Influence as Assimilation and Shifts in Topoi Structures*

In analyzing what happens in intercultural transmission, it seems helpful to me to use models drawn from classical rhetoric.[66] The portions of the social world with which we are concerned in examining traditions of constitutionalism lie in what Aristotle would have thought of as the domain of opinion. Differing opinions are held with differing degrees of conviction. The belief that freedom of speech should be respected is held with greater conviction than the belief, say, that catastrophic health coverage benefits for the elderly should be preserved. But both are matters of opinion as compared with kinds of knowledge we have with respect to matters of hard science – e.g., how the wing of a jet must be shaped in order to provide adequate lift to carry passengers safely. Within the domain of opinion, our belief structures have a very complex topography. As we are confronted with problems, we draw on or shape arguments *(topoi)* to find solutions or resolutions that are socially workable. Some such arguments are concrete and mundane. Think of the arguments lawyers make in negotiating a settlement or pleading a case. Or think of the endless topoi strewn through the pages of West digests. Other topoi are far more general. Constitutional arguments typically have this character.

The topoi in any intellectual landscape have complex interconnections. Topoi in the area of religious liberty have links to those used to defend other types of freedom of expression. Separation of powers topoi can be levelled against judicial activism. Topoi may be patterned in various ways, and topoi can shift. Over the past century, for example, we have witnessed the decline in constitutional analysis of what has been called a »boundary maintenance theory of constitutional law,«[67] and the rise of the model of balancing.[68] In a broad sense, what I have characterized as the rise of the new constitutionalism can be thought of as a shift in the dominant topoi patterns in our age. Within differing topoi structures, differing arguments will have differing measures of persuasiveness. It is as though differing topoi structures are differing sound chambers in which varying arguments will strike different harmonics with differing resonances. The models of facilitating and privatizing freedom appear to me to be contrasting topoi structures of the type I am describing.

To interpret such structures in terms of rhetorical models is not to say they are *merely* rhetorical. At the constitutional level, such structures reflect our deepest and most closely held convictions. The rhetoricity of such models is a reflection of the fact that we are dealing with human affairs, and their humanness means that they remain profoundly open. They are subject to revision, but also to reappropriation by other cultures, or subsequent generations.

With this background in mind, let me attempt to describe what I see as a particularly significant area for interaction between our two cultures. My sense is that the most powerful kinds of interaction occur at the level of theory. The distance between abstract theory and concrete decision is such that it is not always possible to trace direct effects in terms of outcomes, but theory tends to have a broad impact, because it can affect wide-ranging reorientation in topoi patterns.

C. *The Influence of German Thought on American Constitutionalism through Legal Realism*

Consider the example of legal realism. Herget and Wallace have recently demonstrated in a very persuasive article that the roots of American legal realism can be traced to the German free law movement.[69] An influential group of American thinkers, most notably Pound, Gray, and Cardozo, assimilated the writings of the free law movement, repackaged them, and exploited them as part of the critique of the excessive formalism and »mechanical jurisprudence« of the *Lochner* era during the first two decades of this century. By the end of World War I, the free law movement was already on the wane as a persuasive theory in Germany, though it continued to be influential among practitioners, and was available to its discredit during the Nazi era to foster free interpretation of law in the interests of Nazi morality (*gesundes Volksempfinden*).[70] In the United States, in contrast, the movement was entering into its heyday. Younger scholars such as Karl Llewellyn and Jerome Frank entered the fray, typically relying on the works of the earlier American writers and thus avoiding the suspicion that might arise from the »taint« of German theory. Legal realism had a powerful impact in breaking the *Lochner* era's threatened stranglehold on New Deal programs.

Herget and Wallace suggest that philosophically, legal realism was already moribund by 1940.[71] Its skeptical attitude had cut through prevailing myths and had poured Holmes' cynical acid on the prior age's approach to law. But legal realism had little to offer in the way of a positive program. The Holmesian »bad man's view of the law« was a refreshing way of thinking about law for the practicing lawyer, but it didn't provide much guidance for the judge.

While the persuasiveness of legal realism may have gone into decline at the level of theory, however, I think it would be a major mistake to underestimate its residual hold. The generation of lawyers, judges, and professors trained during the height of legal realism is only now reaching retirement. Legal philosophers in subsequent decades may have grown dubious about legal realism, but practitioners and teachers in technical subject matter areas have continued to work in the spirit of the realist tradition. »Learning to think like a lawyer« – the putative aim of American legal education – tends even today to mean learning to think like a legal realist. Legal realism is a fundamental aspect of the topoi structure of post-World War II constitutionalism in America.

My point in all of this is to trace the profound impact one German theory has had on the structure of American constitutionalism. Because legal realism played a central role in undermining the formalist »mechanical« jurisprudence that characterized American constitutional law until shortly before World War II, it provided the intellectual atmosphere for the emergence of the new constitutionalism in the United States. What was in many respects a relatively minor movement in early twentieth century Germany was absorbed, transformed and expanded to become one of the central features of the topoi structure of contemporary American constitutional law. One of the interesting things about this account is the amount of lag time in the process of intercultural absorption. The course of transmission crosses not only cultures, but generations.

D.   Continental Theories of Interpretation and Sympathy for the Idea of an Objective Order of Values

This seems significant to me, because I believe a similar pattern of transmission is in process today that may ultimately have an impact of a similar or even greater magnitude. What I have in mind is a congeries of related doctrines that travel under the rather loosely fitting rubric of »continental theories of interpretation.« These include hermeneutics, deconstruction and rhetorical theory, among others. For most American legal practitioners and academics, these theories seem highly abstruse and inaccessible. Yet on numerous fronts, consciousness of these new theories is percolating into legal academia. This can be seen not only in the writings of the critical legal studies movement, but also in the writings of more mainline theorists such as Ronald Dworkin, Bruce Ackerman, or Michael Perry. It is still too early to discern all the channels through which such influences will flow, and it is impossible to predict the quirks and turns of history that will play the most critical role in determining concrete outcomes. But it seems reasonable to think that within the next generation, these influences may lead to greater sympathy for something akin to the German Constitutional Court's commitment to an objective order of values.

To many American jurists, that commitment seems chronologically aberrational if not downright atavistic. Legal realist teeth are set on edge by anything that remotely smacks of the »brooding omnipresence« of natural law. For Americans, the new constitutionalism was an escape from the conservative excesses of a type of natural law thinking that was dominant until the late 1930's. Hence, American constitutional theorists and judges of the post-war era have sought to avoid being identified with the natural law tradition. One thinks of Justice Black's rather positivistic methodology (his literal textualism) in protecting free speech values that as a functional matter he treated as objective absolutes. Only recently have American theorists with natural law instincts begun to come out of the closet and shake the fear of being labeled as naturalists.

58

The German situation was of course quite different. German constitutionalism emerged from the rubble and guilt of the Nazi debacle, and excessive positivism was seen as at least a contributing factor in that collapse. Thus, in the topoi structure of Germany's new constitutionalism, confession of faith in an objective order of values is a way of exorcising a haunting past that should never recur.

What is interesting about the newer currents in American constitutional theory is the extent to which at least the liberal wing of American theory seems to be converging toward something like the German notion of an *objektive Wertordnung*. One can read Ronald Dworkin's theory, for example, as an argument that even in a pluralistic and relativistic world, law in general and constitutional law in particular consists of the ongoing effort to interpret conceptions of justice in a manner that gives order and coherence to principles across legal subdisciplines and over time. Michael Perry's work can be read in a similar light.

Cultural interaction at the level of theory is a complex and not totally predictable process. But in view of the depth of commitment in both of our societies to certain key values, and the pervasiveness of our intellectual and economic ties, it seems clear that extensive mutual influence will continue. We will both continue to respond to concrete problems slightly differently, because of the differing patterns in the overall topoi structures of our societies, but those structures will continue to be enriched by mutual interaction.

Notes:

1 The pre-World War II cases are a small set. Probably the most notable are the Mormon cases, which provided the earliest definitions of free exercise values. In Reynolds v. United States, 98 U.S. 145 (1878), the Supreme Court affirmed the bigamy conviction of a Mormon polygamist, rejecting a free exercise claim on the ground that the first amendment protected the right to believe, but not the right to act on those beliefs. In Davis v. Beason, 133 U.S. 333 (1890), the Court upheld an Idaho territorial statute that required all voters to execute an oath swearing that they were not a member of an organization that taught beliefs in plural marriage. Confiscation of all property owned by the Mormon Church was sustained in United States v. The Late Corporation of the Church of Jesus Christ of Latter-day Saints, 136 U.S. 1 (1890). These cases, like Bradfield v. Roberts, 175 U.S. 291 (1899), and Quick Bear v. Leupp, 210 U.S. 50 (1908), which dealt with establishment clause issues, were able to reach the Supreme Court because they arose in territories or involved Indian funds, and thus implicated the federal government. Otherwise, the holding in Barron v. Mayor of Baltimore,

32 U.S. (7 Pet.) 243 (1833), that the Bill of Rights constrained only federal power made recourse to the Supreme Court for vindication of religious liberty claims pointless. See Permoli v. City of New Orleans, 44 U.S. (3 How.) 589 (1845) (Catholic priest could not assert first amendment as a defense to conviction under a New Orleans ordinance that proscribed exposing dead bodies, even to bless the deceased during a funeral mass). Church property disputes following a schism in a local congregation managed to reach the Supreme Court on the basis of diversity of citizenship jurisdiction. Watson v. Jones, 80 U.S. (13 Wall.) 679 (1872). With the exception of certain other cases which involved religious issues but did not invoke religion clause protections, see, e.g., Pierce v. Society of Sisters, 268 U.S. 510 (1925)(substantive due process challenge to Oregon statute banning parochial schools), the foregoing are the major religion clause cases in the Supreme Court prior to 1940.

2   Cantwell v. Connecticut, 310 U.S. 296 (1940).

3   Everson v. Board of Education, 330 U.S. 1 (1947).

4   The fact that religious liberty claims were not reaching the federal courts does not imply that there was a parallel vacuum at the state level, but the quantity and style of litigation was more limited there as well. For a review of state constitutional law on this issue, see C. Antieau, P. Carroll, & T. Burke, Religion Under the State Constitutions (1965).

5   See P. Quint, *Free Speech and Private Law in German Constitutional Theory*, 48 Md. L. Rev. 247 (1989).

6   See, e.g., Robert F. Williams, State Constitutional Law: Cases and Materials (With 1990-91 Supplement) (Washington, Advisory Commission on Intergovernmental Relations, 1990); Maltz, Williams & Araten, Selected Bibliography on State Constitutional Law, 1980-89, 20 Rutgers L. J. 1093 (1989); B. Reams & S. Yoak (eds.), The Constitutions of the States: A State-by-State Guide and Bibliography to Current Scholarly Research (1988).

7   My terminology here derives from German sources. See Schenke, 40 Jahre Grundgesetz, 44 JZ 653, 656 (1989); Bachof, in Gedächtnisschrift für W. Jellinek 287 (1955).

8   98 U.S. 145 (1878).

9   83 U.S. (16 Wall.) 36 (1873).

10 94 U.S. 113 (1877).

11 Wisconsin v. Yoder, 406 U.S. 205 (1972).

12 Goldman v. Weinberger, 475 U.S. 503 (1986).

13 See Valley Forge Christian College v. Americans United for Separation of Church and State, Inc., 454 U.S. 464 (1982).

14 Flast v. Cohen, 392 U.S. 83 (1968).

15 See Lemon v. Kurtzman, 403 U.S. 602 (1971).

16 Article 137(1) of the Weimar constitution, which is incorporated in the Basic Law by Article 140.

17 HessStGH, Judgment of October 27, 1965 (Az. P. St. 388), 16 ESVGH 1 = 19 [1966] NJW 31 = 1966 DöV 51 = 1966 DVBl. 29.

18 370 U.S. 421 (1962).

19 W. German Constitutional Court, Decision of October 16, 1979, BVerfGE 52, 223, 235-36.

20 See Cappelletti, The »Mighty Problem« of Judicial Review and the Contribution of Comparative Analysis, 53 So. Cal. L. Rev. 409 (1980).

21 See generally L. Krieger, The German Idea of Freedom: History of a Political Tradition (1957).

22 For an excellent discussion of the significance of the community orientation in German constitutional law, see Kommers, Liberty and Community in Constitutional Law: The Abortion Cases in Comparative Perspective, 1985 B.Y.U. L. Rev. 371.

23 See Currie, Positive and Negative Constitutional Rights, 53 U. Chi. L. Rev. 864 (1986).

24 Reich, The New Property, 73 Yale L.J. 733 (1964).

25 Michelman, Foreward: On Protecting the Poor Through the Fourteenth Amendment, 83 Harv. L. Rev. 7 (1969). Other essays arguing for a more »social« interpretation of the United States Constitution include Miller, Toward a Concept of Constitutional Duty, 1968 Sup. Ct. Rev. 199; Bendich, Privacy, Poverty, and the Constitution, 54 Cal. L. Rev. 407 (1966). But see Bork, The Impossibility of Finding Welfare Rights in the Constitution, 1979 Wash. U.L.Q. 695.

26 See, e.g., Benda, Das sozialstaatliche System der Bundesrepublik Deutschland und seine Grenzen, 23 Zeitschrift für Sozialhilfe und Sozialgesetzbuch 1, 3-4 (1984).

27 The notion of dignity is, of course, not an exclusively Kantian notion. For a wide-ranging analysis of the historical roots of the notion of dignity as a constitutional guarantee, see Starck, Menschenwürde als Verfassungsgarantie im modernen Staat, 36 JZ 457 (1981).

28 I. Kant, The Metaphysical Elements of Justice: Part I of the Metaphysics of Morals §§ 1-9, at 51-67 (J. Ladd trans. 1965).

29 Id., Introduction, §B at 34. 6.

30 Id., § 47 at 81.

31 370 U.S. 421 (1962).

32 Karen B. v. Treen, 653 F.2d 897 (5th Cir. 1981), aff'd mem., 455 U.S. 913 (1982).

33 See HessStGH, Judgment of October 27, 1965 (Az. P. St. 388), 16 ESVGH 1-19 [1966]; NJW 1966, 31.

34 W. German Constitutional Court, Decision of October 16, 1979, BVerfGE 52, 223, 235-36.

35 Id. at 236-37.

36 It is »eine dem Staat zuzurechnende schulische Veranstaltung.« Id. at 240.

37 Id.

38 Id. at 249-50.

39 See Obermayer, Religious Schools and Religious Freedom: Proposals for Reform of the German Public School System, 16 Am. J. Comp. L. 552, 552 (1968); L. Spitz, Impact of the Reformation on Church-State Issues, in Church and State under God 60, 82 (A. Huegli ed. 1964).

40 Obermayer, supra note 39, at 553.

41 Id.; A. von Campenhausen, Staatskirchenrecht: Ein Leitfaden durch die Rechtsbeziehungen zwischen Staat und den Religionsgemeinschaften 101 (1973).

42 Obermayer, Staatskirchenrecht im Wandel, 1967 DöV 9, 12-13, reprinted in H. Quaritsch & H. Weber, Staat und Kirchen in der Bundesrepublik: Staatskirchenrechtliche Aufsätze 1950-1967 382, 390 (1967).

43 Art. 137 (5) WRV, incorporated by Article 140 of the Basic Law, provides for the availability of public corporation status (Körperschaft des öffentlichen Rechts) to all religious bodies which have sufficient membership »to offer an assurance of their permanency.« Art 137 (6) WRV confers taxing power on religious bodies with public corporation status. At least twenty-two religious organizations have received public corporation status. See generally Solte, Die Organisationsstruktur der Kirchen unter Religionsgemeinschaften, in 1 E. Friesenhahn, U. Scheuner, i.V.m. J. Listl (Herausgeber), Handbuch des Staatskirchenrechts der Bundesrepublik Deutschland 341 (1974).

44 J. Locke, A Letter Concerning Toleration 34-35 (Library of Liberal Arts ed. 1955).

45 Id. at 52-54.

46 Quint, Free Speech and Private Law in German Constitutional Theory, 48 Md. L. Rev. 247 (1989).

47 Id. at 339.

48 Id. at 339.

49 Id. at 340.

50 Id. at 345-46.

51 See, e.g., Benda, The Impact of Constitutional Law on the Protection of Unborn Human Life: Some Comparative Remarks, 6 Hum. Rights 223 (1977); Gerstein & Lowry, Abortion, Abstract Norms, and Social Control: The Decision of the West German Federal Constitutional Court, 25 Emory L.J. 849 (1976); M. Glendon, Abortion and Divorce in Western Law (1988); Glenn, The Constitutional Validity of Abortion Legislation: A Comparative Note, 21 McGill L.J. 673 (1975); Gorby & Jonas, West German Abortion Decision: A Contrast to Roe v. Wade, 9 J. Mar. J. Prac. & Proc. 551 (1976); Kommers, Liberty and Community in Constitutional Law: The Abortion Cases in Comparative Perspective, 1985 B.Y.U. L. Rev. 371; Kommers, Abortion and Constitution: United States and West Germany, 25 Am J. Comp. L. 255 (1977); Morris, Abortion and Liberalism: A Comparison between the Abortion Decisions of the Supreme Court of the United States and the Constitutional Court of West Germany, 11 Hastings Int. & Comp. L. Rev. 159 (1988); cf. Stith, New Constitutional and Penal Theory in Spanish Abortion Law, 35 Am. J. Comp. L. 513 (1987).

52 410 U.S. 113 (1973).

53 See City of Akron v. Akron Center for Reproductive Health, 462 U.S. 416 (1983); Simopoulos v. Virginia, 462 U.S. 506 (1983); Planned Parenthood Association v. Ashcroft, 462 U.S. 476 (1983).

54 W. German Constitutional Court, Judgment of Feb. 25, 1975, BVerfG, 39 BVerfGE 1. The Constitutional Court did not recognize gradations moving from trimester to trimester, as the U.S. Supreme Court did. However, its view did have one quirk. It held that the required constitutional protection begins with nidation (the point at which the fertilized egg becomes implanted in the uterine wall) rather than conception, thus leaving roughly the first two weeks following conception without protection. This conveniently avoided issues with respect to

62

contraceptive devices that may take effect after conception, such as morning after pills or intrauterine devices, but otherwise seems rather paradoxical and arbitrary. The biological logic is not much more compelling than that used to justify the American trimester approach.

55 *Id.* at 42-44.

56 The German text of Article 2 provides: »Jeder hat das Recht auf die freie Entfaltung seiner Persönlichkeit, soweit er nicht die Rechte anderer verletzt und nicht gegen die verfassungsmässige Ordnung oder das Sittengesetz verstößt.

57 See 39 BVerfGE 1, 42-43.

58 *Id.* at 43.

59 *Id.* at 43-44.

60 *Id.* at 44.

61 *Id.* at 45-47.

62 *Id.* at 58.

63 *Id.* at 58-59.

64 The precise legal status of such constitutionality is somewhat unclear within German criminal theory. It is not clear whether the indications (threat to the life or health of the mother, rape or other criminological indications, birth defects, and the broad »social« indication, according to which difficult social circumstances might warrant abortion) constitute justifications, excuses, an area ungoverned by the legal order (*rechtsfreier Raum*), or a basis for barring criminal liability extrinsic to questions of culpability.

65 BVerfGE 39, 1, 61-62.

66 I have been heavily influenced in this regard by Theodor Viehweg, Topik und Jurisprudenz (5th ed. 1974).

67 See Seidman, Public Principle and Private Choice: The Uneasy Case for a Boundary Maintenance Theory of Constitutional Law, 96 Yale L.J. 1006 (1987).

68 See Aleinikoff, Constitutional Law in the Age of Balancing, 96 Yale L.J. 943 (1987).

69 Herget & Wallace, The German Free Law Movement as the Source of American Legal Realism, 73 Va. L. Rev. 399 (1987).

70 See *id.* at 418.

71 *Id.* at 435.

Donald P. Kommers

Comments on Part 1

This opening panel has sought to assess the general significance of the Basic Law on the occasion of its 40th anniversary. We have heard two engaging papers, one written from the perspective of a German constitutional scholar - Professor Klaus Stern - and the other from that of an American constitutional scholar - Professor Cole Durham.

Both speakers agree that the Basic Law has served as a successful experiment in constitutional democracy. The Bonn Constitution has provided Germany with four decades of political stability, a viable system of representative government, and a record of protecting basic rights comparable to that of any other western democracy. Equally important is the change the Basic Law has wrought in Germany's constitutional culture. Most Germans regard their Constitution as a law superior in rank to all other laws, they acknowledge its normative force in German society as a whole, and they accept the principle of its judicial enforcement by an independent constitutional tribunal. In short, as our speakers have suggested, the Basic Law has stood the test of time, and it is likely to survive in perpetuity.

Yet Stern worries about a widening gap between constitutional theory and reality in Germany. In the most interesting section of his paper, he discusses what he regards as the principal threats to the German constitutional state. These are (1) the »abundance and complexity« of laws passed in recent years, (2) the expansion of the social welfare state, and (3) recent efforts to incorporate plebiscitary elements into the political system. Stern feels that these developments have undermined the clarity, authority and thus the rule of law, the value of individual responsibility and dignity, and the principle of parliamentary or representative democracy.

His criticism finds a strong echo in the writings of certain conservative critics who find that because of the proliferation of pressure group demands on parliament and the insatiable demand for more social services, financial entitlements, and other favors, Germany is becoming increasingly ungovernable. Critics on the left see the situation differently. In their view, »post-industrial« democracies like the Federal Republic do not and cannot respond adequately to public opinion or to the needs of the »lower« classes. For them, the party oligarchies constitute one of the greatest threats to democracy and the rule of law. These oligarchies, so effective in maintaining existing relationships of power, dominate the constitutional state. To »unfreeze« this system, they contend, forms of direct democracy - *i.e.,* plebiscites and referenda - need to be introduced so that people once again may regain control of their lives. One is constrained to say that there is probably some validity in the views of both Professor Stern and his critics.

Durham's analysis shifts our attention to basic rights. Incidentally, Professor Stern reserves his greatest applause for the Basic Law's provisions on fundamental freedoms, provisions whose ancestry he traces to American and German precedents. Professor Durham, on the other hand, is more concerned with the contemporary development of both German and American constitutionalism. During the last 40 years, in his view, the constitutional law of basic liberties in both countries has been transformed. Rights are now characterized, in his words, by their »federalization«, »subjectification«, and »judicialization.«

Stern would, I think, agree with Professor Durham's analysis, but he strikes a different note in assessing the condition of rights in the affirmative state. Stern's social welfare state is roughly the equivalent of Durham's affirmative state except that the latter sees the welfare state as a threat to individual liberty whereas the former sees it as a threat to personal responsibility. At some stage, however, these differing perspectives would probably converge, for the erosion of personal responsibility is likely to affect the quality of individual *freedom,* just as the erosion of personal liberty is likely to serve as a hindrance to the exercise of individual *responsibility.*

The two papers also strike different notes in their comparison of German and American rights jurisprudence. Stern emphasizes the shared values of the two systems, whereas Durham stresses their differences. »Fundamentally different visions of the ideal of freedom«, Durham writes, »overshadows the many shared characteristics of the two systems.« He distinguishes between the German »facilitative« and the American »privatizing« models of freedom and then proceeds to show, in a captivating analysis, how these different orientations toward freedom manifest themselves in constitutional cases on religious freedom, free speech, and abortion.

Durham clearly feels that we Americans have much to learn from the German - *i.e.,* the facilitative - approach to basic rights. I'm inclined to agree. In his view, as in mine, the *purely* negative freedom of American constitutionalism inhibits the full liberation of the human personality. Although negative rights are clearly necessary to protect individuals against threats posed by the expansion of the state, they are not sufficient for the full realization of human freedom. Needless to say, both Germany and the United States are affirmative states. What is different is that Germany, unlike the United States, has constitutionalized the affirmative - *i.e.,* the social welfare - state. German constitutionalism celebrates not only negative rights but the right of the individual to certain goods only the state can provide.

Stern suggests, however, that German constitutionalism is a long way from resolving the tension between negative and positive rights. He is more critical of the social welfare state than is Durham; yet he applauds the »multidimensional« character of basic rights - *i.e.,* their institutional, negative, *and* positive character. Professor Stern's criticism is aimed not so much at positive rights - indeed he affirms them - as at the *excesses* of the welfare state. But what exactly are these excesses or, alternatively, what precisely does the Basic Law guarantee in terms of those goods only the state can provide? German constitutional scholars seem hopelessly divided over the answer to this quesion.

Finally, I'd like to reemphasize a point made by Professor Durham. He tells us that »in the altered context of the affirmative state« classical liberal values - *i.e.,* negative rights against the state - need to be reinterpreted if they are to have any real meaning at all in the modern world. Using school prayer as an example, he shows how a creative balance between negative and positive liberty can lead to a jurisprudence less dogmatic than that of the American Supreme Court. The notion of an objective value order has of course provided German judges with a convenient tool to reinterpret the meaning of classical liberal values. No one will deny the tension that exists in German constitutional law between objective values and negative rights. That tension leads to considerable controversey when, as in the Abortion Case, an objective value prevails over a negative right. But it is precisely this tension - like the tension between negative and positive rights - that has led to the creative jurisprudence of freedom that Durham applauds, and which he thinks ought to influence American constitutional thought.

We shall hear more about basic rights later in this confernce. For now, we can only agree that the Basic Law is a remarkable document. In terms of its prestige and influence around the world, the Basic Law stands today on an equal footing with the United States Constitution. Both constitutions have given rise to an impressive literature of freedom as well as to grand traditions of constitutional interpretation. And, as a consequence of symposia such as this, we are finding that these traditions can be - and are - mutually enriching.

Part 2:
Federalism

Peter Lerche

Principles of German Federalism

The history of the German nation is also a history of German federalism,[1] if we initially take this word in the broader sense of »belonging to a confederacy«.

1. The Peace of Westphalia in 1648 gave the First German Empire a complex constitution, characterized by the fundamental sovereignty of the individual rulers within a common union. The precise interpretation of that union - whether it was a compound state on the lines of a confederation, or one with greater emphasis on common interests - is controversial. At any rate, it contained federal features, and offered a starting point for early moves towards developing federalistic doctrines.[2]

After the dissolution of the First German Empire, the problem of integrating the German states arose again, initially resulting in the German Federation (1815-1866), an essentially federalistic structure closely interwoven with the European order as a whole.

The defeat of Austria in 1866 sealed the fate of the German Federation. The path lay open to an organization of states which would exclude Austria. The North German Federation, whose constitution was modified and expanded in 1870-71 to produce the constitution of the German Empire, already went beyond the precepts of a mere confederacy. The German Empire as molded by *Bismarck* functioned as a federal state, and indeed, given the powerful position of Prussia, as a hegemonic federal state. In this guise, the German Empire is often referred to as the »League of German Princes,« and *Bismarck* is often praised for his realism in bringing to life this basic concept, providing scope for the development of the »League.« At the same time, however, the term »League of Princes« is also used negatively to express the fact that its legitimacy was not of a democratic, federal nature.

The governmental practice of the German Empire[3] gradually strengthened its centralist and unitarian components, despite the fundamental importance of the Federal Council (the upper house of the German Parliament). The office of Imperial Chancellor, for example, gave rise to the formation of many departmental administrations and the largely unwritten organizational power of the Emperor became a codetermining force. In addition, the exercise of the legislative and administrative mandates granted to the Empire did much to create a uniform system of law.

The Weimar Constitution of 1919 was seen not as the constitution of a new single state, but as a new constitution for the existing Empire, with the dynastic principle being replaced by popular sovereignty. At the same time, this eliminated the previous source of legitimacy for the federal structure. This structure was itself retained in many external forms, with emphasis on the centralized powers, but with a certain weakening of the Prussian position. This necessarily raised the question of what the new legitimacy represented for Weimar's brand of federalism, a question which was never answered with any effective consensus. Several prominent authors[4] have gone so far as to see the Weimar state as being already a unitary state, merely using the organizational forms of a federal state, or at least as a federal state *sui generis*.

2. To some extent the influence of this standpoint is still felt today in evaluating the present constitutional situation, yet the present situation is affected by additional circumstances.

The National Socialist regime smashed the sovereignty of the Länder. In fact, various contentious developments at the end of the Weimar period had in some cases initiated the process of destruction. In this respect, the revival of the federalist concept in the Constitution of the Federal Republic must be seen as the refederalization of a unified state. Conditions in 1949, however, were vastly different than they had been in Weimar. Not only the elimination of Prussia and the establishment of new national frontiers, but also, and in particular, the many material requirements arising out of the imperative need to deal with basic emergencies, including the integration of vast numbers of displaced persons, necessitated a supra-regional view. There was never any doubt, however, that the die would have to be cast in favor of a federal state. This decision was from the start an essentially German decision, whatever the difference of opinion may be regarding the real importance of the Allied interventions aimed at strengthening the authority of member states within the new constitution, including such efforts in the context of the financial system. Towards the end of the formative process of the Federal Constitution, these interventions began to resemble a game of poker.[5]

The external circumstances described above naturally posed the fundamental question as to the individuality and purpose of the Federal Republic as a federal state – designed by the Basic Law as a social federal state. This brings us to the present, and the picture is ambivalent. Seen in light of the past, it is immediately apparent that the development of the German Federal state exhibits a striking continuity in its more particular legal forms[6], combined with profound differences in the fundamental structure of the respective federal state constitutions and the manner of their legitimacy. More specifically:

II.

1. Even at an earlier stage, the legitimacy of a federalist structure, owing to the diversity of the German »tribes,« had not been highly developed. Now it was further weakened by the intermingling and mobility of the population. However, the continuing influence of certain natural ties to traditional regional structures is just as noteworthy as the fact that we have now seen the development of a clear sense of belonging, even to those Länder which did not exist until the postwar era.

2. In this situation, many authors look for the significance of today's German federalism in the concept of governmental separation of powers, a concept not uninfluenced by America. The power-sharing effect of the federalist structure, an idea particularly developed by Hesse, is considered to be both vertical - *i.e.,* the division of governmental responsibilities between the federal government and Länder - and horizontal - *i.e.,* the ways in which the Länder cooperate to shape the will of the Federal Government.

3. No merely rational principle of this kind is in itself sufficient to explain the German population's deep-rooted adherence to the concept of the federal state. No single serious political force does more to promote the unitary state. The federalist structure has indeed been elevated in the constitution itself to the somewhat dubious sphere of the sacrosanct, a status, in other words, which cannot be assailed, even by constitutional amendments (Art. 79, [3].[7] This situation demands additional explanation. Awareness of the expediency of the simultaneous existence of different political decision making centers, including opportunities for change and protection of minorities, is now supplemented, as before, by the weight of regional particularities, a component without which, as Scheuner[8] says, the essential tensions of the federalist structure could not exist. The objective here is to

safeguard individual characteristics of the regions while simultaneously deploying the power of cooperation. In this aim, the concept of a federal government is combined with the more general principle of federalism, which also encompasses non-governmental areas.

4. An underlying assumption here is that the members are fundamentally homogeneous among themselves and in relation to the federation. The Basic Law also supports, in Art. 28 (1) and (3), this homogeneous nature of the fundamental organization of the Länder. We must also acknowledge an unwritten »procedural homogeneity«[9] which goes beyond this.

5. The procedural concept in the German federal state is indeed one of exceptional importance. It is especially in this context that we should consider the principle of loyalty to the federation, highlighted in particular by Smend.[10] This concept was originally forged by Bismarck, who stood firm on the principle of »contractual« loyalty to the federation as more of a mild legal and diplomatic instrument. It has subsequently become an important key to the mutual responsibility and mutual consideration among the Länder, extending particularly to procedural dealings between them and the Federal Government, a principle which, according to the judgments of the Federal Constitutional Court,[11] imposes an obligation on the Federal Government as much as it does on the Länder. The precise hallmark of this unwritten principle is that it creates no rights or obligations extending beyond the legal relationship between the federal states defined by constitutional law, but relates to the manner of exercising rights and complying with obligations arising out of this legal relationship.[12] The Berlin Land Parliament – the House of Deputies, for example – is obliged by loyalty to the federation alone to do everything in its power to ensure that the relevant federal laws are also applied as far as possible in Berlin, regardless of the deputies' political stance towards the content of a particular law.[13]
The full significance of the federal component in the Federal Republic only becomes apparent if we consider the federalist principle in its interaction with the principles of other forms of government against the background of the practical effect of the individual state authorities.

III.

This recalls at the outset the fundamental concept of the German federal state. The emphasis is on legislation and administration, whereas the organization of the administration of justice, which is also a matter for the federal government, may be disregarded. The individual form, as stated, exhibits historical continuity in technical matters of law, but its content is also touched by changes of an internal, structural nature.

1. The fundamental rule of Article 30 emphasizes what is called the normal competence of the Länder. Competences only devolve on the Federal Government if the Basic Law provides for them. However, since important areas of legislation (specifically civil law, criminal law, industrial law, and procedural law), are in fact stated by the Basic Law to be within the federal competence,[14] the significance of Art. 30 is correspondingly reduced.

2. As regards legislation, the following may be said:
a) The individual subjects of legislation in various forms are made the province of the Federal Government (Art. 70 *et seq.*).[15] In the practical foreground is what is known as concurrent federal legislation. This presupposes a need for regulation by federal law (Art. 72 [2]). What remains subject to Länder legislation is essentially – with exceptions – culture and education, local law, and police law. In an important decision based on Art. 30, the Federal Constitutional Court ruled in principle that the organization of broadcasting (apart from transmission technology) was also a matter over which the Länder have jurisdiction.[16]
It is especially here, within the field of legislation, that the unitarian tendencies of today's highly industrialized federal state[17] have exacted their tribute. Modern developments, such as the integration of the Federal Republic's industry into inter-regional and inter-governmental relationships, together with those social and egalitarian tendencies which remain to be examined, have acted as a driving force. Only occasionally and exceptionally (such as in the specific case of Art. 74 [11]) has the theoretical possibility of interpreting existing standards of jurisdiction broadly and flexibly in favor of the Federal Government been exploited. On the contrary, the Federal Constitutional Court is more likely to follow the principle of »strict« interpretation where the exercise of federal power is concerned, albeit not always with perfect clarity.[18] Even in the absence of this

perfection, the Court has become the essential custodian of the Basic Law's federal pillars.[19]

The light shed by constitutional law has, however, failed to illuminate occasional islands which remain highly dubious, such as certain financial allocations which the Länder receive from the Federal Government (cf. Art. 104 a [3 and 4]), even though these must no longer be linked to specific conditions and requirements.[20] This is an area where the former practice of endowments, even more open to attack in its day, still casts a number of dark shadows over the generally brighter present. The courage of the Länder to go to court is often sapped to a remarkable degree if they have to pay to do so, though where there is no plaintiff, there can be no judge.

b) If, then, as we have seen, German constitutional practice seems in principle to be averse to the concept of broad interpretation of federal jurisdiction, the motivational forces of unitarianism are necessarily forced to resort to the machinery of constitutional amendments (Art. 79). In this area, the contrast with the American situation is as logical as it is striking. The Basic Law has undergone a great many explicit textual amendments, most of which have served to extend federal jurisdiction. The Länder have even occasionally permitted deep inroads to be made into their own preserves such as – to take one example – consenting to federal jurisdiction over the payment of Land civil servants (Art. 74 a), even in the teeth of heroic resistance from Bavaria.

c) At the same time, this generous scope for extending the central jurisdiction has reduced the necessity to resort to the safety valve of unwritten federal competencies. German doctrine and precedent admittedly acknowledge such unwritten competencies, both in the form of competence arising from the nature of the case and that of competence arising from the factual context. They are, however, bound to rigid preconditions, and for practical purposes – *cum grano salis* – to the requirement of imperative necessity.[21]

3. By and large, then, the Federal Government is supreme in the domain of legislation. The position of the Länder remains stronger in the field of administration. Here, in sharp contrast to the American concept, the Basic Law follows the dovetailing system which is traditional in Germany. Although the laws of individual Länder are in principle implemented only by the authorities of those Länder (Art. 30), federal laws are nevertheless implemented by federal authorities in regard to specific matters (e.g., Art.

87). The normal case, in both theory and practice, is that federal laws are applied by Land authorities (Art. 83). There are some who would even see this as the key to the sovereignty of the Länder.

Nevertheless, even with this standard practice of local implementation of federal laws, the Federal Government still retains substantial powers of normative influence and supervision of administrative activities. More recent trends towards intensive legal regulation of most areas of life have resulted in a substantial decrease of those areas in which Länder competence in administration can be most forcefully applied, principally in the fields of discretionary powers and »unregulated« initiatives.[22]

4. The unitarian tendencies mentioned above, in legislation as well as administration, are curiously linked with the position of the Federal Council (the upper house of the German Parliament).[23]

a) Through this traditional and independent institution the Länder participate in the legislative and administrative procedures of the Federal Government (Art. 50). The Federal Council consists of Land representatives bound by the instructions of their respective state (Land) governments. The individual Länder have from three to five votes, depending on the number of their inhabitants (Art. 51). To this extent, the Federal Council must be considered part of the executive. Its most important functions, however, lie in its participation in federal legislation.

This participation takes two forms: the possibility of raising an »objection« to a law adopted by the Bundestag, or lower house, and the requirement of »consent« by the Federal Council in matters where the Basic Law prescribes it. Although an objection can under certain conditions be overruled by the Bundestag, a law which requires approval cannot take effect without the endorsement of the Federal Council (Art. 77 *et seq.*). The institution of the mediation committee (Art. 77 [2]) as an instrument of harmonization between Bundestag and Federal Council - an institution also influenced by American examples - has proven its value in German practice, despite the reduction in clear accountabilities which this may sometimes entail.

b) One peculiarity lies in the fact that the number of federal laws requiring approval has undergone a sharp increase since the start of federal legislation, and now amounts to approximately half of all such federal laws.[24] The founding fathers of the constitution probably did not envisage this. They intended the requirement of approval to cover only exceptional circumstances, such as amendments to the constitution or other isolated cases, such as financial matters, which greatly affect the interests of the Länder. But the perfectly legal use of a single provision, namely Art. 84 (1) of the Basic Law, as a lever has resulted in the large number of federal laws requiring approval. The position of the Federal Council as a prime power factor in federal legislation is thus clearly apparent.

c) The emphasis on and expansion of the position of the Federal Council is often seen as a counter-weight to those lines of development noted earlier which reinforce the central jurisdiction. Efforts to neutralize somewhat the inroads into the competences of the Länder include reinforcing the function of the Federal Council. But this picture of, as it were, communicating pipelines[25] has something all too seductive about it. Not only does the Federal Council take majority decisions, but, above all, the function of the Federal Council would lose its internal legitimacy in the long run if it were not truly anchored in the independent statehood of the Länder.

IV.

Keeping in mind the image of the overall federal government structure in legislation and administration, we have a basis to briefly pursue the links between the federal government principle and other essential and more general components of the constitution as recognized by the Basic Law.

1. The effect of the federal structure in promoting democratic elements is often emphasized.[26] In fact, a subdivision into smaller units which are still fairly easily comprehended facilitates opportunities for the citizen's conscious participation as more than just an elector. This is all the more important in that the Basic Law acknowledges (and with good reason) only modest plebiscitary components in the federal sphere. To the extent that the present democracy takes the form of a party democracy, however, the picture becomes complex. On the one hand, the major inter-regional parties produce strong unitarian effects; fundamental political decisions have a tendency to take effect across Land borders. On the other hand, the political parties have to exist within the Federal Government framework and make use of its machinery; this has federalizing counter-effects.

An additional factor is that the natural weight of the interests of the various Länder frequently runs counter, and effectively so, to the parties' political efforts. There is evidence of this in many of the Federal Council's actions, and it also extends to other forms of cooperation between the Federal Government and the Länder. The voting patterns of the Länder in the Federal Council do not always run entirely parallel to their respective party political shades; sometimes quite surprising constellations and coalitions arise. Federalism ensures that the party political scene will be fairly colorful; the colors in Bavaria, in particular, stand out strongly. Nevertheless, the distinctly legalistic spectacles through which the Federal Council tends to observe matters contributes some objectivity.

2.   The relationship of the federalist principle to the conceptual world of the constitutional state is also ambivalent.[27] The two principles are reconciled in the fundamental concept of federal power-sharing mentioned previously. However, constitutional state components exert powerful unitarian effects. In particular, the highly developed fundamental rights jurisprudence under the Basic Law is applicable nationwide.[28] This tendency is reinforced by Art. 33 (1), which guarantees every German in every Land the same civil rights and obligations.

3.   Most of all, it is the concept of the *social* constitutional state,[29] taking the term in a broad sense with overtones of egalitarianism, which has become the main driving force behind unitarian trends. Even the interpretation of such basic rights as so-called partnership rights[30] points in this direction. The formula of »uniformity of living conditions,«[31] only the rudiments of which are incorporated in the text of the constitution, has become the essential mainstay of standardization.[32] Among the reasons given for the major financial reform of 1967/69 is that public opinion no longer accepts fundamental differences in benefits and disadvantages as being a basic way for their own state to solve public problems. Approximately uniform public services have become an automatic requirement even in a federalist state.[33]

V.

It is therefore consistent with this path of development when the concept of harmonization of living conditions is increasingly carried over even into those areas which are central to the competences of the Länder. Application of this concept has been one important reason for the development of a very extensive self-coordination among the Länder (with somewhat unclear limits), which, in a special way, has breathed life into the far-reaching concept of cooperative federalism, even in the German Federal State.[34]

1. This mutual adjustment between the Länder involves the most varied mechanisms, from a plethora of treaties and administrative agreements down to informal understandings. The travels and meetings of members of the ministerial bureaucracy have become an essential feature of today's German Federal State.

2. It is clear that, as a result, the state executive is being strengthened at the expense of the Länder parliaments.[35] This has led to many complaints but few prescriptions and even fewer treatments. Even in the treaties entered into by the Länder (which require the approval of the Länder parliaments) it can be seen how the importance of those parliaments has been reduced: The actual negotiation of the treaties has always had to be left to the government representatives. The Länder parliaments are becoming mere »instruments of ratification.« If the negative aspects of the Länder parliaments reported earlier are also taken into account, it becomes apparent why these parliaments would no longer attract good people, except in leading positions or as temporary appointments.

This trend towards cooperative federalism also has its dark side. Federalism means increased flexibility, pliability, mobility. But, conversely, one consequence of multilateral treaties which can only be concluded unanimously is the correspondingly greater difficulty of securing change (i.e., »federalism with leaden feet«).

3. In addition, cooperative federalism simultaneously affects a Land's relationship to the Federal Government and here federal powers are at issue. In some fields, such as university education, these trends were incorporated into an amendment to the Basic Law, particularly in the section on the so-called »joint tasks« (Arts. 91 a and 91 b).[36] By and large we have not done badly with them, despite a good many criticisms (e.g., blurring the lines of responsibility). But it must be noted that many regulations which sound very enticing and beneficial for the Länder have another side to them. For example, when Art. 91 a (4) says that the Federal Government will bear half the expenditure for these projects in each Land, the Federal Government is at the same time accused, perhaps too harshly, of dictatorship by handout. After all, what Land minister can afford not to approve the project if the Federal Government is bearing half the cost?

VI.

This brings us back to the financial constitution.[37] In fact, this is a central area of cooperative federalism.

1.   Initially, attention should be drawn to an important peculiarity of the German financial constitution. It separates the responsibility for financial legislation – i.e., mainly fiscal legislation – from the power of determining to whom the various taxes are payable, in other words, what is known as the power of allocation, not to mention the question of how financial administration is to be organized. Whereas the legislative sovereignty in the financial sector lies predominantly with the Federal Government (Art. 105), the income from taxation is allocated in accordance with independent principles (Art. 106). This, indeed, is one of the most important mechanisms of cooperative federalism.

2.   It is true that the financial sovereignty of the Federal Government and of the Länder is, in principle, divided – with particular reference to the rights of municipal political subdivisions to self-administration (see particularly Art. 28 [2]; Art. 106 [5]; Art. 107 [2]). In principle, the Federal Government and the Länder are separately responsible for expenditures arising out of the performance of their duties (Art. 104 a [1]), just as they are fundamentally independent of one another in their budget management (Art. 109 [1]). The intention is that the Federal Government should not be the paying guest of the Länder, as seemed to be the case following the Imperial Constitution of 1871, nor should the Länder be paying guests of the Federal Government, as has often been assumed to be the case under the Weimar Constitution. The Basic Law thus attempts to walk a tightrope to reach this balance, including the allocation of income from taxation.[38]

3.   But it is here that the requirements of cooperation immediately become apparent.

a)   For particularly profitable taxes, a compound system exists. Although the Federal Government and the Länder each take a half share in the proceeds of the income tax and corporation tax (Art. 106 [3]), some of the proceeds of the income tax being allocated in advance to local government (Art. 106 [5]), the Basic Law itself does not specify the proportions in which the particularly profitable turnover tax is to be divided. Instead, these proportions have to be defined, and possibly redefined, by a simple federal act, on the basis of certain criteria; this act requires the consent of the Federal Council (Art. 106 [3 and 4]). Even on this central point, therefore, the flexible solution offered by the Basic Law depends on agreement between the Federal Government and Länder.

b)   The concept of cooperation also achieves a special breakthrough in the matter of revenue equalization between the Länder. To the extent that it is due to the Länder, the yield from taxes follows the principle of »local yield« (Art. 107 [1]). This is the main reason why there are »rich« and »poor« Länder. Under the constitution (Art. 107 [2]), a single federal act, requiring approval, must ensure that the differences in the financial capacities of the Länder are »appropriately equalized.« Therefore negotiations are necessary. The Federal Constitutional Court has endeavored – with what long-term success remains uncertain – to bring these negotiations within a framework of rationality and clarity; in this context the Court characteristically refers to the »confederation« principle of mutual responsibility.[39] This, however, must not mislead us into endowing this phrase with »confederal« overtones, the more so since the Basic Law emphasizes the responsibility of the Federal Government; that is, revenue equalization must be guaranteed by a federal act.

4.   The cooperative trend of modern federalism also permeates many other constitutional areas. It should be stressed, for example, that the Federal Government and the Länder have to take account, in managing their respective independent budgets, of the unifying requirements of overall economic equilibrium (see Art. 109 [2]); by a federal act (again requiring approval) regulations of a certain type may be drawn up, with particular principles which apply equally to Federal Government and Länder (pursuant to Art. 109 [3]). The institution of a multi-year financial budget, among other things, has also been set up on the same constitutional basis, as the concept of cooperation undergoes a special process of updating in general terms, and extending beyond the financial sector in many institutions of inter-regional »planning.«[40] Exaggerated manifestations of a kind of planning euphoria, fashionable for a time, seem to have died out in Germany, as evidenced, for example, by the fate of a so-called »global educational plan.«[41]

VII.

If we absorb the implications of the overall picture of present-day German federalism as described so far, two fundamental and interwoven questions arise. The first is whether federalism, despite its perceptible advantages, may not after all be a stumbling block on the road towards giving full validity to that objective which has become the dominant force in all those cooperative forms – the objective of uniform living conditions throughout the federal territory. Second, there is the question of whether, in view of this widespread unitarian tendency, today's Germany is really still a federal state at all - remembering the corresponding and ultimately unsolved problems of the Weimar days.

1.   The first question, whether federalism is a stumbling block, may be answered as follows: Certainly the obligation to strike a balance between many different decision centers does involve numerous delaying factors; also, the manpower required to run the bureaucracy is probably excessive. The original opportunity to eliminate certain gradients by redrawing Land borders (see Art. 29)[42] was wasted in practical terms and is virtually obsolete. But in deeper, more fundamental respects I see no more real contradictions between federal variety and the trend towards creating approximately equal living standards. An important factor here is that today's Federal Republic is a state based not on hegemony but, by and large, on approximate equilibrium. It may even be not merely a misfortune – though it is a misfortune – that we have no real capital city; but, there may be an opportunity here, too. The organizational forms of today's typically equalizing federalism are presumably better suited to bring about uniform standards by way of competition based on approximately equal chances than an organization based on hegemony or centralism. The federal doctrine, which in the past was determined somewhat unilaterally by the concepts of power sharing on the one hand and cooperation on the other, may be capable of extension in this direction. Taking this view, the concept of egalitarian adaptation typical of a social state seems to be not so much a natural enemy, but perhaps even a component of the justification and purpose of modern federalism, a component, of course, as I said initially, to which other components must be added.

From this starting point, we can also answer the second fundamental question:[43] Some people may think that the unitarian tendencies of the present-day Federal State have led the Federal Republic away from the image of a true federalist state, and that in fact it is a unitary state with federalistic window dressing. This view overlooks the fact that there is no such thing as an abstract, »true« federal state, in particular not one which has more the characteristics of a confederation (of states), which tacitly assumes the opposite opinion. Certainly, the Federal Republic is no longer based on a »league« of states; but, it is certainly experienced by the population as a real, functional federal state. The theory of the »true« federal state is incapable of solving even one of the truly important federalistic problems. On the other hand, there is no reason not to detach the material concept of the federal state from one-sided adherence to obsolete notions of an alliance and to see it realized in the specific, living forms of expression chosen by the Basic Law, in forms which should not be dismissed as mere technicalities and facades.

VIII.

However, as we shall note on in this last section, none of this has yet determined how the federalist system as it exists is likely to deal with certain future challenges.

1. If our view is correct, there are two main developments against which the system will again have to prove its worth. The first of these developments is determined by new trends on the industrial and technological fronts. We can consider this in the context of the new media technologies such as cable and satellite broadcasting. The sharing of governmental responsibilities between Federal Government and Länder was influenced by the state of industry and technology at the time the constitution was drawn up, when future trends could be predicted only to a limited extent. It is true that we can still make a theoretical distinction between broadcasting technology, which is in principle the province of the Federal Government, and the broadcasting program sector, which is in principle allocated to the Länder. However, the special characteristic of many new developments, in this field among others, lies in the fact that these distinctions are in many cases becoming inadequate or miss the point altogether; this happens where general material imperatives arise which are characterized by a significant degree of mutual interdependence of the sub-areas. What benefit would the Länder derive from their responsibility for questions of content relating to

the organization of new media if the Federal Government, in charge of the law governing the technology of those media, wanted to steer technological developments into channels at variance with the Länder's strategy (or even block those developments under some circumstances)? And suppose the Länder are unable to agree on decisions which have to be taken on an inter-regional basis? In such cases, the existing channels of responsibility would to some extent be destroyed from within. As mentioned, the appeal to federal loyalty does compel procedural correctness and consideration, but cannot replace a decision in the matter itself. Here again, it is hardly possible to resort to constitutional amendments as a remedy, the more so since they presuppose a broad consensus which will not necessarily exist. German federal doctrine has yet to come up with any effective solutions here. What can be done is to thread the maze on a pragmatic basis.

2.   A second fundamental test is ultimately of much greater practical significance. This springs from increasing international ties, in particular the incorporation of the Federal Republic into the European Communities.

a)   According to Art. 24 (1), the Federal Government can »assign« rights of sovereignty to international institutions by a simple act, which according to prevalent opinion does not even require approval. This assignment, which is not clearly formulated in this respect, is principally understood as the withdrawal by the Federal Republic of its exclusive and absolute right of control within its national territory for the purpose of permitting the direct exercise of sovereign power by another authority within that national territory.[44] In this way it becomes possible, within the territory of the European Community or Communities (EC), particularly the European Economic Community (EEC), for »supranational« law to be directly valid in the Federal Republic under certain circumstances and to be applied as a priority.[45] As a result of the enormous expansion in the supranational law authorized in this way, particularly EEC law, new facts and dimensions are being established on a large scale. The fathers of the constitution could hardly have visualized such modernization.

b)   Problems of a federalist nature principally arise from the fact that it is not only Federal Government competences but also those of the Länder which are »assigned,« and that the EC law thus established takes greater and greater effect directly or indirectly at a Land level. The Federal Government can to some extent compensate for waiving its rights through the fact that the Federal Government exerts an influence principally through the Council of Ministers of the EC; even so, the principle of unanimity enjoys by no means unrestricted supremacy in the EC area.[46] The federal Länder, however, have to rely on the fact that the Federal Government represents their interests in the EC area – understandably, the Federal Republic has to speak with one voice when addressing outsiders.[47] The Treaty of Rome is, as H.P. Ipsen says, »blind to regions,«[48] and, in fact, the Federal Republic is the only fully-developed federalist state in the EC. This has resulted in the development of complex internal agreement procedures between the Federal Government and the Länder, particularly with the aid of the Federal Council,[49] though this has been said to function incorrectly in some cases. Also, the imagination of the Länder has created other subtle forms of indirect diplomatic presence in the EC area, which again has created new situations.[50]

c)   None of this alters the fact that the competences of the Länder, which had already been weakened, are being further constricted by the vastly increasing importance and density of EC law, particularly with a view to the rapid establishment of a single internal market with unrestricted movement of goods, individuals, services, and capital (target date: December 31st, 1992).

Nor is it the case that, in view of the economic character of the EEC, the legislative fields of culture and education,[51] left principally with the Länder, have remained untouched. In fact, full exercise of the competences laid down in the Treaty of Rome also intrudes in these areas. This gives rise to structural uncertainties, one example being the relationship of the general »aims« of the EEC to the significance of restricting the Treaty of Rome to economically relevant spheres. For example, it follows from the decisions of the European Court of Justice that although education policy (as such) does not fall within the scope of the Treaty of Rome, access to instruction, in the broadest sense, does (as provided in detail particularly by Art. 128 of the Treaty).[52] Over and above this, the Federal Government and Länder find themselves in many ways compelled to adopt a community-friendly European education policy.

d)   Recently, these and other currents of development, again, typically, in the field of broadcasting, have highlighted the question of whether or not the fundamental federalist concept, as reflected beyond the governmental field in the significance of the »regions,« might not be put to better use on a supranational basis, ultimately advancing rather than hindering efforts at unification, the more so since there is virtually no direct democratic parliamentary authority for the law established by the EC, in view of the clear predominance of the executive.

e) In conclusion, let me note that it is from this same angle that we should view those considerations that deal with the extent to which unwritten federalist restrictions are attached to Art. 24 (1), in other words, to the national basis of authority for EC law. This issue is now at the heart of a constitutional dispute before the Constitutional Court. In an earlier decision, the Federal Constitutional Court recognized that Art. 24 (1), must not be used to undermine the »identity« of the constitution.[53] It is not only the present speaker who hopes that this statement may be taken as referring to the Federal Government structures, and may be clarified by the high authority of the Court.

Notes:

1 For summaries of German federalism, see P. Badura, Staatsrecht, 1986, pp. 222 *et seq.;* Chr. Degenhart, Staatsrecht I, 4th ed. 1988, pp. 28 *et seq.;* J.A. Frowein, Deutscher Föderalismus der Gegenwart, 1981; R. Hesse, »Bundesstaat« in Evangelisches Staatslexikon I, 3rd ed. 1987, column 317 *et seq.; idem,* Der unitarische Bundesstaat, 1962; R. Herzog in Maunz-Dürig, Grundgesetz, Art. 20, I - IV.; 0. Kimminich in Isensee/Kirchhof (eds.), Handbuch des Staatsrechts I, 1987, pp. 1113 *et seq.;* P. Lerche, Föderalismus als nationales Ordnungsprinzip, Veröffentlichungen der Vereinigung der Deutschen Staatsrechtslehrer, 21 (1964), pp. 66 *et seq.;* Th. Maunz and R. Zippelius, Deutsches Staatsrecht, 27th ed., 1988, pp. 99 *et seq.;* U. Scheuner, »Kooperation und Konflikt in Staatstheorie und Staatsrecht, 1978, pp. 399 *et seq.;* R. Stern, Das Staatsrecht der Bundesrepublik Deutschland I, 2nd ed., 1984, pp. 635 *et seq.*
2 On the history of German federalism, see in particular the multi-volume accounts in E.R. Huber, Deutsche Verfassungsgeschichte seit 1789; Jeserich, Pohl, and v. Unruh (eds.), Deutsche Verwaltungsgeschichte.
3 Summarized in 0. Kimminich, *supra* note 1, at 1130.
4 Cf. for example - apart from E.R. Huber, *supra* note 1 - E. Kaufmann, Bismarcks Erbe in der Reichsverfassung, 1917; H. Triepel, Unitarismus und Föderalismus im deutschen Reich, 1907; *idem,* Die Reichsaufsicht, 1917.
5 R. Smend also found the statehood of the Länder »dubious.« See Die Verfassung des Deutschen Reichs, 1929, p. XI.
6 For further details see R. Mußgnug, Zustandekommen des Grundgesetzes und der Bundesrepublik Deutschland in Isensee-Kirchhof, *supra* note 1, I, pp. 219 *et seq.,* 227 and 228, 245 *et seq.*
7 Cf. for example Badura *supra* note 1, at 222 and 223.
8 Cf. R. Hesse, Bundesstaatsreform und Grenzen der Verfassungsänderung, Archiv des öffentlichen Rechts 93 (1973) 1 *et seq.;* P. Kirchhof, »Die Identität

87

der Verfassung in ihren unabänderlichen Inhalten«, in Isensee-Kirchhof *supra* note 1, at 775 *et seq.*, 807 and 809; and U. Scheuner, *supra* note 1, at 427.

9 P. Lerche, *supra* note 1, at 85 *et seq.*

10 R. Smend, »Ungeschriebenes Verfassungsrecht im monarchischen Bundesstaat,« in Festgabe für Otto Mayer, 1916, pp. 245 *et seq.*

11 See BVerfGE 1, 299 (315).

12 P. Badura *supra* note 1, at 232.

13 For further details see R. Scholz, Der Status Berlins in Isensee-Kirchhof I, *supra* note 1, at 351 *et seq.*, 375 *et seq.*

14 See in particular Art. 74, No. 1 (11) of the Basic Law.

15 Apart from special forms, a distinction is made between the exclusive (Art. 71, 73), concurrent (Art. 72, 74) and skeletal legislation (Art. 75) of the Federal Government; in view of Art. 30, there is no explicit catalog of exclusive Land legislation.

16 BVerfGE 12, 205.

17 Cf. R. Hesse, Der unitarische Bundesstaat, 1962.

18 Cf. e.g. BVerfGE 55, 274 (on the one hand 308 and 309; on the other 319 and 320).

19 See, for example, the survey in W. Rudolf, Die Bundesstaatlichkeit in der Rechtsprechung des Bundesverfassungsgerichts in Bundesverfassungsgericht und Grundgesetz, II, 1976, pp. 233 *et seq.*

20 BVerfGE 39, 96 (120 and 121).

21 See BVerfGE 3, 407 (421 and 422); for further details see M. Bullinger, Ungeschriebene Kompetenzen im Bundesstaat, Archiv des öffentlichen Rechts 96 (1971), 237 *et seq.;* H. Triepel, Die Kompetenzen des Bundesstaats und die geschriebene Verfassung in Festgabe für Laband, II, 1908, pp. 247 and 248.

22 On this general subject, see P. Lerche in Maunz-Dürig, Grundgesetz, Art. 83, note 60 and 61 and Art. 84, note 1 *et seq.*

23 Cf. R. Herzog, Stellung des Bundesrates im demokratischen Bundesstaat in Isensee-Kirchhof, *supra* note 1, at 467 *et seq.; idem* Aufgaben des Bundesrates, pp. 489 *et seq.*

24 For further details see P. Lerche *supra* note 22, Art. 84, note 68 *et seq.*, 78 *et seq.*

25 See P. Lerche, Aktuelle föderalistische Verfassungsfragen 1968, p. 40 *et seq.*

26 E.g., K. Hesse *supra* note 1, columns 319 and 325 (Ev. Staatslexikon).

27 E.g., K. Hesse, Grundzüge des Verfassungsrechts der Bundesrepublik Deutschland 16th ed., 1988, p. 87 *et seq.*

28 With regard to the joint responsibility of the Federal Government and Länder on the distribution of free university places, see BVerfGE 33, 303 (352 *et seq.*, 357 and 358); also R. Wahl, Grundrechte und Staatszielbestimmungen im Bundesstaat,« Archiv des öffentlichen Rechts 112 (1987), 26 *et seq.*

29 Cf. A. Rottgen, »Der soziale Bundesstaat« in Festgabe für Muthesius, 1960, pp. 19 *et seq.;* H. Zacher, »Das soziale Staatsziel« in Isensee-Kirchhof *supra* note 1, at 1045 *et seq.*, 1093 and 1094.

30 Cf. the reports by P. Haberle and W. Martens, Grundrechte im Leistungsstaat, Veröffentlichungen der Vereinigung der Deutschen Staatsrechtslehrer 30 (1972), p. 43 *et seq.*, 7 *et seq.*

31 Cf. P. Lerche, Finanzausgleich und Einheitlichkeit der Lebensverhältnisse, in Festschrift für Berber, 1973, pp. 299 *et seq.;* R. Herzoq in Maunz-Dürig,

Grundgesetz, Art. 20, Notes 89 to IV rightly emphasize that this is a regional problem.

32 U. Scheuner, *supra* note 1, at 425.

33 Begründung des Regierungsentwurfs des Finanzreformgesetzes, Bundestag publication V/2861, heading 10, p.11.

34 See, for example, W. Kewenig, Kooperativer Föderalismus und bundesstaatliche Ordnung, Archiv des öffentlichen Rechts 93 (1968), 433 *et seq.; G. Kisker, Kooperation im Bundesstaat, 1971; F.W. Scharpf, B. Reissert, and F. Schnabel, Politikverflechtung: Theorie und Empirie des kooperativen Föderalismus in der Bundesrepublik, 1976; U. Scheuner *supra* note 1. Uncertainties exist, for example, in the administrative sector on when the limit of unacceptable mixed administration (transfer of responsibilities) is reached or can be taken further; cf. in particular BVerfGE 63, 1 (36 *et seq.*).

35 With respect to these problems see E.W. Böckenförde, »Sozialer Bundesstaat und parlamentarische Demokratie,« in Schafer-Festschrift, 1980, pp. 182 *et seq.; J.* Frowein, Gemeinschaftsaufgaben im Bundesstaat, Veröffentlichungen der Vereinigung der Deutschen Staatsrechtslehrer 31 (1973), pp. 13 *et seq., 24 et seq.*

36 Cf. the reports by J. Frowein and I. V. Münch, Publications of the Association of German Constitutional Jurists 31 (1973), pp. 13 *et seq.,* 51 *et seq.*

37 Cf. in particular the commentaries on Art. 104a *et seq.* by H. Fischer-Menshausen in V. Münch (ed.), Grundgesetz-Kommentar, III, 2nd ed., 1983; by T. Maunz in Maunz-Dürig, Grundgesetz, and by R. Vogel-P. Kirchhof *et al* in the Bonn Commentary on the Basic Law. Also, in particular, P. Badura *supra* note 1, at 489 *et seq.,* 516 *et seq.;* and W. Boning-A. v. Mutius and H. Schlegelberger, Finanzkontrolle im föderativen Staat, 1982. See also R.H. Friauf, »Die Finanzverfassung in der Rechtsprechung des Bundesverfassungsgerichts« in Bundesverfassungsgericht und Grundgesetz, II, 1976, p. 300 *et seq.; R.* Hettlage, »Finanzverfassung und Finanzverwaltung« in Staatslexikon 7th ed., II, 1986, columns 605 *et seq.; H.* Spanner, »Über Finanzreform und Bundesstaat«, in Maunz-Festgabe, 1971, pp. 375 *et. seq.*

38 See for example, BVerfGE 39, 96 (108); 72, 330 (388).

39 BVerfGE 72, 330 (386, 419). At the same time the Court also perceives the limit of the assistance obligation (386 et *seq.)* in this principle, and generally stresses the significance of the normative commitments of the financial system (see especially 388 *et seq.,* 390).

40 See, for example J. Kaiser (ed.), Planung I, 1965; W. Graf Vitzthum, Parlament und Planung, 1978; and Th. Würtenberger, Staatsrechtliche Probleme politischer Planung, 1979.

41 Chr. Degenhart *supra* note 1, at 75.

42 The power of reorganization of Art. 29 was originally worded as an instruction to reorganize.

43 See W. Weber, Spannungen und Kräfte im westdeutschen Verfassungssystem, 3rd ed. 1970, especially p. 63; on the other hand see P. Lerche, Kommende föderalistische Probleme, in Carstens, Goppel, Kissinger, Mann (eds.), Franz Josef Strauss, 1985, pp. 338 *et seq.*

44 See, for example, BVerfGE 59, 63 (90); 68, 1 (90 and 91); 73, 339 (374).

45 See, for example, BVerfGE 73, 339 (375); 75, 223 (242 and 243).

46 See in particular Articles 148 and 235 of the Treaty of Rome.

47 See, Chr. Tomuschat, Bonner Kommentar zum Grundgesetz, Art. 24, revised edition, note 100.
48 See H.P. Ipsen in the Hallstein Festschrift, 1966, pp. 248 *et seq.*, 256 *et seq.*
49 Cf. the so-called Federal Council Proceedings according to Art. 2 of the Act consenting to the Single European Act.
50 See R. Hrbek and U. Thaysen (eds.), Die Deutschen Länder und die Europäischen Gemeinschaften, 1986.
51 See H.P. Ipsen, »Der Kulturbereich im Zugriff der Europäischen Gemeinschaft« in Geck Memorial, 1989, pp. 339 *et seq.*
52 On the »Gravier« judgement of February 13th, 1985, see Th. Oppermann, Europäisches Gemeinschaftsrecht und deutsche Bildungsordnung, 1987.
53 BVerfGE 37, 271 (279 and 280, 291, 296); 58, 1 (40); 73, 339 (375 and 376); 75, 223 (240).

Arthur B. Gunlicks

Principles of American Federalism

I.   *Some Initial Comparisons with Germany*

In spite of many significant differences in their constitutional histories, it is tempting to look for some evidence, however limited, of parallel developments of relevance to the history of federalism in the United States and Germany. A comparison of the German states in the Empire with the thirteen colonies under the British monarch reveals important differences, and the thirty-eight German states that survived as sovereign units after the final collapse of the Empire in 1806 and formed the German Confederation of 1815 and Customs Union of 1834 can also be compared only with reservations to the thirteen independent American states under the Articles of Confederation between 1781 and 1789. Nevertheless, the formation of the United States in 1789 and of the Bismarck or Hohenzollern Reich in 1871 as federal systems was due in large part to the pre-existence of sovereign constituent states that rejected a unitary solution to the problem of national unity.

Federalism in the new United States, as in the new German Reich, was the result of a political compromise between a unitary state and what we would call today a confederation (the American Founders generally referred to their creation as a confederation, but what they meant was later called a federation). In both cases a system of »dual federalism« was created, but this term had a different meaning in each country.

In the United States the idea behind the concept was that the national government has one set of enumerated functional responsibilities, the states and their local governments another set of unenumerated reserve powers. The federal government as well as the state governments legislate, execute and adjudicate their own laws, with the federal courts exercising judicial review over federal (and state) legislative and executive actions and over state supreme court decisions. Each level is responsible for financing its own public policies. There is little overlap; however, in case of conflict in an area of concurrent powers, federal law is supreme. A relatively moderate form of dual federalism existed during the Marshall era until about 1830, but it was followed by a more pronounced focus on the states during the Jacksonian era which took the form of a militant states' rights doctrine in the South. The doctrine of states' rights was modified and severely weakened by the defeat of the South in the Civil War, the policies of the reconstruction era, and the Civil War Amendments; however, dual federalism was revived in other ways by interpretations of the Tenth Amendment[1] that protected the states from federal interference with their traditional police powers in the areas of health, welfare, safety, and morals.

This dual federalism prevailed until federal policies identified mostly with the New Deal brought the federal government into areas previously considered to be the responsibility of the states or, in the view of some critics, to be outside the area of any government's responsibility. Many of these policies called for some form of cooperation, for example, through shared financing, between the federal and state/local governments, which led to what came to be called cooperative federalism. Lyndon Johnson's Great Society programs brought about a dramatic increase in cooperative policies in which the national, state and local governments shared in numerous ways the administrative and fiscal responsibility for most public services and activities. Since then the network of complex interrelationships among governments in the United States has been frequently referred to as intergovernmental relations. In the 1970s dissatisfaction with the confusion, lack of accountability, growing national influence and dependency relationships between the national and state/local governments, and inefficiencies led to severe criticisms of intergovernmental relations and to demands, such as those reflected in the »sorting out« or »swap« proposals of President Ronald Reagan's »new federalism,« that efforts be undertaken to return to something more like the old dual federalism.

German scholars also sometimes refer to the traditional German system of federalism as »dual federalism,« but here the concept can mean something quite different from the American term. What Germans usually mean is that federalism in the German tradition is characterized by policy making in most areas at the national level and policy implementation at the state (since 1919, *Land*) level. The *Länder* are not, however, mere administrative subdivisions of the national government. They enjoy a large degree of autonomy in their administration of national policies. In addition, municipalities – in contrast to the *ultra vires* tradition in the Anglo-Saxon countries that restricts local governments to the activities permitted them in their charters – have had considerable discretionary powers since the early nineteenth century, that is, the right to engage in any activity that does not violate national or *Land* law.

German federalism has also differed from the American model in the German adherence to the continental European practice of »unity of command« (*Einheit der Verwaltung*). In theory at least, this concept requires that the administration of all laws and regulations be combined in each subnational territorial unit. Thus, in addition to administering its own laws, each *Land* is responsible for administering all federal laws and regulations delegated to it. Because most of these national and *Land* laws are then turned over to the local governments for administration, the local units become responsible for the administration of national, *Land* and local laws, regulations and ordinances within their respective territorial boundaries. This territorial or »spatial« system of administration contrasts sharply with the intergovernmentalized and highly dispersed and fragmented »functional« administration (e.g., independent regulatory commissions, special districts) characteristic of American public administration.[2]

Unfortunately, some German scholars also describe German federalism and administration as »functional.« By this they mean, again, that the national government has the function of legislating, while the *Länder* have the function of administering most national laws.

On the other hand, the late Frido Wagener, a leading scholar of German public administration, insisted that functional administration – whether in a federal or a unitary system – is administration by task, examples of which would be the American system of »picket fence« federalism and government by special districts or, in Great Britain, administration by »quangos.« He sometimes referred to this as »vertical administration.«[3] Other authors, for example, Arnold Brecht, have referred to American dual federalism as a »vertical« division of power between the nation and the states,[4] which is a narrower but related application of Wagener's use of »vertical administration.« Gordon Smith makes use of the term »dual administration,« which seems to be the same thing as Wagener's general concept of »functional administration.«[5] Just to confuse matters further, however, some American textbook authors use the term »vertical« in a wholly atheoretical sense of merely describing relations among the national, state and local governments.[6]

Territorial or spatial administration that results from the continental system of unity of command makes the chief administrative officer of each level of administration (whether in a unitary of federal system) legally responsible for all of the public services and activities, whether delegated, mandated or self-generated, within his territory (e.g., the former French prefects). In the Federal Republic even units of administration that are roughly similar to American special districts, e.g., *Zweckverbände*, fall under the administrative responsibility of the chief administrative officer, e.g., county manager (*Landrat*) of a territorial, general purpose unit of administration. This is what Gordon Smith refers to as »fused administration,«[7] though it is more frequently called »horizontal administration.« Frido Wagener and other authors, including Arnold Brecht, used this latter term to distinguish territorial or spatial administration from »vertical« or »functional« administration. But »horizontal« administration, too, is sometimes used atheoretically by American textbook authors to describe relationships among administrative structures within one level or plane of government.

In practice each model of administration, the »functional« and the »spatial,« have been moving toward each other in a mixed system of intergovernmental relations. In the United States numerous nationally inspired programs have been turned over to the states and/or local governments for partial administration, sometimes with very loose federal supervision, while »picket fence« federalism, involving functional experts at the national, state and local levels, continues as well. Functional relationships among experts at different levels (*Fachbrüderschaften*) also exist in German federalism, especially since the finance reform of 1969. Whether characterized by a system of functional administration (Great Britain, United States) or spatial administration (France and Germany), and regardless of their unitary (Great Britain, France) or federal (United States, Germany) organization, Western European countries and the United States have been moving toward a highly complex system of shared powers, or intergovernmental relations (*Politikverflechtung*), that challenges the older, more standard descriptive concepts.

II. The Constitution and American Dual Federalism to 1941

In spite of numerous and significant changes in the constitutional interpretation of the proper relationship between the federal and state governments between 1789 and the immediate post-World War II period, Edward S. Corwin maintained in 1950 that the *structural* features of the American federal system still remain what they have always been, to wit:

1. A written Constitution which is regarded as »law« and »supreme law«;

2. As in all federations, the union of several autonomous political entities or »States« for common purposes;

94

3. The division of the sum total of legislative powers between a »general government,« on the one hand, and the »States,« on the other;

4. The direct operation for the most part of each center of government, acting within its assigned sphere, upon all persons and property within its territorial limits;

5. The provision of each center with the complete apparatus, both executive and judicial, for law enforcement;

6. Judicial review, that is, the power and duty of all courts, and ultimately of the Supreme Court of the Union, to disallow all legislative or executive acts of either center of government which in the Court's opinion transgress the Constitution;

7. An elaborate and cumbersome method of constitutional amendment, in which the States have a deciding role.[8]

Certainly from our perspective today there is a problem with this description of American federalism. From 1787 to the present time, there has been controversy over just what the »assigned sphere« in item 4 is or should be for the federal and state governments. Until the New Deal, this issue was dealt with through the concept of dual federalism. While there was never a consensus about its meaning,[9] Corwin suggested that dual federalism consisted of four postulates:

1. The national government is one of enumerated powers only;

2. Also the purposes which it may constitutionally promote are few;

3. Within their respective spheres the two centers of government are »sovereign« and hence »equal«;

4. The relation of the two centers with each other is one of tension rather than collaboration.[10]

Much of the history of federalism in the United States deals with these four postulates. In the remainder of this paper, I will review briefly some of the major developments in the evolution of the concept of dual federalism to its alleged demise in 1941, its apparent revival in 1976, its renewed burial in 1985, and its constitutional and political status today.

Dual Federalism, 1789-1860[11] - From the beginning, there was a nationalist and a states' rights perspective on American federalism. Supporters of each position differed over the question of whether the Constitution was a contract among the people of the United States or a compact of »sovereign« states.[12] The first, or nationalist, view was that the federal government is the government of all the people and as such can exercise broad powers through the general welfare clause, the commerce clause, and the necessary and proper clause of Article I, Section 8, and the supremacy clause of Article VI. The implications of the second theory are that the federal government is limited to a narrow range of enumerated powers while the states and the people in the states have all residual powers under the Tenth Amendment. These are the views of Hamilton and Jefferson, respectively, and they are reflected in Hamilton's policy initiatives as Secretary of the Treasury in the presidency of George Washington and in the Jefferson and Madison-sponsored Virginia and Kentucky Resolutions of 1798 which were passed in reaction to the Alien and Sedition Acts. The states' rights perspective is also evident in the Hartford Convention of 1814, called in reaction against federal policies in the War of 1812. While these events demonstrated serious disagreement over the nature of the union, they were also partisan disagreements between Federalists and Republicans.[13]

The doctrine of nullification developed by John C. Calhoun was more clearly a conflict between two theories of federalism. In 1831 Calhoun wrote that sovereignty was indivisible and absolute, and in the United States it lay with the states which formed the union for limited purposes. South Carolina claimed in 1828 and 1832 the right as a sovereign state to declare acts of Congress unconstitutional and, if necessary, to secede.

President Andrew Jackson was also a staunch advocate of dual federalism, but even he opposed the doctrinaire states' rights views of Calhoun and his followers. He discouraged a more active federal government in favor of economic policymaking by the states; however, in the final analysis he accepted the thesis of federal sovereignty and rejected the argument that states could annul a law of the United States or secede. Jackson was saved from having to take action against South Carolina when it failed to gain the support of other states and agreed to a compromise settlement of the tariff issue.[14]

The Supreme Court under Chief Justice John Marshall is well known, of course, for its pro-Federalist, national supremacy interpretations of the Constitution. Whether in granting Congress broad powers to regulate interstate commerce (*Gibbons v. Ogden*, 1824),[15] or in intrepreting the »necessary and proper« clause of Article I, Section 8, in such a manner as to maximize federal authority (*McCulloch v. Maryland*, 1819),[16] the Court laid the basis for later expansive interpretations of federal powers that continue to the present day. On the other hand, even Marshall noted limitations on federal powers, when he suggested that the states are »for some purposes sovereign, and for some purposes subordinate« (*Cohens v. Virginia*, 1821).[17]

Roger Taney, Chief Justice from 1836 to 1864, did not share Marshall's views regarding national supremacy and took a much more dual federalist position which expanded the power of the states in relation to the federal government. Thus, in contrast to the Marshall Court, the Taney Court defined commerce narrowly and facilitated the exercise of state police power in ways that affected interstate commerce. It even recognized a concurrent state power to regulate interstate commerce in the absence of congressional legislation.[18]

Without disavowing federal supremacy, the Court treated the existence of the states with their reserved powers as a limitation of federal authority. The state police power, or as Taney preferred to call it, state sovereignty, marked out certain subjects as exclusively within the jurisdiction of the states and beyond the reach of the national government. This feature of dual federalism subsequently enabled it to serve the South's need for an instrument of constitutional power with which to protect slavery against federal intervention.[19]

While the Taney Court's views on dual federalism favored the states, they also had the effect of expanding federal judicial powers. As the Dred Scott (*Dred Scott v. Sandford*, 1857)[20] case demonstrated, »under pressure to defend slavery the Court regarded itself as uniquely qualified to umpire conflicts within the federal system.«[21] It was not just the pressure of slavery, however, that led the Court to support the umpire role; this had also been the position of the Marshall Court.[22] As we shall see later, this view of the Court's role in the federal system was thoroughly and formally rejected in 1985 and 1988.

The Taney Court's attempts to settle the deep political conflicts between North and South by judicial means failed, and it was left to the outcome of the Civil War to determine the future of the American federal system. The Calhoun doctrine of nullification failed in 1832 when other states did not support South Carolina, but it remained the backbone of a militant states' rights doctrine until the Civil War.[23] Not until after the War in *Texas v. White* (1869)[24] did the Supreme Court rule that »The Constitution, in all its provisions, looks to an indestructible Union, composed of indestructible States.« This put to rest the argument that the Constitution was a compact of sovereign states with the right to secede.[25]

Dual Federalism, 1861-1937[26] - Following the Civil War, the passage of the Thirteenth, Fourteenth, and Fifteenth Amendments and civil rights legislation, civil rights were nationalized to a considerable extent. However, the dual-federalist view that national and state citizenship was separate was not rejected, and many civil rights, including voting rights, were left to the states until well into the twentieth century. Also the Court held that federal legislation applied to state actions only, not to private discrimination, which had the effect of limiting the impact of the federal civil rights amendments and laws. The »separate but equal« doctrine of *Plessy v. Ferguson* (1896)[27] was, of course, the best example of the limitations imposed by the Court.[28]

For our purposes, however, the most relevant actions of the Court had to do with its interpretations of the commerce power. The industrial revolution in the United States following the Civil War brought about attempts by the federal and state governments to regulate the economy. Until about 1890 the Court generally upheld especially the federal commerce power and to a lesser extent the police power of the states to regulate the economy.[29] Until the end of the nineteenth century, there was little conflict between the federal and state governments over economic regulation.

No constitutional principle was more fundamental than that which gave the federal government specific powers to deal with matters of general national import, while reserving to the states the general power to govern the social and economic affairs of the people of their local communities. The power to legislate for the health, safety, welfare and morals of the community was called the police power, and it belonged principally to the states. The federal government was not completely excluded from police power considerations, but its chief involvement was negative insofar as it placed restrictions on state legislation. Federal ability to affect the internal welfare of the people by positive legislation consisted mainly in the power over foreign and interstate commerce. But from the beginning of the government to the late nineteenth century little legislation was adopted on this basis.[30]

In the 1890s and after, however, the Supreme Court, under the influence of laissez faire liberalism, sought to protect entrepreneurial liberty against both federal and state regulations that it considered excessive. The Court's substantive interpretation of the due process clause of the Fifth and Fourteenth Amendments came to mean, as the doctrine of vested rights before it had meant, that there were certain things that government, especially legislatures, could not do, regardless of the procedure or process it followed.[31] Thus, »instead of confining itself to the question of whether a legislative power was constitutional, the Supreme Court increasingly concerned itself with the wisdom of legislation.«[32]

Not all efforts of Congress to regulate the economy were rejected by the Court. Indeed, the Interstate Commerce Act of 1887, which regulated the railroads, and the Sherman Antitrust Act of 1890 were only the beginning of significant federal regulatory legislation, especially under the influence of the progressive reformers of the late nineteenth and early twentieth centuries. Congress used its commerce and taxing powers to legislate for the general welfare as though it possessed federal police powers, and the Supreme Court generally went along.[33] However, the Court is also well known for the instances when it said not both to state and federal regulation.

In *Lochner v. New York* (1905),[34] it ruled that the state regulation of working hours in a bakery violated the employer's and employee's liberty of contract under the due process clause of the Fourteenth Amendment. In *Adair v. United States* (1908),[35] it rejected a congressional law that made it a crime for a company involved in interstate commerce to dismiss an employee for membership in a labor union on the grounds that this law violated the employer's and employee's liberty of contract under the due process clause of the Fifth Amendment. And in *Hammer v. Dagenhart* (1918),[36] the Court ruled unconstitutional an act prohibiting the interstate transportation of goods produced by child labor, primarily on the grounds that this was an attempt to regulate production, a state responsibility under the Tenth Amendment, and was not really directed at interstate commerce. The persuasiveness of this decision was not helped by the misquotation of the Tenth Amendment through the addition of »expressly« in »the powers not [expressly] delegated to the national government are reserved to the states.«[37] In a number of cases that followed, the Court upheld these rulings in spite of growing criticism that it was usurping legislative powers and deciding cases on the basis of the justices' social and political attitudes.

With the Depression after 1929, the presidency of Franklin D. Roosevelt, and the advent of the New Deal in 1933, Congress became particularly active in economic and social legislation. Over a sixteen-month period, starting in January 1935, the Supreme Court decided ten major cases involving New Deal legislation.[38] It ruled eight of these unconstitutional, in part on the grounds that the provisions of the statutes violated the Tenth Amendment. There was no dispute over the fact that the President and Congress were attempting to expand dramatically the reach of federal power, even though it was not always clear that this was necessarily at the expense of the states. The Court decisions that negated federal attempts to deal with the economic emergency were greeted by a storm of criticism, and in 1937, following his resounding victory in the presidential elections of 1936, President Roosevelt suggested that the Court's membership be expanded from nine to fifteen and that retirement of federal judges in most cases be set at seventy years of age. While this proposal was met with considerable hostility in Congress, which in the end never acted on it, the Supreme Court began to change direction under Chief Justice Charles Hughes and Justice Owen Roberts. After the introduction of the »court-packing plan« in Congress, the Court upheld several important laws, including a state law establishing a minimum wage, the Farm Mortgage Act of 1935, the Railway Labor Act of 1934, and the Social Security Act of 1935. The case most frequently cited as indicating the »change in time to save nine« is the *National Labor Relations Board v. Jones and Laughlin Steel Corporation* (1937)[39] in which the power of Congress to regulate the economy under the commerce clause was again given wide scope.

Then in *United States v Darby* (1941), the Court said that the Tenth Amendment »states but a truism that all is retained which has not been surrendered.«[40] This ruling seemed to undermine entirely any constitutional role of the Tenth Amendment as a barrier to the exercise of national power under the commerce clause. No longer could the states and their local governments look to the Constitution and the federal courts for protection against an increasingly active and intrusive federal government. Dual federalism was dead.

III. *Cooperative Federalism and Intergovernmental Relations*

In the nineteenth century, grants from the federal government to the states were rare. A federal surplus was distributed in 1837, and various land grants, including the Morrill Act of 1862, were made throughout the century. Not until 1911, however, did federal grants contain provisions for a systematic federal control characteristic of modern grant-in-aid programs.[41] In 1900 five cash grant programs were in effect, and by 1920 six more were added, including the agricultural extension service and highway construction. By 1930 fifteen grant programs were in existence, with highway support replacing education as the most common purpose. The total amount of expenditure was very modest, however, and only about two percent of all state revenues were derived from federal grants in 1927.[42]

With the Depression, the New Deal, and the demise of dual federalism, a new system of federalism, often referred to as »cooperative federalism,« emerged. The competition and conflict which had characterized the American federal system throughout the nineteenth century[43] were replaced to a considerable extent by a sharing of responsibilities between the federal, state, and often also local governments. During the New Deal years, 29 permanent grant programs were enacted, with the total number of programs rising to 71 by the end of the Truman Administration in 1952. Even during the more conservative Eisenhower Administration, another 61 grant programs were added, so that a total of 132 grants were in operation by

1960. Not only federal aid to the states, but also state aid to local governments increased dramatically in the period between 1930 and 1960. Unlike the major focus on education and highways in the period before 1930, the New Deal era grants emphasized health and welfare programs. In 1960 four programs accounted for nearly three-fourths of the federal grant expenditures: highways (43.7 percent), old-age assistance (16.5 percent), aid to dependent children (9.1 percent), and employment security (4.7 percent).[44]

In spite of the growth in federal grant-in-aid programs, federal grant monies were only 10 percent of state and local revenues in the period from 1952 to 1957, rising to 14 percent by 1959. Grants increased from 11.2 percent of nondefense federal expenditures in 1952 to 17.1 percent in 1959.[45] In contrast to German practice, which does not allow direct federal aid to local governments, a growing number of federal grants were for local governments; however, these programs made up only 7 percent of total federal grant funds in 1959.

These federal grant programs and the regulations that came with them »combined to fashion a nonarticulated theory of grants administration that addressed the vertical, functional, bureaucratic linkages and the protective strengthening of administrative counterparts at the recipient level. Under it, the administrative role of elected chief executives and the administrative shaping powers of legislative bodies were de-emphasized, if not ignored.«[46] Bypassing the state and ignoring the administrative role of regional chief executives were and still are features of American cooperative federalism that contrast sharply with German practices; however, cultivating vertical, functional bureaucratic linkages and ignoring legislative bodies are now common to both federal systems.

Between 1960 and 1980 federal grant programs expanded even more dramatically than during the preceding three decades. The five years of President Johnson's Administration alone created 209 new grants, conforming to the theory of »creative« federalism, which reflected a belief that the system was chiefly characterized by a federal-state-local sharing of responsibilities for practically all governmental functions (which the earlier practice of cooperatitve federalism did not).

It assumed implicitly that a division of functions between levels was neither possible nor desirable. It trumpeted the ideal that officials at all levels were allies, not adversaries, under the system. And it accepted the concept that the system was »first conceived as one government serving one people,« hence the president's call for the Great Society.[47]

As a reaction to creative federalism, Richard Nixon's »New Federalism«

attempted to decentralize the increasingly complex system of inter-governmental relations, i.e., a widespread sharing of administrative and financial responsibilities for public policies (a concept close to, but not always the same as, the German *Politikverflechtung*). One of the most important initiatives of the New Federalism was the introduction in 1972 of general revenue-sharing, which offered the states assistance for a range of purposes without most of the numerous conditions of the traditional catego-rical project and formula grants (grants directed at specific, narrowly defined activities). Several block grants, with some conditions but for broader purposes than categorical grants, were also introduced. Nevertheless, in spite of efforts under the New Federalism to reverse the trend toward increasing intergovernmental relations, Congress passed more than sixty new categorical grant programs during the Nixon years and about thirty more during the Ford presidency. By 1976 there were 448 federal aid programs, and by the end of the Carter years there were more than 500.[48] Federal grants-in-aid reached a high of 26.5 percent of total state-local outlays in 1978, or 17 percent of total federal outlays.[49]

The inauguration of the Reagan Administration in January 1981 marked the beginning of a new era in intergovernmental relations. The »New Federa-lism« of the Nixon-Ford years, which saw an effort to reduce the reliance on categorical grants by initiating a new, more flexible program of general revenue-sharing, was replaced by President Reagan's new, »New Federa-lism« which in some respects was reminiscent of the »old« dual federalism. To a remarkable extent, the President made federalism a major agenda item for his Administration, and there has probably been more serious public discussion of federalism since 1981 than in the previous three or four decades combined.[50]

In his efforts to reduce federal expenditures, President Reagan cut back on a variety of federal grant programs. In addition, the Omnibus Reconciliation Act of 1981 consolidated 77 categorical programs into nine block grants, which brought the total of such grants to 13.[51] The number of categorical grants increased to 538 in 1981, but their number declined to 392 in 1984. By 1987 they had increased in number to 422. In that year federal grants-in-aid amounted to $ 109.9 billion, of which $ 94.1 billion was in categorical grants.[52] These figures reflected, however, a reduction in the proportion of federal grants to an estimated 18.2 percent of total state-local outlays and to 10.8 percent of total federal outlays.[53]

General revenue sharing, introduced during the Nixon Administration in 1972, provided federal money with few strings attached for the states and local governments (after 1980, local governments only) to use at their own discretion. By the 1980s all local governments, in spite of need, received general revenue sharing funds without application. In part because it was not targeted to local governments on the basis of need, but also because of the huge federal budget deficit and evidence that many states had budget surpluses, general revenue sharing for 39,000 local government units was eliminated by the Tax Reform Act of 1986.

In his 1982 State of the Union Address, President Reagan proposed a swapping of functions between the federal and state governments. According to the initial proposal, Medicaid was to become a federal responsibility, while Food Stamps and the Aid to Families with Dependent Children (AFDC) program would become state responsibilities, along with 61 (later changed to 31) other federal grant programs. This realignment of functions would be financed by the proceeds of federal excise taxes that would be given to the states. It was assumed that in the end neither the federal government nor the states would suffer or benefit financially from the »swap« and »turnback« elements of the proposal, but such an assumption was based on the premise that Congress would accept a number of cuts in the affected programs.[54] Unable to convince the states that they would not end up with increased costs, the »sorting out« process did not make much progress during the years of the Reagan Administration. When confronted with the choice between a realignment and cutting the federal domestic budget, the Administration chose the latter.

A new focus on »economic deregulation« respecting the private sector was accompanied in the Reagan Administration by a serious effort to effect »social deregulation« as well. The Office of Management and Budget (OMB) was given new, centralized powers to review agency regulations, and the result was a significant decline in regulatory activity in 1981.[55] A President's Task Force on Regulatory Relief was also created to review already-existing regulations and to identify and possibly eliminate rules that were duplicative, inconsistent, or overlapping.[56]

IV.   *Resurrection and Reinterment of the Tenth Amendment*[57]

The idea of »sorting out« federal and state functions in an effort to reduce the complexity of the system of intergovernmental relations did not begin with the Reagan Administration in 1981. The U.S. Advisory Commission on Intergovernmental Relations proposed in the late 1960s that the financial responsibility for AFDC and Medicaid be taken over by the national government while numerous other programs be given to the states.[58]

In 1976 a five-man majority of the Supreme Court also had some ideas about a division of labor between the federal and state governments to be brought about through constitutional interpretation. In the process the Court majority resurrected an interpretation of the Tenth Amendment that many observers had long thought to be dead.

In 1938 Congress passed the Fair Labor Standards Act (FLSA), which set minimum wages and regulated working hours in the private sector. The FLSA, which was based on the commerce clause, was upheld by the Supreme Court in *United States v. Darby* in 1941. In 1974 the FLSA was amended to include employees of the states and their political subunits. In *Maryland v. Wirtz* (1968),[59] the Court upheld the application of the FLSA to public hospitals, schools and other institutions, but in a bitterly contested 5-4 decision in *National League of Cities v. Usery* (1976),[60] the Court overturned its 1968 ruling and held that Congress had not been authorized by the commerce clause to impair the states' »ability to function effectively in a federal system,« and that Congress could not force the states to choose how to conduct »integral governmental functions.« Justice William Rehnquist, who delivered the majority opinion, claimed that »this Court has never doubted that there are limits upon the power of Congress to override state sovereignty, even when exercising its otherwise plenary powers to tax or to regulate commerce which are conferred by Art. I of the Constitution.«[61]

These limits, according to Rehnquist, are found in the Tenth Amendment, in spite of the statement in *Darby* that this Amendment represents nothing more than a »truism.« There is, he suggested, a »dual sovereignty« in the distinction between government regulation of the public and private sectors. The private sector enjoys no sovereignty and therefore cannot be exempted from the power of Congress to regulate commerce. In contrast the states have »functions essential to separate and independent existence,« and they are protected from national interference by the Tenth Amendment.

While Justice Harry Blackmun concurred with Rehnquist's decision, thus creating a majority of five in favor of placing limits on congressional powers under the commerce clause, he did so with the understanding that the decision did not apply to those activities that require national attention, such as environmental protection. In his separate dissenting opinion, Justice John Paul Stevens carried Blackmun's concern much farther by asking by what principle one was supposed to separate the protected traditional governmental functions of state and local governments from many examples of functions that apparently were not protected.[62]

Justice William Brennan, whose dissenting opinion was joined by Justices Byron White and Thurgood Marshall, noted that John Marshall in *Gibbons v. Ogden* had said that »restraints upon the exercise by Congress of its plenary commerce power lie in the political process and not in the judicial process.« Brennan accused the majority of basing its decision on »a line of opinions dealing with the Commerce clause and the Tenth Amendment that ultimately provoked a constitutional crisis for the Court in the 1930's.«[63]

The first challenge of Congress' power to regulate activities in the states that many would argue were among the newly protected »traditional governmental functions« came before the Court in the case of *Hodel v. Virginia Surface Mining and Reclamation Association* in 1981.[64] Here the Court unanimously upheld Congress' use of the commerce power to regulate land-use policies under the Surface Mining Control and Reclamation Act of 1977. The Court rejected the claim that the Act violated the holding of the Court in *NLC* by pointing out that according to this case, three requirements had to be met:

First, there must be a showing that the challenged statute regulates the »States as States.«

Second, the federal regulation must address matters that are indisputably »attributes of state sovereignty.«

And third, it must be apparent that the States' compliance with the federal law would directly impair their ability »to structure integral operations in areas of traditional governmental functions'.«[65]

A fourth requirement was added as a cautionary warning, according to which the commerce power might be used in spite of the above requirements because »the nature of the federal interest advanced may be such that it justifies state submission.«[66] Since not even the first requirement was met in the *Hodel* case, the Act was upheld.

The next challenge to congressional power was brought to the Supreme Court in the case *Equal Employment Opportunity Commission v. Wyoming* in 1983.[67] In 1967 Congress passed the Age Discrimination in Employment Act, which makes it unlawful for an employer to discriminate against any employee between 40 and 70 due to age, except where age is a bona fide occupational qualification. The Act was extended to include state and local governments in 1974. A supervisor in the Wyoming Game Commission was forced by Wyoming law to retire at age 55, and he filed a complaint with the EEOC.

In deciding this case, Justice Blackmun, who had been with the majority in *NLC*, changed sides and helped to form a majority of five in upholding the Act. In the majority opinion, Justice Brennan reviewed the requirements outlined in the *Hodel* case and concluded that the law did address the »states as states.« The second requirement was more difficult to assess, he suggested, because the law »does not ›directly impair‹ the States' ability to ›structure integral operations in areas of traditional governmental functions.‹«[68] The degree of threat to the state's «separate and independent existence« is not sufficient to justify overturning the law, since the state may still assess fitness of its game wardens and dismiss those that are unfit.

Then, in *Garcia* v. *San Antonio Metropolitan Transit Authority*,[69] decided in 1985, the Supreme Court decided to review its *NLC* decision. A District Court had held that the municipal ownership and operation of a mass-transit system is a traditional governmental function and therefore exempt from FLSA provisions concerning wages and hours. The same majority that decided the *EEOC v. Wyoming* case formed in this case to uphold the application of the FLSA to the San Antonio mass transit authority and to overrule *NLC*. Justice Blackmun, whose reluctant concurrence had created a majority in *NLC*, wrote the opinion for the majority of five.

He noted that in *NLC* the Court »did not offer a general explanation of how a ›traditional‹ function is to be distinguished from a ›nontraditional‹ one.«[70] While courts have held that operating ambulance services, licensing automobile drivers, operating a municipal airport, performing solid waste disposal and operating a highway authority are functions protected under *NLC*, the issuance of industrial development bonds, the regulation of intrastate natural gas sales, the regulation of traffic on public roads, the regulation of air transportation, the operation of a telephone system, the leasing and sale of natural gas, the operation of a mental health facility and the provision of in-house domestic services for aged and handicapped are not protected. »We find it difficult, if not impossible,« said Blackmun, »to identify an organizing principle that places each of the cases in the first group on one side of a line and each of the cases in the second group on the other side.«[71] Like Justice Brennan in his dissenting opinion in *NLC*, Blackmun concluded that the protection of state interests lies in the federal political process, not in judicial review of congressional use of the power to regulate commerce.

It was this last assertion that especially aroused Justice Powell in his dissenting opinion that was joined by Justices Burger, Rehnquist and O'Connor. Powell noted that it is the role of the Court, not of elected federal officials, to decide what the Constitution allows. »The States' role in our system of government is a matter of constitutional law, not of legislative grace,«[72] he said, and he accused the majority of ignoring *Marbury v. Madison*.

106

Powell denied that it is impossible to distinguish traditional governmental functions from other functions:

> In *National League of Cities* we spoke of fire prevention, police protection, sanitation and public health as ›typical of [the services] performed by state and local governments in discharging their dual functions of administering the public law and furnishing public services.‹ Not only are these activities remote from any normal concept of interstate commerce, they are also activities that epitomize the concerns of local, democratic self-government. In emphasizing the need to protect traditional governmental functions, we identified the kinds of activites engaged in by state and local governments that affect the everyday lives of citizens. These are services that people are in a position to understand and evaluate, and in a democracy, have the right to oversee. We recognized that ›it is functions such as these which governments are created to provide . . .‹ and that the states and local governments are better able than the national government to perform them.[73]

If one looks for common denominators in the two sides expressed in the cases discussed above, it would appear to be that the majority in *NLC* and minority in the *EEOC* and *Garcia* cases believe there are limits on the power of Congress to interfere with »traditional governmental functions« that are »integral« to the operation of state and local units, and that it is the Court's duty to determine through judicial review what the limits are in specific cases. The other side disputes each of these arguments, and asserts that in the final analysis the only protection available to state and local governments is to be found in the political process.

This view was confirmed in 1988 in the case *South Carolina v. Baker*.[74] South Carolina, joined by The National Governors' Association, contested the provision of the federal Tax Equity and Fiscal Responsibility Act of 1982 (TEFRA) requiring that most state and local bonds must be sold as »registered« bonds that are subject to federal taxation. South Carolina objected that this provision violated the Tenth Amendment and the doctrine of intergovernmental tax immunity enunciated in *Pollock v. Farmers' Loan and Trust Co.* (1895).[75] The Court reaffirmed its decision in *Garcia*, overturned the *Pollock* ruling, and said that intergovernmental tax immunity did not exist with respect to federal taxation of state and local bonds. Again, the Court said that the states had to find protection in the political process against federal government incursions, not in the federal courts. Again, dual federalism as constitutional doctrine was declared dead. »American federalism has been construed by the Court as a political and administrative relationship rather than a constitutional one.«[76] It should be noted, however, that, especially under the new Chief Justice Rehnquist, the narrowly divided Court could change its mind again, overturn *Garcia* and *South Carolina*, and return to the views expressed in *NLC*.[77]

V. *Some Comparisons with West Germany*

In West Germany the national parliament has taken on an increasing number of responsibilities since the early 1950s on grounds of promoting some form of equality, especially »uniform living conditions« (Art. 72, Paragraph 2 [3]; Art. 91a, Paragraph 1; also Art. 104a, Paragraph 4). In the United States the interstate commerce clause has been used by Congress to regulate the economy, to protect health and welfare, and to nationalize provisions of the Constitution concerning civil rights. The result is that in both countries certain constitutional provisions (In the United States, the Tenth Amendment; in the Federal Republic, Article 30 BL) which some observers saw as placing limits on national powers proved ineffective in protecting the states/*Länder* from federal regulation.

In spite of the apparent similarities in constitutional law between Germany and the United States concerning regional governments in their respective federal systems,[78] a significant difference exists in the law of the two countries concerning the protection of local governments from incursions by national or even state/*Land* governments. This is reflected most clearly by the inclusion in the German Basic Law of a provision that guarantees local governments self-government and by Federal Constitutional Court decisions and the conventional view of German jurists that there is a *Kernbereich* – certain core functions – of local governments that must be protected. In contrast, a narrow majority of the American Supreme Court decided in *Garcia* in 1985 that there are no »traditional governmental functions« of state or local governments that can be protected by the federal courts *via* the Tenth Amendment, and it reaffirmed the view in *South Carolina* in 1988 that incursions on state and local powers can be resisted only through the political process.

In spite of this important legal difference, it is not so easy to distinguish between the American and German views concerning the role of state/*Land* and local governments in their respective federal systems. In *Hodel*, it was made clear that three important tests would have to be met in any complaint that there had been an infringement of a »traditional local government«

function by national policy; yet even then, the national interest in an area such as environmental protection could still justify a federal incursion where local authority was otherwise thought paramount, namely land-use control. Also, in spite of the constitutional protection of local governments in the Basic Law, the German Federal Constitutional Court has allowed numerous national and *Land* government incursions in local government affairs on grounds of the common good.[79]

While the highest court in each country has concluded that incursions in state and local affairs by the national legislature may be justified in spite of certain constitutional provisions, there is a legal difference that distinguishes the roles of the two courts. With the *Garcia* and *South Carolina* decisions, the U. S. Supreme Court has removed itself from disputes between the national government and state/local governments regarding their respective powers and functions. In spite of a number of decisions by the German Constitutional Court approving national and *Land* incursions in local government activities, the German Court, in contrast, due to such provisions of the Basic Law as Article 28, Paragraph 2, and to its rhetoric about protected core functions, remains a watchdog over disputes between governments concerning their respective functions in the federal system.[80]

That leaves the American subnational governments with the political process as a protective shield. Many American students of federalism have severe doubts that the American political process in the last decade of the twentieth century is designed to offer the states protection from federal incursions. They point to the popular election of the Senate since 1913, the nationalization of the electoral process, the national impact of current campaign finance practices, and iron triangle relationships that transcend questions of federalism.[81] And they suggest that all members of Congress, »regardless of party or section of the country from which they come, have a stake in creating a situation in which they can claim local credit for national actions that are beneficial to their constituents.«[82] Thus, in spite of rhetoric in favor of federalism, »Congress has virtually no incentives to consider the principles of the federal division of powers in making concrete decisions.«[83] Perhaps for these reasons more than one-half of the states now have lobbyists in Washington, D. C., in order to protect and further their interests in federal policymaking involving the states.

Whether reliance on the political process in the United States can protect state and local governments from intrusive federal regulation is still an open question. The Advisory Commission on Intergovernmental Relations is skeptical. It published a report on the implications of the *Garcia* decision in which a number of alternative strategies are reviewed and recommendations are made for one or more constitutional amendments that would presumably strengthen the federal system and promote a sorting out of governmental functions.[84] Given the German experience with explicit constitutional protection of local governments accompanied at the same time by trends toward growing dependence of local governments on *Land* and national financial assistance, ever more intergovernmental regulation and sharing of powers, and increasing pressure for »uniformity of living conditions,« there is also room for some skepticism that legal remedies alone can arrest the developments in either country away from separate functions and toward a complex, intertwined system of intergovernmental relations.

VI. *The States in Political Practice*

While it appears that there is a degree of constitutional protection of state and local governments in Germany that no longer exists in the United States, one might ask whether this should lead one to conclude that the American states are somehow »weak« or have become mere agents of the federal government. I would argue together with Gunter Kisker that American states are in a much »stronger« position in practice than are the German *Länder*,[85] in spite of the superior constitutional protection enjoyed by the latter.

A systematic and thorough comparative case cannot be made here, due to restrictions of space; however, a brief summary of the role of the states shows that any talk of their decline is surely premature. In spite of *Garcia* and *South Carolina*, American states remain major actors in the American federal system. Until well into the twentieth century, the states had primary responsibility for domestic government in the United States. They have been

»(1) the foremost instruments of public choice in certain areas, such as public morals; (2) direct service providers in their own right, particularly in the fields of criminal justice, health and hospitals, transportation, higher education and business relations through commercial codes; (3) prime regulators in guarding the public health, safety, welfare, food order and convenience of their citizens through the use of their police power; (4) architects and empowerers of local governments; (5) innovators in public policies; and (6) to some degree, middlemen in federal grant-in-aid programs.[86]«

In the United States in 1986 all governments combined had receipts of $ 1,339,300,000,000, or 31.6 percent of GNP. The federal share of these receipts was 61.9 percent, the state share 22.5 percent, and the local share 15.7 percent. With federal aid, total state and local receipts amounted to 46.2 percent of the total of all government receipts.[87] If outlays for national defense and international relations are excluded, federal government expenditures were only 38.9 percent of total expenditures; states and local governments had 24.7 percent and 36.4 percent, respectively.[88]

In West Germany the *Länder* receive the bulk of their tax revenues through an elaborate system of shared financing and fiscal equalization measures.[89] While the federal, *Land*, and local governments have some own source revenues, these are relatively minor in comparison with the proportion of shared taxes each level receives.

In contrast to the German *Länder*, American states have significant own source revenues. The major source of revenue for the states is the sales tax, and income taxes are important in most states as well (Because German law prohibits two levels of government from applying the same kind of tax, the value-added sales tax [VAT] and income tax are shared). Local governments also have significant own source revenues from taxes, charges and fees, utilities, and liquor stores. Local governments in Germany receive substantial income from user fees and utilities, but most of their tax revenue comes from the *Länder* and fiscal equalization measures. Some American municipalities, especially in Pennsylvania, have their own income taxes; 29 states permit their local governments to levy a state sales tax, frequently as an added percentage or more to the state sales tax; and virtually all local governments have property (mostly real estate) taxes, the latter of which are the major »own source« of tax revenue.[90]

While there are some differences among the German *Länder* in certain policy areas, especially in areas such as education, law and order, and background checks of candidates for civil service positions, most of the discussion among federalism experts in Germany revolves around the pressure for »uniformity of living conditions.« There are, of course, pressures for national standards in the United States as well, but there is also considerable variation among the states in areas such as public assistance, punishment for certain crimes, e.g., death penalty, abortion policy, ERA ratification, public sector collective bargaining, and right-to-work laws.[91]

As a result of the numerous cuts in federal grant programs during the

Reagan years, many observers predicted dire consequences for state and local governments. By the mid-eighties, however, it was clear that the worst fears of many experts were exaggerated.[92] What seems to have happened in a majority of cases is a revival of these governments and a strengthening of American federalism.[93] According to one rather optimistic school of thought, the »Reagan Revolution« brought about »a renewal and invigoration of long-dormant state and local governments,« the enactment of tax increases by state and local governments, numerous reforms in public schools and welfare policies, and efforts by state legislatures to give local governments more authority to raise new taxes and to end other policy restrictions. More than half of the states have raised their personal income or sales taxes, virtually all have increased user fees, and 27 states had established lotteries by 1987.[94] Given the desolate condition of the federal budget, local governments and various interest groups have turned to the states for the funds no longer available from Washington, and in general the states have responded. It should also be noted that a recent unanimous decision by the Texas Supreme Court that the state's system of school finance was unconstitutional due to »glaring discrepencies« between rich and poor school districts[95] should force widespread action by state legislatures in a policy area that has been generally ignored since the early 1970s.

If one looks at some of the assumptions and predictions made only a decade ago about an increasing dependence of the states on federal grants, an increasing dominance of the federal government in domestic policymaking, and a generally decreasing role of the states overall,[96] the relative strength of the states today seems remarkable.[97] A combination of federal policies toward the states (including deregulation and benign neglect), the federal deficit (which discourages virtually all new program initiatives), and state court decisions will probably place continuing pressure on the states to play a significant and perhaps an increasing role in the American federal system.

Notes:

1 »The powers not delegated to the United States by the Constitution, nor prohibited by it to the States, are reserved to the States respectively, or to the people.«

2 For a more detailed discussion, see Arthur B. Gunlicks, *Local Government in the German Federal System* (Durham: Duke University Press, 1986), Chapter 11.

3 Frido Wagener, »Äußerer Aufbau von Staat und Verwaltung,« in *Öffentliche Verwaltung in der Bundesrepublik Deutschland*, eds. Klaus Koenig, H.J. von

Oertzen, and Frido Wagener (Baden-Baden: Nomos Verlagsgesellschaft, 1981), p. 77.

4 Arnold Brecht, *Föderalismus, Regionalismus und die Teilung Preussens* (Bonn: Ferd. Dümmlers Verlag, 1949), p. 85. For the original English edition of this book, see his *Federalism and Regionalism in Germany: The Divsion of Prussia* (New York: Oxford University Press, 1945).

5 Gordon Smith, *Politics in Western Europe* (4th ed.; New York: Holmes & Meier Publishers, Inc., 1984), pp. 223-226.

6 See, for example, David Caputo, *Urban America: Policy Alternatives* (San Francisco: W. H. Freeman and Company, 1976), Ch. 8. For a German example of the use of »vertical« in this atheoretical sense, see Werner Thieme, »Die Gliederung der deutschen Verwaltung,« in *Handbuch der kommunalen Wissenschaft und Praxis,* vol 1: *Grundlagen,* 2d ed., ed. Gunter Püttner (Heidelberg, Berlin and New York: Springer Verlag, 1981), p. 149.

7 Smith, *Politics,* pp. 223-226.

8 Edward S. Corwin, »The Passing of Dual Federalism,« *Virginia Law Review* (February 1950), reprinted in: *American Constitutional History: Essays by Edward S. Corwin,* eds. A. T. Mason and G. Garney (New York: Harper & Row, 1964), pp. 147-148.

9 For a discussion of different views of the location of »sovereignty,« and whether it is to be found in the separate states, in the people, or in a »mixed« form, see Raoul Berger, *Federalism: The Founders' Design* (Norman and London: University of Oklahoma Press, 1987), pp. 48-60.

10 Corwin, »Dual Federalism,« p. 148.

11 Cf. David B. Walker, *Toward a Functioning Federalism* (Cambridge: Winthrop Publishers, Inc., 1981), pp. 46-54.

12 For a brief comparison between the United States and Germany on the issue of sovereignty, see Gunter Kisker, »The West German Constitutional Court as Guardian of the Federal System,« in *Federalism and Intergovernmental Relations in West Germany: A Fortieth Year Appraisal,* ed. Arthur B. Gunlicks, special issue of *Publius: The Journal of Federalism* 19, No. 4 (Fall 1989), pp. 47-50.

13 Alfred H. Kelly, Winfred A. Harbison, and Herman Belz. *The American Constitution: Its Origins and Development* (6th ed.; New York: W. W. Norton and Co., 1983), pp. 211 and 244.

14 *Ibid.,* pp. 209 and 217.

15 9 Wheaton 1 (1824).

16 4 Wheaton 316 (1819).

17 6 Wheaton 264 (1821).

18 Kelly, Harbison, and Belz, *American Constitution,* p. 238.

19 *Ibid,* p. 242.

20 19 Howard 393 (1857).

21 Kelly, Harbison, and Belz, *American Constitution,* p. 242.

22 Walker, *Toward a Functioning Federalism,* p. 55.

23 Kelly, Harbison, and Belz, *American Constitution,* pp. 301-315.

24 7 Wallace 700 (1869).

25 Kelly, Harbison, and Belz, *American Constitution,* p. 448.

26 Cf. Walker, *Toward a Functioning Federalism,* pp. 54-65.

27 163 U. S. 532 (1896).

28 Kelly. Harbison, and Belz, *American Constitution*, p. 368.
29 *Ibid.*, p. 402.
30 *Ibid.*, p. 428.
31 *Ibid.*, p. 399.
32 *Ibid.*, p. 415.
33 *Ibid.*, p. 428.
34 198 U. S. 45 (1905).
35 208 U. S. 161 (1908).
36 247 U. S. 251 (1918).
37 Kelly, Harbison, and Belz, *American Constitution*, p. 460.
38 *Ibid.*, p. 488.
39 301 U. S. 1 (1937).
40 312 U.S. 152 (1941).
41 Kelly, Harbison, and Belz, *American Constitution*, pp. 471-472.
42 Walker, *Toward a Functioning Federalism*, pp. 60-62.
43 Kelly, Harbison, and Belz, *American Constitution*, p. 515.
44 Walker, *Toward a Functioning Federalism*, pp. 66-67, 76-79, 81.
45 *Ibid.*, p. 81.
46 *Ibid.*, p. 84.
47 *Ibid.*, p. 104.
48 *Ibid.*, 109-110, 174.
49 ACIR, *Significant Features of Fiscal Federalism, 1989 Edition*, Vol. 1, M-163 (Washington, D. C.: Advisory Commission on Governmental Relations, 1989), p. 21.
50 For an excellent review of federalism in the first term of the Reagan administration, see George E. Peterson, »Federalism and the States: An Experiment in Decentralization,« in *The Reagan Record*, ed. John L. Palmer and Isabel V. Sawhill (The Urban Institute, Cambridge: Ballinger Publishing Company, 1984,), 217-259; see also Richard P. Nathan, Fred C. Doolittle, and Associates, *Reagan and the States* (Princeton: Princeton University Press, 1987).
51 For a listing of programs that were consolidated, see ACIR, *A Catalog of Federal Grant-in-Aid Programs to State and Local Governments: Grants Funded FY 1981* (Washington, D. C.: Advisory Commission on Intergovernmental Relations, 1982), pp. 67-69.
52 ACIR, *A Catolog of Federal Grant-in-Aid Programs to State and Local Governments: Grants Funded FY 1987* (Washington, D. C.: Advisory Commission on Local Government, 1987).
53 ACIR, *Significant Features 1989*, p. 21.
54 J. Edwin Benton, »Economic Considerations and Reagan's New Federalism Swap Proposals,« *Publius: The Journal of Federalism* 16, No. 2 (Spring 1986), pp. 20-21; Peterson, »Federalism and the States,« pp. 219-220.
55 ACIR, *Regulatory Federalism: Policy, Process, Impact and Reform* (Washington, D. C.: Advisory Commission on Intergovernmental Relations, 1984), pp. 189, 198.
56 *Ibid.*, pp. 228-234.
57 This section draws on a portion of my article, »Constitutional Law and the Protection of Subnational Governments in the United States and West Germany,« *Publius: The Journal of Federalism* 18, No. 1 (Winter 1988), pp. 144-148.

58 ACIR, *Intergovernmental Perspective* 11, No. 4 (Fall 1985), p. 5.
59 392 U.S. 183 (1968).
60 426 U.S. 833 (1976).
61 *Ibid,* 842.
62 *Ibid.,* 856, 881.
63 *Ibid.,* 868.
64 452 U.S. 264 (1981).
65 *Ibid.,* 287-288.
66 *Ibid.,* 288.
67 460 U.S. 226 (1983).
68 *Ibid.,* 239.
69 105 S. Ct. 1005 (1985).
70 *Ibid.,* 1007.
71 *Ibid.,* 1011.
72 *Ibid.,* 1026.
73 105 S. Ct. 1031.
74 108 S. Ct. 1355 (1988).
75 157 U. S. 429 (1895).
76 Margaret T. Wrightson, »The Road to *South Carolina*: Intergovernmental Tax Immunity and the Constitutional Status of Federalism,« *Publius: The Journal of Federalism* 19, No. 3 (Summer 1989), p. 52.
77 For a critique of Justice Rehnquist's opinion in *NLC*, based on a review of the development of American federalism from 1789 to the present, see David M. O'Brien, »Federalism as a Metaphor in the Constitutional Politics of Public Administration,« *Public Administration Review* 49, No. 5 (September/October 1989), pp. 411-418.
78 Gunlicks, »Constitutional Protection,« pp. 148-149.
79 For a discussion of several cases in which the Federal Constitutional Court has upheld incursions into local government autonomy on the grounds of the common good, see Gunlicks, »Constitutional Protection pp. 151-155. For a somewhat briefer German version of this article, see »Die Eigenständigkeit der Länder und die kommunale Selbstverwaltungsgarantie in den Vereinigten Staaten,« *Archiv für Kommunalwissenschaften* I (1988), pp. 108-115.
80 For an up-to-date discussion of German constitutional law regarding local government, see Friedrich Schoch, »Zur Situation der kommunalen Selbstverwaltung nach der Rastede-Entscheidung des Bundesverfassungsgerichts,« *Verwaltungsarchiv* 81, Heft 1 (1990).
81 Cf. A. E. Dick Howard, »*Garcia*: Federalism's Principles Forgotten,« *Intergovernmental Perspective* 11 (Spring/Summer 1985): 13; also, by the same author, »*Garcia*: Of Federalism and Constitutional Values,« *Publius: The Journal of Federalism* 16 (Summer 1986): 22-23.
82 Randall Ripley, »Congress and Federalism,« OSU Mershon Center *Quarterly Report* 9, No. 3 (Winter 1985), p. 4.
83 *Ibid.,* 3.
84 ACIR, *Reflections on Garcia and Its Implications for Federalism: An Information Report* (Washington, D. C.: ACIR, February, 1986); see also Lawrence A. Hunter and Ronald J. Oakerson, »An Intellectual Crisis in American Federalism: The Meaning of *Garcia*,« *Publius: The Journal of Federalism* 16 (Summer

115

1986), pp. 33-50, and ACIR, *Is Constitutional Reform Necessary to Reinvigorate Federalism? A Roundtable Discussion* (Washington, D. C.: Advisory Commission on Intergovernmental Relations, 1987).

85 Gunter Kisker, »200 Jahre US-Föderalismus,« in *Zweihundert Jahre amerikanische Verfassung,* Raimund Borgmeier and Bernhard Reitz (eds.), *Anglistik & Englischunterricht,* Band 34 (Heidelberg: Carl Winter Universitätsverlag, 1988), p. 59.

86 ACIR, *The Question of State Government Capability* (Washington, D. C.: Advisory Commission on Intergovernmental Relations, 1985), p. 6.

87 ACIR, *Significant Features of Fiscal Federalism 1988* (Washington, D. C. Advisory Commission on Intergovernmetal Relations, 1988), pp. 6-7.

88 *Ibid.,* p. 193.

89 For a discussion of public finance in West Germany, see Arthur B. Gunlicks, *Local Government in the German Federal System* (Durham: Duke University Press, 1986), Chapter 7; same, »Financing Local Governments in the German Federal System,« in *Intergovernmental Relations and Public Policy,* ed. J. Edward Benton and David R. Morgan (New York: Greenwood Press, 1986), pp. 77-92; and Rüdiger Voigt, »Financing the German Federal System in the 1980s,« in *Federalism and Intergovernmental Relations in West Germany,* ed. Arthur B. Gunlicks, special issue of *Publius: The Journal of Federalism* 19, No. 4 (Fall 1989), pp. 99-113.

90 Deil Wright, *Understanding Intergovernmental Relations* (3rd ed.; Pacific Groves: Brooks/Cole Publishing Co., 1988), pp. 128-129, 157.

91 ACIR, *State Government Capability,* p. 21.

92 George E. Peterson and C. W. Lewis (eds), *Reagan and the Cities* (Washington, D. C.: The Urban Institute, 1986), pp. 4-5, 29-31.

93 Richard Nathan, »The Role of the States in American Federalism,« in *The State of the States,* ed. Carl Van Horn (Washington, D. C.: Congressional Quarterly Press, 1989), pp. 15-32.

94 J. Herbers, »The New Federalism: Unplanned, Innovative and Here to Stay,« *Governing the States and Localities,* Vol 1, No. 1 (October 1987), pp. 30, 34.

95 *New York Times,* 3 October 1989, p. A1.

96 See, for example, Michael D. Reagan and John G. Sanzone, *The New Federalism,* 2d ed. (New York: Oxford University Press, 1981), pp. 164-168.

97 For the views of several authors who argue that the American states have assumed a larger role in the American federal system in the past two decades, see Carl Van Horn (ed.), *The State of the States* (Washington, D. C.: Congressional Quarterly Press, 1989).

Francis X. Beytagh, Jr.

Comments on Part 2

Federalism in a conceptual sense presents, at least initially and at a level of some generality, questions involving governmental structure. In that respect, it does not present difficult definitional questions, although federalism can of course, and does in fact, take a variety of forms. It is more at the functional or operational level that comparative assessments of various federalist systems are likely to be most useful. Both the Lerche and Gunlicks papers proceed in this fashion, to their credit.

In endeavoring an overview of the threshold question of »why federalism«, as distinguished from a unitary state, the two papers concentrate primarily on the differing, yet not wholly dissimilar, historical circumstances that led both in Germany and the United States to the adoption of federalism as a way of organizing the state and at the same time dividing governmental authority between national and regional instrumentalities. But neither history nor cultural differences adequately respond to the need in a constitutional democracy for a contemporary, continuing justification for a structural concept as important as federalism. To the extent that the two papers take federalism in Germany and the United States more or less for granted, and proceed to deal descriptively and analytically with its various manifestations, they address only indirectly the necessity for periodic evaluation of the benefits of and detriments flowing from the incorporation and application of such a governmental theory to the situation of major, modern democratic states. Indeed, the perceived decline in significance of state governments, noted in both papers as to Germany as well as the United States, may in essence be a reflection of some of the deficiencies that are inherent in such a structure in the latter years of the 20th century.

At the same time, there is considerable vitality in the federalism notion in both Germany and the United States, and a number of practical as well as theoretical justifications for its continuing use. Government closest to the people creates a greater sense of participation of the citizenry, and may be more responsive to their needs, especially in a time of considerable confusion about the effectiveness of government generally. Division of power in a vertical manner, even with a supremacy clause contained in both the German and American constitutions, provides a check against misuse and abuse of authority. States in a federal system can serve as »laboratories of experiment,« as Justice Brandeis observed. And the American States and the German Länder continue to perform a wide variety of important governmental functions in a generally effective manner.

The two papers obviously provide an opportunity for contrasting the somewhat varying styles of federalism employed in the two countries. In this respect, each can learn from the other, and perhaps improve upon, or at least experiment or innovate, in different ways. This also illustrates the necessity for a constant rethinking of the changed (and changing) role of federalism in a vital democratic state.

Perhaps the most enduring issue raised – and to some extent addressed – by the two papers is the future of federalism in two of the world's most important democracies. The German Länder perform valuable administrative functions that relieve the national government of this responsibility. In America the States continue to deal with vital matters such as public education. Moreover, in the U.S. at least, State courts are increasingly deciding significant policy questions in litigation brought under State (as distinguished from the U.S.) constitution. Scholars as well as politicians need to identify the enduring strengths and contributions of federalism – to the end that a *purposeful, examined federalism* is maintained, both in Germany and America. Both the German and American constitutional systems, whether desired or not, serve as examples to other nations around the world seeking to organize or reorganize their governmental systems in efficient and workable ways. And, as further political along with economic integration of Europe proceeds toward 1992 and beyond, federalism in another and very important sense will inevitably be with us, for Europe represents a major part of the world with a population in excess of 300 million persons.

In conclusion, comparative law conferences such as this one are extremely valuable, for all can learn much from each other. Congratulations should go to the Federal Republic of Germany on the fortieth anniversary of the 1949 Basic Law. Now a mature, stable constitutional system, Germany has both the responsibility – as does America – of constantly examining and rethinking the essential premises of its system, while at the same time helping to shoulder the burden the United States has endured for some time – that of being examined, imitated and, sometimes at least, criticized, by others. Lastly, there is a growing need for the establishment of a *center for comparative constitutional studies*, probably located in Europe, perhaps in Germany, to carry on and effectively institutionalize the potential of existing conferences and interchanges. The time is ripe, the need is considerable, and the likely benefits would be substantial.

118

Part 3:
Representative Democracy

Helmut Steinberger

Political Representation in Germany

Preface

German political theory has long wrestled with the concept, content and principles of representation.[1] It is no surprise that the debate reached a climax in the 1920s with the standard works of Carl Schmitt and Gerhard Leibholz.[2] These were the years of the Weimar Republic, that period of German history in which, for the first time, representation could no longer be conceived of as being primarily the representation of the entire population through parliament, in confrontation with a monarchical head of state who had not been democratically elected.[3] At the same time, this was the period in which the traditional, liberal parliamentarianism, which had in the past seemed indissolubly linked to the idea of representation, came into its phase of deepest crisis with the strengthening of the political parties to become central power factors in political life, to the point where one-party states developed in Italy, Spain and eventually Germany. The more it became apparent that the ideal of parliament as a civilized assembly of the »best of the nation,« reaching the »right« decisions exclusively by the guiding light of reason through the exchange of arguments, with complete freedom of discussion and decision (»free mandate«), was very far from reality, the more urgent became the question of reorienting or even overcoming the principle of representation. Although 40 years after the Basic Law came into force this controversy has not died away,[4] it has diminished in intensity, despite a good deal of verbose lamentation,[5] as modern party democracy has found its feet; in the meantime, the focal points have shifted.

Today, politicians and political scientists understand representative democracy to be primarily the antithesis of direct democracy.[6] It may be doubted whether such an interpretation of »representation« fully exhausts the historical content of this concept;[7] nevertheless, it can serve as a starting point for considering whether, and if so how, democratic political representation is achieved under the supremacy of the Basic Law. The applicable criterion here for *political* representation will be whether a particular state institution is called upon by constitutional law to exert a fundamentally active influence on the shaping of the future, and whether it is therefore also assigned the responsibility and jurisdiction for so-called key political decisions.

I. *The Concept and Content of Political Representation*

1. Political representation in the representative democracy of the Basic Law is understood primarily as the representation of the people, pursuant to Art. 20 (2) [1][8] by the political State institutions provided for by the Basic Law within their respective constitutional competences.[9]

2. We can speak of political representation in a broader, social sense where, in relation to the political field, we are concerned with the representation of groups and their interests, such as trade unions and employers' associations, farmers' associations, organizations for refugees, war victims and taxpayers, as well as organized leisure interests in sporting associations, to mention just a few of the countless forms of representation of organized interests. The political significance of such associations and unions may be very important, not only regarding the political influence of their members and adherents in elections, but also in the continuing process of shaping and articulating public opinion in the acceptance or rejection of governmental policy. This extends even to parameters which can hardly be influenced at all by the state political institutions, such as the salaries and wages policy of the parties' collective bargaining agreements,[10] or the defense of ownership interests which are politically irreversible, except by recourse to the cynical expedient of inflationary currency devaluation, which of course only affects recipients of cash benefits, or savers.
In a libertarian, pluralistic democracy, the representation of social groups and their respective interests is a highly legitimate matter under constitutional law. This representation is guaranteed via basic rights, particularly freedom of association - which in Art. 9 (3), includes the right to take industrial action, particularly the right to strike - freedom of assembly and the freedoms of speech and action. These rights are subject to the limitations of general law, which in turn must be constitutional, must not violate the essential content of a basic right, and which must observe the prohibition of excess and the constitutional principle of certitude.

Nevertheless, social representation in this sense is not democratic representation in the sense of the principle of popular sovereignty set out in Art. 20 (2), since the legitimation is based not on democracy but on membership, and rather than State authority being exercised by part of the people, freedom is being exercised by one group of the people. Social groups do not enjoy the sovereign right vested in the State authority to call the general public or individual third parties to their duty. They exercise the authority of a private association over its members, who can evade that authority by withdrawing from the association.

3. a) In the process by which organs of public authority form intentions and arrive at decisions, representatives of social groups are sometimes institutionally involved on a statutory basis. Examples here are the broadcasting councils of the public law broadcasting corporations, advisory committees of all kinds in public commercial law, regional development and planning law, or the law governing nature conservation and the preservation of historic buildings.

The Standing Orders of the Bundestag, the Federal Government and the Federal Council provide them with the option of formally hearing relevant expert opinion. The parliamentary legislature increasingly includes not only individuals but relevant associations in its hearing procedures, in order to obtain a spectrum of concerned interests and opinions. It is also noteworthy that the Federal Constitutional Court quite frequently, when proceedings are pending, provides social associations with the opportunity to express an opinion on matters of either fact or law, even if those associations do not have the procedural status of participants to the action. As a result, parts of the procedure, such as oral proceedings, sometimes acquire the character of a hearing.

b) There are also cases where, on legal authority, associations under public law have been formed into corporations or public law institutions on the basis of specific features, usually relating to professional status or the law of social insurance. They are granted sovereign powers for specifically limited purposes of self-administration; in other words governmental authority is exercised indirectly, as in the case of chambers of industry, commerce and crafts or other professional corporations, universities and their staff associations, or persons insured by public social insurance institutions. Even in these cases, however, the bodies representing these associations are not democratic bodies representative of the people in the sense of Art. 20 (2), but representative of specific interests arising out of membership in the associations.

The same applies where, for legal authority, employees exercise their rights of participation in the civil service through staff meetings or bodies elected to represent the staff, particularly in determining working conditions, and in cases of appointments, transfers, termination of employment, and so on. Similar considerations apply to other group-specific representative bodies in the government sector, such as parent's associations in schools.

The granting of *political* rights of participation, or even codetermination, to such groups affecting the decisions taken by the political institutions of the state would very rapidly come up against barriers created by constitutional law; such privileged status in comparison with that enjoyed by citizens in general would be incompatible with the principle of popular sovereignty.

c) Similarly, in the private enterprise sector, the rights which legal authority gives to employees or unions to exercise powers of codetermination through works meetings, elected works councils or their representatives in the governing bodies of private companies are again not a case of political representation of the people.

d) This is because legitimation, in the sense of the principle of representative democracy, and particularly a general political mandate for the political representation of the nation, is bestowed under the Basic Law exclusively by the electorate on the basis of direct, general, equal, free, and secret elections, and is conferred on the political supervisory bodies by the popular representatives thus elected, within the context of their respective constitutional competencies.

4. By contrast, democratically legitimized political representation does exist in the case of the municipal representative bodies and their directly elected officials. Art. 28 (1) provides that these officials must be chosen in general, direct, free, equal, and secret elections (unless these are replaced by a town meeting of all citizens). This legitimation is not conferred by the entire population of the country in the sense of Art. 20 (2), though one can reasonably speak of a legally formed sub-population and the existence of a structural equivalence to the national population, since the franchise is linked to the general qualification of citizenship of a district or municipality, but not to other qualifications specific to individuals or groups. This is because Art. 28 (1) [2] refers to the people »in the Länder, districts and municipalities.« The function of political representation in these cases does

not, of course, extend beyond the constitutionally and statutorily defined jurisdiction of the municipalities and districts which, in the case of the municipalities, for example, is restricted to the affairs of the local community. Thus, for example, it does not lie within their jurisdiction to express an opinion on matters of foreign policy or to conduct surveys among the townspeople on the arming of the Federal Army.

5. The political parties occupy a special position with respect to political representation, and I will return to this issue in due course.

II. *Political Representation of the People by the Political State Institutions*

1. The Basic Law formed the Federal Republic of Germany as a representative democracy. Art. 20 (2) [1] which provides that all state authority emanates from the people, represents the normative commitment to the principle of popular sovereignty, and hence to the principle that any exercise of sovereign power requires democratic legitimation, (i.e., reference back to the people as the repository of such power, whether to one direct act by the population of the state or via an uninterrupted chain of acts of legitimation extending back to that population.

2. At the federal level, the central democratic act of legitimation is the election of deputies to the Bundestag, which according to Art. 38 (1) is to take place in general, direct, free, equal, and secret elections. With a single exception, relating to the reorganization of the federal territory, this is the only case in which, at the federal level, the entire population of the state exerts state authority directly, that is, not through representatives.[11]
Apart from the constitutional provisions regarding active and passive electoral rights – Art. 38 (2) – the Basic Law leaves to the federal legislature the details of the right of election to the Bundestag. In the present context, there are two essential elements of the current statutory form of the electoral law: First, the federal territory does not constitute a single electoral district in which the candidates are chosen from among the electoral nominations in accordance with the highest numbers of votes received; rather, the entire federal territory (in the sense of §§ 54, 55 of the Federal Electoral Act [BWG]) is divided into territorial constituencies – 259 of them, or half of the statutory number of deputies (§ 1 BWG). In each of these constituen-

cies, one deputy is elected by simple majority, making a total of 259 deputies.[12]

The other half of the deputies, possibly with excess mandates, are selected in accordance with electoral lists which are drawn up separately for each federal Land; in other words, they in turn are territorially subdivided.[13] This regional orientation of the electoral districts and the Land lists is intended to ensure that deputies from all parts of the federal territory are sent to the Bundestag, and consequently that the people are represented on a territorial basis, as well.

The *second* essential element is the proportional representation system introduced by law.[14] The distribution of the mandates obtained through Land lists, and ultimately the overall distribution of the mandates as a result of the list proposals, is based on principles of proportional representation; this is not the place to deal with details, such as excess mandates. With a relative majority voting system, for example, it would have been likely in the past that long periods of time would have seen only two political parties represented in the Bundestag – considering the CDU and CSU as one party in this exceptional case – so that many coalition governments would not have come about, and political representation by these state institutions would have followed a different pattern in each case.

3. a) Whether elected by the electors of his electoral district or by the Land electorate via a Land list, each deputy is nevertheless regarded as representing the people as a whole, is not tied to mandates and instructions and is subject only to the dictates of his conscience (Art. 38 [1], clause 2). Together with the franchise principles of clause 1, the limitation of the duration of the mandate to 4 years in principle (Art. 39 [1]) and the right of the Bundestag to convene itself, Art. 38 [1], clause 2) is the central norm of parliamentary representative democracy under the Basic Law. It expresses a specific concept of representation. The norm excludes the imperative mandate, which for centuries characterized professional corporate representation in Europe.[15] The free mandate, an achievement of the French Revolution, does not regard the deputy as a mere messenger subject to certain demoscopic ties, and responsible for implementing the empirical will of the people in the electoral district, the Land or the entire electoral territory. The deputy is not required to introduce a supposedly arbitrary or hypothetical popular will into the Bundestag's process of forming intentions and taking decisions. He is to have the freedom to introduce his own ideas and evaluations into that process. In doing so, he will generally take into account an empirically ascertainable and genuinely existing popular will,

126

such as he perceives it. He will be guided by key political programs, such as those of his party. In the legislative process, because of the complexity of modern life, he will often trust the expert knowledge of a few specialists inside or outside parliament. He will weigh the repercussions on his prospects of reelection, should he wish to be reelected - and this is not a deprecating factor, since it is with a view to reelection that the element of responsibility and responsiveness of the deputy becomes apparent. This and much more may be and will be involved in shaping the deputy's intentions.

Although Art. 38 (1) does not express it in these terms, the free mandate is intended to make it possible for the deputy to base his decisions on the common good. The concept has sometimes not been too highly regarded in recent German constitutional jurisprudence. This was justified to the extent that it does not imply a predetermined material order, whose content is fixed once and for all, ready to hand, and only needs to be packaged in parliamentary decisions. More recently the concept of the common good - secularized in content, however - seems to be coming back into vogue.[16] The Federal Constitutional Court - and, I believe, the Supreme Court - have not shied away from the concept.[17] The Federal Constitutional Court refers cautiously to the »common good which has to be defined according to the situation in each case.« Ernst Fraenkel is right when he refers to a »refined will« of the people which is to be expressed by the representative institution, though whether this should be called a hypothetical popular will is another question, concerned more with terminology.

The determination of the common good under the Basic Law is not made the absolute prerogative of the majority. In Article 1, the Basic Law obliges all state authority, and thereby also the deputy in the exercise of his mandate, to respect and protect human dignity as the supreme legal value of the constitution. Limits are set here on majoritarian policy by the necessity of observing the essential content of the basic rights, and ultimately by the principles of Arts. 1 and 20, which are exempt from constitutional amendment. At the same time, they define material elements of the common good and represent constitutionalized basic criteria of the common good. That, of course, is not the end of the matter; a more detailed definition is always required in a specific situation, and here lies the defining power of the majority. The Federal Constitutional Court once expressed this in a decision which denied the state institutions - in this case the Federal Government - the right to influence an electoral contest by means of advertising and partisanship:

»where the Basic Law yields to the rule of the majority in State institutions, it does not exempt them from the fundamental constitutional obligation entrusted to all State authority to protect the dignity and freedom of all and protect social justice to all and consequently always has to be oriented towards the good of all citizens. And only when the majority has been produced by a free, frank and regularly repeated process of formation of opinion and will, in which all enfranchised citizens are always enabled to participate with equal rights, only when the majority, in its decisions, has an eye to the common good (which always has to be determined according to the situation), and also in particular respect the rights of the minority and takes its interests, too, into account and in particular does not deprive the minority of the opportunity to become the majority of tomorrow, or reduce that opportunity, only then can the decision of the majority in exercising the State authority be regarded as the will of the entire people and develop a power of obligation in accordance with the idea of free self-determination for all citizens. . . . Because it provides an institutional framework for the free self-determination of all, with a guarantee of peace and order, the State enjoys sovereign authority *i.e.*, the power to pass Acts which are binding on all.«[18]

The possibility of political representation through a free mandate ultimately rests on confidence that the representative is able and willing to place the general good above individual and group interests, to base his decisions on this guiding principle, and to decide in such a way that the freedom of one and the freedom of the other can coexist in accordance with a general law.

b)   The status of deputies has, of course, long been doubted whether political reality corresponds to the ideal of the free mandate and to its traditional formulation from the period of early constitutionalism and civil/ liberal parliamentarianism, and has not in fact become altogether obsolete. The party allegiance of virtually all deputies is said to have resulted[19] in a basic change in the free mandate, in a fundamental change in the conventional, liberal form of representative democracy to produce a completely new type, the party state.[20] The consequences for constitutional law derived by Leibholz from this sharpening of terms are now predominantly regarded in current German constitutional jurisprudence as going too far. The deputy of today sees himself exposed, from his nomination as candidate through his activity in parliament up to his departure, to manifold influences from the party to which he belongs. Virtually the only way he can break free of these ties is to accept that he will not be nominated again as a candidate for the coming election. In the first post-war decades, in particular, this was the origin of a much-debated »state of conflict« between the constitutional status of the deputy on the one hand, and that of the parties which, according to Art. 21 (1) »participate« in forming the political will of the people, on the other. In more recent constitutional jurisprudence and precedent, this situation of conflict seems to have become more relaxed, and to have given way to an understanding which places both regulations in a relationship of concordance.[21]

In legal terms, there is extensive unanimity that Art. 38 is unaffected by Art. 21. The essential element of the deputy's right not to be subject to any kind of legal sanctions because of his voting behavior (Art. 46 [1]) also applies with respect to the parties. A deputy whose parliamentary behavior deviates from the line adopted by his national or parliamentary party can indeed be sanctioned by the party with internal sanctions, and particularly with exclusion from that party; but he cannot for this reason forfeit his mandate against his will.[22] Even a corresponding »voluntary« declaration of submission by the deputy brought forward at the time of his candidacy has no continuance in the eyes of the law.[23]

On the other hand, Art. 21 entitles the parties, particularly through the parliamentary groups, to exert an influence on the process by which »their« deputies reach decisions. In contrast to associations and social interest groups which attempt to influence the deputies, the political parties have a much stronger position because of their *de facto* monopoly in the nomination of candidates, which gives them the opportunity to apply party discipline in many ways. If this kind of »circumscribed mandate«[24] is nevertheless not considered as dubious today as it was 20 years ago, one of the most important reasons for this is that today's party scene differs in one essential from that of the Weimar period, the experiences of which influenced not only Leibholz: in principle, all parties – particularly the two major parties, without which it seems inconceivable that a government could be formed in the Federal Republic, at least in the long run – are regarded as »popular parties« which aim to be open to all social groupings and, as regards their programs, are oriented towards the general good and not towards specific group interests.[25] The fact that the deputy who comes into conflict with the discipline of his party or parliamentary party, and therefore leaves the party association either voluntarily or by exclusion, nevertheless does not as a result lose his mandate before the expiry of the legislative period may not seem to him to be much consolation if the parliamentary procedural order reserves essential rights of participation to the parliamentary parties, or indirectly to deputies belonging to those parties. Certainly a parliament like the German Bundestag, with more than 500 deputies, cannot, in the interests of performing its duties, abandon the search for ways of streamlining its work. It must not be overlooked, however, that the parliamentary parties, via an extensively used procedural autonomy, reduce non-party deputies to *de facto* »second class« deputies, and so can indirectly exert an increased pressure on their members not to secede from the party association. With regard to the resultant situation of conflict between deputy status and procedural autonomy, the Federal Constitutional Court recently commented with specific reference to the non-party deputies. In its judgment of June 13th, 1989,[26] the Court emphasizes that all members of the Bundestag, regardless of whether or not they belong to parliamentary parties, have the same rights and obligations. According to the decision, every deputy's rights include minimal rights of participation, without which the deputy could never be truly representative of the people. The Court said:

> Accordingly, every deputy is entitled to participate in the proceedings of the Bundestag and in its transactions and decisions . . . the consequent rights of the deputy include, in particular, the right to speak and the right to vote, participation in the exercise of the parliament's rights of interrogation and information, the right to participate in the elections to be held by the parliament and to take parliamentary initiatives, and finally the right to combine with other deputies to form a political group.[27]

To this list of recognized rights of participation, the Federal Constitutional Court adds another: the right to participate in a parliamentary committee after election of the Bundestag or of its presiding committee, with the right to speak and right of proposal.[28] However, the same decision denies the non-party deputy the right to vote on the committee assigned to him, together with a right to participate in the Council of Elders and in the Commissions of Inquiry called by parliament to prepare decisions on the merits in difficult points of substance.[29] Finally, the non-party deputies are also not to be paid, in addition to the daily allowances and expenses payable to every deputy, additional appropriations corresponding to those which the parliamentary parties receive to defray their specific costs.[30] The Court has denied the non-party deputy the right to determine for himself on which committee he will serve.

4.   Only in the context of reorganization of the federal territory (Art. 29) does the Basic Law envisage direct exercise of state authority by the people, outside of elections.[31] This institutes plebiscitary forms of deciding by conducting and petitioning for referenda.
Such plebiscitary forms of direct democracy are found in a number of Land

constitutions. The homogeneity guaranty of Art. 28, paragraph 1, 3 is not in conflict with this; the Länder must of course observe the federal allocation of jurisdiction.

These plebiscitary forms at Land level are not often used – only in cases of importance to Land policy. One example occurred in Bavaria, with respect to the retention of the public-law organization of the broadcasting system, a field which of course is subject to restrictions imposed by the federal constitution and cannot, for example, prevent the establishment of private broadcasting enterprises.[32]

Recently, there has been lively debate as to whether further infractions of the representative form of democracy under the Basic Law would be admissible, either by simple act or by an act amending the constitution, going beyond Art. 29.[33] This coincides with politico-legal demands for the introduction of plebiscitary processes at the federal level also, for example in the draft of an SPD commission for a new general policy program to replace the Godesberg Program of 1958; the proposal has not gone uncontested by some Land party associations. The prevalent view in constitutional literature rightly rejects this as regards the introduction of such plebiscitary procedures by simple act.[34] It can be indirectly inferred from the comprehensive regulation, in the Basic Law itself, of preconditions and procedures for referendum and plebiscite with regard to the reorganization of the Länder, on the occasion of the amendment to Art. 29 in 1976, that the introduction of further instances either of plebiscites or referenda by simple act is still contrary to the intent of the constituent assembly and therefore inadmissible.[35] By contrast, it is necessary to be more cautious in answering the question of whether Art. 20 (2) [2], in combination with its »implementing provisions,« is also to be interpreted as a prohibition of extensive introductions of plebiscitary elements by constitutional amendments.[36] There is a danger here of overstretching the scope of the so-called perpetuity guarantee of Art. 79 (3) of the Basic Law.[37]

A different question altogether is whether the introduction of such institutions into the constitutional structure would result in an increase in democracy, as its proponents believe. Considerable doubts exist on this matter. E.W. Böckenförde[38] has made the relevant point that the will of the people, in order to be articulated, must be formed through procedures. In this context – whether it be in the form of the plebiscitary decision, the referendum or the petition for a referendum – the people are necessarily restricted to the acceptance or rejection of predetermined questions; the plebiscitary act is inevitably merely responsive in nature. An additional point relates to who has the right to ask the question, and hence the ability to influence the popular will. In the case of the referendum petition in particular, a position of political power is assigned to individual citizens or groups of citizens who will be quick to articulate their specific interests. What these plebiscitary forms particularly lack, however, is the institutionalized venue for the clear, dialogue-style resolution of conflicts, and the balancing of interests against the guiding principle of the common good, sometimes provided by the political representative institutions in the »checks and balances« system and procedures. Plebiscitary forms provide not more but less frank, clear discussion, and hence less libertarian democracy. The fundamental mainstay of libertarian democracy is that the democratically legitimated political representative institutions, over and above elections, bring out the popular will in the first place, and give it form and immediacy.

5. At the federal level, political representation is provided by the principal political institutions: the Bundestag, the Federal Chancellor and Federal Government, the Federal Council, and the Federal President.

a) Historical development alone ensures unequivocally that parliament is a political representative institution of the state population. German constitutional literature, however, is noticeably reticent with regard to the representative function of the other supreme political federal institutions, particularly the government.[39] By contrast, Leibholz,[40] for example, took it for granted that in a parliamentary governmental system the population of the state is also »represented« by the government. Even if the representative's independent authority to take decisions is seen as an essential feature of representation, the Federal Government cannot be denied a representative character. The fact that the government, as part of the executive authority, is bound by »law and justice« (Art. 20 [3] subclause 1), whereas parliament is bound only to the »constitutional order« (Art. 20 [3] subclause 1) changes nothing here. The field of foreign relations, for example, and the courts' tendency to reserve substantial independent organizational scope to the executive, provides emphatic proof of this autonomous power of decision from which the Federal Government derives its character, like that of the Federal President, as a political representative institution. Nor is it any argument against the view that the government, too, is a representative institution in that it, unlike the Bundestag, is not directly elected by the national population. This special feature certainly raises parliament to a prominent position in the overall constitutional structure. But the concept of representation does not presuppose such a direct democratic legitimation; the parliamentary responsibility of the government, through the Federal Chancellor, to the popularly elected parliament is, to this extent, indispensable on the one hand but adequate on the other. Even those who are reluctant to become enmeshed in the terminological toils of representative theory, but lay claim to a realistic understanding of democracy, will be unable to avoid the conclusion that Bundestag elections during 40 years of the Basic Law have been principally »chancellor elections« and hence »government elections.«

b) All the federal institutions referred to have democratic legitimation. The Bundestag is comprised of deputies who have been elected directly by the people in general elections, and so have direct democratic legitimation. The other federal institutions referred to have indirect democratic legitimation: the Federal Chancellor is elected by the Bundestag; the members of the Federal Government are nominated by the Federal Chancellor and appointed by the Federal President. In contrast to what is the case in most Länder, neither the Federal Government as a body, nor its individual members require the consent, confirmation or confidence of the Bundestag for their inauguration. The Federal Council - a federal institution - consists of members of the Land governments which appoint them and remove them from office, governments which derive their democratic legitimation from the directly elected Land parliament, usually through the minister-president elected by the Land parliament. The Federal President is chosen by the Federal Assembly, which is equally comprised of Bundestag members and members elected by the Länder parliaments.

6. In the Federal Republic, the political representative institutions of the Länder supplement those of the Federal Government. The people in the Länder directly elect the parliaments, which in turn elect the minister-presidents; the governments in most Länder (usually[41] decided by the minister-president) require endorsement as a body, or parliamentary approval or election of individual members.[42] In some cases, as in Hesse, all that is required is notification of the ministers to the Land parliament.[43] Political representation by these state institutions of the Länder plays an extremely important role in the political process of the Federal Republic. The Federal Republic is a living federal state, and the federal elements enjoy a political importance which is matched only, if anywhere, in the United States and Switzerland. Thus, for example, the Federal Republic is permanently engaged in election campaigns, since the legislative periods of the municipal representative institutions, the Land parliaments, and the

Bundestag are not coterminous. Municipal elections in a Land, mayoral elections in major cities, and parliamentary elections in each federal Land all attract considerable nationwide attention. Federal politicians often campaign in Land parliamentary and municipal elections, and federal issues play a substantial part in these campaigns. A party's successes and failures in federal policy have an effect on electoral attitudes in Land parliamentary and municipal elections too. The scandal surrounding a Lend minister-president has nationwide repercussions on electors, especially the so-called floating voters, who are now estimated to account for approximately 50% of the electorate. Land parliamentary elections quite often have explosive consequences for federal policy in light of the majority situation in the Federal Council. The results of municipal and particularly Land parliament elections are regarded as a barometer of political opinion and a significant trend indicator for Bundestag elections, even for impending elections in another Land. Quite frequently, events in municipal politics and Land politics form a breeding ground for influence and positions in federal politics:[44] Land minister-presidents (Governing Mayors) become Federal Chancellors, Lord Mayors become Land minister-presidents and opposition leaders in the Bundestag. The Federal Republic lives – culturally, economically, and specifically politically – essentially in and on its Länder.

The federal structure of the Federal Republic is also of prime importance from the standpoint of political representation of the people, to the extent that it enables political parties without working majorities at the federal level to take on governmental responsibility if they have appropriate majorities at the Land level. Provided they are also represented in the Bundestag, they therefore do not have to rely on appearing solely in an opposition role. Through their elected representatives (in the context of Land jurisdiction) they represent the people in the Land as state institutions, and exert an influence on federal policy through the Federal Council. It has been pointed out that this counteracts a feeling of frustration among these parties, and enables them to acquire governmental experience, expertise and specialist personnel which will be available to them should they take over governmental responsibility. Experience over 40 years confirms this assumption.

Despite this importance of the Land level for political representation in the Federal Republic, the time available here means that the following remarks will have to be confined to federal level.

1. As already mentioned, the Basic Law has established a strictly representative democracy. Art. 20 (2) provides that state authority is to be exercised by the people in elections and polls and through specific institutions of the legislature, the executive authority and the courts. Apart from the direct forms of participation in the reorganization of the federal territory, the people, at the federal level, exercise state authority directly only in the electoral act.

Political representation of the people, therefore, is to be found largely in the exercising of authority, but also in the limits to the constitutional competences of the political state institutions. In terms of constitutional law, this refers to the separation of powers as designed by the Basic Law.

Art. 20 (2) and (3) lays down the fundamental principle of separation of powers and the functional distinction between powers. Further distinctions are drawn in the provisions relating to the Länder institutions and their areas of competence.

2. The system of separation of powers, as laid down by the Basic Law, is characterized by two fundamental features.

First, in Art. 20 (3), the Basic Law distinguishes between three functions of state authority: the legislative, the executive and the judicial. Additional functions exist in constitutional precedent and in German constitutional jurisprudence, in particular the governmental function as the epitome of the principal political power of decision, and the supervisory function, which distinguishes between the political and the legal supervisory function.

Second, the Basic Law, through its allocation of competences, assigns these functions, with the exception of the judicial function, not to a single specific institution or institutional structure in each case, but to various, organizationally separate institutions or institutional structures. Only the judicial authority, whose function is to provide a binding decision of what is right within the context of specific legal processes and procedures – a decision which is also binding on the other branches of the state authority – is entrusted, in Art. 92, exclusively to the judiciary. By contrast, the legislative function involves the Bundestag, the Federal Government, the Federal Council, possibly the Mediation Committee which is made up of members of the Bundestag and the Federal Council, and the Federal President, each with its own powers. In the normal case, for example, the powers of the Federal Government in legislation are formally restricted to the right to initiate legislation and the right of its members to be heard at any time (in other words, including during legislative proceedings) in the Bundestag and its committees (Art. 42 [2]), and to countersign the bills signed into law and promulgated by the Federal President. It also has, for a limited time, the right of consent to laws which increase expenditure or reduce income as compared with its budget proposals.[45] In material terms, the right of the Federal Government to initiate laws is of prime importance. It is perceived as a normal function of government that the Federal Government takes the legislative initiative and pursues a legislative program in order to implement »its« policy.[46] Accordingly, in practice, the great majority of draft laws come from the government, which also has the competent ministerial apparatus for the preparation of laws. The German Bundestag has so far not equipped itself with any »legislative service« comparable with that available to the U.S. Congress.

In particular, in addition to the right to initiate laws and the right of its members to be heard in the Bundestag and its committees at any time (Art. 43 [2]), the Federal Council has important powers of participation in legislation. In principle, every adoption of a bill by the Bundestag must be passed to the Council; the Council can apply the good offices procedure to every bill adopted. For certain types of laws specially defined in the Basic Law, particularly in the field of fiscal and financial legislation, and in amendments to the Basic Law, the Council's consent is required in order for the law to be enacted.[47] With all other Federal laws, leaving aside instances of legislative and national emergency, it has a right of opposition, which the Bundestag nevertheless can overrule. The practical importance of the Federal Council's right of consent is sufficiently apparent from the fact that the Federal Council has dealt with approximately half of all past federal laws as laws requiring consent; whether rightly so, in each individual case, cannot not be discussed here.

The Federal Council is, however, not merely a legislative entity; it also participates in the executive authority of the Federal Republic, for example, in the form of its power of consent to the enactment of general administrative regulations for the implementation of federal laws by the Länder[48] and to the enactment of certain types of statutory instruments by the Federal Government or a federal minister unless federal statutes rule to the contrary.[49] Very generally it participates in the enactment of statutory instruments based on federal laws which require the consent of the Federal Council or which are implemented by the Länder, either on their own initiative or at the behest of the Federal Government.[50] The Federal Council is also involved in the federal supervision of the Länder's implementation of federal laws, and in the event of so-called federal enforcement when a Land fails to comply with its federal obligations under federal law. In 40 years of the Basic Law, no use has been made of either of these instruments.[51]

It is through the Federal Council that the Land administrations' experience of implementing the laws, and their expert knowledge, pass into the legislative and administrative activity of the Federal Republic. The reason why there is such a great store of this kind of experience and expert knowledge in the Land executives is that in the Federal Republic, in contrast to the United States, the federal laws too are in principle implemented by the Länder; therefore, feedback on the effects, practicability, costs and other aspects of enforcing the laws can pass primarily through the Land executives and their administrations, and thus be introduced into the Federal Council.

IV. *Political Representation and the Parliamentary System of Government*

1. The separation of powers, as prescribed by the Basic Law, is principally shaped by the parliamentary system of government.[52] This system is the culmination of the ideas of representative democracy, of the general, equal and free franchise, of the deputy's free mandate, and of the separation of powers, particularly the acknowledgement of an independent area of government authority.[53] These ideas have been molded by the Basic Law into a unique system of »checks and balances.«

This system is integrated into a structure of additional fundamental constitutional principles and institutions. It is only in its interaction with these that this system of checks and balances takes on its full constitutional and political effectiveness. Particular mention should be made of the federalist organization, which, through its subdivision of the state authority, acts as a supremely important element in vertical political separation of powers even at the constitutional level, and not merely through decentralization at the administrative level. It includes the principle of political exercise of authority for a limited period because of the requirement that the democratic legitimation be periodically renewed, and the principle of libertarian democracy, which, in accordance with a pronouncement by the Federal Constitutional Court,[54] prescribes as standard an order which, excluding any rule of force or arbitrariness, represents a constitutional system of control based on the self-determination of the people in accordance with the

137

will of the current majority, and with freedom and equality. The basic principles of this order include, together with popular sovereignty and the separation of powers, at least the following: respect for the human rights defined in the Basic Law, the responsibility of the government, the binding power of the laws on the executive authority, the independence of the courts, the multi-party principle with equality of opportunity for all political parties, and the right to form an active opposition. The Basic Law system of checks and balances includes the jurisdiction of a constitutional court which has no equal in the world with regard to the scope of its responsibility, and whose importance in the political process is exceeded, if at all, only by the Supreme Court of the United States, notwithstanding the differences between them.

With the parliamentary form of government, the system of checks and balances under the Basic Law is essentially different from the American presidential regime. Both, of course, are based on the same fundamental concept which has grown out of the political ideological history of the western world: guaranteeing the liberty of individual citizens and the community as a whole through a separation of powers in the form of allocating essentially autonomous functional areas of the state authority to organizationally different responsible bodies, through equal distribution of the respective powers of the state institutions, and through mutual supervisory mechanisms which interconnect the powers.

2. A focal point of the parliamentary governmental system under the Basic Law lies in the fact that, substantively, the appointment and removal of the Federal Chancellor – again excepting the case of a national emergency, when he is elected by the Joint Committee (Art. 53a, 115h [3]) – resides exclusively with the Bundestag. This contrasts with the situation under the Weimar Constitution, where the State President had the exclusive power to nominate the Chancellor, and also the power to dismiss him conditioned upon a vote of no confidence by the Reichstag. This is not the place to examine the detailed procedure for electing the Federal Chancellor (cf. Art. 63). Although the Federal President has an exclusive right of nomination for the first ballot, his nomination has in practice always been influenced in advance by those political parties which have enjoyed a governing majority in the Bundestag. Even the electoral campaigns of the major parties are overshadowed by the question of candidates for the office of Chancellor, and perhaps potential members of the government. The composition of the government, which constitutionally lies in the hands of the Federal Chancellor, with the Federal President having the formal right to appoint (Art.

64), is also essentially influenced by the party leaders, and particularly by partners in a coalition; all Federal Governments since 1949 have been coalition governments, even during legislative periods in which the CDU/CSU had an absolute majority in the Bundestag. To what extent the Federal Chancellor, when forming a government, has to give political thought to his own party and its possible partner or partners in a coalition is crucially dependent on the relative strengths of the parliamentary parties in the Bundestag, the coalition agreement, and the political importance of the Chancellor within his own party and with the public. It may also depend on the political importance of potential ministerial candidates. In the past, for example, the Chancellor has been politically obliged to appoint certain people within his own party, or in a coalition party, as economic or foreign ministers.

A somewhat controversial question is whether the Federal Chancellor, once in office, requires the confidence of the Bundestag. According to the Basic Law, it is not necessary for the Federal Government or the individual ministers to be endorsed by the parliament, as is the case in most Länder constitutions. Nor is the Chancellor obliged to step down if he no longer has a majority in the Bundestag, such as after the collapse of a coalition. He can hold office as a minority chancellor and indeed can even take office as such, provided he receives the most votes – though not an absolute majority – on the third ballot, and provided that the Federal President does not thereupon dissolve the Bundestag within seven days (Art. 63 [4]). However, the Federal Chancellor can ask for a vote of confidence from the Bundestag. If this motion is not carried by the majority of members of the Bundestag, he is not obliged to step down. In this *constitutional* sense, the Chancellor does not require the confidence of the Bundestag. How far he can go *politically* in such a situation, and whether he can still fulfill his legislative program with changing majorities, is another question.

The Bundestag, on the other hand, can express its lack of confidence in the Chancellor and thus bring about his downfall – but only if a majority of its members elects a new Federal Chancellor; in other words, only by what is called a constructive vote of no confidence (Art. 67). This form of vote is intended to stabilize the Federal Government, and aims at preventing a government from being overthrown by a parliamentary majority which is not willing or able to take governmental responsibility on its own shoulders. The intention of the founding fathers of the Basic Law here was to prevent the recurrence of a Weimar situation. Admittedly, there were very few instances during the Weimar period in which the government fell as a result of a vote of no confidence from such heterogeneous majorities in the

139

Reichstag; but this was only so because the Reich President often fore-stalled the fall of the government by dissolving the Reichstag. Not a single Reichstag under the Weimar Republic held office throughout the complete legislative period.

The Federal Chancellor's option of asking for a vote of confidence, insti-tuted in Art. 68, is likewise conceived as an instrument for stabilizing the Federal Government. Either the Federal Chancellor uses it as an attempt to regain what has become the precarious support of the existing government majority in the Bundestag – for example, to discipline dissident factions within his own party or his coalition partner's deputies – or the Bundestag finds it necessary to elect a new Federal Chancellor by a constructive vote of no confidence and thus bring about stable conditions of government. So it would not be wrong to assume that Federal Chancellor Schmidt, during the last phase of his period in office on February 3, 1982, called for a vote of confidence with the intention of bringing back certain factions of his own parliamentary and national party to support his policies.[55]

The means of bringing pressure to bear on the deputies, which is associated with the confidence vote, is the Federal Chancellor's option, where the vote of confidence is refused, of proposing to the Federal President that the Bundestag be dissolved. As a rule to which there have certainly been excep-tions, parliaments tend to be wary of their dissolution, especially in the case of government majorities, at least in political situations – and this is what Art. 68 primarily aims for – in which the Federal Chancellor sees reason to ask for a vote of confidence in order to reunite behind him what has become a precarious government majority in the Bundestag. In cases like these, the popularity of the government majority with the electorate will not exactly be at its apogee. Even when elections follow the normal expiry of the legislative period, the percentage of deputies who are not returned to the Bundestag is substantial. Normally, a deputy forming part of the government majority prefers his present mandate in the hand to a risky re-election in the bush of the future.

In practice, the option of dissolution provided by Art. 68 has taken on another dimension. The Basic Law makes no provision for the Bundestag to dissolve itself. The German situation is different from that in Great Britain, where a constitutional convention decrees that the Prime Minister, within the last year of the legislative period, can decide the date for new elections to the House of Commons in accordance with his political judgment; in other words, he can set it for the time which he estimates to be most favorable for himself and his party. In Germany, the Basic Law grants no such authority to the Federal Chancellor, the Federal President or the

Bundestag itself. Nevertheless, Art. 68 was applied in 1972 and 1983 to bring about premature dissolution of the Bundestag and hence premature new elections. In both cases, though the initial situations were quite different in terms of parliamentary politics, the Federal Chancellor's call for a vote of confidence was defeated, because the great majority of deputies in the government parliamentary parties abstained. This, of course, was agreed upon between the Federal Chancellor and the leaders of the national and parliamentary parties involved in the governing coalition at the time. In both cases the Federal President dissolved the Bundestag, in response to a proposal by the Federal Chancellor, and ordered new elections.

The constitutional legality of this procedure was not unchallenged.[56] In the second case, four Bundestag deputies - three belonging to the government parties and one non-party deputy who had previously been a member of the parliamentary SPD - initiated litigation proceedings against the Federal President.

Art. 68 prescribes a multi-stage procedure for the dissolution of the Bundestag. At each of these stages, one of the bodies involved - Federal Chancellor, Bundestag and Federal President - is granted scope for an independent political judgment as to whether to carry the procedure forward to the next stage or to discontinue it. While these procedural stages are in progress, the Bundestag has the option of bringing down the Federal chancellor at any time by way of a constructive vote of no confidence (complying with the 48-hour term required by Art. 67 [2]). The first procedural stage of Art. 68 is the Federal Chancellor's call for a vote of confidence, a call which is left to his political judgment. The second stage is the Bundestag's decision to carry this motion with a majority of its statutory quorum (in which case there is no dissolution) or not to carry it, in which case the third phase is initiated. In this phase, it is left to the political judgment of the Federal Chancellor to propose to the Federal President the dissolution of the Bundestag, or not to make such a proposal and hence not to initiate the dissolution proceedings. If the Chancellor does propose dissolution, the next stage is for the Federal President to decide within a period of 21 days, in accordance with his political judgment, whether he will dissolve the Bundestag or not. If he decides in favor of dissolution, the dissolution order requires the countersignature of the Federal Chancellor, which is a matter for his judgment, so that the Federal Chancellor can prevent the dissolution at the last moment.

It has been disputed whether Art. 68 requires, in addition to these procedural and jurisdictional preconditions, the existence of a crisis situation under substantive law. In particular, there is uncertainty as to whether the Federal Chancellor, in calling for a vote of confidence, is in fact ultimately forced to try to secure such a vote, rather than attempting to procure the dissolution of the Bundestag in what are really stable majority conditions as a devious way of, for example, fixing a time that suits him for new elections.[57] In the case of the dissolution of the Bundestag early in 1983, the deputies in the coalition government had, on the day before the vote of confidence, approved the 1983 budget proposed by the Federal Government by 266 votes, a clear majority. The Federal Constitutional Court decided that Art. 68 (1), clause 1, did not grant a free right of dissolution and did not entitle the Federal Chancellor to institute the dissolution procedure at his discretion. Instead, according to the Court, the article in question contains an unwritten substantive feature to the effect that a Federal Chancellor who wishes to dissolve the Bundestag may only initiate the procedure if he is no longer politically assured of continuing to govern with the relative forces existing in the Bundestag. These conditions, said the Court, would have to impair or disable his ability to act to such an extent that he would be incapable of reasonably pursuing a policy supported by the continued confidence of the majority.[58] An interpretation to the effect that Art. 68 entitles a Federal Chancellor with an unquestionably adequate majority in the Bundestag to arrange the failure of a vote of confidence, at what seems a suitable time, with a view to bringing about the dissolution would, according to the Court, not be in the spirit of this constitutional provision. The Court has said that by granting scope for assessment, evaluation, and judgment on key political decisions to three supreme constitutional bodies in Art. 68, the Basic Law entrusts the question of the dissolution of the Bundestag primarily to the system, laid down in that same provision, of mutual political control and political balance between the bodies involved. The constitution itself, therefore, had also withheld opportunities for revision by the Constitutional Court to a greater extent than in the fields of legislation and executive action. Only where constitutional yardsticks for political behavior were standardized could the Federal Constitutional Court take action against their infringement. What this means in practice is that the scope for assessment, evaluation and judgment granted to the three bodies involved could only be examined by the Court with respect to blatantly improper use. In the specific case, the Court ruled that there had been no such breach of constitutional law.

In its decision, the Federal Constitutional Court rejected with uncharacteristic sharpness opinions expressed by a number of current opposition politicians after the fall of Federal Chancellor Schmidt in September 1982 as a result of a constructive vote of no confidence, namely that a Federal Chancellor elected via the constructive vote of no confidence required, in addition to his constitutional legality, democratic legitimation by new elections. On this point, the Court says:

> In particular it is fundamentally at odds with the spirit of Art. 68 BL, and of the representative democracy shaped by the Basic Law, to demand the dissolution of the Bundestag and new elections on the assertion that a Federal Chancellor newly elected through a constructive vote of no confidence requires, in addition to his constitutional legality, legitimation provided by new elections. The following constitutional argument is against this: even a Federal Chancellor elected by way of Art. 67 enjoys full democratic legitimation, because of the constitutional legality of his election. With a view to the preservation of the democratic constitutional state, as created by the Basic Law, it would be an irresponsible undertaking to depreciate or undermine constitutional proceedings with the assertion that they require additional further forms of legitimation. Under the Basic Law, constitutional legality is synonymous with democratic legitimacy. Any other interpretation would strike at the purpose of the fundamental democratic principle of free elections and of the free representative mandate of the deputies in the sense of Arts. 38 and 40 (1).[59]

3. The constructive vote of no confidence, which brings about the downfall of the previous Federal Chancellor, and with him the Federal Government, is the sharpest means by which the Bundestag can recall the Federal Chancellor and his government to its political responsibility, and exercise and sanction political control over the government. Parliamentary responsibility naturally presupposes an independent area in which the government can take political action and decisions; otherwise there would be no responsibility here except merely to implement the instructions of parliament.

The concept of the »executive authority« alone, as used in Art. 20 (2) and (3) may not in itself automatically suggest an independent area in which the government (in the organizational sense) can take political action and decisions. Other regulations contained in the Basic Law, however, leave no doubt that it normatively assumes such an area, and not merely as a de facto condition. Art. 65, clause 1 refers to the Federal Chancellor as determining the guidelines of policy and bearing responsibility for them. However one defines the individuals and institutions to which this provision is addressed, it does express the existence of an independent area of political decision for the Federal Chancellor which implies more than purely executive functions. The right to initiate laws, the initiatory right of the Federal Government in connection with the budget plan and budget act, and its »right of veto«

against laws which increase expenditure or reduce income all confirm this, as does the historical context of the institution of countersignature to orders and decrees issued by the Federal President (Art. 58). The Federal Chancellor's powers to bring about the dissolution of the Bundestag are similarly powers of taking decisions of high policy, which would have been difficult to grant to a merely executive body. Finally, the powers of the Federal Government in a legislative emergency (Art. 81) and in a national emergency (Art. 115a *et seq.*) confirm this normative finding. In constitutional precedent[60] and constitutional jurisprudence,[61] there is substantial agreement in principle on this.

The Basic Law also assigns to the Bundestag powers to take key political decisions. Legislation, budget legislation, granting of regulatory authorizations, and appointing and removing the Federal Chancellor, to name only the most important, are the Bundestag's central instruments for controlling the political process. This is why Ernst Friesenhahn and others have said that the power of making key political decisions are collectively in the hands of both government and parliament,[62] and that a bipolar form of state leadership exists.[63] Such formulae are plausible ways of classifying a theory of state or form of government, but it is necessary to be cautious, even wary, if they are converted into normative constitutional principles from which specific legal consequences are then derived. The farthestreaching normative deduction attempted in constitutional jurisprudence – echoed to some extent in various decisions by the Federal Constitutional Court – was the statement that key political decisions by the Federal Government are, in cases where the Basic Law does not clearly give that Government exclusive powers to take such decisions, subject to a general parliamentary reservation which stems from the political position of the Bundestag as the sole representative institution directly elected by the people.

The Federal Constitutional Court has opposed this in two more recent decisions. In the first case a Higher Administrative Court referred to the Federal Constitutional Court the question, which it had itself answered in the negative, of whether a provision of the Atomic Energy Law permitting the licensing of nuclear power stations by the administration was compatible with the Basic Law to the extent that the licensing of fastbreeder-type nuclear power stations could also be subsumed under this provision. To this extent the referring Court had found a breach of, *inter alia,* the principle of separation of powers pursuant to Art. 20 (2), clause 2, and of the principle of parliamentary democracy pursuant to Art. 20 (1) and (2). It submitted that key political decisions on subjects as far-reaching as breeder technology, and the plutonium fuel cycle necessarily associated with it, must be taken by parliament itself, in accordance with the principle of separation of powers, and be specified in a formal law.

On this, the Federal Constitutional Court commented, *inter alia:*

> The Basic Law does not give parliament an all-embracing priority to make fundamental decisions. By apportioning authority on the basis of separation of powers, it sets limits to parliament's authority. Wide-ranging decisions, specifically including political decisions, are assigned to the jurisdiction of other supreme institutions of state, for example the determination of the guidelines of policy by the Federal Chancellor (Art. 65, clause 1,), the dissolution of the Bundestag (Art. 68), the declaration of legislative emergency (Art. 81) or important decisions in foreign policy such as the establishment or breaking off of diplomatic relations. The parliament which disapproves such decisions retains its supervisory powers; it may be able to elect a new Federal Chancellor and thus bring about the fall of the existing Federal Government; it may make use of its budgetary powers – but the Basic Law does not recognize its power of decision in these matters. The specific arrangement of the distribution and equilibrium of state authority which the Basic Law intends to guarantee must not be circumvented by a monistic interpretation, in the form of an all-embracing parliamentary reservation, erroneously derived from the democratic principle. The fact that only the members of parliament are directly elected by the people does not mean that other institutions and functions of the state authority are devoid of democratic legitimation. Even the fact that an issue may be the subject of political dispute cannot displace the powers of decision assigned by the constitution.[64]

In the second case, the Greens in the Bundestag had opposed the USA's deployment on Federal German territory of Pershing 2 and Cruise Missiles equipped with nuclear warheads. The applicant claimed that the constitution had been infringed upon by the fact that the Federal Government had neglected to obtain statutory authorization for its consent to the deployment.

The Federal Constitutional Court rejected the application. The heart of the matter was the question of whether acts of high-level foreign policy by the responsible authority which were not in the nature of a treaty required the consent of the Bundestag. The Court classified the Federal Government's consent to the deployment of the rockets not as a treaty regulating political relations – the conclusion of which requires the consent of the Bundestag in the form of a law, pursuant to Art. 59 (2), clause 1, of the Basic Law, but as an act of defense policy under the auspices of a collective security alliance and its implementation, which did not possess the legal status of an independent declaration of conclusion of a treaty. The Court ruled that the consent requirement contained in Art. 59 (2), clause 1, was not directly applicable to acts of this nature. Was it, as an act of high policy, nevertheless subject to a general parliamentary reservation? We may think of the connection with the American-Soviet disarmament talks in Geneva and the Soviet deployment of SS 20 rockets. The Court examined this in light of the question of whether Art. 59 (2), clause 1, was applicable by analogy.

Its findings were, inter alia: the Basic Law granted the Bundestag, to a substantial extent, powers of participation in the formation of intent for undertaking acts in the field of foreign relations. Effects of this on areas and forms of action were so important, both politically and legally, they could not be referred to as exceptions. However, Art. 59 (2), clause 1, restricted this participation substantively to treaties, and in terms of content to a mere declaration of consent to the conclusion of the treaty in the form of a law. Nevertheless, the Bundestag could not, for example, under Art. 59 (2), clause 1, either prevent or compel the Federal Government's refraining from, engaging in, or discontinuing treaty negotiations. It could not compel the executive to conclude a treaty to which an act of consent had been passed, nor to conclude it or maintain it in force following its conclusion under international law. Nor was it possible to infer from the provision that whenever an act by the Federal Government in dealings under international law regulated the political relations of the Federal Republic, it was necessary to select the form of a treaty requiring legislative consent.

This strict limitation of the powers conferred on the legislature by Art. 59 (2), clause 1, was, said the Court, an element of separation of powers as framed by the Basic Law. The separation of powers established as an axiom in Art. 20 (2) served to distribute political power and responsibility, and to control the holders of power. The concentration of political power which would result from allocating central powers of an executive nature to the Bundestag in foreign affairs – over and above the powers assigned to it by the constitution – would run counter to the structure of distribution of power, responsibility and supervision which the Basic Law established at the time. This argument was unaffected by the fact that only the members of the Bundestag were directly elected by the people. The specific arrangement of the distribution and equilibrium of State authority which the Basic Law intended to guarantee must not be circumvented by a monistic interpretation in the form of an all-embracing parliamentary reservation, erroneously derived from the democratic principle; here the Court is again emphasizing the stance it adopted in the fast-breeder case. »Even the principle of the parliamentary responsibility of the government necessarily presupposes a central area of executive independent responsibility (BVerfGE 67, 100, [139]). The democracy laid down by the Basic Law is a *constitutional* democracy, which means, as regards the mutual relations of the state institutions, that it is primarily a *power-distributing* democracy.«[65] That democracy was not based on referring to parliament all acts and decisions which, in themselves or in their consequences, were of politically far-reaching or vital importance, or involving parliament in them in the form of an act. The executive, and particularly the government within the executive, was also designed as a »political« authority and not, for example, restricted ab initio to decisions of lesser political significance. The state authority in all its functions was democratically constituted and legitimated under the Basic Law, though in different ways. »It is therefore by no means a shortcoming in democracy if the executive also possesses exclusive powers in the field of foreign affairs to take far-reaching, possibly vital decisions. Therefore any risks associated with this distribution of powers must constitutionally be accepted.«[66]

4.   However, the Federal Constitutional Court has inferred from the principle of democracy based on separation of powers that the legislature must itself fulfill its legislative function.

a.   As regards the highly economically developed democracies of Western Europe, it can be said that, in purely quantitative terms alone, well over half the norms of the written law are no longer passed in the form of acts but in the form of sub-statutory norms – orders, decrees, ordinances, executive orders, or whatever the terms and the legal nature of the details may be. The reasons for this are found in the rapidly changing and highly complex circumstances encountered, especially in the fields of industry and technology, which require constant adaptation of, for example, the law relating to industrial safety. Formal legislation must increasingly resort to regulating general policy alone, since, on purely practical grounds, it is now impossible for the wealth of inevitable detailed regulations to be dealt with in good time by the legislative bodies.
In Art. 80, the Basic Law grants the executive a legislative authority in the form of a regulatory power. However, in contrast to, for example, the situation under the French constitution of 1958, the Basic Law does not recognize any regulatory power of the executive which is independent of the law, and in that sense autonomous. According to Art. 80 (1), every statutory instrument requires authorization by a formal act. The wording of

147

the statutory instrument must expressly include this principle. The act only represents a constitutionally adequate basis for authorization for the enactment of an order if it is sufficiently specific in defining the content, purpose, and scope of the authorization granted. A statutory provision which merely read that »the Federal Government is empowered to enact statutory instruments in the field of foreign trade« would fall far short of being a constitutionally adequate authority for enactment of orders.

It follows from the so-called priority of the law, laid down in Art. 20 (3), that the statutory instrument itself, and its application in the individual case, must remain within the scope of the statutory authorization, otherwise the order is void and the individual exemtive act based upon it is illegal.

b.   However, the Federal Constitutional Court has gone farther in its judgments. Since the beginnings of German constitutionalism in the early 19th century, the question of when a legal regulation required a formal authoring act and when it could be left to the executive had to be dealt with by such regulations, developed as a criterion, that interference with the liberty or property of the citizen was permissible only by the law itself or only on the basis and within the limits of a suitably empowering law – the so-called proviso of legality. The formula dates back to Freiherr vom Stein, and can be found as far back as the Bavarian Constitution of 1818. This criterion – interference with liberty or property – remained crucial for determining the scope of the proviso of legality for a considerable time even after the Basic Law came into force. Even today, it remains an essential criterion for the necessity of a law, a criterion which the Federal Constitutional Court has expanded in a series of decisions. Particularly as regards the ever-increasing state interventions in the social and economic domain – administration of benefits and public services may be mentioned as key phrases which increasingly affect the individual basic rights, as well – the Federal Constitutional Court has developed the doctrine that the legislature itself must, even outside the sphere of the application of Art. 80 (1), take the fundamental normative decisions and be answerable for them,[67] and must not leave them to the executive. In this decision the Court moved away from the strict concept of intervention[68] and took into account the intensity of the regulation for the area of basic rights of those concerned in each case, where this area is constitutionally accessible to State regulation in the first place. The decisive reason for this expansion of the proviso of legality was that State action which guarantees the citizen benefits or opportunities is often no less important for a free existence than refraining from intervention.[69]

In the decision in the fast-breeder case, mentioned earlier, it was stated that the legislature was obliged »to take all essential decisions itself in fundamentally normative areas, particularly in the area of exercising basic rights, where this is accessible to State regulation.«[70] It must not delegate it to the executive and its methods of action. The Court justifies this so-called doctrine of materiality with particular reference to the democratic principle, with the greater openness of debate and the clarity of parliamentary legislation in comparison with the executive forms of action.[71] At the same time, the Court requires the legislature to accept the political responsibility for this, in the eyes of the electorate, the general public.

This development was closely linked with the Court's decision on the so-called special authority relationship. The German theory of civil law distinguishes the general legal relationship which exists between the citizen and the public authority, whose content is primarily determined by the basic rights, from narrower, specifically purpose-oriented legal relationships such as the civil service, military, school and university relationships, the convict relationship, and so on, which are summarized under the general definition of special authority relationships. An opinion which found support over a considerable period of time was that, within the framework defined and limited by the purpose of such a special authority relationship, the executive could enact regulations which restricted the basic rights and which, in the general authority relationship, could be enacted only by law or on a legal basis, provided that the basic right is subject to a proviso of legality at all; in other words, that the proviso of legality has only limited applicability here. By contrast, in a fundamental decision of 1975, the Federal Constitutional Court found[72] that a »special authority relationship,« however defined, cannot obviate the need for a regulation by formal act or a statutory instrument in accordance with the provisions of Art. 80 (1) where the proviso of legality, which the Court deems to be enshrined in Art. 20 (3) applies. In further decisions relating to schools, the Court defined it as a function of the legislature to impose the essential normative regulations itself, such as compulsory exclusion from a school or the obligatory introduction of sex education, and not to leave it to the administration.[73] In this decision the Federal Constitutional Court has defined the legislative function and responsibility of parliaments emphatically, and perhaps not always to the complete happiness of the parliaments. The same purpose and tendency are reflected in a number of decisions which find the existence of an obligation on the part of the legislature to scrutinize and, if necessary, amend the statutory regulation if the basis of a regulation previously in force is

149

critically called into question by new, originally unforeseeable developments.[74]

In this context, the Court commented as follows in the fast-breeder decision:

> In a situation where reasonable doubts may exist as to whether hazards . . . of the feared type may or may not arise, the State institutions, and consequently the legislature also, are, on the basis of their constitutional obligation to serve the common good, and in particular because of the objective legal obligation arising from Art. 1, (1), clause 2, for all State authorities to protect the dignity of man, called upon to make every effort to identify possible dangers in good time and to counter them with the necessary constitutional means. Should there be indications in the future that hazards of this type are at all likely to arise from nuclear power stations of the fast-breeder type . . . the legislature would be obliged to take further action.[75]

5. The supervision of the Federal Government and the Bundestag's right of inquiry is another principle of democracy based on separation of powers.

a) A clear-sighted observer of the parliamentary system once pointedly commented that, in a functional parliamentary regime, it is not parliament which supervises the government but the government which supervises its parliamentary majority. This comment referred to the British parliament, in which at times as many as a hundred MP's of the governing party may simultaneously hold government office. In the Bundestag, there are in practice – not as a result of a constitutional imperative – generally a few dozen deputies of the governing parties holding government office, from the Federal Chancellor – who need not be a Bundestag deputy – down to the more or less influential ministers of state and parliamentary under-secretaries. It is not exactly the most colorless deputies who are called to government office, either. The office of party whip does not exist only at Westminster; the history of the Bundestag has seen various leading figures in this role.

In view of this circumstance, and in view of the very natural endeavors to win the next elections, can the governing parties be expected to exercise effective parliamentary supervision – which means, in particular, supervision before the public eye, in public debate? In political terms, the supervision of the government has to a considerable extent been transferred to the parliamentary parties and senior committees of the governing parties, and is therefore largely out of the public eye. It would of course be politically and constitutionally erroneous to regard the political supervisory function of parliament as outmoded. The constitutional supervisory instruments and their sanctioning still remain, from questions and interpellations, debates arising out of current concerns, government statements, bill and budget deliberations, rendering of accounts, and any obligations to report required by statute, through the right of the Bundestag and its committees to demand the presence – and not merely the silent presence – of any member of the Federal Government, and the right to institute committees of inquiry, up to the constructive vote of no confidence.

There is no doubt that, in the parliamentary government system as shaped by the Basic Law, the parliamentary opposition has a particularly important part to play and responsibility to bear in the parliamentary supervision of the government. This is because, politically at any rate, the system includes no guarantee that a Bundestag dominated by a government majority will make use of its constitutional supervisory powers in such a way that the government is effectively subjected to political supervision – the parliamentary majority will always have its eyes on the next election; and, as noted earlier, there are virtually always election campaigns in progress somewhere in the Federal Republic.

This places the emphasis on the so-called minority rights as regards the supervisory powers of parliament. In the time available here, only the right of inquiry is given detailed consideration.

b)   The right to institute committees of inquiry has developed into one of the sharpest instruments for the supervision of the legislature in the United States – where the phrase »government by committees« was quite often heard – and also in the Federal Republic of Germany. This instrument is on the cutting edge of parliamentary supervision because the committee of inquiry – with the exception of the Defense Committee as a committee of inquiry (Art. 45a [2] and [3]) – always conducts its necessary investigations in public proceedings (Art. 44 [1]), so that alleged dubious circumstances or misconduct can be depicted and criticized before the public eye, particularly through the media.

The Bundestag is obliged to institute a committee of inquiry if called upon to do so by a quarter of its members, and the majority may not essentially alter the mandate, which this minority wishes the committee of inquiry to be given, against the minority's will.[76] According to the Standing Orders of the Bundestag,[77] the members of committees of inquiry are appointed by the parliamentary parties but not elected by the plenum. Constitutional misgivings that this may be an infringement of the principle of democratic legitimation have been rejected by the Federal Constitutional Court in light of the status and function of the parliamentary parties.[78]

In this form, the German parliamentary right of inquiry as (also) a law in favor of the minority goes much farther than the equivalent under other constitutions.[79] The right of inquiry provided by Arts. 44, and 45a (2) is of course not designed purely as a minority right. This is true not only in the sense that the majority can also resolve to institute committees of inquiry – it goes without saying that, in a parliamentary democracy, the minority does not at any event have more rights than the majority – but also in the sense that the parliamentary majority of today can, for example after a change of government, investigate the performance of yesterday's government, and certainly avails itself of that opportunity.

As an auxiliary institution for the Bundestag, a committee of inquiry must observe the limitations which the Basic Law places on federal authority; an inquiry mandate cannot authorize the overstepping of these limits.[80] The committee of inquiry exercises the investigatory right of the Bundestag, not an investigatory right of its own. This is not affected by the fact that the Bundestag, if it wishes to employ for the purposes of an inquiry the special powers conferred by the Basic Law, in particular the hearing of evidence by an analogous application of the regulations relating to the criminal law process (Art. 44 [2], clause 1), may do this only by means of the instrument of a committee of inquiry. The committee of inquiry is therefore also bound to the scope of the duties and powers of the Bundestag, its institutional authority. The Basic Law, however, does not restrict this institutional authority, for example, to the sphere of supervision of the executive. The purpose of the right of investigation is to enable the Bundestag to obtain the necessary information to perform all its functions independently of other state institutions; it is based on the complete range of functions of the Bundestag.[81] The Bundestag is also the political forum of the nation which is entitled to deal with all issues relating to the State as a whole;[82] the right of inquiry corresponds to the width of its jurisdiction.[83] However, a central segment of this jurisdiction is the supervision of the executive. The constitutional principle of the parliamentary responsibility of the government arises from the association of ideas between the number of constitutional provisions which assign supervisory powers to the Bundestag.[84] The right of inquiry is particularly aimed at the exercise of powers of supervision relative to the executive.

Supervision means measuring performance against a yardstick, evaluating it, and, if necessary correcting it. The principle of separation of powers in the Basic Law, however, excludes the possibility that one authority can countermand decisions taken by another authority or replace them with decisions of its own. For a *legal* correction, only judicial recourse is available here, particularly recourse to the Federal Constitutional Court. The Bundestag can object to the performance of the executive on the basis of the result of a committee of inquiry, can take that performance as grounds for a constructive vote of no confidence, can draw conclusions for the future in terms of budget law or other law, and can refuse to give formal approval to the actions of the Federal Government (Art. 114). What it cannot do is reverse a criticized decision by the executive or replace it with a decision of its own; in other words put itself in the executive's place for jurisdictional purposes.

In addition to the federalist restrictions and those arising out of the institutional jurisdiction of the Bundestag, there are substantive limitations on the parliamentary right of inquiry. It is regarded as an immanent substantive limitation that, in order for the right of inquiry to be exercised in a specific case, there must be a sufficiently substantial public interest in the inquiry.[85] A public interest only exists when there is a relationship to the common good. The courts could scrutinize the existence of this prerequisite only to the extent of determining whether the Bundestag has blatantly misused its scope for judgment and evaluation – if, for example, a private enterprise is to be exposed or discredited without soundly based factual evidence of illegal action.

In order to be constitutional, an inquiry mandate must be sufficiently specific in terms of object and subject, particularly if it is to serve as a basis for methods of hearing evidence which are supported by sanctions. The witness, for example, must know how far he is under an obligation to tell the truth.

The Bundestag is not vested with a general supervisory right over the executive in the sense of being authorized, in the manner of an auditor, to scrutinize a specific section of the executive in order to determine *whether* an irregularity has occurred, without any factual evidence of an irregularity.[86] In all inquiries into irregularities, there must be factual evidence that irregularities may have occurred.

Under Art. 44 (1), clause 1, the committee of inquiry has the direct right to inspect, for evidential purposes, records and other papers in the official safekeeping of the federal authorities, and to order production of such documents for this purpose.[87] The disputed though relevant view is that their production can be compelled,[88] in the event of refusal, by judicial seizure under the Code of Criminal Procedure.[89] Pleading the good of the Federal

153

Republic or of a German Land as grounds for refusal to produce[90] is not generally an acceptable defense to a committee of inquiry if those interests are safeguarded by adequate secrecy precautions on the part of the committee.[91]

A special limitation on the hearing of evidence by the committee of inquiry may arise with reference to what is called the central area of sole executive responsibility. The Federal Constitutional Court has deemed that the government's responsibility to parliament and the people[92] necessarily presupposes such an area, which includes an area of initiative, consultancy, and action that in principle cannot be investigated even by committees of inquiry. These areas include the internal deliberations of the government itself, as regards both cabinet discussion and the preparation of cabinet and departmental decisions, current negotiations and preparations for decisions. Even in the instance of events which have already been concluded, however, cases are possible in which the government, on the basis of this central area of self-executive responsibility, would not be obliged to disclose facts that were to be kept secret.[93] The dame will necessarily apply to the granting of permission to testify in the sense of §§ 96, 54 Code of Criminal Procedure.

Parliamentary committees of inquiry exercise sovereign powers; therefore, according to Art. 1 (3), they too must observe the basic rights. The right of inquiry and the basic rights have equal constitutional priority, and a balance has to be struck between them. The difficult problems this entails cannot, however, be pursued here.[94]

Parliament's right of inquiry has become to a great extent a political weapon in the conflict between the government and government parties on the one hand and the parliamentary opposition on the other. In a parliamentary democracy, this is anything but illegitimate. A political error or a failure by one's political opponent will be displayed before the public eye, in public proceedings. The Basic Law also designed it as a minority right; a parliamentary opposition which meets the minority quorum can wield it as an effective supervisory instrument against the government, and can hence counteract the danger, inherent in a parliamentary form of government, of a lack of supervision of the government by the majority parties sustaining it. In this sense, the instrument has certainly proven its value in practical politics in the Federal Republic of Germany. The German Bundestag is one of the most »inquiry-friendly« parliaments among the western democracies.

For decades, there has been a justified call for statutory harmonization of the inquiry procedure. In my opinion the right of the minority in the inquiry committee to hear evidence is in particular need of clarification. Without

154

this right, the right of inquiry would be a blunt sword. In addition, it is advisable to regulate by statute the position of witnesses before committees of inquiry. The practical functioning of the right of inquiry as a political weapon all too easily jeopardizes the freedoms guaranteed by basic rights. In particular, the status of a citizen relative to the state, and hence relative to the committee of inquiry also, is not that of a »glass man,« from whom the state can extract any information whatsoever it wishes.

V. *Representation by Political Parties*

1. According to Art. 21 (1) clause 1, the political parties participate »in the development of the people's will.« Although political parties have become powerful factors in the German political process since as long ago as the mid-19th century, and particularly since the introduction of universal suffrage,[95] the Basic Law represented the first positive recognition of the political function of the parties.[96]

2. In Art. 21 (1), clause 2, the Basic Law guarantees the freedom to establish political parties. This freedom is not subject to any obligatory license or permission of any kind.[97]

3. The political parties do not enjoy any constitutional monopoly of the right to participate in the political development of popular objectives. The citizen (through his political basic rights of communication),[98] other social groupings and associations and, not least, the media, also participate in that process. A statutory monopoly for the political parties, for example in the matter of nominating candidates for elections to the parliament, would be incompatible with the franchise principles of Art. 38 (1).[99]

4. In practice, however, the parties' contribution to the development of political objectives is predominant. No non-party candidate has been elected to the Bundestag since the Bundestag elections of 1953; there have been isolated cases of non-party deputies, resulting from their resignation or expulsion from their parties. Although there has been no constitutional requirement to that effect, the offices of Federal Chancellor and Land minister-president have in all cases, and those of federal and Land ministers in almost all, been held by people who belonged to a political

party or immediately joined one. The creation of the political institutions of State – exclusively at the federal level and in the Länder, predominantly in the municipalities – lies for practical purposes in the hands of the political parties.

The Federal Constitutional Court has described the function of the political parties as follows:

> The political parties participate in the political formation of objectives by the people principally through their participation in the elections, which could not be held without the parties. They are additionally links between the citizen and the State institutions, agents through whom the will of the citizens can be implemented even between elections. They accumulate opinions, interests and endeavors directed towards political power and its exercise, balance them internally, and shape them into alternatives among which the citizens can choose. The political parties exert a decisive influence on the occupancy of the highest government offices. To the extent that they form the parliamentary majority and support the government, they create and maintain the most important link between the people and the directing political institutions of the State. As minority parties they form the political opposition and make that opposition effective. They influence the development of national objectives by exerting an influence on the system of the State institutions and offices, doing so particularly by influencing the resolutions and measures of parliament and government.[100]

Even in one of its earliest decisions, the Federal Constitutional Court categorized the parties as »integral constituents of the constitutional structure,«[101] which had been raised by Art. 21, (1) from the area of the politico-sociological into the area of a constitutional institution.«[102]

Parallel to this constitutional development of the German party system, a change has also taken place in the parties' understanding of their own policies and programs. Beginning as early as the 19th century with bourgeois parties, and increasingly in the Weimar era, the parties since 1945 have more and more tended to abandon specific class, professional, confessional, or local association orientations in favor of endeavoring to be national parties aiming to secure the participation of all strata and groups in society, and to integrate and balance their often conflicting interests, claiming to base their programs and practical policies on the general good. This does not rule out programs including key benefits for certain social strata – the older generation, the employees, the professional middle classes, the farmers, and so on. However, attempts to justify these are regularly made by pleading that they, too, indirectly serve the general good, at least in the sense of a more humane society and quality of life.

156

5. However, the political parties - an opinion shared by the Federal Constitutional Court[103] - do not form part of the organized apparatus of government, being not agencies of State authority, but

> freely formed groups rooted in the social sector (BVerfGE 1, 208 [224]); 3, 383, [393], called upon to participate in the formation of political objectives by the people and to exert an influence on the area of the institutionalized apparatus of State.[104] They are political agencies which democracy needs in order to combine the electors into groups capable of political action and so to enable them to exert an effective influence on State events . . .[105]

Section 1 clause 2 of the Law on Political Parties describes the function imposed by Art. 21 (1), clause 1, as a public function;[106] this, however, is not meant to invest that function with the power of public authority, but to describe it as a function in the political process.[107]

As agencies rooted in the social sector, the political parties are not representative institutions of the national population in the sense of Art. 20 (2). As such, unlike those who carry their mandates in the parliaments as a result of general elections, they are popular groups whose legitimation is not democratic, but rather based on membership. Their relation to the citizen is not that of sovereign authorities but that of a private association;[108] federal and Land governments are answerable to the parliaments, not to the parties. In contrast to other representatives of organized interests, however, the specific aim of the parties is to fill the political institutions representing the national population, and in this way directly implement their political programs as government policy. This is a crucial distinction between them and all other groupings from the social sector. These other groups will, indeed, often attempt to exert direct influence on the members of political state institutions, or to have their own members or adherents elected as deputies to the parliaments through the political parties; but they do not attempt as such to obtain mandates in the political state institutions at federal or Land level, nor do they pursue political programs aimed at comprehensively shaping government policy, both of which are essential to the political parties.

6. This two-dimensional nature of the political parties - on the one hand rooted in society, legitimated only by some groups among the population, but on the other hand exerting an influence on the organized apparatus of the State since political representative institutions at federal and Land level are almost entirely recruited from party members - necessarily results in constitutional conflicts which seem far from resolved under the Basic Law.

The Basic Law itself attempts to resolve some of these conflicts by prescribing, in Art. 21 (2), clauses 3 and 4, that the internal organization of the parties must »conform« to democratic principles and that accounts must be publicly rendered showing the source and application of their funds. One such conflict, mentioned earlier, is that between the deputy's free mandate according to Art 38, (1), and the constitutional status of the parties according to Art. 21. Another question which encapsulated this conflict related to the constitutional legality of the public financing of the parties, shown in a series of judgments of the Federal Constitutional Court, whose tenor deviates considerably a straight line,[109] and also in the sequence of statutory regulations on this question, which however cannot be further pursued here.[110] The key problem, as Kunig[111] pertinently puts it, is whether Art. 21 (1), clause 1, also protects the functionality of the parties and compels reimbursement of electoral campaign costs to maintain that functionality. This too depends on the other sources of finance actually available to the parties, and their productivity. In my opinion, it is possible to infer this kind of protective functioning as a principle from Art. 21 (1), clause 1, a principle which the legislature needs to specify in each case, but substantively covers only the reimbursement of absolutely essential campaign costs. What is »absolutely essential« is something the legislature must determine within the limits of a properly formed assessment, and in this case the yardstick to be applied by the Federal Constitutional Court – extending also to questions which are not strictly concerned with the equal franchise – should be more stringent than for normal, arbitrary examination because of the obvious danger of the parties »helping themselves.«

7.   There has for some years been almost daily speculation in the public media, increasingly extending to professional legal circles and even the deliberations of the Association of German Jurists,[112] relating to a »party depression,« even a crisis of the party state. Many symptoms have been mentioned, such as the frustrations in the civil service and those relating to the awarding of government contracts through a widespread party accounts system; the small proportion of party members among the population at large, currently about 4 to 5 percent; spectacular scandals surrounding top politicians. In particular, the rise and – admittedly limited – electoral successes of parties on the fringes of the democratic spectrum, and also the many citizens' initiatives which have been proliferating for some time, are attributed to a failure by the »established« parties to come to grips with concerns which motivate the people, or to be sufficiently prompt in recog-

nizing urgent problems, such as ecological threats, and outlining solutions to them.

There is a good deal of justification in these analyses, particularly regarding the complaints about the party accounts system.[113] The rise of new parties as such is no crisis, but more a testimony to the openness of a pluralistic, libertarian democracy. If the parties concerned happen to be on the fringe of the democratic spectrum, this is certainly not entirely harmless from the standpoint of a democracy based on libertarian ideas. The question is left open as to whether the increase in the popularity of, say, the Republican Party at the latest elections to the European Parliament and in the municipal elections really heralded the long-term formation of a party and policies of the extreme right, or whether it was merely a matter of a »warning shot« fired for the benefit of the parties represented in parliaments and governments, indicating electoral dissatisfaction with certain political issues of the day, such as the policy on political asylum, believed to be a mistake, or inadequate living conditions. On the other hand, it should not be forgotten that those parties which are firmly rooted in the soil of libertarian, constitutional democracy were and are accustomed to garnering about 90 percent of votes cast, and of political mandates.

VI. *Citizens' initiatives*

1. Citizens' initiatives and movements are not all of the same stamp. Many of them have their origins in local or regional issues, such as transport, building or waste disposal projects, the construction of airports or industrial plants, the transfer of teachers, closing of schools and so on. At the other end of the spectrum are initiatives characterized by general ideas associated with ecology or a specific region of politics (disarmament initiatives, peace movements and the like). In between these two are various shadings and hybrids, in which local concerns, such as the building of certain large-scale industrial plants, are taken up and then argued in light of general ecological or socio-political ideas.

2. These initiatives do not involve political representation of the national population in the sense of Art. 20 (2). The creation and active pursuit of such initiatives, provided it remains within the bounds of the constitutional

laws, represents the exercise, by certain groups among the population, of their freedoms which are protected by the basic rights. The political freedom of action of the individual citizen is not, as it were, consumed by the act of participating in elections to the representative institutions of the state. The fact that these initiatives arise outside the political parties may be due to various causes: the parties may consider the general political objectives of such a movement to be mistaken, which cannot be qualified as a crisis of the parties, since the parties are under no obligation to incorporate into their programs what they believe to be misguided objectives; supporters of such an objective retain the freedom to form a political party themselves, and to try by this route to obtain a voice in the representative institutions of state. Particularly in the case of citizens' initiatives arising from local or regional causes and motives, their adherents may be under the impression, rightly or wrongly, that the political parties will not take up their concerns – at least not quickly enough – are not sensitive to the problem, or, for a variety of reasons, will not be honest or energetic enough in their commitment, not least because the contested plans or decisions emanate from governmental or municipal institutions whose personnel, in turn, have been provided by the parties. If such cases accumulate, the citizens feel that their concerns are no longer being taken up by the parties. Citizens' initiatives of this caliber are entirely in harmony with the idea of libertarian representative democracy, and are in this sense legitimate types of phenomena in the »market place of ideas.« They make the political institutions of state, the bureaucracies and the political parties aware of certain concerns, and ensure that they do not forget their responsibility to the citizen. In actual practice, their sound common sense has often prevented foolish projects through political pressure.

3. There are initiatives, however – admittedly usually organized only by relatively small groups – which do become suspect from the standpoint of representative democracy. This occurs when, as in the second half of the 1960s, they are reshaped under the banner of democratic »participation« into a demand for »political action« to circumvent and destroy the constitutionally instituted political organs of the state with slogans such as »public action« and »extra-parliamentary opposition;« when they lay claim to a form of democratically legitimated counter-authority, and proclaim self-chosen areas of »irreconcilable differences« going beyond the limits of the inviolable basic rights.[114] They then run the risk of setting themselves up in opposition to the legitimation principle of the free and general election of representative institutions and the democratic majority principle. The »participatory«

calls for the introduction of a system of Soviet-style councils (under whatever name), for example in the university sector, is an attempt by groups to appropriate to themselves sovereign functions, which in reality concern all citizens of the state. The slogan which calls for the politicization of such institutions is a devious attempt to obtain a general political mandate and to cut loose from the only foundation for legitimation which is recognized in a libertarian democracy, namely free election by all active citizens. The associated calls for »autonomy,« such as »police-free« areas, are intended to eliminate the general political representative institutions, and can thus be seen as an attempt to disenfranchise the ordinary citizen of the state, who alone is entitled, in person or through his freely elected parliaments, to grant a general political mandate. Participatory ideas of this kind are the culmination of corporate state ideas, Soviet ideas and intellectual elite ideas, and become linked with the belief in the abstract, perfectionist »new man« whose »wrong convictions« must be driven out (with energetic assistance, if necessary), resulting in the Utopia of an authority-free state of Marcusian provenance – let the people again endure its happiness.

This kind of participatory movement has been nurtured principally in intellectual circles among the universities, and flourished to a certain extent at the end of the 1960s in the Federal Republic, as it did elsewhere in the western world. So far it has not been of any lasting significance in the Federal Republic, or been able to pose a serious threat to the constitutional, representative democracy in which the political parties play such an important part, although the political representative institutions have occasionally shown considerable signe of weakness, at least at the local level, in implementing the rule of law against violent groups, proclaimed by them to be »limited infringements of rules.«

VII. *Substantive Representation under the Basic Law*

There is no doubt that the people have been strongly »mediafied« by political parties and social groups and associations. A number of authors see this as a depoliticization of the democratic public, of the democratic opinion-shaping and decision-making process, and hence of representative democracy which has alienated the civil society from the consumer society, and especially from the intellectual and political consumer society.[115]

This touches – no less for the parties than for the political representative institutions of the people in the sense of Art. 20 (2) – on the question of substantive representation, concerned with content, in contrast to the formal representation organized through acts of legitimation of a democratic or associative nature. This concerns the possibility of the citizen's identifying with the representative's behavior, his »responsiveness.«[116] With each additional link in the chain by which democratic legitimation is conferred, the danger of alienation of the represented person tends to increase. The constitution cannot guarantee substantive representation concerned with content. At best it can create the preconditions for it, including, in particular, the requirement of regular elections in which the elector can reward the representative but also »settle scores.« Substantive representation can, in the long run, be achieved only through performance; it does not come about automatically as a result of formal legitimation and the acts which confer it.

1. It is in this context that we must view considerations of a reform in the Basic Law which have been developed over the past 20 years. If we except the Marxist-Leninist radical criticism of »bourgeois parliamentarianism,« which has never achieved any significant importance in the practical political process in the Federal Republic, the basic structures of political representation as disclosed by the Basic Law are not in question; there is, in fact, no alternative to them. Equally, no serious consideration is being given to altering the parliamentary form of government in favor of the presidential one, as had been advocated in isolated cases even while the Basic Law was being drafted, particularly by the F.D.P. (Thomas Dehler), though thought is occasionally given to the possibility of the Federal President's being directly elected by the people.

Among the wealth of reformist ideas,[117] we will find the advice and recommendations of the Committee of Inquiry into Constitutional Reform instituted by the German Bundestag,[118] where it is relevant to the topics under consideration here. On the question of the possible strengthening of citizens' rights of participation, the Committee discussed
- the introduction of petitions for, decision by and conducting of referenda,
- a change in the procedure for nominating electoral candidates for the Bundestag elections (primaries, internal nomination within parties of the candidates for electoral districts and of the Land lists),
- the introduction of the model of the semi-open list for the allocation of the second vote in the Bundestag election (following the example of the

162

Bavarian Land parliament franchise, (i.e., the opportunity for the elector to influence the sequence of the candidates on the list),
- popular election of the Federal President.

Rightly, in my opinion,[119] the Committee did not recommend the introduction of the plebiscitary forms or the popular election of the Federal President. Relevantly, it called attention to the irreconcilable conflict between the forms of organization and legitimation based on representative democracy and those based on plebiscitary democracy, and to the functional powers of the executive national leadership.[120] If plebiscitary forms of legislation were extended to constitutional amendments, many of their advocates would probably experience quite a few surprises, regarding for example the reintroduction of the death penalty or an amendment to the basic right of political asylum. Also to be welcomed are the recommendations regarding the semi-open list for the second vote in Bundestag elections,[121] and the possibility of giving party members an absentee vote in the nomination of candidates.[122] More extensive proposals regarding the influence of, for example, citizens (primaries) were not recommended.

On the position of the Bundestag, the Committee recommends that the institution of the dissolution of parliament under Art. 68 be replaced by the option of terminating the legislative period prematurely on the basis of a resolution adopted by two-thirds of its members.[123] In view of the constitutional controversies about the two previous dissolutions of the Bundestag, this recommendation also is to be welcomed.

Furthermore, the Committee recommends an extensive revision of the parliamentary right of inquiry which would appropriately strengthen the rights of the minority (particularly the right to request and compel the production of evidence).[124]

Further recommendations by the Committee, where thematically relevant in the present context, relate to proposals for a more streamlined, simplified and clear legislative procedure in the Bundestag, which are also intended to strengthen its powers of supervision of the Federal Government.[125]

Although nothing has been heard in recent years about the implementation of these recommendations by the Committee, apart from the right of inquiry, they do merit further attention from the legislators concerned with amending the constitution (and with ordinary legislation). They are moderate and balanced, they fit smoothly into the structure of the parliamentary regime established by the Basic Law, and they permit the continuance of proven regulations. They may be of value to the substantive representative nature of the political institutions of state and of the political parties. This, however, can only be demonstrated by the citizens of that state itself.

Whatever value one may place on the content of the policies of the political representative institutions under the Basic Law since 1949, it is difficult to detect any forms of political representation of the people which would promise substantial improvements. The party scene may change in view of a high potential of floating voters, stable government majorities may be more difficult to achieve, the test of minority governments may not yet have been passed – but there is no convincing reason to make substantial changes in the forms of political representation in the Basic Law as currently drafted.

2.   Finally, if we pose the question of whether the political state institutions and the political parties have provided such representation, with respect to content, over the past 40 years under the Basic Law, it will be difficult to answer in the negative. Certainly, political representative institutions of the national population and political parties have made mistakes, and have been very slow to deal with issues such as the threat to the environment. This, however, is not the exclusive privilege of political parties in the Federal Republic of Germany. Another danger seems much greater: that of the demoscopically controlled democracy of complaisance, in which the function of creative and innovative policy which also demands sacrifices can become paralyzed. Nonetheless, the Basic Law does at least permit this kind of representation as regards content.

My opinion is that over the past 40 years – within the limits of the fragility of all human endeavor – this type of representation has been provided by the political institutions.[126] The electors in the Federal Republic of Germany are not departing in droves either from this state or from the political parties. Even citizens' initiatives and, at times, so-called extraparliamentary opposition have seen, and do see, no reason to call, for example, for free and secret elections under the supervision of the United Nations. Elections to the parliaments in the Federal Republic, and hence the fundamental act of democratic legitimation for the political representation of the people are free, and the »market place of ideas« is no less free.

3.   The events of these weeks of September 1989 may recall another act of political representation in the Basic Law. In the preamble, it is stated that the German people have adopted this Basic Law for the Federal Republic of Germany on the basis of its constituent authority. »It has also acted on behalf of those Germans who were denied the right to participate.« At present, there are some 700,000 Germans in another part of Germany who

have applied for permission to travel to the Federal Republic. Since 1949, several million of them have migrated to the Federal Republic of Germany – an indication of the representative nature of this constitution and of the achievement of its political representative institutions during the past 40 years?

Notes:

1 Carl Schmitt, Verfassungslehre, Munich/Leipzig 1928, reprinted without amendments Berlin 1957, pp. 204 *et seq.*

2 Die Repräsentation in der Demokratie, 1st ed., Berlin/Leipzig 1929, 3rd (1966) edition reprinted without amendments, Berlin/New York 1973.

3 Under the Imperial Constitution of 1871, it was not the Kaiser but the Federal Council which was the supreme body in the state; the Kaiser was merely the formal leader of the Presidium of the Federal Council, a largely monarchical committee. Nevertheless, the Kaiser did in fact act to a large extent as a Head of State, for example when declaring war on Tsarist Russia by telegram in 1914, without consulting the Federal Council.

4 Cf. more recently e.g. Suhr, Repräsentation in Staatslehre und Sozialpsychologie, in Staat, 1981, pp. 517 *et* seq; Oppermann/Meyer, Das parlamentarische Regierungssystem des Grundgesetzes, in Veröffentlichungen der Vereinigung der Deutschen Staatsrechtslehrer 33 (1975), pp. 7 *et seq,* 69 *et seq,* 120 *et seq.*

5 See the description in Oppermann/Meyer, *supra* at 10 - 11 and 68 - 69.

6 Cf., for example, Zippelius, Allgemeine Staatslehre, 10th ed., Munich 1988, pp. 170 *et seq;* Degenhart, Staatsrecht I, 4th ed., Heidelberg 1988, marginal notes 4 *et seq;* Badura, Staatsrecht, Munich 1986, D 10.

7 This is the case, at any rate, if we maintain together with C. Schmitt and Leibholz. (See also Herzog, in Art. 20 II; Stern, Staatsrecht der Bundesrepublik Deutschland I, 2nd ed., Munich 1984, p. 963) that the freedom of decision of the »representatives« is an essential feature of a representative system, since a system of councillors characterized by the imperial mandate may be seen as indirect democracy, but in the light of what has been said cannot be seen as representative democracy. However, a substantial part of the literature is critical of the conceptual association between representation and freedom of decision on the part of the representatives. See, Scheuner, Das repräsentative Prinzip in der modernen Demokratie, in Festschrift for Hans Huber, Bern 1961, pp. 221 *et seq.,* especially pp. 225 - 6; Badura, in Bonner Kommentar zum Grundgesetz, Bonn Commentary on the Basic Law, marginal note 67 on Art. 38 (second revised edition, 1966); Hasso Hofman, Repräsentation - Studien zur Begriffsgeschichte, (Berlin 1974), pp. 21 - 2 who all criticize the interpretation quoted above as being an unacceptable adherence to an early liberal concept of representation.

8 Art. 20, paragraph 2, clause 1 of the Basic Law reads: »All State authority emanates from the people.«

9 The initiators of the symposium suggested that the constitutional position of the political State institutions should also be dealt with under the given theme. This is relevant to the extent that political representation of the people in the sense of Art. 20, paragraph 2, of the Basic Law is exercised constitutionally through these competences and within their limitations.

10 The significance here for governmental industrial, economic and - through the possible link with pension levels - social policy, and their effects on the national budgets, are obvious. The State, by guaranteeing autonomy in collective bargaining, has in this case renounced its legislative sovereignty, with the exception of the facility to declare the general application of collective agreements, but is otherwise restricted to more or less plausible appeals to economic discipline and good sense on the part of the partners to the agreement. This is not intended as criticism: in a social market economy, autonomy in collective bargaining is the only appropriate means of reconcility interests in the normal situation.

11 The constituent right reserved by the Basic Law in Art. 146 will not be considered here.

12 The electoral districts must conform to Länder borders, and are required, if possible, to conform to the borders of municipalities, districts and towns, and to form a cohesive area. The population of an electoral district must not vary by more than 25% from the average population figure for all electoral districts; in the event of variations of more than one third, boundaries must be redefined.

13 Each elector has two votes, a primary vote for the election of the electoral district deputy, and a secondary vote for the election of a Land list.

14 It is not my intention to deal here with the question of whether, so far as the principle of equal franchise is concerned, a franchise exercised by a majority vote requires that votes be equal not only numerically but also in terms of their success value. In any case, it has not become a current constitutional problem, but has remained in the sphere of party political threats.

15 See Badura *supra* note 7, at Art. 38.

16 Cf., for example Chr. Link and G. Ress, »Staatszwecke im Verfassungsstaat - 40 Jahre Grundgesetz.«

17 Cf. inter alia Decisions of the Federal Constitutional Court (BVerfGE) Tübingen, 1952 *et seq;* BVerfGE 5, 85, 197 *et seq* (1956); 44, 125, 142-3 (1977).

18 BVerfGE 44, 125, 142-3 (1977).

19 A detailed and particularly pointed account is given by G. Leibholz, Die Repräsentation in der Demokratie (1st ed., 1928, 3rd edition reprinted without amendments, 1973), pp. 224 *et seq.*

20 Whereas the concept still enjoys a considerable vogue in constitutional jurisprudence, it has virtually disappeared from the terminology of the Federal Constitutional Court since 1975. It would not be unjustified to assume that this has occured not accidentally but, by contrast, as a result of a certain caution about deriving specific normative statements from such classificatory concepts of general State theories, and not for example, from the court's distancing itself from the political parties and their function in the political process of a libertarian democracy to which the parties made a vital contribution.

21 Cf. BVerfGE 2, 1, 72-3 (1952); 41, 399,416 (1976).

22 Cf. Stern, *op. cit.,* vol. I, § 24 IV 3a, with numerous references.

23 All summarized in Degenhart, Staatsrecht I (4th ed., 1988), marginal note 335.

24 N. Achterbert, Das rahmengebundene Mandat, 1975; the same in Parlaments-
    recht (1974), pp. 216 *et seq.*
25 Cf. in similar vein Stern, *op. cit.*, Vol. 1, § 24 I 1: »Representation and party alle-
    giance are only mutually exclusive opposites when the parties abandon the prin-
    ciple of being popular parties and become transmuted into groups or class
    parties which then cease to be aware of any aims other than those of their
    groups«; see also, Achterberg, *op. cit.* pp. 224-5.
26 Europäische Grundrechte-Zeitschrift 1989, pp. 288 *et seq.*
27 *Ibid.*, p. 295.
28 *Ibid.*, p. 297.
29 *Ibid.* pp. 299 *et seq.*
30 *Ibid.* pp. 299-300.
31 Art. 29 in its original version has become relevant on eight occasions, though not
    since it was revised in 1976; the additional reorganization regulation of Art. 118
    was disposed of as a result of the amalgamation, during the 1950's, of three
    federal Länder to form the Land of Baden-Württemberg. A referendum of June
    7th, 1970, did not produce the majority needed to reconstitute the Land Baden.
    In this context, the Federal Constitutional Court decided in 1951 that the result
    of the plebiscite according to Art. 118, clause 2 of the Basic Law is binding on
    the federal legislator as regards the form of reorganization and is not merely a
    non-binding guideline. (BVerfGE 1, 14 [1951]).
32 Cf. BVerfGE 57, 295, 319 (1981); 74, 331 (1982).
33 Cf. in particular Bleckmann, »Die Zulässigkeit des Volksentscheides nach dem
    Grundgesetz«, in JZ 1978, 217 *et seq.*, and Pestalozza, »Volksbefragung – Das
    demokratische Minimum«, in NJW 1981, 733 *et seq.*
34 Cf. in particular Herzog in Maunz-Dürig, *op. cit.* marginal notes 44-5 on Art. 20,
    paragraph 2, and also Stern, *op. cit.*, Vol. II, § 25 II 1 b. The Federal Consti-
    tutional Court has not yet expressed an opinion, though Herzog (*op. cit.*,
    marginal note 45) believes that the decision (BVerfGE 8, 104 [1958]) implies
    that the Court, if it had come to the point, would have decided against the
    admissibility of referendum by simple act; a contrary interpretation will be found
    in Stein, Alternativ-Kommentar zum Grundgesetz, marginal note 39 on Art. 20,
    paragraphs 1-3.
35 For a different opinion see Bleckmann, Pestalozza, Stein, *op. cit.*
36 Herzog (*op. cit.*, marginal note 42), for example, believes that even after a
    corresponding amendment to the constitution »the focal point of political
    decision-making« would have to remain with the state institutions.
37 That the decision between representative and direct democracy is at the
    discretion of the constitutional legislator is also assumed, for example, by
    Maunz-Dürig, in Maunz-Dürig, marginal note 47 on Art. 79, paragraph 3, and
    also Bryde, in GGR, Vol. 3, marginal note 40 on Art. 79.
38 »Demokratische Willensbildung und Repräsentation«, in Isensee/Kirchhof,
    Handbuch des Staatsrechts, II, § 30, pp. 29 *et seq*, 31 *et seq.*
39 Stern, *op. cit.* I, 5 22 II 5a, (see also Herzog, Allgemeine Staatslehre, Frankfurt
    1971, p. 216, fn. 57 and p. 296) raises the question without ultimately taking a
    position; in favor, Degenhart, *op. cit.*, maginal note 8; against, Alternativ-Kom-
    mentar. H.P. Schneider (Neuwied, 1984), marginal note 5 to Art. 38, according
    to whom the Bundestag is the only representative institution; similarly H. Meyer,
    op. cit., p. 80 (but on the other hand cf. p. 89).

40 *Op. cit.*, pp. 79 *et seq.*
41 In Bremen and Hamburg the senators are elected by the citizens, Art. 107 I Bremen Land Constitution; Art. 34 I Hamburg Land Constitution.
42 As in Baden-Württemberg, Art. 46 III Land Constitution; Bavaria Art. 45 Land Constitution; Berlin Art. 41, paragraph 2, Land Constitution; Lower Saxony Art. 20 III Land Constitution; Rhineland-Palatinate Art. 98 II; Saarland Art. 89 Land Constitution.
43 In Hesse and North Rhine-Westphalia the minister-president merely indicates to the Land parliament the ministers he has appointed. Art. 101 I, II Hesse Land Constitution; Art. 52 III North Rhine Westphalia Land Constitution; in Schleswig-Holstein no formal notification is required, but the ministers take the oath before the Land Parliament. Art. 21 II, 23 II Land Constitution.
44 The question of the constitutionality of a municipal franchise for foreigners will have to take this fact into account.
45 Art. 113 of the Basic Law.
46 Cf. also H. Meyer, *op. cit.*, p. 87.
47 Cf. arts. 29, 79, 81, 84, 85, 87b, 106, 107, 108, 120a, 134, 135 of the Basic Law.
48 Cf. art. 84, paragraph 2; 85, paragraph 1; 108, paragraph 7, BL.
49 E.g., those relating to the charges for the Federal railroad, mail and telecommunications systems. See art. 80, paragraph 2, of the Basic Law.
50 Art. 80, paragraph 2.
51 Art. 37, paragraph 1; 91, paragraph 2, clauses 2 and 3.
52 For the very extensive academic literature on the parliamentary system, the American reader is referred to U. Bermbach, (ed.), Hamburger Bibliographie zum Parlamentarischen System der Bundesrepublik Deutschland 1945-1970, 1973.
53 Stern, Das Staatsrecht der Bundesrepublik Deutschland I (2nd ed.1984), 22 I c, pp. 948, 959 *et seq.*
54 BVerfGE 2, 1, 12 *et seq.* (1952).
55 German Bundestag, Reports of Proceedings, 84. Sitting of February 5th, 1982, pp. 5050-1, 5070; Bundestag Drucksache 9/1312; the vote of confidence was passed by the votes of the deputies of the governing SPD and FDP parties.
56 Among the extensive literature, cf. *inter alia* Bull, Parlamentsauflösung - Zurückverweisung an den Souverän in ZRP 1972, pp. 201 *et seq.;* H.P. Schneider, Die vereinbarte Parlamentsauflösung, in JZ 1973, pp. 652 *et seq.;* Kremer (Ed.), Parlamentsauflösung (1974).
57 This view was held not only by those who called for the vote but also, in particular, by two of the dissenting votes in the case of the decision of the Federal Constitutional Court which was eventually passed by 6 votes against two, cf. BVerfGE 62, 1, 70 *et seq.,* 108 *et seq.* (1983).
58 BVerfGE 62, 1, 41 *et seq.* (1983).
59 BVerfGE 62, 1, 43 (1983).
60 Cf. only BVerfGE 9, 268, 281 (1959).
61 Friesenhahn, VVDStRL 16 (1958), p. 38; Stern, *op.cit.,* 5 33 II 5 d), pp. 966 *et seq.* with further references.
62 *Ibid.,* p. 38.
63 Friesenhahn in A. Randelzhofer, German-Spanish Constitutional Law Colloquium (1982), p. 43.

64 BVerfGE 49, 89, 124 *et seq.* (1978).
65 BVerfGE 68, 1, 85 *et seq.,* 87 (1984).
66 *Ibid.,* p. 89.
67 Cf. BVerfGE 33, 125 (158); 33, 303 (346); 40, 237 (249-250); 47, 46 (80); 45, 400 (417); 49, 89 (126127); 58, 257 (268).
68 Cf. even the early BVerfGE 8, 155, 167 (1958).
69 BVerfGE 40, 237, 249 (1975).
70 BVerfGE 49, 89, 126 with further references (1978).
71 BVerfGe 40, 237, 249 (1975). Although, in fact, the legislative work of the Bundestag and the Federal Council inevitably takes place largely in the committees, which do not meet in public, the possibility of plenary debate and the published committee reports ensure incomparably greater clarity – even if only because the opposition receives a hearing – than is the case with executive legislation. Quite often, however, only a very few experts in parliamentary parties understand the regulations introduced, for example in the fields of social or fiscal law.
72 BVerfGE 40, 237, 254 (1975).
73 BVerfGE 45, 400, 417 (1977); 47, 46, 80 (1977); 58, 257, 268 (1981); cf. also 53, 185, 204 (1980).
74 Cf. BVerfGE 49, 89, 130 *et seq.* (1978); 50, 290, 352, 377 *et seq.* (1979); 53, 30, 58 (1979); 55, 274, 308 (1980); 56, 54, 79 (1981); 57, 139, 162 (1981); 59, 119, 127 (1981); 65, 1, 55 (1983); 68, 287, 309 (1984).
75 BVerfGE 49, 89 (guiding principle 3), 130 *et seq.* (1978).
76 BVerfGE 49, 70, 86 *et seq.* (1978); 67, 100, 126 (1984).
77 Art. 57, paragraph 2.
78 BVerGE 76, 363, 376, 381 (1987); 77, 1, 39 (1987).
79 Cf. Kipke, Die Untersuchungsausschüsse des Deutschen Bundestages (1985), pp. 78 *et seq.;* Gascard, Das Untersuchungsrecht in rechtsvergleichender Sicht (Dissertation, Kiel, 1966); F. Meyer, Die Untersuchungskompetenzen des amerikanischen Kongresses (Bern, 1968).
80 BVerfGE 77, 1, 44 (1987); M. Schröder, Empfiehlt sich eine gesetzliche Neuordung der Rechte und Pflichten parlamentarischer Untersuchungsausschüsse, in Proceedings of the 57th Conference of German Jurists in Mainz 1988, Vol. I, part E (1988), pp. 7 *et seq.,* E 30 *et seq.*
81 R.J. Partsch, »Empfiehlt es sich, Funktion, Struktur und Verfahren der parlamentarischen Untersuchungsausschüsse grundlegend zu ändern« in Proceedings of the 45th Conference of German Jurists, I/3 (1964), p. 13.
82 Kölble, DVBl. 1964, 701 *et seq.;* Böckenförde, in AöR 103 (1978) 1, 8 *et seq.;* Stern, Staatsrecht, II, p. 47, Schenke, in JZ 1988, 808.
83 BVerfGE 77, 1, 44 (1987).
84 These articles, in addition to Arts. 44 and 45a, particularly Art. 67 (constructive vote of no confidence), 43 paragraph 1 (so-called right of summons against every member of the Federal Government), 45b (the regulation expressly refers to the »exercise of parliamentary supervision«), and Art. 17 in combination with Art. 45c and Art. 114 (rendering of accounts).
85 BVerfGE 77, 1, 44 (1987). The constitutional literature is virtually unanimous. See, Böckenförde, AöR 103 (1978) 1, 14; Scholz, AöR 105 (1980), 564, 594.
86 Cf. Constitutional Court of the German Reich, RGZ 104, 423, 428 *et seq.;* Constitutional Court of Baden-Württemberg, ESVGH 27, 1, 11.

87 The production of records and papers in the safekeeping of authorities which are not subject to the federal authority, and of court records, requires recourse to administrative assistance as provided by Art. 44, paragraph 3, of the Basic Law. See, BVerfGE 67, 100, 128-9 (1984).

88 Kramer, NJW 1984, 1502-3.

89 § 94 Code of Criminal Procedure.

90 § 96 Code of Criminal Procedure.

91 Cf. in this connection, and in connection with the possible levels of precautions to be applied in individual cases, BVerfGE 67, 100, 133 (1984) and Schröder, *op. cit.,* p. E 97 *et seq.*

92 Cf. BVerfGE 9, 268, 281 (1959).

93 BVerfGE 67, 100, 139 (1984). Important military secrets, for example, will be covered by this.

94 See comments on this in the following judgments of the Federal Constitutional Court: BVerfGE 67, 100, 130 (1984); 77, 1 *et seq.* (1987); BVerfG (Preliminary Examination Committee) NJW 1984, 2276; DÖV 1984, 759, 760 with criticism by Badura, *ibid.,* p. 760. Schröder, *op. cit.,* p. E 20 *et seq.;* Masing, Parlamentarische Untersuchungen gegenüber Privaten in Der Staat, 1988, pp. 273 *et seq.*

95 As early as 1848, the Frankfurt National Assembly was elected on the basis of universal suffrage for the male population of voting age; the Imperial Constitution of 1871 introduced, at the Reich level, the universal right to vote in Reichstag elections for all male Germans over the age of 25 whereas in the kingdom of Prussia, for example, a so called three-category suffrage prevailed until 1918; women suffrage was not introduced until 1918.

96 Art. 130 paragraph 1, of the Weimar Imperial Constitution of 1919 did so in a somewhat defensive manner with the provision that civil servants were »servants of the people at large, not of a party«.

97 The civil law administrative regulations governing the chosen legal form – usually that of the unincorporated association, but in isolated cases among Land party associations that of the incorporated association – do not provide grounds for any licensing right on the part of the State.

98 In particular through the freedom of expression under Art. 5 and the freedoms of assembly and association under Art. 8 and 9 Basic Law.

99 Kunig, Parteien, in Isensee-Kirchhof, Handbuch des Staatsrechts II, § 33, pp. 103 *et seq.,* 111.

100 BVerfGE 52, 63, 82-3 (1979); cf. also BVerfGE 3, 19, 26 (1953); 14, 121, 133 (1962); 20, 56, 99, 101 (1966); 44, 125, 145-6 (1977).

101 BVerfGE 1, 208, 225, 227 (1952). Since then the established precedent has been BVerfGE 73, 40, 85 (1986).

102 BVerfGE 2, 1, 73 (1952).

103 Cf. BVerfGE 1, 208, 225 (1952); 20, 56, 100-101 (1966).

104 BVerfGE 20, 56, 101 (1966); 52, 63, 83, 85 (1979).

105 BVerfGE 69, 92, 110 (1985).

106 See also BVerfGE 61, 1, 11-12 (1982).

107 In the same way as the Federal Constitutional Court sometimes refers to the public function of the press.

108 Kunig, Parteien in Isensee-Kirchhof, *op. cit.,* II, § 33, p. 129.

109 See BVerfGE 8, 51, 63 (1958); 20, 56 (1966); 24, 300 (1968); 52, 63 (1963); 73, 40, 70 *et seq.* (1986).

110 As one of many examples in the literature, see Kunig, *op. cit.,* pp. 136 *et seq.* with the most important references from court judgments and literature.

111 Kunig, *op. cit.,* p. 139.

112 Cf., for example, the report by M. Stolleis, Parteienstaatlichkeit – Krisensymptome des demokratischen Verfassungsstaats in VVDStRL 44 (1986), pp. 7 et *seq.,* who – rightly, in my view – is notable for a cautious composure.

113 Another factor which has also been the subject of quite frequent and specific criticism in expert legal circles is the great influence of the parties on the composition of the Federal Constitutional Court. See R.W. Geck, Wahl und Amtsrecht der Bundesverfassungsrichter (1986), in particular pp. 31 *et seq.* What is quite absurd, however, is the radical criticism expressed by Uwe Wesel, Nach Karlsruhe gehen, in: Kursbuch 77 (1984), pp. 123 *et seq.* On the one hand Wesel deplores the influence of the parties on the selection of the judges; but on the other hand he presumes to accuse a judge such as Wolfgang Zeidler of a form of party treason because he concurred in the judgment against his own political party (*ibid.,* p. 130). Whether the parties have always been most fortunate in the selection of »their« candidates for the judiciary may be judged from an impartial position. The Federal Constitutional Court is no more proof against wrong decisions than other supreme court, but it remains to be proved that such wrong decisions are specifically attributable to the strong influence exerted by the political parties in the selection of the judges. It is also noteworthy that, since the appropriate annual representative surveys were instituted in the 1970's, the Federal Constitutional Court had always enjoyed the highest esteem of any institution in West German public life – and this despite the fact that the identities of the judges are in practice controlled by the political parties.

114 Art. 19, paragraph 2, of the Basic Law.

115 Cf., for example, J. Habermas, Strukturwandel der Öffentlichkeit (1961), pp. 165 *et seq.,* 193 *et seq.*

116 Böckenförde, Demokratische Willensbildung und Repräsentation, in Isensee-Kirchhof, *op. cit.,* Vol.II, § 30, pp. 39-40.

117 Cf. *inter alia,* Oppermann, *op. cit.,* pp. 38 *et seq.* and Meyer, *op. cit.,* pp. 104 *et seq.*

118 Cf. Zur Sache 3/76, Beratungen und Empfehlungen zur Verfassungsreform, Schlußbericht, Teil I published by the Press and Information Center of the German Bundestag. Only a few of the Committee's recommendations have so far been taken up by the legislators concerned with amending the constitution. Cf., for the present context, the 33rd Act Amending the Basic Law of August 23rd, 1976 (Federal Law Gazette I, p. 2381); the redrafted Arts. 29, 39, paragraphs 1, 2 and 45 and Arts. 45a, paragraph 1, clause 2 and 49 were deleted. The 35th Act Amending the Basic Law of December 21st, 1983, Federal Law Gazette I, p. 1481 redrafted Art. 21, paragraph 1, clause 4 to the effect that the parties must in the future render a public accounting regarding the application of their funds and their assets.

119 See *supra,* p. 19.

120 Report, *op. cit.*, p. 21-2.
121 There is of course a political price to be paid for this model: it may curtail, or at least jeopardize, the parties' option of using their Land lists to help secure mandates for people who may, for example, be highly qualified but are not very suited to fighting election campaigns.
122 The Committee regarded the current influence of the individual party members as unsatisfactory. Action to counter what is perhaps the most serious argument, the top-heaviness of the vocational composition of the Bundestag, which has increasingly become a parliament of civil servants and party and association functionaries, cannot of course be taken by way of a provision in the Act Concerning the Political Parties; this would fail because of the freedom of political parties under Art. 21, paragraph 1, of the Basic Law.
123 Report, *op. cit.*, pp. 20 *et seq.*
124 *Op. cit.*, pp. 24 *et seq.*
125 For details see, Report, op cit., pp. 29 et seq.
126 In libertarian democracies, it is virtually a compulsory exercise, when they celebrate their anniversaries, to highlight the weaknesses of their own constitutional order as pitilessly as possible; this is what happened two years ago in the United States, and it is also happening abundantly in the Federal Republic of Germany, where the role and behavior of the political parties have been caught in a particularly intense crossfire. If no attempt has been made to follow that trend in this lecture, this is not an attempt to give the impression that everything is perfect in the constitutional world, or to minimize shortcomings in substantive representation concerned with content, but because all that has been attempted here is to give an outline, even if fragmentary, of the constitutional framework of political representation as imposed by the Basic Law.

*Walter F. Murphy**

Excluding Political Parties: Problems for Democratic and Constitutional Theory

Both the United States and the Federal Republic of Germany are constitutional democracies. Yet the systems differ in many obvious and consequential ways. Not least striking among those differences is the manner in which the two polities articulate the sibling political theories of constitutionalism and democracy. The purpose of this paper is to explore some of those differences by examining the specific issue of excluding from participation in the electoral processes political parties that embrace authoritarian values and aim to destroy constitutional democracy.

I. *The German and American Models of Constitutional Democracy*

A. *Government by the Consent of the Governed*

The constitutional texts of the Federal Republic and the United States clearly, albeit problematically, commit their polities to the once revolutionary[1] but now commonplace[2] norm that governments derive »their just powers from the consent of the governed.« The Basic Law opens with the assertion: »The German people . . . [h]ave enacted, by virtue of their constituent power, this Basic Law. . . . They have also acted on behalf of those Germans to whom participation was denied.«

In 1948-49, this myth of »we, the people« had a certain irony in Germany, though hardly equal to the similar invocation in Japan's »MacArthur Constitution.« Unless one accepts an ultra-Burkean view of virtual representation, the »people« of East Germany had no voice whatever in exercising any »constituent power«; even citizens of West Germany played only a limited role. Not only did Britain, France, and the United States set the basic guidelines for the new order,[3] but their military governors were also frequent, if seldom effective, kibitzers in the drafting process.[4] In addition, the Parliamentary Council that wrote the Basic Law had been chosen not by popular vote but by the legislatures of the Länder. And ratification was neither by plebiscite, as in Ireland and Spain,[5] nor by conventions specifically chosen for this task as in the United States; rather, the legislatures of the Länder provided a touch of political symmetry by accomplishing that task themselves.

The American constitutional text also purports to speak in the name of »We, the People,« but that claim is problematic as well. The Continental Congress that adopted the Declaration of Independence in 1776, setting out the standard of popular sovereignty, had not been elected to decide the issue of separation from Britain, nor did that Congress submit the Declaration or the Articles of Confederation, the first constitution for the American nation, to any sort of referendum.

More specifically, there are also serious questions about how much legitimacy, democratic or otherwise, the body of the constitutional text of 1787 could initially claim. With good reason, some Anti-Federalists charged that the document conceived at Philadelphia was born out of wedlock. First, the delegates exceeded the authority that Congress conferred. It had called a convention »for the sole and express purpose of revising the Articles of Confederation.«[6] But, after deliberating their mandate, the delegates decided to exceed their commissions and proposed an entirely new set of constitutional arrangements, one that would claim to speak in the name of »the people of the United States,« a group who, some Anti-Federalists charged, had no corporate existence except in the individual states. »What right had they to say, *We, the people?*« Patrick Henry angrily asked. »Who authorized them to speak the language of *We, the people,* instead of We, the States?«[7]

Second, some Anti-Federalists contended that Congress could not have validly conferred on the convention the authority it exercised. The Articles of Confederation – the document through which the peoples of the several states, acting as separate political entities, had seemingly, albeit indirectly, consented to limited, though permanent, cooperation with each other – did not allow for a constitutional convention. A third objection claimed that the method prescribed for ratification violated the plain words of Article XIII, which required amendments be unanimously supported by the states:[8] Rhode Island had neither answered the call for a convention nor agreed to the congressional resolution submitting the proposed constitutional text to the states. More critically, the proposed text provided that approval of nine states would be sufficient to bring the new covenant into effect among

174

assenting states, thus potentially depriving as many as four states of their explicitly protected right to veto changes in the Articles and presenting them with an end to a union that all the partners had pledged would be »perpetual.«

Fourth, the people of the several states had delegated their sovereign powers to their legislatures. Under the principle that delegates may not further delegate, those who had such awful authority could not yield it to popularly chosen conventions but had to exercise it themselves, in accordance with Article XIII's procedures for amendment.

In addition, some modern commentators, most notably Charles A. Beard, have charged that the ratifying conventions of 1787-88 did not speak words of consent for »We, the people,« much less exercise the people's »constituent power.« Rather, these commentators argue, a small cabal who stood to profit from the new institutional arrangements clothed their private interests in public garb and, thanks to the limited suffrage of the time, secured a false measure of approval. That no woman, Indian, or slave could vote lends weight to this claim, though by standards of the late eighteenth century, the elections were remarkably »democratic.«[9]

Such objections to the genuineness of German and American claims to speak in the name of »the people« raise fundamental - and vexing - questions about who the people are, *how* they can consent to merge themselves into a larger whole, and how new generations can *continue* to exhibit such agreement. Nevertheless, popular acceptance and public practice have covered these shortcomings with patinas of legitimacy. Few citizens outside of academe now challenge textual assertions that »the people« consented to either political system, but that acceptance tells us little about what it was that either people have accepted.

B. *Democratic Government*

»Government by consent« is not the same as »government chosen by and responsible to the people,« for the people may consent to any kind of government they wish. The Basic Law implicitly recognizes this distinction by baptizing the new polity as »a democratic and social federal state« in which all public authority »emanates from the people. It shall be exercised by the people by means of elections and voting and by specific legislative, executive, and judicial organs.«[10] Furthermore, Article 38 stipulates that deputies to the Bundestag »shall be elected in general, direct, free, equal, and secret elections. They shall be representatives of the whole people, not bound by orders and instructions, and shall be subject only to their own conscience.«

The original American text included elements of democratic theory. An interpreter, however, must largely read those elements *into* rather than *out of* the document's plain words, for they contain no endorsement of democratic theory that even closely parallels the German. Indeed, among the Anti-Federalists' principal criticisms of the proposed document was that it was anti-democratic. It was a charge to which some Federalists would have, in private, pleaded guilty. In truth, most Federalist leaders were at least ambivalent about democracy. Some were fundamentally distrustful, even contemptuous, of the common man. Others, initially ardent democrats, had become disenchanted by what they viewed as the near-tragic experience under popularly responsive state governments.[11] Madison, for instance, told Jefferson that he had come to believe that:

> the invasion of private rights is *chiefly* to be apprehended, not from acts of Government contrary to the sense of its constituents, but from acts in which Government is the mere instrument of the major number of its constituents.[12]

Others feared that universal manhood franchise, with voting - as it then often was - public and oral, would merge political and economic power. As Gouverneur Morris, who drafted the final version of the Convention's proposal, purportedly told the other delegates at Philadelphia:

> If the suffrage were open to all *freemen* - the government would indubitably be an Aristocracy. . . . It would put into the power of opulent men whose business created numerous dependents to rule at elections. Hence so soon as we erected large manufactories and our towns became more populous - wealthy merchants and manufacturers would elect the house of representatives.[13]

It is worth noting that neither the document of 1787, the Bill of Rights, nor any later amendment recognizes a general right of citizens to vote. Article II declares that those eligible to cast a ballot for the most numerous house of a state legislature can vote in congressional elections, and the Seventeenth Amendment extends those terms to senatorial contests. But neither clause sets any standards for eligibility to vote for state legislators. Later amendments merely forbid governmental discrimination against voters because of their race, sex, failure to pay a tax, or age (if over 18).[14]

Madison went so far as to boast in The Federalist Nos. 10 and 51 that the new political system would make it extremely difficult for interests, even if together they constituted a majority, to coalesce in such a way as to control the federal government. He proved to be an accurate prophet. The webs of separated institutions sharing power, staggered elections, and distributions of power between nation and state have, in fact, typically fractured and often frustrated the popular will.

Still, the American system has become much more democratic over the past two centuries. Practice in the states as much as or even more than formal amendments brought about that change; and constitutional interpretation by judges, willing to read the text's prohibitions against assorted forms of discrimination as circumlocutions for positive acceptance of democratic theory,[15] have propelled the change forward.[16]

C. *Limited, Constitutional Government*

The text of the Basic Law also plainly reflects a commitment to limited, constitutionalist government. Article 1 begins with an assertion dear to hearts of constitutionalists:

(1) The dignity of man shall be inviolable. To respect and protect it shall be the duty of all state authority. (2) The German people therefore acknowledge inviolable and inalienable human rights as the basis of every community, of peace and justice in the world.

Moreover, the Basic Law clearly spells out the *Bundesverfassungsgericht's* authority to invalidate governmental action and the obligation of other agencies to conform to the Court's interpretations. Here, too, the German document is much more specific than the American, which bows in very broad terms to constitutionalism in its Preamble[17] and more particularly in the Ninth Amendment:

The enumeration, in the Constitution, of certain rights shall not be construed to deny or disparage the existence of others retained by the people.

The very notion, however, of a government of delegated powers implies limited government, as does establishment of separate institutions with overlapping grants of power. Whether the American framers meant to establish the judiciary as what Gouverneur Morris would, 14 years after the Convention adjourned, reverentially term »that fortress of the Constitution«[18] is not completely clear. The document, however, made such authority easy to infer. Adoption of the Thirteenth and Fourteenth amendments (1866-68), passage of legislation authorizing federal courts to interpret these provisions,[19] and judicial interpretations of them and the Bill of Rights have solidified constitutionalism as part of the larger political system, though one should not underestimate legislative and executive action[20] or the synergistic effects of political institutions and culture.[21]

Of course, formal endorsements of constitutionalism and democracy are of themselves weak indicia of political reality. Some constitutions, like Stalin's, Mao's, or, for much of its slim decade of existence, Pinochet's, have functioned as political fig leaves, not as codifications of fundamental rules of the political game. Indeed, no constitution is completely authoritative in the sense of being always and completely obeyed; moreover, a constitutional authority varies over time. Certainly neither the German nor the American system has consistently lived up either to its ideals or its specific commands, though on a relative scale each polity has done rather well.

D.   *Formal Roles of Political Parties*

Here again the differences appear striking. Article 21 (1) of the Basic Law establishes parties as legitimate political institutions, recognizes the right to establish such organizations, and imposes on them a critical duty: »The political parties shall participate in the forming of the political will of the people.« In addition, Article 21 requires parties to »publicly account for the sources of their funds« and, by fiat, tries to rid the Federal Republic of the near-universal organizational tendency toward oligarchy: »[parties'] internal organization must conform to democratic principles.«[22]

Although the Constitutional Court Act allows parties represented in Parliament to bring *Organstreit* proceedings in the *Bundesverfassungs-gericht* to challenge the validity of governmental policies touching on their activities, the judges have only partially accepted Judge Gerhard Leibholz's theory that the Federal Republic is a »party state,« resting on universal suffrage and an electoral system in which unified, programmatic parties compete with each other to inform as well as form public opinion and so perform public functions.[23] Still, the Judges have gone a long way down road, or so it would seem to people whose base line is constitutional interpretation in other polities. German jurisprudence has, as Donald P. Kommers puts it, viewed parties »as integral to German *democracy* as are the representative organs of government.«[24] In »the reality of the large modern democratic state,« the Constitutional Court has said, the »popular will can emerge only through parties operating as political units.«[25] And the Basic Law, the Judges later added, »has consciously taken the step of

›constitutionalizing‹ political parties. By raising them so the rank of constitutional institutions, the Basic Law has also included parties in the ›integral factors‹ of the state.«[26]

On the other hand, neither as originally written nor as amended does the American constitutional text so much as mention the word »party.« The omission is interesting, for the drafters and ratifiers of all amendments proposed after 1801 were intimately involved in the work of political parties. Even the framers, with their British roots, must have been familiar with the crude form of party competition between Whigs and Tories. In fact, some founders may have feared parties. Madison wrote eloquently about the dangers of »faction,«[27] but admitted that there were only two ways to remove its causes: »the one by destroying the liberty which is essential to its existence; the other, by giving to every citizen the same opinions, the same passions, and the same interests.«[28]

In any event, the issue of ratification quickly split the founding generation into Federalist and Anti-Federalist camps. Then, within a decade of ratification, new problems generated somewhat different cleavages leading to the creation of the Democratic-Republican party[29] in opposition to the remnants of the old Federalists; and these fissures remain visible today. The persistence of those divisions and rival organizations legitimized political parties more than any consciously articulated version of democratic theory.

Although the First Amendment[30] provides a firm constitutional basis for parties, dissidents were almost as slow as judges to reason that freedom to speak and write, to assemble peacefully, and to petition government for redress of grievances, taken together, implied a right not only to oppose governmental policies but also to organize political parties to make that opposition effective. In 1798, for example, even Jefferson and Madison initially opposed the Sedition Act,[31] which resurrected the British law of seditious libel, on grounds that Congress had invaded the authority of the states rather than violated the First Amendment.[32]

In recent decades, federal judges have frequently and formally recognized not only the importance of parties and the country's interest in a stable party system, but also that the »freedom of association protected by the First and Fourteenth Amendments includes partisan political organization. ›The right to associate with the political party of one's choice is an integral part of this basic constitutional freedom.‹«[33] Furthermore, the Supreme Court has also stressed the connection between the individual's constitutional rights and those of his or her party: »Any interference with the freedom of the party is simultaneously an interference with the freedom of its adherents.«[34]

Nevertheless, judges and legislators in the United States have stopped far short of endorsing the concept of the »party state.« Its proponents are likely to be eloquent but lonely academics.[35]

Moreover, the prevalence of primary elections as *the* means of selecting parties' candidates for all important public offices, individual candidates' utilization of television and other mass media of communication, and voters' frequent crossings of party lines within and across elections make it clear that the American people, however they feel about parties in the abstract, do not rejoice in the pair they have.[36] Certainly the role of »party leader« does not generally confer much prestige in American culture; nor, in practical politics, is it necessarily a position of great power.

II. *The Exclusion of Political Parties*

The differing formal roles of parties in the two polities raise several sets of important questions. Out of prudence, I shall attack only two. The first requires a descriptive answer: To what extent have the Federal Republic and the United States attempted to exclude some parties from participation in the normal political processes? The other question raises normative as well as practical issues: What do these policies, different and/or alike, portend for the actualization of constitutional and democratic theory?

A. *German and American Policies*

1. *The German Practice*

The notion of »militant« or »fighting democracy« precedes the founding of the Federal Republic.[37] First, this concept distinguishes between, on the one hand, opposition to specific institutional arrangements and/or to particular policies, however important, and, on the other hand, utter rejection of the entire political order. The fundamental thesis of militant democracy is that the polity need not commit suicide by allowing those people who fall in the latter category to utilize its free and open processes to demolish those very processes. In short, a democracy may punish or exclude those whose clear aim is to destroy the system. Indeed, it may even strike back at those opponents.[38]

180

The notion of »fighting democracy« suffuses much of the Basic Law. Article 5 (3) notes that »Freedom of teaching shall not absolve from loyalty to the constitution.« Article 9 (2) prohibits »Associations, the purposes or activities of which conflict with criminal laws or which are directed against the constitutional order or the concept of international understanding.« Article 18 provides for judicial removal of the fundamental rights of those who »combat the free democratic basic order.«[39] It is, however, the second paragraph of Article 21 which contains the most famous of these »militant« provisions:

> Parties which, by reason of their aims or the behavior of their adherents, seek to impair or abolish the free democratic basic order or to endanger the existence of the Federal Republic of Germany, shall be unconstitutional. The Federal Constitutional Court shall decide on the question of unconstitutionality.

In only two instances during the Federal Republic's first 40 years did the government ask the *Bundesverfassungsgericht* to outlaw a party.[40] The most obvious mark, the Socialist Reich Party, a neo-Nazi group, provided an easy case for the Court. The organization modelled itself on the old NSDAP and its auxiliaries on the SA and SS; its youth groups used the same uniforms as the Hitler Youth; many of its slogans, jingoistic as well as anti-semitic, were recycled from Joseph Goebbels; and it openly professed contempt for liberal democracy in general and the Federal Republic in particular. Moreover, the SRP was a relatively small association whose bloody roots made it unlikely to appeal to large segments of opinion inside or outside Germany.

The second target, the German Communist Party, raised more serious problems. Although the normative issue seemed clear – »The dictatorship of the proletariat is incompatible with the free democratic order of the Basic Law«[41] – the case presented enormous practical difficulties: The KPD was much larger than the SRP and, in the previous general election, had polled 1.4 million votes and won 15 seats in Parliament; the Social Democrats, then the Federal Republic's largest opposition party, were also Marxist in origin, though long shed of most of that ideology; the old KPD had fought valiantly against Hitler and its leaders had been killed or exiled; and, not least, West Germany was bordered on the east by communist states, with one of whose people the Basic Law pledged reunification.

In a vain hope that the case might disappear, the Judges waited almost five years before handing down the inevitable decision that the KPD was unconstitutional. To run afoul of the Basic Law's criteria, the Judges ruled, a party must not merely reject the polity's highest values, it must also demonstrate an intent to destroy the constitutional system.[42] And even these strict standards condemned the KPD: Its organization, tactics, political style, and ultimate goal were all contrary to the basic norms of the constitutional order and directed against its continued existence.

As with the SRP, the Court ordered the KPD dissolved, its assets confiscated, and its deputies in Parliament dismissed. The order, however, did not extend beyond the actual party and its suborganizations. And, although the Judges specified that no substitute party could be established in the KPD's place, they kept the door open to reunification: »Banning the KPD is not legally incompatible with reauthorization of a Communist party were elections to be held throughout Germany.«

2. *American Practice*

The popular image of the American notion of constitutional democracy is radically different from that of »fighting democracy.« »Freedom for the thought we hate«[43] is supposedly not merely the ideal but also the operative constitutional rule. As Justice Oliver Wendell Holmes wrote:

[W]hen the men have realized that time has upset many fighting faiths, they may come to believe even more than they believe the very foundations of their own conduct that the ultimate good is better reached by free trade in ideas – that the best test of truth is the power of the thought to get itself accepted in the competition of the market, and that truth is the only ground upon which their wishes safely can be carried out.[44]

Or as he said six years later:

If, in the long run, the beliefs expressed in the proletarian dictatorship are destined to be accepted by the dominant forces of the community, the only meaning of free speech is that they should be given their chance and have their way.[45]

In both instances, however, Holmes wrote neither for the Supreme Court nor in agreement with its decisions. Rather, his were dissenting views. The tenor of both American constitutional history and law have been quite different, providing an analogue closer to »fighting democracy« than to Holmes's picture – whether charmingly Miltonesque or wonderfully relativistic – of truth »successfully« grappling with falsehood. One of the major differences between the German and American systems, however, is that the United States has been less concerned, though surely not *un*concerned, about organized parties than about the ideas and policies they advocate. Another difference lies in constitutional style: On these issues, as on many others, American constitutional interpretation has been episodic and *ad* *hoc,* without the *Bundesverfassungsgericht*'s conscious adoption of a systematic jurisprudence.

The Alien and Sedition Acts of 1798[46] went far beyond control of immigration, naturalization, and attempts to overthrow the government by force. Together they represented efforts to protect the country from the more radical ideas of the French Revolution and, not coincidentally, to suppress the Democratic-Republican party that was emerging under the leadership of Jefferson and Madison.[47]

During the Civil War, Lincoln jailed, often without formal charges, hundreds, perhaps even thousands, of political opponents. Some of these were armed, pro-Confederate guerrillas,[48] but many were loyal citizens who took the position – which they were willing to test in the market place of the normal electoral processes – that Lincoln had incorrectly interpreted the Constitution in claiming it authorized the federal government to use force to keep states in the Union.

After the war, Republicans' plans focused as much on reconstructing southern whites as on rebuilding the Union. Radical Reconstruction was motivated not only by revenge against »rebels« – though that was surely a critical element – but also by a fear that these rebels would resume their allegiance to the Democratic party, which had been, on the whole, sympathetic to slavery and, to a lesser extent, to the right of secession. In sum, the Radicals could legitimately fear that the sweeping constitutional changes they had won by blood might be lost by ballots.

The obvious solution was to create a new electorate in the South, first by enfranchising blacks, next by disenfranchising southern whites, and last by excluding southern states from the national political processes until they had been thoroughly purified. Military orders, statutes, and finally the Fifteenth Amendment carried out the first step. Acting under the Reconstruction Acts, military commanders executed the second by denying ballots to whites whom they thought had fought for, served in public office under, or supported the Confederacy.[49] The military also barred such people from serving in the conventions that redrafted state constitutions. Moreover, § 3 of the Fourteenth Amendment excluded from state or federal office any former public official, again state or federal, who had »engaged in insurrection or rebellion against [the United States], or given aid or comfort to the enemies thereof.« Some of the »reconstructed« state constitutions in the Old Confederacy had similar provisions. Had these terms been meticulously carried out, a full generation of southern Democratic leaders would have been kept out of public office.[50] The last step was to deny southern states representation in Congress or even full control over their local governments until they had been politically cleansed by years of military rule and had »freely« accepted the Fourteenth Amendment.

During the First World War, the Sedition and Espionage Acts of 1917 went far beyond punishing efforts to overthrow the government by force, to obtain information by spying, or to commit sabotage. Their principal targets were critics of the war – Socialists like Eugene Debs[51] and Victor Berger,[52] trivial pamphleteers,[53] petty printers,[54] or Russian emigrés who opposed American intervention in the civil war raging in their homeland.[55]

Later the Great Red Scare and the Palmer Raids, which arrested thousands and deported about 500 aliens, were aimed at the Left in general, not only anarchists and communists but also socialists, radical labor groups like the Industrial Workers of the World, and Left-liberal intellectuals, who seemed to conservative Americans to be all of the same evil ilk.[56] Indeed, in 1920, the New York state legislature refused to seat duly elected socialists.[57] By putting some leftists in jail, deporting others for their political ideas, and depriving socialists of elective office, the government – Democratic and Republican, state and federal – effectively restricted the sorts of organizations that could operate in the political arena and thus narrowed the electorate's choices.

During the 1920s the Supreme Court sustained a further restriction on political choice by upholding legal attacks on the Ku Klux Klan, the American group closest, at that time, to the Nazis. New York state required that all incorporated and unincorporated societies of more than 20 members which imposed an oath as a condition of membership file with the secretary of state a copy of its constitution, by-laws, and oath along with an annual list of officers and members. It was a crime for anyone to remain a member of such a society that had failed to file the specified documents. Reacting to the remarkable revival the Klan was enjoying, New York began to enforce this statute and convicted George W. Bryant, who had stayed in the KKK after it had failed to register.

On appeal, the U.S. Supreme Court sustained the action by a vote of 8-1.[58] The justices rejected out of hand Bryant's arguments that the statute violated due process: »There can be no doubt that under that [the police] power the state may prescribe and apply to associations having an oath-bound membership any reasonable regulation calculated to confine their purposes and activities within limits which are consistent with the rights of others and the public welfare.«[59] The Court also gave short shrift to Bryant's second argument that by exempting some organizations, such as the Masons and the Knights of Columbus, New York had denied the KKK equal protection. The justices »assumed« that the legislature was familiar with the Klan's long and sordid history of intimidation and violence against blacks, Catholics, Jews, and foreign-born, and so had ample cause to treat the Klan differently from peaceful, fraternal societies.[60]

It was the Left, however, that remained the principal target of governmental action. The centerpiece of federal policy was the Smith Act of 1940. Section 2 (a) made it a crime:

(1) »to knowingly and wilfully advocate, abet, or advise, or teach the duty, necessity, desirability or propriety of overthrowing or destroying any government in the United States by force or violence, or by the assassination of any officer of such government«;

(2) with the intent to carry out any of the ends proscribed in (1) »to print, publish, edit, issue, circulate, sell, distribute, or publicly display any written or printed matter. ...«

(3) »to organize or help organize any society, group, or assembly of persons who teach, advocate, or encourage« ends forbidden by (1) »or to be or become a member of, or affiliate with, any such society, group, or assembly of persons, knowing the purposes thereof.«

Section 3 forbade attempting or conspiring to commit any of the forbidden deeds.

As drawn, this statute was broad enough to include Nazi and neo-Nazi groups; but Nazis were scarce,[61] and its main target became the Communist party. Dennis v. United States (1951)[62] upheld the conviction of 13 of the party's leaders for violating §§ 1 and 2. The six justices[63] in the majority could not agree on opinion, but none found a constitutional flaw in the statute or its application, though two of the six, Felix Frankfurter and Robert H. Jackson, expressed discomfort.

Justice William O. Douglas's dissent pointed out that the evidence against the accused demonstrated nothing more than that they had read and taught Stalin's *Foundations of Leninism,* Marx and Engels's *Communist Manifesto,* Lenin's *State and Revolution,* and the official *History of the Communist Party of the Soviet Union.* The record showed no attempt or even plan to overthrow the government. Thus, Douglas argued, the Smith Act, as applied in this case, did not merely guard against sedition but restricted free expression of ideas:

Full and free discussion has indeed been the first article of our faith. We have founded our political system on it. It has been the safeguard of every religious, political, philosophical, economic, and racial group amongst us. We have ... trusted the common sense of our people to choose the doctrine true to our genius and to reject the rest. ... We have deemed it more costly to liberty to suppress a despised minority than to let them vent their spleen. We have above all else feared the political censor.[64]

Douglas's views never fully won out, but a few years later *Yates v. United States*[65] took a more restrictive interpretation of the statute, construing it to outlaw only »incitement« to action, not advocacy of ideas. *Yates* went on to hold the evidence was insufficient to support a conviction[66] and, as one critic said, »gutted« the act.[67] Not since 1957 has the Department of Justice prosecuted anyone for advocacy or even incitement under this law, but *Yates* largely rested on statutory, not constitutional, interpretation. Thus, the Smith Act remains available as a weapon against dissidents if the moods of the public, prosecutors, and judges change.

The government also moved on several occasions against individual communists for being »members« of a party that advocated violent overthrow of the government.[68] In 1961, the Court sustained one conviction[69] under this clause and reversed another.[70] In affirming the conviction of Junius Irving Scales, who had once been chairman of the party in North and South Carolina,[71] the Court interpreted the statute as reaching »only ›active‹ members having also a guilty knowledge and intent.«

In addressing problems of the First Amendment, the majority opinion, written by John Marshall Harlan, the author of *Yates,* relied less on that reasoning[72] than on the plurality opinion in *Dennis.* Not since 1961, however, has the federal government prosecuted anyone for membership in a political party.

During the heat of the Cold War, Congress passed the Internal Security Act of 1950[73] and the Communist Control Act of 1954.[74] These statutes, *inter alia,*[75], declared the existence of »a world Communist movement« which, »by treachery, deceit, infiltration . . . espionage, sabotage, [and] terrorism,« threatened to install totalitarian dictatorship around the globe and revoked any legal privilege earlier granted to the Communist party or any of its subdivisions. In addition, the new laws:

1) Forbade any person »knowingly to combine, conspire, or agree with any other person to perform an act which would substantially contribute to the establishment within the United States of a totalitarian dictatorship . . . *Provided, however,* That this subsection shall not apply to the proposal of a constitutional amendment.«

2) Made it criminal for any member of a »Communist organization« - defined in detail - to hold, seek, or accept federal elective office without first disclosing such membership.[76]

3) Forbade any member of a communist organization to hold any

186

nonelective federal office or employment, engage in work in a defense industry, or hold office or employment for a labor union.

4) Denied passports to any member of a communist organization.

5) Required every communist organization to file with the Attorney General elaborate reports about the sources and uses of its funds.

6) Created the Subversive Activities Control Board (SACB) with authority to designate organizations as communist, require them to register, divulge their memberships lists,[77] and be entitled only to restricted use of the mails or other means of interstate and foreign commerce.

7) But »[n]either the holding of office nor membership in any Communist organization shall constitute *per se* a violation« of any criminal statute nor shall the fact of registration »be received in evidence against such person in any prosecution« under any criminal statute.

As one can imagine these regulations triggered a great deal of litigation. The Supreme Court invalidated the prohibitions against employment in defense industries[78] and issuance of passports.[79] Enforcement of registration of communist organizations, the heart of the effort to »control« communism, bogged down in litigation for more than a decade. In 1961, the justices ruled, 5-4, that the requirement of registration did not constitute a bill of attainder or violate members' rights under the First Amendment. The majority also held »premature« the claim that registration involved self-incrimination.[80] Four years later, however, the Court addressed the latter issue and said that forbidding registration's use in evidence did not go far enough to preserve the Fifth Amendment's protection against self-incrimination. The government could not introduce registration in evidence at a trial, but it could still use that fact in its own investigations to uncover other evidence it might utilize in criminal proceedings.[81] Invalidation of the requirement of registration left the SACB without any real work to do, but it continued to exist – and its members and staff to draw salaries – until 1973, when it became a victim of budgetary restrictions.[82]

B. *The Practical Effects*

The American mishmash of legislation and judicial rulings by no means forms the equivalent of the Federal Republic's formal ban on the Communist or Socialist Reich Party. In the United States, such outlawry would probably constitute a bill of attainder. Still, one might argue that the American policies were more restrictive than the German because they reached deeper into individual lives than did simply banning political organizations. That argument is valid as far as it goes; but the Germans also moved, in ways similar to the American way, against political dissidents.[83] Section 88a of the AntiConstitutional Advocacy Act reads much like the Smith Act; and § 90a echoes the Sedition Act of 1798 by providing up to three years in prison for anyone who »insults or maliciously maligns the Federal Republic of Germany or one of its Länder, or its constitutional order.« Not unexpectedly, the charge of McCarthyism has been raised in the Federal Republic.[84] Kenneth H. F. Dyson has asked the fundamental question about this program: »[W]hether the purpose . . . is to protect the constitution's free democratic basic order or whether it seeks by restrictive constitutional interpretation to protect a particular economic and social system against criticism and reform?«[85]

The practical results of these policies have been mixed. In the Federal Republic, the rulings of the *Bundesverfassungsgericht* allowed the government to push its loyalty-security programs and, in turn, provoked new litigation.[86] Further, the Minister of the Interior has on several occasions used the Socialist Reich Party Case to move against other neo-Nazi parties and confiscate their property – including a half-track, an anti-aircraft gun, assorted small arms, uniforms, leaflets, and office equipment. Still, such parties remain a part of the political scene in the Federal Republic; and, while they have never gained significant national power, their allies, such as the National Democratic Party or the Republican Party, have sometimes been a force in Länder and local elections.

Despite the Constitutional Court's order against reestablishment of the KPD, that deed was done after a decent interval had elapsed. A dozen or so years later a refurbished and rechristened German Communist Party (DKP) emerged. Although somewhat influenced by the pragmatism of Euro-Communism, its share of the popular vote has remained tiny. It is difficult to know what impact the Constitutional Court's ruling may have had. Alfred Grosser claimed »the ban appeared positively unsporting, and it did the KPD at least as much good as harm. . . .«[87] In the long run, the failures of the East German regime and the testimony of its refugees did far more than the *Bundesverfassungsgericht* to demolish any attractions a communist party might have claimed to offer the Federal Republic.

In the United States, the effect of the most recent anti-communist crusade is easier to gauge. The Supreme Court eventually invalidated some important statutory provisions and administrative regulations, but even had the ramshackle program stayed in effect its curtailment of communism within the United States would have been puny. American mistakes in foreign policy sometimes generated anger at whatever administration controlled the White House; but Stalin's purges in the 1930s, his pact with Hitler, and the capacity of Marxist governments to offer their people only oppression leavened with poverty[88] did far more to discredit communism than all the test oaths, legislative investigations, black listings, and criminal prosecutions. Perhaps even more fundamental, Marxism's avowal of historical determinism and economic collectivism scraped as painfully as sandpaper over sunburn against the pugnacious self-determination of America's individualist culture.

The hard fact is that a communist menace in domestic political processes was largely the figment of Senator Joseph McCarthy's drunken imagination, the overweening ambitions of men like J. Edgar Hoover and Richard M. Nixon, and the nativism of racists like Senator James O. Eastland. Not even among blacks, surely a downtrodden minority, could communists make many converts.[89] They remained, as Justice William O. Douglas said, »miserable merchants of unwanted ideas.«[90] There was more truth than humor in the joke, circulated while *Dennis* was underway, that most of the dues paid to the Communist party came from the FBI, whose undercover agents and informants outnumbered committed members of the party. The American efforts were epitomized by the fact that Junius Irving Scales, the only person to go to jail for »knowing« membership in the Communist party, had rejected that affiliation before his conviction.

Lacking much of a real target, the American program could accomplish little of its purported objective. It did, however, succeed in gaining election, reelection, and national prominence for its more vocal prophets like McCarthy and Nixon; and it did limit what was open to political debate about domestic and foreign policy. Thus, to some extent, it advanced the goals of some of its sponsors – people who, in their own way, were also opponents of constitutional democracy.

More generally, Article 21 of the Basic Law served as the model for Article 8 of Pinochet's constitutional document, which, though ostensibly aimed at communists, also provided a weapon against all those who tried to organize peacefully against his military rule.[91] Still, even that clause did not succeed in stifling effective political opposition, as the General's humiliation at the polls in 1988 demonstrated. The repeal of Article 8, wrested from the Junta less than a year after the election, was high on the opposition's agenda.

Italy has had a similar experience with the Extreme Right. Despite the Italian constitutional text's forbidding the reconstitution of the Fascist party,[92] the *Movimento Sociale Italiano,* a blatantly neo-Fascist party, continues to exist, garners about five per cent of the popular vote, and has deputies in Parliament. Indeed, on occasion, the Christian Democrats have utilized the MSI's support to keep its coalition in office. In return for that service and for the MSI's toning down its rhetoric, the government has never enforced the »Scelba Law,« which buttresses the Constitution's ban with criminal sanctions.[93]

As Justice Jackson noted in his concurrence in *Dennis:* »This prosecution is the latest of never-ending, because never successful, quests for some legal formula that will secure an existing order against revolutionary radicalism.«[94] Banning ideas is not likely to be effective unless one is both ruthless enough and skillful enough to kill all those who entertain the forbidden thoughts – or fortunate enough, as the United States was, to confront an intellectually bankrupt opposition.

III.   *The Theoretical Implications*

A.   *The Party State*

Despite American refusals to recognize the fact, some form of party state is inevitable in modern industrialized nations that wish to make democratic theory work. If parties did not exist, we would have to invent them – or institutions quite like them – to inform and organize opinion, aggregate interests, simplify and communicate possible choices, and present candidates for elections.[95] The alternatives would be various forms of anarchy or dictatorial rule. Even the American voters, who in recent years have displayed such lean loyalty to any particular party, continue to choose their national representatives from the two traditional organizations.

Some version of the party state is almost as necessary to transform constitutionalism into political reality. Both anarchy and dictatorship inevitably violate constitutionalist values.

B.   *Democratic Legitimacy, Constitutional Validity, and Political Prudence*

As an abstract proposition, outlawing espionage, sabotage, or efforts to overthrow the government by violence poses no problems for either democratic or constitutionalist theory. But when outlawry moves from deeds to

190

doctrines, as it almost invariably does when the government moves against sedition or tries to exclude certain kinds of parties, difficulties multiply, even more for democratic than for constitutionalist theory. For proscribing a political doctrine, excluding a party, or punishing membership in a party – again absent violence or other transgressions of »normal« criminal law – narrows both the information the electorate can obtain and the options citizens can exercise.

There is, of course, no single democratic[96] or constitutionalist theory, but the essence of democracy is that the people rule either directly or through their freely chosen representatives. What makes a policy valid is not its conformity to ostensibly objective standards of morality and justice – about those things, democratic theorists generally say, reasonable people can and do reasonably differ. What does make a policy valid is that the people had a fair opportunity to discover the alternatives, could express their choices in free elections, could even run for office themselves if they wished, and chose the officials who made the policy.[97] The people are thus both the subjects and the authors of the law. They are sovereign; and, if they are sovereign, they may, consistenty with the basic tenets of democratic theory, enact whatever substantive policies they wish,[98] *as long as* these policies do not curtail the democratic processes themselves – for example, restrict freedom of speech, press, association, assembly, limit the right to vote, or weigh some votes more heavily than others.[99] In this sense a democracy opens up to public choice all important issues.

The American Internal Security Act of 1950 clumsily fumbled with this issue by exempting »the proposal of a constitutional amendment« from its prohibitions against furthering »totalitarian dictatorship.«[100]

But a theory of »militant democracy« allows government to exclude certain kinds of peaceful efforts to change the system. In effect, it authorizes government to substitute its judgment for whatever preference the supposedly sovereign people might express if they had a free choice – not, on its face, a »democratic« decision. And, not insignificantly, such a governmental decision increases the job security of incumbent public officials.

Nevertheless, one can make a strong argument that »militant democracy's« exclusionary policy is compatible with the basic tenets of democratic theory. Although the people's decision to move to a totalitarian system might be the result of free choice resulting from open political processes, that decision will inevitably deny most citizens in the polity the right to further meaningful participation in self-government. Thus, a democratic government may validly protect its people's basic right to self-rule.

191

This sort of argument requires a more sophisticated understanding of democratic theory than that which Oliver Wendell Holmes expressed in *Gitlow*.[101] There, like some other proponents of democracy, the Justice saw government's objective as merely *aggregating* the people's current preferences. A democratic theory that postulated such an objective could not, at least with any logical coherence, sanction government's preventing a group from peacefully offering the supposedly sovereign people any options whatsoever for peaceful change of the system.

If, however, democracy has temporal as well as spatial and substantive dimensions,[102] the issue of restraining peaceful political expression becomes more complex. A temporal dimension extends democracy's objective to the more difficult one of *integrating* current preferences with those, and perhaps changed, preferences the people would, in the future, have a right to make. At minimum, a democracy would be obliged to leave open to the people at a later time a similar right to self-government.[103] Thus, insofar as democratic theory conceives of its political system as stretching across time, it could not validate the current generation's depriving future generations of the right to express their own preferences; that is, such a theory would not allow the destruction of democracy even by »democratic« means.[104]

This sort of argument from democratic theory is not only complex, it also requires self-policing both to invoke militancy when democracy is truly threatened and not to invoke militancy as an excuse to stifle legitimate opposition, as the Federalists did in the closing years of the eighteenth century, Richard Nixon's cronies did in the early 1970s, and Mrs. Gandhi did in India during her first regime (1971-77). For this reason, some commentators have argued,[105] democracy needs more clearcut, institutionally imbedded restrictions, such as those offered by constitutionalism, lest it self-destruct.

In contrast to the competing responses of various versions of democratic theory, the logic of constitutionalism takes a firm position on the legitimate scope of political change. For constitutionalism, democracy's procedural criteria are, at most, only necessary not sufficient conditions for a policy's validity. Constitutionalist legitimacy has an additional criterion: A policy must also accord with certain substantive values, not merely those listed in a constitutional text but also with principles relating to the dignity and autonomy of the individual which undergird that text. For, as the *Bundesverfassungsgericht* pointed out in its very first decision, not only might an amendment to the constitutional text be unconstitutional, but a provision of that text itself could also be invalid because it conflicts with more fundamental principles within or underlying the document.[106] And, establishment of a totalitarian dictatorship is squarely at odds with constitutionalism's principles. Thus, it would brand as illegitimate all efforts, peaceful as well as violent, to replace a constitutionalist polity with a totalitarian state.

Armed more with intuition than articulated understanding, American justices have groped with these problems of competing theoretical claims. The Constitutional Court of the Federal Republic has not displayed theoretical brilliance either; but at least the German Judges, instructed by democracy's self-destruction in Weimar, have been conscious of the basic problem and tried to confront it. In the Communist Party Case, the *Bundesverfassungsgericht* addressed the central issue of the validity of Article 21 (2) itself:

> The Basic Law represents a conscious effort to achieve a synthesis between the principle of tolerance with respect to all political ideas and certain inalienable values of the political system. Article 21 (2) does not contradict any basic principle of the Constitution; it expresses the conviction of the [framers], based on their concrete historical experience, that the state could no longer afford to maintain an attitude of neutrality toward political parties. [The Basic Law] has in this sense created a »militant democracy«, a constitutional decision that is binding on the Federal Constitutional Court.[107]

It would have been conceptually more neat had the Court said »constitutional democracy« rather than »militant democracy,« or explained its understanding and use of the temporal dimension of democratic theory. Either usage would have permitted the Judges to offer a more persuasive demonstration that Article 21 (2) does not conflict with the principle which Article 20 declares »basic«: »The Federal Republic of Germany is a democratic . . . state.«

The practical compromises the Federal Republic and the United States have struck are uneasy and the theoretical problems they have created are enormous. It may well be true both that democratic theory makes more complex demands than those envisioned by Holmes's majoritarianism of the moment and that constitutionalism and democracy need each other to flourish, perhaps even to survive with any integrity. Still, to be viable, a complex democratic theory needs public officials to be clear about its terms and how they are applying those terms. Moreover, the tensions between democratic and constitutionalist theories are always present; and sometimes those tensions can produce sharp conflict. The severity of the conflict is likely to be directly proportional to the failure of officials, legislative and executive as well as judicial, to recognize how deeply that conflict goes into the underpinnings of the political system. In these senses, German and American judges as well as legislators and executives failed their people, the American officials even more than their cousins.

There is yet another danger, one that Justice Felix Frankfurter spoke of in his concurring opinion in *Dennis:* The temptation to equate constitutionality with wisdom.[108] Many policies that are unwise, even foolish, can pass muster under the terms of a constitutional text – and even be congruent with democratic and/or constitutionalist principles.

These two theories impart a great deal of prudence by charting all sorts of hidden reefs, but neither alone nor in combination can they force public officials to make wise choices within the channels of the law or compel voters to choose representatives who can discern wise from foolish courses. Constitutionalism as well as a more sophisticated theory of democracy may permit the polity to exclude parties that are trying to establish a totalitarian state, but utilizing that authority, as the United States has, may be utterly inane and destructive of basic values. So, too, simpler forms of democratic theory may demand freedom for totalitarian movements; and that demand may be tantamount not merely to national suicide but to collective slavery, as the sometime citizens of Weimar learned.

Notes:

*   I am indebted to Rosemary Allen Little of the Firestone Library of Princeton for help above and beyond the call of duty and to Peter Jerdee of the Princeton Class of 1989 for research assistance. Prof. Mark E. Brandon of the University of Oklahoma read the manuscript with care as did Professors Stanley Kelley, Jr., of Princeton and Donald P. Kommers of the University of Notre Dame. This paper is part of a larger project on constitutionalism conducted by the American Council of Learned Societies under a grant from the Ford Foundation. The William Nelson Cromwell Fund of Princeton University and the Boesky Family Fund of the Center of International Studies, Princeton University, also supported this study.

1   Robert R. Palmer claims that the idea of the people as exercising the constituent power »was a distinctively American one. European thinkers, in all their discussion of a political or social contract, of government by consent and of sovereignty of the people, had not clearly imagined the people as actually contriving a constitution and creating the organs of government. They lacked the idea of the people as a constituent power. Even in the French Revolution the idea developed slowly. . . .« *The Age of Democratic Revolution* (New York: Putnam's, 1959), I, ch. 8. The quotation is from p. 215.

194

2   For example: »We, the people of Eire,« the Irish constitutional text reads, ». . . do hereby adopt, enact, and give to ourselves this Constitution.« The Indian document begins: »WE, THE PEOPLE OF INDIA, having solemnly resolved to constitute India into a SOVEREIGN DEMOCRATIC REPUBLIC . . . do HEREBY ADOPT, ENACT AND GIVE TO OURSELVES THIS CONSTI-TUTION.« The Japanese preamble opens: »We the Japanese people . . . do proclaim that sovereign power resides with the people and do firmly establish this Constitution.« The Spanish preamble is less populist, opening with the words »The Spanish Nation,« but the second section of the first article says: »National sovereignty resides in the Spanish people from whom emanate the powers of the state.« The Australian and Canadian texts are among the more notable exceptions to this populist model. True to the euphemisms of the British Commonwealth, they label themselves as gifts from »the Queen's Most Excellent Majesty.«

3   Document I that emerged from the Tripartite Conference at London in the spring of 1948 authorized governments of the West German Länder to convoke an assembly to »draft a democratic constitution which will establish for the partici-pating states a governmental structure of federal type . . . and contain guarantees of individual rights and freedoms.« Given recent German history, there could have been no doubt that the delegates would have opted for a constitutional democracy without the Allies' directive. It is far less certain, however, whether that government would have been federal or as federal as the Basic Law stip-ulates. See John Ford Golay, *The Founding of the Federal Republic of Germany* (Chicago: University of Chicago Press, 1958), chs. 1-2.

4   *Ibid.,* espec. pp. 92-108. See also Lucius D. Clay, *Decision in Germany* (New York: Doubleday, 1950); and Jean Edward Smith, ed., *The Papers of General Lucius D. Clay: Germany 1945-1949* (Bloomington: Indiana University Press, 1974), 2 vols.

5   Even Pinochet, when he decided in 1980 to cloak himself in a mantle of respectability, submitted his constitution to a plebiscite – of sorts.

6   Resolution of February 21, 1787, reprinted in Max Farrand, ed., *The Records of the Federal Convention of 1787* (New Haven, Conn.: Yale University Press, 1966 – originally published, 1911), III, 13-14. (Farrand's title is misleading; the Convention kept no official »records,« other than a journal, which turned out to be jumbled and inaccurate.)

7   Herbert J. Storing, ed., *The Complete Anti-Federalist* (Chicago: University of Chicago Press, 1981), V, 211. The Basic Law contains language that, under other circumstances, might have led to a claim that the new polity was a »confederation« rather than a true federation. The Preamble begins: »The German people in the Länder of . . .« not simply »The German people.«

8   The article read in part: »And the Articles of Confederation shall be inviolably observed by every state, and the union shall be perpetual; nor shall any alteration at any time hereafter be made in any of them; unless such alteration be agreed to in a congress of the united states, and be afterwards confirmed by the legislatures of every state.«

9   For Beard's argument, see his *An Economic Interpretation of the Constitution* (New York: Macmillan, 1913); for one of many responses, see Robert E. Brown, *Charles Beard and the Constitution* (Princeton: Princeton University Press, 1956).

10 Art. 20 (1) and (2).
11 It is interesting that Judge Robert H. Bork, who is convinced that the United States is a representative democracy and professes to ground his interpretation of the Constitution on »original intent« or »original understanding,« ignores the facts that neither the text nor what we can glean from incomplete materials about »intent« and »understanding« do much to advance his cause. See his *The Tempting of America: The Political Seduction of the Law* (New York: The Free Press, 1990).
12 October 17, 1788. A convenient source is Marvin Meyers, ed., *The Mind of the Framer* (Indianapolis, Ind.: Bobbs-Merrill, 1973), p. 206. (Italics in original.)
13 Farrand, *op. cit., supra* note 6, II, 209-210. The quoted passage is actually a summary of Morris's remarks jotted down by another delegate, James B. McHenry, who added that »Mr. Maddison [sic] supported similar sentiments.« McHenry's complete notes are reprinted in Charles B. Tansill, ed., *Documents Illustrative of the Formation of the Union of the United States* (Washington: Government Printing Office, 1927), pp. 923-952. (Italics in original.)
14 The Fifteenth, Nineteenth, Twenty-fourth, and Twenty-sixth amendments. The Twenty-third Amendment allocates the District of Columbia three votes in the Electoral College, but does not state who has a right to participate in choosing the three electors. Even § 2 of the Fourteenth only lowers a state's representation in Congress if it denies the franchise »to any of the [state's] male inhabitants« unless as a punishment for a crime. Section 1 of the Fourteenth Amendment, which has become the judiciary's most potent weapon for democratization, forbids states to deny »the equal protection of the laws,« hardly a ringing affirmation of the sacredness of the right to vote. And, historically, it is very uncertain that the Congress that proposed the amendment thought it applied to voting at all – hence adoption of the Fifteenth Amendment to forbid racial discrimination at the ballot box.
15 *Reynolds v. Sims,* 377 U.S. 533 (1964), offers the clearest statement of the Court's endorsement of democratic theory.
16 Representative democracy must, of course, protect more than the right to vote, and the German and American texts, practices, and interpretations have so recognized.
17 »We, the People of the United States, in Order to form a more perfect Union, establish Justice, insure domestic Tranquility, provide for the common defense, promote the general Welfare, and secure the Blessings of Liberty to ourselves and our Posterity, do ordain and establish this Constitution for the United States of America.«
18 Debate on the Judiciary Act of 1802, *Annals of Congress,* 7th Cong., 1st Sess.; parts of the debate are reprinted in Walter F. Murphy, James E. Fleming, and William F. Harris, II, *American Constitutional Interpretation* (Mineola, N.Y.: Foundation Press, 1986), pp. 203-211; the quotation is from p. 209.
19 See espec. 42 *U.S. Code* §§ 1981-1986.
20 In the United States, for example, long before the School Segregation Cases, 347 U.S. 483 (1954), President Harry S Truman had urged Congress to pass legislation protecting equal rights and, as commander-in-chief, had ordered the armed forces to desegregate. These actions, along with the Civil Rights Acts of 1964 and 1968, Voting Rights Act of 1965, and the Bill of Rights for the Handicapped (1973) – see John E. Finn, »Implied Rights of Action Under the Rehabi-

196

litation Act of 1973,« 68 *Geo. L. J.* all tolics 1229 (1980) – echo Justice Oliver Wendell Holmes's assertion: »legislatures are ultimate guardians of the liberties and welfare of the people in quite as great a degree as the courts.« *Missouri, Kansas, & Texas R'way v. May,* 194 U.S. 267, 270 (1904).

21 As Madison said in introducing the Bill of Rights in the First Congress:
It may be thought that all paper barriers against the power of the community are too weak to be worthy of attention. I am sensible they are not so strong as to satisfy gentlemen of every description who have seen and examined thoroughly the texture of such a defence; yet, as they have a tendency to impress some degree of respect for them, to establish the public opinion in their favor, and rouse the attention of the whole community, it must be one means to control the majority from those acts to which they might otherwise be inclined. [*Annals of Congress,* June 8, 1791, p. 455.]

22 See, for instance, Robert Michels: »Who says organization says oligarchy.« *Political Parties: A Sociological Study of the Oligarchical Tendencies of Modern Parties,* trans. E & C. Paul (New York: Collier, 1962), p. 365. There is a long standing debate on whether the »iron law of oligarchy« is a law in the sense of the natural sciences, a general tendency, or merely a pathological condition. Scholars as eminent as Vilfredro Pareto and Gaetano Mosca have argued for the existence of a law (for an excellent analysis see James H. Meisel, *The Myth of the Ruling Class* [Ann Arbor: University of Michigan Press, 1958], while some more empirically oriented theorists, such as Robert A. Dahl, take a less rigid view. See Dahl, *Who Governs?* (New Haven, Conn.: Yale University Press, 1961).

23 See, for example, his *Politics and Law* (Leyden: Sythoff, 1956). Donald P. Kommers notes that the First Party Finance Case, 20 BVerfGE 56 (1967), rejected some aspects of Liebholz's theory and treated parties as fundamentally »voluntary associations« serving as »constitutional institutions« only in their electoral role and not when functioning more generally to form public opinion. »Politics and Jurisprudence in West Germany: State Financing of Political Parties,« 16 *Am. J. of Jurisp.* 215, 235 (1971). The Court has also recognized that Art. 20 of the Basic Law does not give parties monopolies even in the electoral process: The Daniels Case, 41 BVerfGE 399 (1976); discussed in Kommers, *Constitutional Jurisprudence of the Federal Republic of Germany* (Durham, N.C.: Duke University Press, 1989), pp. 213ff.

24 *Judicial Politics in West Germany* (Beverly Hills, Cal.: Sage, 1976), p. 240.

25 The Socialist Reich Party Case, 2 BVerfGE 1 (1952); translated and edited in Walter F. Murphy and Joseph Tanenhaus, *Comparative Constitutional Law* (New York: St. Martin's, 1977), pp. 602-607. The quoted passage is at p. 603.

26 The Communist Party Case, 5 BVerfGE 85 (1956); trans. in Murphy and Tanenhaus, *op. cit., supra* note 25, pp. 621ff; the quoted passage is at p. 626.

27 Which he defined as »a number of citizens, whether amounting to a majority or minority of the whole, who are united and actuated by some common impulse of passion, or of interest, adverse to the rights of other citizens, or to the permanent and aggregate interests of the community.« *Federalist,* No. 10.

28 *Ibid.*

29 This party was the forerunner of the modern Democratic party. On the early history of American parties, see espec. Noble E. Cunningham, *The Jeffersonian Republicans: The Formation of Party Organization* (Chapel Hill: University of

North Carolina Press, 1957); and Roy F. Nichols, *The Invention of the American Political Parties* (New York: The Free Press, 1967).

30 The first ratified not the first proposed. The relevant part reads: »Congress shall make no law . . . abridging the freedom of speech, or of the press, or the right of the people peaceably to assemble, and to petition the Government for a redress of grievances.« Judicial interpretation of the Fourteenth Amendment has made the First – and most other portions of the Bill of Rights – binding on state governments as well.

31 1 Stat. 596 (1798). Sec 2. made it a crime for any person to »write, print, utter, or publish, or [] cause or procure to be written, published, uttered or published . . . any false, scandalous and malicious writing or writings against the government of the United States, or either house of the Congress of the United States, or the President of the United States, with intent to defame the said government, or either house of the said Congress, or the said President, or to bring them, or either of them, into contempt or disrepute; or to excite against them, or either or any of them, the hatred of the good people of the United States. . . .«

32 See, generally, the work of Leonard W. Levy: *Legacy of Suppression: Freedom of Speech and Press in Early American History* (Cambridge, Mass.: The Belknap Press of Harvard University Press, 1960); »The *Legacy* Reexamined,« 37 *Stan. L. Rev.* 767 (1985); and *The Emergence of a Free Press* (New York: Oxford University Press, 1985). As late as 1874, the U.S. Supreme Court unanimously held unenforceable a contract between a lobbyist and his principal on grounds that such activity was »pernicious.« *Trist v. Child,* 21 Wall. 441.

33 *Tashjian v. Republican Party,* 479 U.S. 208, 214 (1986); the internal quotation is from *Kusper v. Pontikes,* 414 U.S. 51, 57 (1973).

34 *Democratic Party v. Wisconsin,* 450 U.S. 107, 122 (1981).

35 See, for example: James McGregor Burns, *The Deadlock of Democracy,* rev. ed. (Englewood Cliffs, N.J.: Prentice-Hall, 1963); Austin Ranney *et al., The Doctrine of Responsible Party Government* (Urbana: University of Illinois Press, 1954); and Elmer E. Schattschneider, *The Struggle for Party Government* (College Park: University of Maryland Press, 1948).

36 For a different view, see Sandra Kayden and Eddie Mahe, Jr., *The Party Goes On: The Persistence of the Two-Party System in the United States* (New York: Basic Books, 1985).

37 Karl Loewenstein's two-part article, »Militant Democracy and Fundamental Rights,« 31 *Am. Pol. Sci. Rev.* 417 (1937) and 31 *ibid.* 638 (1937), is one of the earliest and most comprehensive analyses in English. See also his two-part article »Legislative Control of Political Extremism in European Democracies,« 38 *Colum. L. Rev.* 591 and 38 *ibid.* 725 (1938). The opinion of the Court in the Socialist Reich Party Case (1952), *supra* note 25, offers a more recent exposition but from *within* the framework of »fighting democracy« itself.

38 One of the charges against the Weimar Republic was that it took a politically neutral stance toward parties, including extremist groups. In fact, Weimar had ample legislation to cope with Nazism, including sedition laws, a ban against paramilitary organizations, and special statutes allowing the government to implement its authority under Article 48 – which allowed the President to declare a state of emergency. The Republic also kept intact § 128 of the *Criminal Code* of 1871, which forbade secret political societies. The government did react

swiftly and harshly against Communists; but, for a variety of reasons, enforcement against all groups from the Right was typically feeble. See: Office of the U.S. Chief of Counsel for the Prosecution of Axis Criminality, *Nazi Conspiracy and Aggression* (Washington, D.C.: Government Printing Office, 1946), II, 10ff; and John E Finn, *Constitutions in Crisis: Political Violence and the Rule of Law* (New York: Oxford University Press, 1990), ch. 4.

39 More generally, Art. 5 of the Fifth Republic's constitutional text reads: Political parties »are obliged to respect the principles of national sovereignty and democracy.« The document, however, does not command parties to adhere to democratic principles in their internal organization and makes no provision for declaring a party »unconstitutional.«

40 See, however, the National Democratic Party Case, 40 BVerfGE 287 (1975), discussed in Kommers, *Constitutional Jurisprudence,* at p. 231. There the Ministry of Labor had branded the NPD as a »party engaged in anti-constitutional goals and activity« and »a danger to the free democratic basic order.« The party challenged the ministry's statement as a violation of »party privilege,« but the Constitutional Court held that the government had authority, perhaps even a duty, to make public its finding about a party's being opposed to the constitutional order, even if the Court had not declared that party to be illegal under Art. 21 (2). See, more generally, Dan Gordon, »Limits on Extremist Political Parties: A Comparison of Israeli Jurisprudence with that of the United States and the Federal Republic of Germany,« 10 *Hast. Intern'l & Comp. L. Rev.* 347 (1987); and Paul Franz, »Unconstitutional and Outlawed Parties: A German-American Comparison,« 5 *B. C. L. Rev.* 57 (1982).

41 Communist Party Case, 5 BVerfGE 85 (1956), translated and edited in Murphy and Tanenhaus, *op. cit., supra* note 25, pp. 621-627. Wolfgang P. von Schmertzing, *Outlawing the Communist Party: A Case History* (New York: Bookmailer, 1957), has a longer but still incomplete translation.

42 To this extent, *KPD* clarified *SRP,* for the earlier opinion had left open the possibility that deep-seated opposition to the values of the constitutional order was sufficient to justify outlawry under Art. 21 (2), for example: »a party may be eliminated from the political process only if it denies the supreme principles of a free democracy.« Murphy and Tanenhaus, *op. cit., supra* note 25, p. 603.

43 Holmes dissenting in United States v. Schwimmer, 279 U.S. 644, 655 (1929).

44 *Abrams v. United States,* 250 U.S. 616, dis. op., 630 (1919).

45 *Gitlow v. New York,* 268 U.S. 652, dis. op., 673 (1925).

46 For the core of the text of the Sedition Act, see note 31, *supra.*

47 See James Morton *Smith, Freedom's Fetters: The Alien and Sedition Laws and American Civil Liberties* (Ithaca, N.Y.: Cornell University Press, 1956); and Levy's writings, cited *supra* note 32.

48 See *Ex parte Merryman,* 17 Fed. Cases 145 (1861); and *Ex parte Milligan,* 4 Wall. 2 (1866) and M. E. Neely, Jr., *The Fate of Liberty* (New York: Oxford University Press, 1991).

49 President Andrew Johnson, a Democrat, pardoned many ex-Confederates and so restored their civil liberties. He also accepted the opinion of his Attorney General that the taking of an oath denying such aid to the Confederacy qualified a man to vote, whether or not the oath was truthful. Congress, however, overrode this executive action by a specific statutory clause. The Test Oath Cases, *Cummings v. Missouri,* 4 Wall. 277 (1867), and *Ex parte Garland,* 4 Wall. 333

(1867), invalidated the requirement that those in public office or in certain professions, such as law and the ministry, swear they had never aided the rebellion. But those rulings left untouched the barriers against former Confederates. Still, although it is impossible to be absolutely certain, the number of white southerners actually disenfranchised was probably small. See also note 50 infra.

50 The last sentence of § 3 reads: »But Congress may by a vote of two thirds of each House, remove such a disability.« Far from opening a path to grace, this clause admits of an interpretation that it vested the power to absolve exclusively in the Congress and so *prevented* the President from restoring his fellow Democrats' right to hold office by pardoning them.

51 249 U.S. 211 (1919).

52 The Supreme Court eventually reversed Berger's conviction because of prejudicial conduct of the trial judge. Berger v. United States, 255 U.S. 22 (1921).

53 Schenck v. United States, 249 U.S. 47 (1919).

54 Frohwerk v. United States, 249 U.S. 204 (1919).

55 Abrams v. United States, supra note 44.

56 See generally: Paul L. Murphy, *World War I and the Origin of Civil Liberties in the United States* (New York: Norton, 1979); and Zechariah Chafee, Jr., *Free Speech in the United States* (Cambridge, Mass.: Harvard University Press, 1954), chs. 1-12. Frederick Lewis Allen's *Only Yesterday: An Informal History of the Nineteen-Twenties* (New York: Harper, 1931), espec. ch. 3, still provides the most graphic account of the »Great Red Scare.«

57 Congress also refused to seat Victor Berger, who had been elected to the House from Wisconsin, but the official reason was not his being a socialist but his speeches against the war. Berger was reelected and again the House refused to seat him. Only after the Department of Justice dropped all criminal charges against him, did the House allow him to take his place.

58 James C. McReynolds, himself a notorious anti-Semite who refused to speak to the two Jewish justices, Louis D. Brandeis and Benjamin N. Cardozo, with whom he served, dissented on grounds that the Court lacked jurisdiction to review the conviction. Thus, he, too, would have let the conviction stand.

59 New York ex rel. Bryant v. Zimmerman, 278 U.S. 63, 72 (1928).

60 One can see obvious opportunities here for government to obtain information about associations of political dissidents. Indeed, after the School Segregation Cases, 347 U.S. 483 (1954), almost every southern state tried to obtain the NAACP's membership lists. See Walter F. Murphy, »The South Counterattacks,« 12 *West. Pol. Q.* 371 (1959), and Robert H. Birkby and Murphy, »Interest Group Conflict in the Judicial Arena,« 42 *Tex. L. Rev.* 1018 (1964). Eventually the Supreme Court struck down these efforts, recognizing constitutional rights both to »political privacy,« NAACP v. Alabama, 357 U.S. 349 (1958), and to utilize the judicial process to achieve individual or organization aims, NAACP v. Button, 371 U.S. 415 (1963). In sustaining federal legislation subsidizing presidential campaigns and requiring parties to report the names of contributors, the Court recognized that, under some circumstances, publicizing donors' names might inhibit legitimate political activity and promised to examine carefully any such claims. Buckley v. Valeo, 424 U.S. 1, 64ff (1976). In Brown v. Socialist Workers Party, 459 U.S. 87 (1982), the justices made good on their pledge and invalidated a state requirement that parties reveal donors'

200

names where the party was an unpopular, left-wing group whose members had in the past been harassed.

61 During World War II, the federal government prosecuted Elmer Hartzel for writing articles that allegedly attempted to cause disloyalty, insubordination, and mutiny within the armed forces. Hartzel, however, was tried and convicted under the Espionage Act of 1917, not the Smith Act. The Supreme Court reversed his conviction because of lack of evidence. Hartzel v. United States, 322 U.S. 680 (1944).

62 341 U.S. 494.

63 Justice Tom Clark, who had been Attorney General while the prosecutions were in progress, recused himself, and Hugo L. Black and William O. Douglas dissented.

64 341 U.S. at 584-585.

65 354 U.S. 298 (1957).

66 A majority of the Court also construed the term »organize« as the original act of organizing, not the day-to-day operations necessary to keep an association functioning. Congress, however, amended the statute to include the broader definition.

67 For reactions to Yates and a bevy of other decisions defending civil liberties by the press, interest groups, executive officials, and legislators, see Walter F. Murphy, Congress and the Court (Chicago: University of Chicago Press, 1962).

68 For a discussion of some of the earlier cases, see the annotations: »Supreme Court Decisions Involving Membership in Communist Party,« 95 L. Ed. 875 (1951); 96 L. Ed. 605 (1952); 100 L. Ed 661 (1956).

69 Scales v. United States, 367 U.S. 203 (1961).

70 Noto v. United States, 367 U.S. 290 (1961). The Court held that the prosecution had produced insufficient evidence to show that the Communist party had advocated direct action to overthrow the government.

71 For an intriguing study of the Communist party – and of Scales himself – see Junius Irving Scales and Richard Nickson, Cause at Heart: A Former Communist Remembers (Athens: University of Georgia Press, 1987).

72 I think the explanation lies in the justices' timidity in the face of the fierce counterattack that southern Democrats and conservative Republicans launched against the Court from 1957 to 59. See also the Court's retreat in Barenblatt v. United States, 360 U.S. 109 (1960), from Watkins v. United States, 354 U.S. 178 (1957). See generally my Congress and the Court, supra note 67.

73 Pub. L. 81-831, 64 Stat. 987. This and other statutes, administrative regulations, congressional hearings, and judicial opinions are conveniently collected in U. S. Senate, Internal Security Manual, 2 vols. (Revised), Document No. 126; 86th Cong., 2d Sess. (1973).

74 Pub. L. 83-637, 68 Stat. 775.

75 Because of paucity of space and plenitude of mercy for the reader, I pass over the various state and federal efforts to make public servants, including school teachers, and members of learned professions such as plumbers, swear they were not and never had been members of the Communist party and, sometimes, any Fascist party. For West German efforts to cleanse its civil service of »subversives,« see Kommers, Constitutional Jurisprudence, pp. 229ff. I also do not discuss the various efforts by congressional committees to punish former communists by public exposure as well as the efforts of private organizations to »blacklist« former communists.

76 Some election boards and courts interpreted this and similar clauses as together banning Communist-party candidates from the ballot. But, despite the fact that such a course was several times proposed in Congress, the laws as passed contained no such express language, and the party has continued to run presidential candidates. Moreover, as the Court pointed out in Communist Party v. SACB (1961), cited *infra,* note 80, such a bar would probably constitute a bill of attainder, forbidden by Article I, § 9.

77 Cf. Brown v. SWP, *supra* note 60, but that decision came down in 1982, decades after these statutes became law.

78 United States v. Robel, 389 U.S. 258 (1967).

79 Aptheker v. United States, 378 U.S. 500 (1964).

80 Communist Party v. SACB, 367 U.S. 1 (1961).

81 Albertson v. SACB, 382 U.S. 70 (1965).

82 Cf. Samuel Huntington, *Political Order in Changing Societies* (New Haven, Conn.: Yale University Press, 1968), pp. 17-18: »an organization which has many purposes is better able to adjust itself to the loss of any one purpose than an organization which has only one purpose.«

83 See Finn, *op. cit., supra* note 38, ch. 5, and Donald P. Kommers, »The *Spiegel* Affair,« in Theodore L. Becker, ed., *Political Trials* (Indianapolis, Ind.: Bobbs-Merrill, 1971).

84 See Peter Weiss, »Joe McCarthy is Alive and Well and Living in West Germany,« *9 N. Y. U. J. of Intern'l L. & Pols.* 61 (1976).

85 »Anti-Communism in the Federal Republic of Germany: The Case of the ›Berufsverbot,‹« 28 *Parl. Affrs.* 51 (1974).

86 See Kommers, *Constitutional Jurisprudence,* pp. 229ff.

87 *Germany in Our Time: A Political History of the Postwar Years,* Paul Stephenson, trans. (New York: Praeger, 1971), p. 140.

88 For all its failures, many of them murderously brutal, Mao's regime did manage to feed almost all Chinese, no small feat.

89 See Wilson Record, *The Negro and the Communist Party* (Chapel Hill: University of North Carolina Press, 1951). See, more generally: Theodore Draper, *The Roots of American Communism* (New York: Viking, 1957); and Irving Howe and Lewis Coser, *The American Communist Party: A Critical History* (New York: Praeger, 1957).

90 Dissenting in Dennis v. United States, *supra* note 62, at 589.

91 With exquisitely ironic references to violence the Article read in part:
Any action by an individual or group intended to propagate doctrines which are antagonistic to the family, or which advocate violence or a concept of society, the State or the juridical order, of a totalitarian character or based on class warfare, is illegal and contrary to the institutional code of the Republic.
The organizations and political movements or parties which, due to their purposes or the nature of the activities of their members, tend toward such objectives, are unconstitutional.
The Constitutional Tribunal shall have cognizance of violations of the provisions set forth in the preceding paragraphs.

92 Article XII of the section entitled »Transitional and Final Measures« reads: »The reorganization in any form whatever of the now dissolved Fascist party is prohibited.«

93 One might also recall here the fate of the tangled history of Prime Minister Eamon De Valera's campaign against the »blue shirts« or Young Ireland Association, which ended in 1933 in a legal banning of the organization. As is typical of such action, it is unclear how much De Valera was concerned about a civil war (at that time he made no parallel moves against the armed and well organized Irish Republican Army) and how much with curtailing peaceful political opposition. For a brief account of the episode, see Donal O'Sullivan, *The Irish Free State and Its Senate* (London: Faber & Faber, 1940), ch. 19.

94 341 U.S. at 561.

95 For a set of studies on the apparent decline of parties in modern democracies and the rise of organizations that attempt to replace some or all of their functions, see Kay Lawson and Peter H. Merkl, *When Parties Fail: Emerging Alternative Organizations* (Princeton: Princeton University Press, 1988).

96 In recent years, the most elegant and eloquent explanation has been that of Robert A. Dahl: *Democracy and Its Critics* (New Haven, Conn.: Yale University Press, 1989).

97 See Murphy, Fleming, and Harris, *op. cit., supra* note 18, ch. 2.

98 Michael Walzer argues eloquently for the sovereignty of the people and the illegitimacy of external checks, such as judicial review, on the popular will. »Philosophy and Democracy,« 9 *Pol. Th.* 379 (1981). He claims that the popular will, to be valid, must will generally, and not be aimed at specific minorities, because it is the people as a whole who are sovereign. But »the people« are typically divided on public issues of any significance. To survive, then, any polity must have rules for decision making other than unanimity, and any rule that allows a majority (of whatever size) to triumph over a minority and to express the will of the »sovereign people« threatens substantive values and quite possibly substantive rights of the minority. I have developed this point at somewhat greater length in »The Nature of the American Constitution,« The James Lecture (Urbana: Department of Political Science, University of Illinois, 1989), pp. 17-20. For an analysis along the same lines as Walzer but more oriented toward modern American constitutional interpretation, see John Hart Ely, *Democracy & Distrust* (Cambridge, Mass.: Harvard University Press, 1980).

99 Which is not to say these limitations are trivial. Indeed, they include, I have argued, protection of substantive rights, such as privacy, which are necessary to truly free electoral decisions. »The Right to Privacy and Legitimate Constitutional Change«, in Shlomo Slonim, ed., *The Constitutional Bases of Social and Political Change in the United States* (New York: Praeger, 1990).

100 See text ca. notes 73-74, *supra*. A decade earlier, Wendell Wilkie, who had been the Republican candidate for the presidency in 1940, made a more direct argument on this point. The government had tried to revoke the naturalization of William Schneiderman on grounds that he had fraudulently obtained citizenship: Because he had been a member of the Workers [Communist] Party, the government contended, he could not have truthfully sworn that he was »attached to the principles of the Constitution of the United States.« Wilkie, however, claimed before the Supreme Court that the real test of attachment to the Constitution is not the scope of changes an alien wanted to make in the political system but, rather, his or her willingness to pursue change peacefully in accordance with the terms of Article V, which provide for consti-

tutional amendment. And Schneiderman was on record that he thought »the dictatorship of the proletariat« meant no more than that »a majority of the people shall really direct their own destinies and use the instrument of the state for these truly democratic ends.« Demonstrating to an unusual degree their usual prudence, the justices avoided any decision on this very difficult point. Schneiderman v. United States, 320 U.S. 115, 140-142 (1943). Here, as often, I am indebted to Sanford V. Levinson. See his *Constitutional Faith* (Princeton: Princeton University Press, 1989), pp. 135-138.

101 *Supra* note 45.

102 For a discussion of the temporal dimension of democratic theory, see James G. March and Johan P. Olsen, *Rediscovering Institutions: The Organizational Basis of Politics* (New York: The Free Press, 1989), pp. 118, 146-47, and sources cited; and Dahl, *op. cit. supra* note 96, p. 71 and chs. 12-13. As March and Olsen say, pp. 146-47:

Unless a democratic system can solve the problem of representing the future, changing interests of the unborn, it violates a rather fundamental underlying premise of democracy – that those who bear the costs of decision should have their interests adequately reflected in the choice.

If aggregative democracy cannot be extended to the unborn, or to the future (changed) preferences of current citizens, the criterion of political equality is compromised as a foundation of democracy. Aggregative democracy based on subjective political equality among current citizens appears to be only a crude approximation to political equality. It is conceivable that it is the best practical solution to a complicated problem. But the assertion of practicality is a claim that the flaws of such a system as an instrument of the ideals of democracy are less than the flaws of procedures that seek to provide some kind of basis for interpersonal and intertemporal comparisons; and such a claim is not self-evidently justified.

103 This is the sort of problem to which Walzer was apparently alluding in »Philosophy and Democracy,« *loc. cit. supra* note 98, in which he denied that people had a right, even under democratic regime, to opt to surrender democracy. This way of looking at problem also solves the dilemma Walzer, seemingly without awareness, presents: If a polity cannot, even by open democratic processes, reject democracy, then a democratic people might well have to choose extinction by a foreign power over some kind of negotiated settlement that would force the democratic nation to adopt a different kind of regime. For extinction would deprive future generations of a right to choice with a finality that even a radical change of the system would not.

104 There are, of course, further complications. For instance, the refractions caused by every known means of representation make it difficult to be certain about a people's current preferences. How can one then speak of the preferences of the future other than by, as Judge Learned Hand would have put it, »shoveling smoke«? Perhaps the one preference we can say with assurance that rational men and women would prefer is the right to have some significant choices about the kinds of lives they could lead. In the political realm, so a democratic theorist would argue, such a preference would require a form of democratic governance. But that sort of conclusion rests on a typical - and typically unspoken - assumption of modern western societies like those of West Germany and the United States: There will be enough basic necessities

like food available to sustain life so that human beings may make choices. Obviously, this conclusion might not hold in large areas of the world, such as the Horn of Africa. In places like that, preference for survival would probably come first. »Being,« as Franklin Roosevelt remarked, »comes before well being.«

The problem becomes even more complex when one adds dimension of past. One might, as Thomas Jefferson did, simply say that »life belongs in usufruct to the living.« But then one runs afoul of the legitimacy of all sorts of traditional bonds that tie a people together and validate processes of decision making as well as more overtly substantive values.

105 For instance: Stephen Holmes's two papers: »Gag Rules or the Politics of Omission,« and »Precommitment and the Paradox of Democracy,« both in Jon Elster and Rune Slagstad, eds., *Constitutionalism and Democracy: Studies in Rationality and Social Change* (New York: Cambridge University Press, 1988); for a quite different view, see Dahl, *op. cit., supra* note 96.

106 The Southwest Case, 1 BVerfGE 14 (1951), trans. and ed. in Murphy and Tanenhaus, *op. cit., supra* note 25, pp. 208-211. See also the Privacy of Communications Case, 30 BVerfGE 1 (1970), reprinted *ibid.,* pp. 659-666 (Kommers, *Constitutional Jurisprudence,* refers to this ruling as the Klass Case, pp. 230-31). There the Court said:

Constitutional provisions must not be interpreted in isolation, but rather so they are consistent with the Basic Law's fundamental principles and system of values.... [I]t is especially significant that the Constitution ... has decided in favor of a »militant democracy« that does not submit to abuse of basic rights for an attack on the liberal order of the state. Enemies of the Constitution must not be allowed to endanger, impair, or destroy the existence of the state while claiming protection of rights granted [sic] by the Basic Law. [Murphy and Tanenhaus, p. 660.]

107 Quoted in Kommers, *Constitutional Jurisprudence,* p. 228.

108 341 U.S., 553-556.

Donald P. Kommers

Comments on Part 3

These two papers are fascinating accounts of the theory and practice of political representation in Germany and the United States. The two speakers, however, have approached the topic in different although complementary ways. Professor Steinberger's approach is telescopic: His wide angle lens takes in all the articles of the Basic Law that implicate or create structures of political representation. Drawing heavily upon the jurisprudence of the Federal Constitutional Court, he examines each of these articles – they are both numerous and complex – and their relationship to one another. His analysis concludes with an assessment of various popular movements as well as recent constitutional reform proposals designed to modify the prevailing concept or pattern of political representation in Germany. Professor Murphy's approach, by contrast, is microscopic: He focuses on Article 21 of the Basic Law, particularly the clause banning unconstitutional political parties, and then compares the practical effects of this clause – one among several clauses incorporating the idea of a »militant democracy« – with similar practices in the United States. He concludes his study by examining these effects and practices in terms of their compatibility with both democratic and constitutional theory.

Professor Steinberger, by the way, does not consider the topic of militant democracy. Here, I think, the organizers of the conference missed a golden opportunity for an interesting exchange between the two presenters. After all, Steinberger's *Konzeption und Grenzen freiheitlicher Demokratie* (Berlin: Springer Verlag, 1974) is, to my knowledge, one of the most exhaustive studies to date – by a European or by an American – of internal security legislation and political censorship in the United States. This massive 600 page work, published in German, examines American anti-subversion legislation ranging from the Alien and Sedition Acts of 1798 down to the anti-communist legislation and loyalty-security programs of the 1950s, including the *Schenck-Brandenburg* line of constitutional cases. Philosophically and legally, Steinberger takes a more benign view of militant democracy than does Murphy. In any event, the Americans in the audience should know that Steinberger has well-developed views of his own on the subject of Murphy's paper. We just didn't ask him to address the topic. On the other hand, he may have served his American listeners better by focusing on other aspects of political representation in Germany, for his detailed sketch of the German idea of representative democracy gives Americans some cause for reflection about the nature – and future – of their own system.

Professor Murphy's comparative study is helpful in this respect because it highlights the similarities and differences in the constitutional texts and practices of our two countries. In examining these texts and practices, Murphy finds that both countries qualify as serious constitutional democracies notwithstanding their efforts over time to suppress political parties and activities allegedly subversive of the political order. He finds it easier to justify the theory than the practice of militant democracy because of the difficulty in drawing a bright line between legitimate and illegitimate speech on political matters. Murphy's argument – it is both nuanced and complex – suggests that there is no perfect balance between democracy and constitutionalism; indeed, from his point of view they are in perpetual and unavoidable conflict. In the final analysis, however, his paper manifests a strong civil libertarian – or constitutionalist – mistrust of militant democracy.

In any event, the two papers are very different and I'm afraid that if I focus too long on one I'll neglect the other. So what I'd like to do in these remaining moments is to highlight some of the differences in the German and American idea of representation as well as some of the differences in perspective that I find implicit in the two papers. We should of course bear in mind that the two presenters are writing out of their respective traditions of constitutional governance, and that their views on representation are likely to reflect predominant themes in those traditions.

First, the papers manifest different perspectives on constitutionalism itself, although I hasten to add that this difference is one of emphasis. Murphy and Steinberger, if brought into conversation with one another, would agree more than they disagree on the nature of constitutionalism. In my reading of their papers, however, Steinberger sees less conflict between democracy and constitutionalism than does Murphy. This difference between the two perspectives – if indeed my perception is correct – flows from the different aspects of the constitution that they have chosen to stress. Steinberger emphasizes the Basic Law's capacity to serve as a force for political stability. It is seen as a mechanism for structuring political decision-making as well as for tempering the winds of political change. Constitutional governance in this view is essentially preservative; it seeks to make change difficult, not to hasten it. Murphy, on the other hand, sees the constitution as an ordered way of legitimating - and fostering - change, for which reason he would vigorously protect individual and group rights. Still, it would be misleading to suggest that the Basic Law is any less committed to individual rights than the U.S. Constitution. In some senses, as Murphy himself has pointed out - and Steinberger would agree - it is more constitutionalist than the text of the U.S. Constitution.

Second, and relatedly, Steinberger associates constitutionalism much more with institutional structures and relationships than does Murphy. Indeed, the bulk of his paper is devoted to a close analysis of separation of powers and checks and balances as manifested in Germany's system of parliamentary government. German constitutionalism, as a consequence, places a heavy accent on what Steinberger calls »power-sharing.« Germany is a power-sharing democracy in contrast to the predominately rights-oriented democracy of American constitutionalism. In recent years, separation of powers has made something of a comeback in America constitutional law, but as a principle of limited government it has far less bite than its German equivalent. Steinberger's discussion of the delegation doctrine under Article 80 of the Basic Law is one illustration of the vigor with which the Federal Constitutional Court applies the doctrine.

Third, the idea of popular democracy itself has served as a limit on governmental activity, as Steinberger's discussion of the Political Propaganda Case (44 BVerfGE 125 [1977]) suggests. Popular democracy is a highly textured concept having no exact equivalent in American constitutional law. The popular will as expressed by the rule of the majority in state institutions must be oriented to the common good, a jurisprudential approach that prompts the Federal Constitutional Court to examine the activities of government and the legislative process with considerable scrutiny. The strong anti-interest group orientation that informs this jurisprudence is very much at odds with the theory of group conflict that undergirds the American perspective on political representation. The closest the American Supreme Court has come to common good reasoning of this character is the heightened scrutiny it brings to bear on legislative classifications based on sex and race.

In his discussion of popular democracy, Steinberger refers to »the liberty of the community as a whole.« This notion too creates an odd ring in American ears. It can only be explained by the communitarian ethos that informs the German theory of popular democracy. This notion seems to be reflected in German constitutional cases vindicating the parliamentary rights of individual legislators who have either resigned or been expelled from their parties. The Constitutional Court has enforced their right to represent not their parties but their constituents. It is reflected as well in the constitutional right of legislative minorities to institute committees of inquiry empowered to supervise the actions of parliament as a whole, a new and exciting twist on the German understanding of separation of powers. Again, there is no exact American equivalent of this approach to constitutional review.

Finally, as both papers suggest, our two countries represent diverging as well as converging views with respect to the role of political parties. Our highest courts have stood firm in supporting the electoral rights of political parties. In the United States, however, these rights are cast in terms of the *individual's* right to vote or to associate for political purposes. The German cases, by contrast, as Murphy recognizes, tend to emphasize the corporate rights of parties as organizations, stemming in part from their special status under the Basic Law as participants in »forming the political will of the people.« Thus, for electoral purposes, they are part of the state's constitutional structure, yet they are not constitutionally part of the government, a distinction that allows the state to reimburse parties for the essential expenses they incur during an election campaign but forbids the state to finance their general operations.

Americans are likely to be impressed if not perplexed with the ambiguity as well as the strong anti-interest group ethos that pervades Germany's jurisprudence of political representation. Parties are entitled to special protection because they speak for - or are uniquely capable of speaking for - the general interest. Yet, as Steinberger points out, parties do not embrace all of the »people« within the meaning of Article 20. Moreover, the governments the parties elect are responsible to parliament and not to the parties *per se*, and under the terms of Article 38 parliamentary representatives represent »the people as a whole, unbounded by orders and instructions.« Indeed, representatives are »subject only to their conscience.«

These German views of political representation pose a challenge to American Constitutional Theory. It would be interesting to explore, at another time and place, the relevance of these views to the development of American constitutional doctrine.

Part 4:
Basic Rights and Liberties

Kurt Sontheimer

Principles of Human Dignity in the Federal Republic

The first part of the constitution of the Federal Republic of Germany, following the preamble, deals with basic rights. Article 1 of the Basic Law forms the impressive overture to the detailed basic rights set out in the Articles which follow. The language of Article 1 is also striking, combining clarity of content with a degree of solemn rhetoric. It reads as follows:

Art. 1

(I) The dignity of man is inviolable. It is to be respected and safeguarded with the full authority of the State.

(II) The German people therefore declares its belief in the unassailable and inalienable rights of man as the foundation of every human community and of peace and justice in the world.

(III) The basic rights which follow shall be binding on the legislature, the executive authority and the judiciary as directly applicable law.

In the American constitution, the basic rights were added to the original constitution in the form of Amendments. This procedure does not, of course, diminish the constitutional status of the basic rights in American constitutional life. However, in formulating the constitution of the Federal Republic, the Founding Fathers had the opportunity to demonstrate visually their conviction of the primary importance of the basic rights for the social coexistence of people within a state. For this reason they decided – departing from the example of the Weimar imperial constitution, in which the basic rights were found in the second part of the text – to place the basic rights at the head of the text of the constitution. It would hardly be possible to express the commitment of the authors of the Basic Law to the basic rights more clearly and resolutely than has been done in Article 1. The unshakable nature of this commitment was additionally underlined by the provisions of Article 79, according to which Article 1 together with Article 20 forms that central essence of the Basic Law which was declared to be immune from any constitutional amendment. Article 1, then, is the absolute central Article of this constitution. It imposes an obligation on the state and the citizen. In simple terms: the citizen is not there to serve the state, but the state to serve the citizen.

In the order established by the Basic Law, the inalienable and inviolable rights of man are deemed to be the foundation of human society, and of peace and justice in the world. This does not go far enough. The constitution is not content merely to invoke these high principles of western civilization, but also requires, in paragraph 3 of Article 1, that the legislature, the executive and the judiciary be bound to observance of the basic rights as »directly applicable law.« With these words, the authors of the constitution elevated the rights of man, as derived from the principle of human dignity, to be the guiding principle of the authority of the state, whose bounds it may not overstep.

The importance of the value of human dignity in the Basic Law is, therefore, impossible to overestimate. It is the express intention of the authors of the constitution that man stands at the center of the governmental system, and that therefore any action by the public authority must be based on a specific image of man, as expressed in the concept of human dignity.

The reasons for this extreme emphasis on the principle of human dignity and on the rights of man derived therefrom, and their significance for the actions of the state, are generally known. The men and women in the constituent assembly of the Parliamentary Council who formulated and passed the Basic Law desired to inaugurate a completely new beginning after the national disaster of the Third Reich. They were endeavoring to bring into existence a political order which would be a denial of the preceding criminal, totalitarian regime of National Socialism, with its contempt for mankind, an order which would make it possible to bring Germany back among the world's civilized states with respect for human dignity.

There can be no doubting the high ideals of the Founding Fathers in this respect. Their intention, as had constantly been proclaimed in the years following the catastrophe, was to »re-establish the image of mankind« which had been destroyed by the National Socialist dictatorship.

In the commentary on Article 1, for example, given by the former President of the Constitutional Court, Ernst Benda,[1] it is emphasized that despite the elevated language, the article is not a »transfiguration of reality;« rather, the respect for human dignity in the constitutional system of the Federal Republic is the supreme principle of every governmental activity. Although the inalienable rights of man had been adopted from the political tradition of the West, no German constitution had elevated the safeguarding of freedom and human dignity to the status of supreme constitutional principle as emphatically as the Basic Law.

The Basic Law is a 20th-Century constitution. It can only be interpreted appropriately against the background of the historical experience of totalita-

214

rianism. The quintessence of this experience was the state's blatant disregard for the dignity of man, a disregard practiced by the totalitarian system both against its own citizens and against people in other states who came under the domination of barbarism. In the liberal conception of the nineteenth century, there was no state obligation to respect the dignity of man. The foundation of the liberal state was that the freedom and dignity of man could best be ensured by the creation of a society which permitted freedom of action. As the state expanded, however, and increasingly encroached on social development and hence on the sphere of the individual, so the danger grew that human freedom and dignity would be threatened by the state itself, a danger which reached its apogee with totalitarianism. Hence the Basic Law attaches great importance to an obligation on the fort of the state and its institutions to respect human dignity. The state must itself become the guarantor of human dignity. This is the meaning of Article 1.

The »image of man« is a popular German concept, and attempts have been made to define the »image of man under the Basic Law.« The following definition was adopted by the Federal Constitutional Court: »The image of man under the Basic Law is not that of isolated, sovereign individual; rather, the Basic Law resolves the conflict between the individual and the community by relating and binding the citizen to the community but without detracting from his individuality.« In reality this implies a departure from classical individualism, but at the same time rejects any form of collectivism. A state which is required to respect the dignity of man must also be careful to ensure that the needs of the community receive as much consideration as individual freedoms. A conflict inevitably arises, however, between the individual's claims to freedom and the general needs of the community, a conflict that must be balanced in a way that is detrimental to neither. This makes it necessary to reconcile the rule of Article 1 with that of Article 20, which requires the Federal Republic to be a »social state.« This obligation is the modern trend of the Basic Law, which looks beyond classical liberalism. The social state clause imposes an obligation on the State not only to respect the dignity of man and safeguard his individual rights, but also to ensure the creation of the most equitable social conditions possible, in which the individual can develop that dignity and exercise those rights. Article 1, then, must be considered in combination with Article 20. Under modern conditions, this is impossible unless the state intervenes, where appropriate, in the development of society, for it is social conditions that determine the extent to which the individual is truly able to safeguard his own human dignity.

»Over and above the entitlement not to be subjected to arbitrary actions, the citizen increasingly expects the state also to guarantee his material existence. Article 1, paragraph 1, of the Basic Law requires at any event that the individual be allowed those goods which are irrefutably necessary for a dignified existence. In particular, governmental encroachments on private property, for example by way of taxation, must not go so far as to destroy the most modest foundation of existence.«[2]

In the course of the debate on constitutional law, the majority opinion expressed in the Federal Republic today is that the state is under an obligation to guarantee a minimal subsistence to the individual citizen. The state is a social state to the extent that it is required to guarantee this vital security. Therefore, the citizen who, through no fault of his own, finds himself in hardship has a subjective civil right to state assistance. This right has been expressly specified in the Federal Social Security Act.

On this point, the German constitution is substantially at variance with the still prevalent conception of the American constitution. The social state is thus directly charged with safeguarding the foundations of human dignity. Not only is it required to refrain from any interference with human rights, but, in accordance with this conception, it is also under an obligation to assist its citizens to exist according to the principles of human dignity.

The reality of constitutional life

It has been the task of practical politics to translate the lofty principles of Article 1 into the reality of political life. Overall, it may be said that the Federal Republic has become, not only by the rules of its constitution but also in the reality of its constitutional life, a state in which the elementary rights of man are guaranteed, a state which has taken seriously its obligation to create favorable external conditions for its citizens to achieve a life in conformity with human dignity.

Nevertheless, numerous situations have arisen during the growth of the Federal Republic which raised the question of how adequately the Federal Republic has complied with its constitutional obligation to be a libertarian social state which respects the dignity of man. The Constitutional Court has played a critical role in this controversy by handing down specific judgments. Public opinion and legal authorities in general acknowledge the Court to be a reliable »guardian of the constitution« and to take particularly seriously the safeguarding of basic rights against the authority of the state.

Without doubt, it has acquired a substantial authority through its cautious and responsible decisions on constitutional questions. It has consolidated the libertarian constitutional state of the Federal Republic, although its individual judgments also reflect the conflict between libertarian individual interests and community needs, a conflict to which the Court must find an answer in each specific case. These answers have not always been consistent.

Fundamentally, there is an essential state of conflict between freedom and equality. Democracy demands equality desiring free individuals, who produce inequalities as a result of their free activities. It is the state's function, as far as possible, to strike a balance between freedom and equality, a never-ending process in which there are no definitive results. This process is naturally dependent on political and social development and the ideas which shape them. Commitment to the fundamental principles of the constitution, therefore, does not exclude a permanent dispute over the implementation of these fundamental principles in political practice. Constitutional jurisprudence and its interpretation are woven into the intellectual and political process of democratic argument even where they endeavor to judge constitutional life from the standpoint of human dignity.

The Federal Republic was not a fully fledged libertarian constitutional state from the beginning. Initially, it took time to eradicate the traces of National Socialism in legislation. Many members of the judiciary had previously served in the Third Reich. There had been little intensive effort among the ranks of the German judiciary to come to terms with its National Socialist past, and so, during the early days of the Federal Republic, the judiciary tended towards conservatism. In practice, the liberties of citizens who were not in agreement with the new democratic consensus of the Federal Republic, particularly those who professed socialist or communist ideas, were severely restricted. Overall, the protection of minorities was not as strong a feature as it is today. This in particular is an area where the judgments of the Federal Constitutional Court have opened up more possibilities: »It is difficult to overestimate the achievement of the Federal Constitutional Court during the early years of the Federal Republic in clarifying and implementing the basic rights ... The fundamental guarantees were fleshed out; more and more, they also influenced the judgments of the other courts, where the Supreme Courts were established in the early 1950s, and where the pre-democratic traditions were still deeply rooted. The option of the constitutional complaint, in particular, became an effective instrument for safeguarding the basic rights of the individual citizen.«[3]

The terrorism of the 1970s repeatedly brought the constitutional state into situations of crisis, raising the need for more effective means of combating terrorism by amending the laws and hence by restricting individual freedoms for certain groups. This was not always seen in the right perspective. Critics frequently voiced fears that the libertarian constitutional state was being undermined in the Federal Republic. This controversy reached its climax in the dispute over what were called »occupational prohibitions,« in other words, the constitutional loyalty of current and prospective members of the civil service. But it is precisely in such critical situations that the constitutional state must be able to prove itself. The Federal Republic did not always convincingly succeed in meeting such challenges in a constitutionally satisfactory and convincing manner.

In recent years, the tensions between community needs and individual interests have been particularly reflected in the field of environmental protection and privacy of data. Both are relatively modern trends, against which citizens have taken up arms, in some cases on a massive scale, and often without understanding the existing statutory rules. On the one hand there is a call to adapt existing law to these new developments, while on the other hand it is necessary to bring individual liberties and safeguards into alignment with the needs of the general public as represented by the state and its bureaucracy. This is not always easy, and will continue to cause difficulties and problems in the future. There is a certain social tendency to place such a broad and radical construction on the protection of minorities, in relation to environmental questions, that the overriding interests of the community fall by the wayside. However, the state and the legislature cannot overlook the fact that the technological progress of civilization has created new needs for protection which they simply cannot ignore. Similar considerations apply to privacy of data, where the needs of the general public and the justified interests of the individual in protecting his privacy often come into conflict.

In the field of social legislation, too, the conflicts and tensions between the state's willigness and ability to provide benefits under the social state principle and the increased individual need for security are ever present. The Federal Republic is among those western countries which have a particularly highly developed social legislation, and indeed can pride themselves upon it, but in this case the growing interest in social security has resulted in frequently unjustified expectations of services to be provided by the state. The consequence is that the principle of individual responsibility is increasingly thrust aside in favor of overall responsibility by the state for the economic and social conditions of *all* citizens. As a result of this tendency, the German social state is coming closer and closer to its economic limits, which during the past decade have also resulted in a certain adjustment to the collective public services provided by the state.

The predominant mentality of the majority of citizens means that it will not be easy to solve these problems in the future. On the one hand, the need for individual self-realization has been intensified, but often without consideration for the community demands, so that the principle of solidarity – which is also part of the idea of human dignity – suffers and has to be implemented by the state through bureaucratic means. On the other hand, there has been an extraordinary increase in the extent to which the state is expected to help the citizen, and in the security it is required to provide. The willingness to act freely on one's own responsibility, which is part of the formation of the dignity of man, is unilaterally concentrated on purely private needs without consideration for others or for the community as a whole.

This is not a new phenomenon, but it has become even more marked in recent years, not least under the pressure of technological and economic change. The most important thing here will be to find a constructive balance between the right to self-determination and social welfare. My impression is that the United States still has some way to go along the road of developing the modern state into the social state. The Federal Republic, however, must examine the extent to which the development of the social state can be brought into a healthy balance with the necessary responsibility and freedom for the individual.

A chief problem of the future will be determining how far it will be possible to combine the wealth of conceptions and blueprints for living into a constitutional consensus. Today we are having to bring more and more areas within the scope of statutory regulation, because uniform, common moral values are becoming increasingly unimportant and insignificant in society. It is true that a free democratic process includes respecting differences of opinion in the spirit of tolerance and coming to an acceptable result by a regulated procedure; but, that process also sincludes a willingness for frank dialogue – dialogue between state and citizen, dialogue between the constitutional institutions and the political public. It is here, precisely in the Federal Republic, that the danger repeatedly arises that the state will react too harshly and too massively to new challenges, or even provocations to the existing constitutional order. The Federal Republic has existed for 40 years, and in that time we have certainly made substantial progress towards a fully functional and constitutionally acceptable democracy. But, as yet, we are far from perfect.

Notes:

1 E. Benda, W. Maihofer, and H.-J. Vogel (eds.), Handbuch des Verfassungsrechts, Part 1, 1984, pp. 107-8.
2 Benda, *op. cit.*
3 W. Benz (ed.), Geschichte der Bundesrepublik, I and H. Hege, Recht und Justiz, p. 185.

John B. Attanasio

Personal Freedoms and Economic Liberties: American Judicial Policy

Introduction

The American constitutional experience has been characterized both by profound constants and remarkable transformations. One central feature is a government in which power is separated both horizontally among coordinate branches, and vertically between a national government and a number of states.[1] Other fixed aspects include a written constitution construed by the judiciary, and some sphere of private or civil society protected against government interference.[2] Co-existing with these relatively stable elements have been a number of remarkable transformations. For example, we have moved from a position of constitutionalized slavery[3] to constitutionally proscribing that terrible institution.[4] Within our system of federalism and separation of powers, we have witnessed tremendous shifts in the balances of power between the states and the national government,[5] and between coordinate branches of the national government.[6] More importantly, for purposes of this essay, our notions of what counts as an individual right have changed dramatically over the course of American constitutional history.[7]

In loose and somewhat imprecise terms, this shift is often described as moving away from safeguarding property or economic rights, to guaranteeing personal rights. As simplistically articulated, this statement is laden with imprecision and related controversy, but controversy can often prove illuminating. Differentiating between personal and economic rights immediately embroils us in at least two difficulties. First, can we articulate a satisfying difference between them? Second, do adequate reasons exist for affording these purportedly different categories of rights very different levels of constitutional protection?

This essay examines the dramatic shift away from protection of property rights and toward protection of personal rights that occurred during this century. As I will attempt to demonstrate, however, the shifts in the

Supreme Court's position are much more complex than one overarching move.

The paper is divided into three parts. The first part attempts to sketch some analytical markers for distinguishing between personal and property rights. More historical in nature, the second part traces the transformation in protection of personal and property rights. The focus of this section is on the watershed case of *United States v. Carolene Products Co.*,[8] which not only exemplifies the metamorphosis but also explains it. Finally, the third section etches the contours of the Court's strong protection of personal rights and its diminished protection of property rights. In this part, I hope to demonstrate that whatever the explicit protection of property rights, the Court still strongly safeguards property interests through its protection of certain personal rights.

I.   *Personal Versus Property Rights: The Elusive Distinction*

A logical starting point is to grapple with what personal and property rights mean in American constitutional jurisprudence. A coherent comparison should begin by defining these constituent terms with some precision. Most basically, can we articulate satisfying lines of demarcation between personal and property rights? In an oft-quoted statement, Justice Potter Stewart of the United States Supreme Court once said:

> [T]he dichotomy between personal liberties and property rights is a false one. Property does not have rights. People have rights. The right to enjoy property without unlawful deprivation, no less than the right to speak or the right to travel, is in truth a »personal« right, whether the »property« in question be a welfare check, a home, or a savings account. In fact, a fundamental interdependence exists between the personal right to liberty and the personal right in property. Neither could have meaning without the other. That rights in property are basic civil rights has long been recognized. J. Locke, Of Civil Government 82-85 (1924); J. Adams, A Defence of the Constitutions of Government of the United States of America, in F. Coker, Democracy, Liberty, and Property 121-132 (1942); 1 W. Blackstone, Commentaries * 138-140.[9]

This rich quotation has a number of interesting facets. For example, the Court indicates that property rights are important, and indeed its modern jurisprudence clearly evidences the Court's continued attention to property

222

rights. Perhaps most importantly, the Court continues to afford substantial defense against governmental takings of private property through the Fifth Amendment of the Constitution. The »Takings Clause« of the Fifth Amendment requires that government pay »just compensation« as recompense for having appropriated private property.

This continuing importance of certain kinds of property rights engages a second, larger point. Although one may be tempted to distinguish between property and personal rights for purposes of constitutional protection, this distinction is not the correct one. As we shall see in greater detail, the modern Court does protect certain property rights, having departed from the past practice of safeguarding freedom of contract or freedom from economic regulation. During the first third of this century, the Court invoked such broadly conceptualized economic rights to invalidate such regulatory measures as minimum wage[10] and maximum hours laws.[11]

Contrasting these economic regulation cases with takings cases involving government seizure of property readily illustrates that property rights is a variegated concept. Indeed, in a recent article, Professor Edwin Baker breaks property down into six separate functions and argues that the amount of constitutional protection should vary according to the specific function of the property involved.[12] For instance, Professor Baker would extend greater protection to the welfare function of property by affording each individual the resources for »a meaningful daily life« rather than to the allocative function which involves the distribution of societal resources generally.[13] Professor Baker introduces this scheme to dispute Justice Stewart's claim in *Lynch* that property rights are just another kind of personal right.[14] Professor Baker posits his functional differentiation of constitutional protection for property partly as a normative ideal and partly as a description of how the Court already has been treating property rights. Professor Baker's article simply reinforces my second point that property rights are multi-faceted, and that constitutional protection for property rights does and should vary accordingly.

A third difficulty with any distinction between property and personal rights involves the ambiguity infecting the very notion of personal rights. After all, the term does not tell us very much. Considerable legal and philosophical thinking about rights examines the rights of people, or personal rights.[15] At some level, the term personal rights is even more vague than the term property rights; and in a broad sense, Justice Stewart is certainly correct in maintaining that all property rights ultimately attach to persons.[16] To alleviate the ambiguity that afflicts both the terms personal rights and property rights, I propose that we overlook the common or ordinary meaning of these

223

terms. Instead, we should infuse these terms with the meanings ascribed to them by the modern Supreme Court.

In a general sense, then, personal rights receiving strong constitutional protection can be summarized as follows: the largely procedural safeguards protecting the rights of those accused of a crime; the more general procedural guarantees concerning civil lawsuits; the vast array of First Amendment protections comprehended by freedom of expression and religion; the proscriptions in equal protection jurisprudence against discrimination based on race, gender, and several other impermissible categories; and the guarantee of a sphere of individual liberty primarily confined to procreation and the family.

Because the modern Court has displayed such ambivalence in safeguarding property rights, the constitutional protection of these rights is more difficult to define. As a starting point, we can say that the modern Court's protection of property is at least the following: procedural protections in a civil trial before one can be deprived of property; just compensation for governmental takings of private property; enforcement of government's contractual obligations with private entities; procedural protections, particularly for statutory entitlements; and the right not to be excluded from certain prerogatives like appellate review because of indigency. Of course, some of the categories that I have defined as property rights could easily be thought of as personal rights. Particularly susceptible of overlap are the last two categories of statutory entitlements and distributional rights of poor people.[17]

I readily concede what many others have argued, namely, that this distinction between personal and property rights is not airtight. Nevertheless, it aptly describes a general difference in the level of protection that the modern Supreme Court has afforded these two kinds of rights.

I appreciate of course that my method of distinguishing between personal and property rights only begs the question of whether the different levels of protection that the Court has attached to each of these concepts are justifiable. This question is bound up with a still more interesting question: has the Supreme Court afforded any satisfying justifications for the disparate protection that it affords personal rights and property rights?

II. Protection of Personal and Property Rights: The Transformation

a. The Ascendancy of Property Rights

During the first third of the twentieth century, the Supreme Court appeared more interested in protecting property rights than personal rights. To some degree, this interest in property rights existed from the first days of the Republic and continued to develop during the nineteenth century. The Framers of the Constitution were powerfully influenced by the property theories of John Locke.[18] Locke posited a labor theory of property:

> Whosoever, then, he removes out of the state that Nature hath provided, and left in, he hath mixed his *labor* with it, and joined to it something that is his own, and thereby makes it his *property*. It being by him removed from the common state Nature placed it in, it hath by this *labor* something annexed to it that excludes the common right of other Men.[19]

Many of the Supreme Court's cases during the nineteenth century concerned property interests of various sorts.[20] During this time, the Court protected a fairly significant number of property interests. Starting with the Marshall Court, let me briefly mention a few widely discussed examples. In *Fletcher v. Peck*,[21] the Marshall Court invoked the Contracts Clause of Article I, § 10 to invalidate a Georgia statute nullifying - for reasons of corruption - a land grant after the grantees had sold the land to purchasers for valuable consideration.[22] In *Dartmouth College v. Woodward*,[23] the Court again invoked the Contracts Clause to invalidate a New Hampshire law altering the corporate charter of Dartmouth College as granted by the British Crown.[24]

During the antebellum Taney Court, in *Dred Scott v. Sandford*,[25] the Supreme Court guaranteed an owner's property interest in a slave against congressional intervention. After the Civil War, the Court extended broad-ranging constitutional protection to corporations, holding them persons within the meaning of the Fourteenth Amendment.[26] It also held the national income tax unconstitutional thus necessitating the adoption of the Sixteenth Amendment.[27]

Of course, during the nineteenth century, the Court often refused to protect property rights. For example, in the *Slaughter-House Cases*,[28] the Court upheld a Louisiana law that granted a monopoly over the slaughterhouse business to a particular company. The Court so held despite a challenge by

New Orleans butchers that the law deprived them of their freedom to conduct their chosen trade. In *Munn v. Illinois*,[29] the Court upheld the power of States to regulate the rates of grain elevators.[30]

Despite such limits on property guarantees, protection of personal rights paled against protection of property rights during the past century. Perhaps, the most egregious holdings came in the area of racial discrimination. I have already recounted the infamous holding in *Dred Scott v. Sandford* that contributed to insulating the slave system against legal attack and thereby helped to spark the American Civil War. After the Civil War, the Court held unconstitutional Federal anti-discrimination laws that reached racial segregation in »›inns, public conveyances on land or water, theatres, and other places of public amusement.‹«[31] It also upheld the notorious doctrine of separate but equal that codified a racially segregated society.[32] Protection for freedom of speech was still virtually undeveloped. In the freedom of religion area, the Court sustained the application of a federal ban on polygamy to a member of the Mormon faith despite his claims that polygamy was a religious practice.[33]

b. *Increasing Protection for Property and Economic Liberty*

Around the turn of the century, the Supreme Court dramatically enlarged the scope of protection for property. The Court used the Due Process Clauses that proscribe governmental deprivations »of life, liberty or property without due process of law.«[34] From those clauses, it fashioned a doctrine called substantive due process to strike down laws that violated substantive rights of liberty and property. Although the Court at this time occasionally applied the doctrine to guarantee certain personal rights,[35] it primarily used this doctrine to shield freedom of contract from government interference. From an economic perspective, this ideal of freedom of contract was a logical extension of property rights: if a society guaranteed the right to retain property, then the next logical economic step would be to guarantee one's right to acquire it.[36] The very term »liberty of contract« also signals an important aspect of the understanding of property rights at this time. Around the turn of the century, the Justices of the Supreme Court viewed liberty as »the opportunity to acquire property.«[37] Moreover, liberty of contract was a personal right.[38]

The decision epitomizing the substantive due process notion of freedom of contract was *Lochner v. New York*.[39] In 1897, the State of New York enacted a law requiring bakery employees to work no more than 60 hours per week.

226

The Supreme Court struck down the law as violating the freedom of contract of both employees and employers. Writing for the majority, Justice Peckham rejected the state's assertion that the law advanced worker health:

> It is manifest to us that the limitation of the hours of labor as provided for in this section of the statute under which the indictment was found, and the plaintiff in error convicted, has no such direct relation to, and no such substantial effect upon, the health of the employee, as to justify us in regarding the section as really a health law. It seems to us that the real object and purpose were simply to regulate the hours of labor between the master and his employees (all being men, *sui juris*), in a private business, not dangerous in any degree to morals, or in any real and substantial degree to the health of the employees. Under such circumstances the freedom of master and employee to contract with each other in relation to their employment, and in defining the same, cannot be prohibited or interfered with, without violating the Federal Constitution.[40]

Lochner was one of a number of cases in which the Court invoked the doctrine of substantive due process to protect freedom of contract. For example, during this era the Court invalidated laws protecting labor unions,[41] guaranteeing minimum wages,[42] fixing prices,[43] and regulating business in other respects.[44] *Lochner* and its progeny have been criticized on two grounds. Focusing on substantive due process as a method of adjudication, some inveighed against the Justices' injecting their own substantive values into Due Process Clauses that appear to concern procedural rather than substantive values. Others complained about the specific outdated ideas of freedom of contract that the Justices were enforcing.[45]

Substantive due process was not the only technique that the Court used during the first third of this century to protect property or economic rights. Notably, the Court invoked federalism concepts to invalidate a wide variety of congressional regulation of business interest. Measures invalidated included wage and price controls,[46] laws prohibiting child labor,[47] and other business regulations.[48] While these decisions technically left open the possibility of states regulating these areas, the economic milieu itself often rendered this option impractical. Often states wanting to impose such regulations feared that businesses would be driven to other states that lacked similar restrictions. Consequently, in many instances, the national government was the only viable regulator.[49]

The Court also indirectly protected property interests by restricting the amount of regulatory power that Congress could delegate to administrative agencies.[50] Congress simply could not feasibly engage in daily regulatory activities on any widespread basis. Consequently, to restrict its delegation

227

power effectively restricts not only the methods it can use to regulate but also the realistic possibility of regulating at all. While such structure of government techniques less directly protected property interests than substantive due process theory, they were highly effective. Ironically, as I shall discuss later in the paper, the Court has recently again moved to extend strong protection to property interests using different but equally indirect methods that distort the structure of our democratic decision-making process.[51]

During the 1930's, Supreme Court decisions involving federalism and other areas invalidated key portions of President Roosevelt's New Deal.[52] In reaction to these decisions, the President proposed a »court packing« plan that would allow him to appoint a new Justice for every one then over 70 years of age. »During the critical spring of 1937, the Supreme Court made the famous ›switch-in-time-that-saved-nine,‹ upholding key federal and state legislation, through the shifting votes of Chief Justice Hughes and Justice Roberts.«[53] The story of this transformation is captured in *United States v. Carolene Products.*[54]

c. *The Decline of Economic Rights and the Ascent of Personal Rights.*

Although slightly earlier cases reversed protection for economic rights through such doctrines as federalism[55] and substantive due process,[56] *Carolene Products* encapsules – and indeed to some degree provides the formula for – this historic watershed change. The metamorphosis marked the decline of property rights and the ascendancy of personal rights. While the case surely stands as one of the most discussed in modern American constitutional law,[57] commentators generally focus on its famous footnote four that provides the blueprint for safeguarding of personal rights by the modern Court. What we often overlook are the holdings of the case rejecting several claims of protection for property rights. The reason for this neglect is probably that *Carolene Products* was not the first case generally to vitiate protection for certain previously important property rights. Nevertheless, for purposes of this essay, both the property rights and personal rights aspects of the case are worth examining. The reason is that *Carolene Products* outlines the contours of a kind of political settlement in which the Court shed much of its past protection of property rights and moved toward embracing strong protection of personal rights.

The basic issue in the case was simple:

The question for decision is whether the »Filled Milk Act« of Congress of . . . 1923 which prohibits the shipment in interstate commerce of skimmed milk compounded with any fat or oil other than milk fat . . . transcends the power of Congress to regulate interstate commerce or infringes the Fifth Amendment.

Thus, the issue statement implicated two of the most common methods that the Court had used to strike down economic regulations. One entailed a federalism challenge asserting that the statute lay beyond Congress' power to regulate interstate commerce.[58] The other involved a substantive due process challenge using the Due Process Clause of the Fourteenth Amendment to object to Congress' rationale for the law.[59] In rejecting both of these claims, the Court applied a relaxed rationality standard in which it almost completely deferred to Congress' judgment on the commerce issue, that the restriction related to interstate commerce and on the due process issue, that the measure »was an appropriate means of preventing injury to the public.«[60] With these holdings, the Court reinforced its decisions of the previous 1937 term that had declined to employ either the Commerce Clause or the Due Process Clause to strike down, or even to scrutinize seriously, a governmental regulation.[61]

Ironically, the true importance of *Carolene Products* lies not so much in its holdings, as in the famous footnote four of the opinion. At the same time that the Court was relinquishing protection for property, it proposed safeguarding what have come to be called personal rights:

There may be narrower scope for operation of the presumption of constitutionality when legislation appears on its face to be within a specific prohibition of the Constitution, such as those of the first ten amendments, which are deemed equally specific when held to be embraced within the Fourteenth.
It is unnecessary to consider now whether legislation which restricts those political processes which can ordinarily be expected to bring about repeal of undesirable legislation, is to be subjected to more exacting judicial scrutiny under the general prohibitions of the Fourteenth Amendment than are most other types of legislation. On restrictions upon the right to vote, on restraints upon the dissemination of information, see . . .; on interferences with political organizations, see . . .; as to prohibition of peaceable assembly, see. . .
Nor need we enquire whether similar considerations enter into the review of statutes directed at particular religious or national, or racial minorities; whether prejudice against discrete and insular minorities may be a special condition, which tends seriously to curtail the operation of those political processes ordinarily to be relied upon to protect minorities, and which may call for a correspondingly more searching judicial inquiry.[62]

This brief passage nicely summarizes most of the constitutional rights guaranteed by the modern Court. In contrast with substantive due process analysis in particular, each of these rights is buttressed by comparatively explicit support in the text of the Constitution. The first part of the footnote talks about incorporating provisions of the Bill of Rights against the states. Many of these involve the rights of the accused. For example, the Fourth Amendment that prevents unreasonable searches and seizures, the Fifth Amendment that codifies the right against self-incrimination, and the Sixth Amendment that affords the accused the rights to counsel and jury trial.[63] The second part of the footnote primarily implicates freedom of expression and association as protected by the First Amendment. The third part concerns both the Equal Protection Clause of the Fourteenth Amendment and freedom of religion as guaranteed by the First Amendment.

Why in this footnote did the Court seek to protect these rights and forsake the property rights that it had previously defended? A cynical response is political pressure from President Roosevelt.[64] This answer, however, only begs the questions of what engendered such pressure and why has such pressure not so dramatically curtailed the modern Court's protection of personal rights.

Over time, commentators have offered a number of reasons as to why the Court allows government substantial discretion to regulate property. One set of reasons preys on the subtlety and ambiguity in Locke's thought. After he posited his influential labor theory of property that was quoted earlier,[65] Locke immediately qualified that theory in several important ways: »For this *Labor* being the unquestionable Property of the Laborer, no Man but he can have a right to what that is one joined to, at least where there is enough, and as good left in common for others.«[66] In the state of nature, Locke allows people to possess only so much property as they could combine with their labor without spoiling or destroying it. Arguably, then, the labor theory of value inherently limited how much property one person could acquire. As some commentators construed the theory, then, it tended to ensure a measure of equality in the amount of property each person could appropriate and to facilitate adequacy of property for all. For Locke, introducing money allowed substantial inequality in the possession of property. This inequality necessitated government intervention. While government could not forcibly take property, it could tax and regulate it.[67]

Another line of argument permitting greater government regulation of property rights simply dismisses Locke, or the reading of Locke that buttresses strong property rights. Those who advance this position note that Locke wrote for an agrarian society: »the subjects of ownership in Locke's pages are consumption goods, land used by its owner, and the tools of handicraft. Corporate wealth and the apparatus of large-scale production and business enterprise are absent from his discussion.«[68] Advocates of Lockean property rights also overlooked that Locke posited these property rights to combat the House of Stuart's attempt to assert absolute power.[69]

A third series of reasons for this shift in protection of property rights is related to the large, industrial structure of modern America. The *Lochner* Court professed to safeguard the liberty of contract of both employers and employees.[70] This view may have been plausible in a society in which wealth and economic power were relatively evenly distributed. As indicated by the facts of *Lochner* itself, however, that society had become a fading memory even before that case was decided.

Adam Smith himself noted that the absence of concentrated economic power favored economic liberty.[71] Conversely, grossly unequal bargaining power between employer and employees often made it difficult to defend liberty of contract based on the economic liberty of employees. In this milieu, the correct way to treat economic liberty was to view the property interests of employers, employees, and perhaps other groups as often being in competition with each other. In the *Carolene Products* settlement, protecting economic liberty was reconceptualized as a complex task that necessitated the careful balancing of competing interests in a highly complex, modern economic milieu. This daunting task hardly seemed well-suited for the judiciary.

With regard to the substantive due process rights guaranteed by the *Lochner* Court, judicial involvement was further compromised by the lack of a firm textual basis in the Constitution to get involved in this area in the first place.[72] Thus, the Court abandoned scrutiny of economic regulation under the Due Process Clause and various other provisions including the power of Congress to regulate interstate commerce.

If one message of the *Carolene Products* settlement was that the legislature should balance this confluence of competing economic interests, the other was that the process of legislative decision making should be fair. This was the over-arching message of the famous *Carolene Products* footnote. I leave to one side the criminal procedure part of the footnote that generally concerns fairness in the judicial process.[73]

The remaining two parts both ensure some level of fairness in the democratic process that was to decide property rights and other important questions of public policy. The goal was that everyone get a fair shake in the formulation of policy including the distribution of resources in society. In this connection, the second prong of the footnote talks explicitly about

231

protecting the political process, particularly the freedom of expression and association that is so vital to that process. The third part of the *Carolene Products* footnote talks about protecting discrete and insular minorities. Definitionally, these are groups that the political process has historically excluded or disfavored, such as black persons in American politics. In his celebrated explanation of the footnote, Professor John Ely aptly summarizes the work of the modern Court as »representation-reinforcing.«[74]

Unlike the enterprise of advancing freedom of contract, the judiciary was better able than the legislature to promote these personal rights. First, as previously noted, each of the three parts of the footnote had distinctive grounding in the text of the Constitution.[75] Second, the tasks outlined in the footnote were ones that the judiciary was functionally and structurally better-suited to perform then the executive or the legislature. Obviously, protecting the rights of the accused directly concerns trial and judicial process. Turning to the two parts of the footnote that more closely relate to this paper, those holding political power would have difficulty fairly policing the political process. Instead, the democratic games should be monitored by some referee removed from the electoral process.[76] Similarly, defending discrete and insular minorities is a task that the majoritarian process has definitionally failed to accomplish. Consequently, the need arises for some sort of countermajoritarian body like the judiciary that is removed from the political process.[77] Again, the countermajoritarian Court seems a natural choice.[78]

III. *Contemporary Protection for Personal and Property Rights*

Where has the dust settled? What protection does the modern Court currently afford personal and property rights? Time constraints dictate only a brief sketch, but in my view the story is more complicated than, »The Court protects personal rights but not property rights.«

a. *Personal Rights*

As I have indicated, the term personal rights is rather vague.[79] Essentially, the Court's personal rights tend to cluster around safeguarding three values: liberty, equality,[80] and procedural fairness.[81] The First Amendment guaran-

232

tees of freedom of speech and freedom of religion generally advance liberty as does the revived doctrine of substantive due process. The Equal Protection Clause obviously stands as one of the key safeguards of equality. The various protections afforded the accused in a criminal case, and litigants in a civil case, focus on procedural fairness. Certainly overlap exists. For example, the religion clauses of the First Amendment also guarantee a measure of equality, and the rights of the accused also advance the value of liberty. I take this simple schematic of clauses and values as a useful starting point.

Perhaps, the most lucid way in which to expand on protection for these values is to track the *Carolene Products* footnote. I will not treat the rights of the accused or procedural protections in civil cases in any detail. The basic thrust of the modern Court's efforts has been to apply against the states the procedural guarantees of the Bill of Rights. The process has been called selective incorporation.[82] My summary treatment does not in any way reflect the importance of these rights. The rights of the accused in particular advance not only procedural fairness but guarantee a measure of liberty as they shield against the terrible prosecutorial forces of government. Lacking such safeguards as a right to jury trial,[83] a right to counsel,[84] a privilege against self-incrimination,[85] and protection against unreasonable searches and seizures[86] allows authoritarian regimes to spawn.[87]

The second part of the *Carolene Products* footnote concerns the political process. This directly implicates the free speech portion of the First Amendment. The part of the First Amendment of the United States Constitution protecting freedom of speech reads as follows:

> Congress shall make no law . . . abridging the freedom of speech or of the press; or the right of the people peaceably to assemble, and to petition the Government for a redress of grievances.

These are but thirty-three words among the several thousand in the Constitution. Given this context, one scarcely would have expected the position of prominence, if not primacy, that the First Amendment occupies among American constitutional values.[88] Essentially, the amendment can be viewed as a bedrock of American democracy and political freedom. Indeed, Justice Benjamin Cardozo once remarked, »of freedom of thought, and speech . . . one may say that it is the matrix, the indispensable condition, of nearly every other form of freedom.«[89]

The reach of First Amendment protection of speech extends to advocating government overthrow,[90] freedom of assembly,[91] freedom to associate in political parties,[92] political advertising,[93] and criticism of the highest officials of government.[94] Protection is not limited to political speech; it also includes artistic speech, scientific speech, academic speech, commercial advertising,[95] et cetera.[96] Nor is the First Amendment confined to rational speech, or even to spoken or written words. First Amendment doctrine preserves the emotive as well as the cognitive function of speech;[97] it also extends beyond words to protect conduct that expresses an idea. For example, the Supreme Court has extended constitutional protection to high school students wearing black armbands to protest the Vietnam War[98] and recently to burning an American flag as a political protest.[99] Two very important decisions of the modern Court define the nature of its First Amendment jurisprudence. These are *New York Times v. Sullivan*[100] and *Brandenburg v. Ohio.*[101]

Exemplifying the degree or depth of protection, *Brandenburg* safeguards speech advocating overthrow of the government:

> [F]ree speech does not permit a State to forbid or proscribe advocacy of the use of force or of law violation except where such advocacy is directed to inciting or producing imminent lawless action and is likely to incite or produce such action.[102]

Focusing on actions rather than words, the standard requires a specific purpose to incite activity that is both imminent and lawless. Beyond having such intent, the words must appear actually likely to succeed in inciting such action.[103] The importance of *Brandenburg* ranges well beyond subversive speech. The case is paradigmatic in providing stringent protection for freedom of speech generally.

If *Brandenburg* exemplifies the depth of protection for expression, *New York Times* signals its breadth. It establishes that virtually no categories of expression are completely bereft of First Amendment safeguards:[104]

> In deciding the question now, we are compelled by neither precedent nor policy to give any more weight to the epithet »libel« than we have to other »mere labels« of state law . . . Like insurrection, contempt, advocacy of unlawful acts, breach of the peace, obscenity, solicitation of legal business, and the various other formulae for the repression of expression that have been challenged in this Court, libel can claim no talismanic immunity from Constitutional limitations. It must be measured by standards that satisfy the First Amendment.[105]

With these words, the Court during the 1960's embarked on the path toward much greater protection for all types of speech.

Beyond outlining broad protection for freedom of speech generally, *New York Times* specifically pertains to speech that defames government officials. The decision severely limits the actionability of such speech in civil lawsuits.[106] The theory is that government officials can protect their reputations by responding in the press themselves. Criticizing the government without impugning the reputation of specific officials is essentially not actionable. Finally, both *Brandenburg* and *New York Times* curtail criminal[107] and civil liability for speech after it has been uttered. First Amendment jurisprudence takes a particularly dim view of government imposing prior restraints on speech before it has come to light.[108]

Emphasizing egalitarian concerns, the third paragraph of the *Carolene Products* footnote talks about protecting minorities. It begins with protection for religious minorities. Although the footnote stresses egalitarian concerns, the religion clauses emphasize notions of both liberty and equality. The Establishment Clause requires separation of church and state. It prohibits both discriminating among religions[109] and promoting the interests of religion generally.[110] While the Establishment Clause enforces separation between church and state, the Free Exercise Clause is designed to safeguard each individual's pursuit of her own religious beliefs.[111] This Clause is meant directly to enforce the footnote's articulated goal of protecting religious minorities.[112]

Turning more completely to egalitarian concerns, the third part of the *Carolene Products* footnote proceeds to discuss protecting discrete and insular minorities. The basic device that the Court has used to effectuate this goal is the Equal Protection Clause.[113] There are two basic strands of equal protection jurisprudence, one involving suspect class cases and the other involving fundamental rights cases. The suspect class strand is much better developed. It also lies closer to the discrete and insular minority concerns articulated in the *Carolene Products* footnote. The types of suspect classifications that receive the highest level of scrutiny are ones based on race, ethnicity, or national origin. Legislative or other governmental classifications based on one of these criteria must be necessary to serve a compelling state interest.[114] Particularly in cases involving these types of classifications, this standard is almost never met. A number of classifications – those relating to alienage,[115] illegitimacy,[116] and gender[117] – receive somewhat lesser levels of scrutiny. For example, in the case of gender discrimination, the Court has required »at least that the classification serves ›important governmental objectives and that the discriminatory means employed are ›substantially related to the achievement of those objectives.‹«[118] In the suspect class strand of equal protection analysis, the Court has rejected heightened scrutiny for certain classifications, such as, those based on wealth.[119]

Turning briefly to the fundamental rights strand of equal protection jurisprudence, the Court has enforced some measure of equality with respect to governmental distribution of certain fundamental rights. It has largely confined protection to the right to vote,[120] travel,[121] and access to the judicial process.[122] Finally, even when neither a suspect class nor a fundamental right is involved, the Court occasionally has struck down a law using a heightened rationality standard of review.[123]

While the core agenda of the modern Court's protection of personal rights has been the *Carolene Products* footnote, there is an important group of decisions that lies beyond the concerns articulated in the footnote. This area involves the revival of substantive due process jurisprudence, focused this time on procreation and familial matters rather than on liberty of contract.[124] The right is sometimes loosely referred to as a right of personal autonomy and other times, as a right of privacy.[125] Although some differ as to precisely when this revival began,[126] *Roe v. Wade*,[127] which enforces a woman's constitutional right to elect an abortion, is clearly its most widely discussed decision. The many decisions following *Roe* have fashioned a rather stringent right to elect an abortion;[128] however, *Webster v. Reproductive Health Services*,[129] decided just this last term, may signal some relaxation of this right.

The modern substantive due process cases cluster around the ideas of procreative liberty and the family.[130] The majority of the cases involve abortion with birth control a distant second. Several years ago, the Court upheld the constitutionality of a law criminalizing homosexual sex.[131] It thus declined to expand modern substantive due process theory to protect privacy or autonomy in sexual matters generally.

As the theory underlying the *Carolene Products* footnote does not buttress substantive due process analysis, commentators have sought to find other reasons on which to ground it. Much debate and controversy focuses on *Roe v. Wade* itself.[132] The revival of substantive due process has also catalyzed a larger discussion about the extent to which the Supreme Court should adhere to the text of the Constitution in adjudicating constitutional cases.[133]

236

b. *Property Rights and Property Interests*

As I will try to illustrate in the ensuing discussion, the modern Court's protection for property rights is characterized by four basic themes. First, as I have previously indicated, it is a mistake to say that the Supreme Court has abandoned protection for property rights. The Court, however, does accord personal rights far more protection than property rights.

Second, the way in which the modern Court thinks about property has changed to take into account the property interests of poor people. Third, the modern Court has sometimes moved toward guaranteeing strong property rights, but generally shied away from this process. Recall that in the *Carolene Products* settlement, the Court relegated much of the protection of property interests to the political process. The Court instead focused on the political process itself to ensure that it fairly represents all interests.[134] This »shy away« point must be tempered by my fourth, most important point: despite the weakened protection of property rights, the Court's recent free speech jurisprudence has so skewed the marketplace of ideas that property interests are doing quite well.

To begin with traditional property rights analysis, the most important constitutional provision still shielding such rights is the Takings Clause of the Fifth Amendment. This prevents governmental takings of private property without just compensation. The Fifth Amendment does not safeguard ownership or possession of a particular piece of property. The government can take private property for virtually any purpose that it desires.[135] The Takings Clause merely exacts just compensation for governmental takings of property.

While many cases directly concern using the eminent domain power to take land, the Clause extends to personal and intangible property as well.[136] Of course, to the extent that they distort the normal workings of the market, many government regulations diminish the value of property used in a given activity. The modern Court has largely declined to exact compensation for such »regulatory takings.«[137] While the Court has ratcheted up the level of Fifth Amendment protection for property to some extent,[138] it has thus far shrunk back from using the Takings Clause to afford strong protection for property rights.[139]

A second source of modern property rights is the Contract Clause of Article I,[140] which provides »No State shall . . . pass any . . . law impairing the Obligation of Contracts.« While the Court made some move during the 1970's to strengthen protection of property using this clause,[141] it subsequently has shied away from this position, particularly when government is not a party to the contract.[142]

The modern Court has expanded its conception of property rights to comprehend protection for the poor, government employees, and others generally less advantaged than those protected during the *Lochner* era. Again, however, the Court has shied away from strong guarantees. The movement began during the late 1960's when the Court struck down a New York state requirement of one year of residence for receipt of welfare benefits.[143] Some thought that the Justices would hold wealth a suspect classification and that broad-ranging property rights for necessities would emerge for the poor. As I have already recounted in the discussion of equal protection, however, such a result did not eventuate.[144] Instead, the Court has satisfied itself with guaranteeing that people not be deprived of certain fundamental rights – the vote,[145] travel,[146] and judicial access[147] – based on their indigency. These cases generally are consistent with the *Carolene Products* quest of ensuring access to influence the levers of power. Both the vote and even appellate review implicate such influence.

While the modern Court has narrowly circumscribed substantive constitutional protection for necessities based on indigency, it has fashioned certain procedural requirements that must be satisfied before one can be deprived of property. Many of these cases have disproportionately benefited the less advantaged. The cases split along two doctrinal lines. One guarantees notice and an opportunity to be heard before property can be attached by a court. The early cases in this line involved the wages and goods of poor consumers.[148]

The other line of constitutional cases procedurally protecting property impose certain procedural safeguards before government can deprive someone of a government entitlement such as welfare,[149] disability benefits,[150] or government employment.[151] In contrast to the claims for substantive constitutional rights to education or welfare, these decisions simply require fair procedures before government can deprive people of entitlements that the government itself has opted to give. The source of the entitlement is a statute rather than the Constitution. These features both fit nicely into the *Carolene Products* framework: the source of the entitlement is legislation and the right afforded is procedural.

The *Carolene Products* vision is appealing because it is democratic and fair: »Give everyone some say in who gets what, and let the majority decide.« Indeed, even the Takings Clause itself only safeguards property rights in the short run. In the long run, the majority can redistribute wealth to its heart's content through, for example, progressive taxation.

How is it, then, that in America so few people have so much and so many have relatively little? In 1983, 34.3 % of the wealth of this country was concentrated in 1 % of the population.[152] By 1987, that figure was approaching 36 %.[153]

I readily grant that market considerations may favor a certain amount of concentrated wealth. For example, highly redistributive systems of taxation may well cause capital flight. Moreover, some concentration of wealth can benefit all by providing the kind of capital formation that can facilitate risk-taking and innovation.[154] As I shall presently discuss, however, an historically excessive concentration of wealth occurred just before the depression of the 1930's, a time when property rights were strongly guaranteed.[155] Leaving to one side the economic or ethical[156] merits of particular distributions of wealth, I simply wonder why so much concentration exists in a constitutional system that has comparatively weak property rights. At the same time that the rich have been growing richer, a number of commentators maintain that the poor – and many members of the middle class – have been growing poorer.[157] How did all of this transpire under the *Carolene Products* regime? Did society consent?

I submit that within the past 15 years or so the Court has dramatically increased constitutional protection not for property rights but for property interests. Ironically, this protection has largely been the product of the First Amendment jurisprudence of freedom of speech. These developments guarantee that the wealthy will have grossly disproportionate opportunity to speak and influence the marketplace of ideas.[158]

Even under the best of circumstances, a democracy with a free economy will be saddled with some disparities in the abilities of citizens to express themselves. Speech requires money and some inequalities in its distribution will entail disparate abilities to communicate. In recent years, however, the jurisprudence of the United States Supreme Court has greatly exacerbated these natural difficulties. For example, the Court has given great advantage to the wealthy in the electoral process.[159] In *Buckley v. Valeo*,[160] it struck down those parts of a federal statute restricting how much money people could spend on their own campaigns for political office. The Court thereby has given candidates a distinct advantage. It has afforded the wealthy further advantage by not allowing restrictions on the amount that particular individuals or Political Action Committees (PAC's) might spend to support the election of a particular candidate, so long as they do not contribute directly to a particular political campaign. At the same time, the *Buckley* Court left in place severe restrictions on how much a person could contribute directly to a candidate's campaign. Such restrictions effectively

239

narrow the chances of the less wealthy candidate to raise adequate funds from outside sources.

To take another area, the Court has severely constricted the places where people can engage in free expression for »free,« that is, without cost.[161] In *Perry Education Association v. Perry Local Educators' Association*,[162] the Court narrowed the places in which speakers have a right to communicate on public parks, streets, and sidewalks. Government can close off all other public property. The Court has even limited access to speak in traditional public forums, such as, streets and parks. In *Members of City Counsel v. Taxpayers for Vincent*, [163] it upheld a ban on placards being placed on city utility poles. In *Clark v. Community for Creative Non-Violence*,[164] it upheld a ban on sleeping in certain parks in Washington, D.C. as applied to homeless persons who wanted to demonstrate their plight.

As to private property, not even shopping centers – where many middle class Americans now congregate – are public forums where speakers have a right to communicate.[165] Consequently, the decision of who can speak on the premises is made by the private owner. Even an owner who is sympathetic to the needs of poor people and other disadvantaged may be driven by market forces not to afford access. If his competitors at the mall nearby do not afford such access, he may lose lots of business of shoppers who find the sight of such protests uncomfortable or unpleasant.

The public forum and political campaigns are not the only areas in which judicial decisions have distorted the political process and the marketplace of ideas in accordance with wealth. For example, in *C.B.S. v. Democratic National Committee*,[166] the Court denied a right of access to the media – even a paid right of access. In that case, the Court denied the Democratic Party the right to purchase television time to call for an end to the Vietnam War. The only way left to guarantee access was to own one's own media source. The Court also has afforded protection to commercial advertising, which moves toward constitutionalizing a *laissez faire* economy. The stronger such protection is, the more it revisits the central problem with *Lochner* and its progeny.[167] Finally, the Court has afforded corporations the right to speak.[168] This move allows wealthy shareholders the possibility of combining their personal wealth and corporate wealth to advance their ideas.[169]

At bottom, contrasting property and personal rights is a tricky business. It is surely simplistic to say that the modern Court protects personal rights and not property rights. Instead, the modern Court offers weakened protection for property rights. More importantly, its recent First Amendment jurisprudence has skewed the political process and the marketplace of ideas so as to favor property interests. The crux of protection for personal rights is the *Carolene Products* footnote. Rather than favor particular interests, the footnote advances the rights of all individuals to participate in a fair political process. Unfortunately, the Court's recent free speech jurisprudence has distorted that process.

Whether it is coincidental or not, during about the same time that the Court has been strengthening protection for property interests, some commentators have noted a sharp increase in the concentration of wealth. In 1987, 1 % of the population possessed nearly 36 % of the wealth of the United States.[170] This compared with 24.9 % of the wealth being so concentrated in 1969. It also may or may not be coincidence that this near 36 % concentration is the highest since 1929, when 36.3 % of America's wealth was so concentrated.[171] Of course, around 1929, the Supreme Court also offered strong protection for property rights. By 1933, the concentration declined to 28.3 %, but a phenomenon other than protection of property had accounted for this decline.[172] Thus, both the contemporary case law and the distribution of wealth both suggest strong protection for monied interests. While protection of property rights has diminished, protection of property interests is alive and well.

I first discussed some of these ideas in a paper on freedom of expression presented at another exchange between German and American constitutional scholars at the University of Notre Dame. During the discussion, I briefly inquired about the respective importance of a right of expression as against rights to necessities like food. On a napkin, a German scholar poignantly responded, »In order to tell that he is hungry he will have to speak.«

Notes:

* I would like to thank Michael Slinger, David McClamrock, and Andor M. Laszlo for their outstanding research and other assistance. I would like to thank Mary Ann Glendon, Donald Kommers, Walter Murphy, and Kathleen Spartana for their helpful comments. Finally, I would like to thank Mead Data Central, Inc. for their generous research support.

1 *See* Federalist No. 51, in The Federalist (J. Cooke ed. 1961).

2 In terming certain ideas in American constitutional thinking »constants,« I do not mean to suggest that these concepts are bereft of controversy. For example, controversy even surrounds the bedrock institution of judicial review, *see, e.g.*, Attanasio, *Everyman's Constitutional Law: A Theory of the Power of Judicial Review*, 72 GEO. L. J. 1665 (1985).

3 *See, e.g.*, Dred Scott v. Sandford, 60 U.S. (19 How.) 393 (1856).

4 *See* U.S. CONSTI. amend. XIII.

5 *Compare* Carter v. Carter Coal Co., 298 U.S. 238 (1936) *with* Wickard v. Filburn, 377 U.S. 111 (1942) (congressional power to regulate interstate commerce).

6 *Compare* Panama Refining Co. v. Ryan, 293 U.S. 388 (1935) *with* Yakus v. United States, 321 U.S. 414 (1944) (congressional delegation of legislative authority to administrative agencies).

7 Indeed, the method for protecting the individual against government interference has itself been altered. For many years, the core strategy for protecting individual rights was to limit the power of government. Necessarily, a government of limited powers would also be limited in the extent to which it could interfere in the private affairs of its citizenry. In the face of the historical exigencies of big government, the Supreme Court grudgingly has relinquished this indirect strategy of containing government power to protect individual rights more directly: the Court has explicitly elaborated specific individual rights against which government could not infringe. *See generally* Attanasio, *supra* note 2, at 1678.

8 304 U.S. 144 (1938).

9 Lynch v. Household Finance Corp., 405 U.S. 538, 552 (1972).

10 *See* Adkins v. Children's Hosp., 261 U.S. 525 (1923).

11 *See* Lochner v. New York, 198 U.S. 45 (1905). *See also infra* text accompanying notes 33-44.

12 *See* Baker, *Property and Its Relation to Constitutionally Protected Liberty*, 134 U. PA. L. REV. 741 (1986).

13 *See id.* at 760, 767.

14 *Id.* at 742 n.2.

15 Of course, some have advocated protection for animal rights. *See, e.g.*, Goodkin, *The Evolution of Animal Rights*, 18 Colum. Hum. Rts. J. 259 (1987); McDonald, *Creating a Private Cause of Action Against Abusive Animal Research*, 134 U. PA. L. REV. 399 (1986).

16 *See supra* text accompanying note 9.

17 On the overlap between personal rights and property rights in the statutory entitlements area, see N. Redlich, B. Schwartz, & J. Attanasio, Constitutional Law 548 (2d ed. 1989).

18 *See* Hamilton, *Property - According to Locke,* 41 YALE L.J. 864, 873-75 (1932); Comment, *Property Versus Civil Rights: An Alternative to the Double Standard,* 11 N. KY. L. REV. 51, 53 (1984).

19 J. Locke, The Second Treatise of Government § 27 (P. Laslett ed. 1988).

20 *See, e.g.,* Weis, *The Constitution's Second Century: The Shift in Emphasis From Property Rights to Personal Rights,* 26 DUQUESNE L. REV. 1, 3-4 (1987).

21 10 U.S. (6 Cranch) 87 (1810).

22 The legislature had invalidated the land grant for reasons of political corruption.

23 17 U.S. (4 Wheat.) 518 (1819).

24 For additional discussion of protection of property by the Marshall Court, see Mann, *The Marshall Court: Nationalization of Private Rights and Personal Liberty from the Authority of the Commerce Clause,* 38 IND. L.J. 117 (1963).

25 60 U.S. (19 How.) 393 (1856).

26 *See* Santa Clara County v. Southern Pacific R. Co., 118 U.S. 394 (1986); Covington & Lexington Turnpike R. Co. v. Sanford, 164 U.S. 578 (1896). For discussion of the extensive constitutional protections afforded corporations, see First Nat'l Bank of Boston v. Bellotti, 435 U.S. 765, 778 n.14 (1978).

27 *See* Pollock v. Farmer's Loan & Trust Co., 157 U.S. 429 (1895).

28 83 U.S. 36 (1873).

29 94 U.S. 113 (1877).

30 *Cf.* Ogden v. Saunders, 25 U.S. (12 Wheat.) 213 (1827) (upheld state bankruptcy laws against Contracts Clause challenge); Mugler v. Kansas, 123 U.S. 623 (1887) (upheld state law prohibiting the sale of intoxicating beverages and thus effectively outlawed the liquor business).

31 Civil Rights Cases, 109 U.S. 3, 9 (1883); *see United States v. Harris,* 106 U.S. 629 (1883).

32 Plessy v. Ferguson, 163 U.S. 537 (1896). *But cf.* Strauder v. West Virginia, 100 U.S. 303 (1880) (striking down a law that limited jury service to white males over 21 years old).

33 *See* Reynolds v. United States, 98 U.S. (8 Otto) 145 (1878). Perhaps, a quick way to see the different levels of development of personal and property rights is to compare Constitutional Law casebooks of different eras. *Compare, e.g.,* O. Field, Cases and Authorities on Constitutional Law (2d ed. 1936) with N. Redlich, B. Schwartz & J. Attanasio supra note 17.

34 Both the Fifth and Fourteenth Amendments contain Due Process Clauses. The clause in the Fifth Amendment applies to the federal government and the Fourteenth Amendment clause applies to the states.

35 *See infra* note 125.

36 *See* Siegel, *Understanding the Lochner Era: Lessons from the Controversy over Railroad and Utility Rate Regulation,* 70 VA. L. REV. 187, 260-61 (1984).

37 *See* Hamilton, *supra* note 18, at 877.

38 *See* Ashley, *Personal Rights v. Property Rights,* 20 A.B.A. J. 49, 53 (1934). In *Allgeyer v. Louisiana,* the Supreme Court summarized its view of the liberty guaranteed by its doctrine of substantive due process accordingly:

> The liberty mentioned in [the 14th amendment] means not only the right of the citizen to be free from the mere physical restraint of his person, as by incarceration, but the term is deemed to embrace the right of the citizen to be free in the enjoyment of all his faculties; to be free to use them in all lawful ways; to live and work where he will; to earn his livelihood by any lawful

calling; to pursue any livelihood or avocation, and for that purpose to enter into all contracts which may be proper, necessary and essential to his carrying out to a successful conclusion the purposes above mentioned.
165 U.S. 578, 589 (1897).

39 198 U.S. 45 (1905).

40 *Id.* at 64.

41 Coppage v. Kansas, 236 U.S. 1 (1915); Adair v. United States, 208 U.S. 161 (1908).

42 Adkins v. Children's Hosp., 261 U.S. 525 (1923).

43 *See, e.g.*, Williams v. Standard Oil Co., 278 U.S. 235 (1929).

44 *See, e.g.*, Allgeyer v. Louisiana, 165 U.S. 578 (1897).

45 *See* Michelman, *Property as a Constitutional Right*, 38 WASH. & LEE L. REV. 1097, 1101 (1981).

46 Schechter Poultry Corp. v. United States, 295 U.S. 495 (1935).

47 Hammer v. Dagenhart, 247 U.S. 251 (1918).

48 *See, e.g.*, United States v. Butler, 297 U.S. 1 (1936) (Agricultural Adjustment Act); Carter v. Carter Coal Co., 298 U.S. 238 (1936) (Bituminous Coal Conservation Act).

49 For Justice Cardozo's famous elaboration of this argument, see Steward Machine Co. v. Davis, 301 U.S. 548 (1937).

50 *See, e.g.*, Panama Refining Co. v. Ryan, 293 U.S. 388 (1935).

51 *See infra* text accompanying notes 154-70.

52 *See, e.g., id.*

53 N. Redlich, B. Schwartz & J. Attanasio, *supra* note 17, at 418. For additional discussion of this crucial period, *see, e.g.*, R. Jackson, The Struggle for Judicial Supremacy (1941); Currie, *The Constitution in the Supreme Court: The New Deal, 1931-1940*, 54 U. CHI. L. REV. 501 (1987); Leuchtenberg, *The Origins of Franklin D. Roosevelt's »Court-Packing« Plan*, 1966 SUP. CT. REV. 347.

54 304 U.S. 144 (1938).

55 *See*, National Labor Relations Board v. Jones & Laughlin Steel Corp., 301 U.S. 1 (1937).

56 *See* West Coast Hotel v. Parrish, 300 U.S. 379 (1937). The Court also allowed Congress broad discretion to delegate authority to administrative agencies. *See, e.g.*, Yakus v. United States, 321 U.S. 414 (1944).

57 *See, e.g.*, J. Ely, Democracy and Distrust 75-77, 151-53 (1980); L. Lusky, by what Right? (1975); Attanasio, *supra* note 2, at 1678-81; Cover, *The Origins of Judicial Activism and the Protection of Minorities*, 91 YALE L.J. 1287 (1982); Powell, *Carolene Products Revisited*, 82 Colum. L. Rev. 1087 (1982).

58 U.S. CONSTI. art. I, § 8, cl. 3.

59 U.S. CONSTI. amend. XIV.

60 *Carolene Products, supra* note 8, at 148.

61 *See* N. Redlich, B. Schwartz & J. Attanasio, *supra* note 17, at 418-19.

62 *Carolene Products*, 304 U.S. at 152 n.4 (citations omitted).

63 Of course, the incorporation process also includes other amendments – notably the First. The guarantees of the First Amendment are more explicitly discussed in the second and third paragraphs of the footnote.

64 *See supra* text accompanying notes 51-53.

65 *See supra* text accompanying note 19.

66 J. Locke, *supra* note 19, § 27.

67 *See* Leeson & Sullivan, *Property, Philosophy and Regulation: The Case Against a Natural Rights Theory of Property Rights,* 17 Willamette L.J. 527, 560-62 (1981).

68 *See* Hamilton, *supra* note 18, at 868. *See also* Reich, *The New Property,* 73 YALE L.J. 733 (1964).

69 Hamilton, *supra* note 18, at 865-70.

70 *Lochner,* 198 U.S. at 53.

71 *See* A. Smith, Lectures on Jurisprudence 83-84, 363-64, 471-72, 497-98, 529 (R.L. Meek, D. Raphael, and P.G. Stein eds. 1978); A. Smith, The Wealth of Nations 278 (E. Cannon ed. 1976).

72 *See supra* text accompanying notes 42-43; Attanasio, *supra* note 2, at 1677-78.

73 *See generally* N. Redlich, B. Schwartz & J. Attanasio, *supra* note 17, at 392-408.

74 *See* J. Ely, *supra* note 57, at 101.

75 *See supra* text accompanying notes 62-64. *See also* Attanasio, *supra* note 2, at 1681-84.

76 *See* J. Ely, *supra* note 57, at 73.

77 Members of the federal judiciary including the Supreme Court are not elected but appointed by the President with the advice and consent of the Senate. U.S. CONSTI. art. II, § 2, cl. 2. Moreover, they have lifetime tenure, can only be impeached for lack of good behavior, and cannot have their salaries decreased during their terms of office. *See* U.S. CONSTI. art. III, § 1.

78 *See* Attanasio, *supra* note 2, at 1680.

79 *See supra* text accompanying notes 15-16.

80 *See generally* Attanasio, *The Constitutionality of Protecting Human Genetic Engineering: Where Procreative Liberty and Equal Opportunity Collide,* 53 U. CHI. L. REV. 1274 (1986).

81 My comment on procedural fairness primarily involves judicial proceedings. As I previously stated, one could view the portions of the *Carolene Products* footnote protecting the political process and discrete and insular minorities as advancing fairness in the democratic process. *See supra* text accompanying notes 70-71. *See also* J. ELY, *supra* note 57, at 102; Attanasio, *supra* note 2, at 1680,

82 *See* Duncan v. Louisiana, 391 U.S. 145 (1968); Israel, *Selective Incorporation Revisited,* 71 GEO. L.J. 253 (1982).

83 U.S. CONSTI. amend. VI.

84 *Id.*

85 U.S. CONSTI. amend. V.

86 U.S. CONSTI. amend. IV.

87 One of the most important ways that the Court has used to enforce the rights of the accused is the exclusionary rule. This excludes evidence that the government obtained illegally by, for example, an unreasonable search and seizure or by violating the privilege against self-incrimination. *See, e.g.,* Weeks v. United States, 232 U.S. 383 (1914) (adopting the exclusionary rule); Mapp v. Ohio, 367 U.S. 643 (1961) (applying the rule to the states); United States v. Leon, 468 U.S. 897 (1984) (qualifying the exclusionary rule in the search and seizure context).

88 In *Murdock v. Pennsylvania,* the United States Supreme Court established the notion that the First Amendment occupies a »preferred position« among American constitutional values. 319 U.S. 105 (1943). Although the Court no longer tends explicitly to use this rhetoric, the decisions of the Supreme Court continue

to reflect this preferred position. *See* J. Nowak, R. Rotunda & J. Young, Constitutional Law 837-38 (3d ed. 1986).

89 Palko v. Connecticut, 302 U.S. 319, 327 (1937).

90 *See, e.g.*, Brandenburg v. Ohio, 395 U.S. 444 (1969).

91 *See, e.g.*, Cox v. Louisiana (No. 24-Cox I), 379 U.S. 536 (1965).

92 *See, e.g.*, United States v. Robel, 389 U.S. 258 (1967); Branti v. Finkel, 445 U.S. 507 (1980).

93 *See, e.g.*, New York Times v. Sullivan, 376 U.S. 254 (1964).

94 *See, e.g.*, *id.*

95 Virginia State Bd. of Pharmacy v. Va. State Consumers Union, 425 U.S. 748 (1976). Understandably, the Supreme Court affords considerably more protection to political advertisements than to commercial ones.

96 Prominent First Amendment theorist Alexander Meiklejohn stressed the role of freedom of speech in protecting the political process. *See, e.g.*, A. Meiklejohn, Free Speech and its Relation to Self-Government (1948); A. Meiklejohn, Political Freedom (1965). Nevertheless, Meiklejohn did not limit constitutional protection to political speech. He also guaranteed other forms of speech – scientific, artistic, academic, *et cetera* – as these inform the political deliberative processes of society. Meiklejohn, *The First Amendment Is an Absolute*, 1961 SUP. CT. REV. 245.
For a recent account of the various rationales advanced for protecting freedom of expression, see Greenawalt, *Free Speech Justifications*, 89 COLUM. L. REV. 119 (1989).

97 *See, e.g.*, *Cohen v. California*, 403 U.S. 15 (1971).

98 Texas v. Johnson, – U.S. –, 109 S. Ct. 2533 (1989).

99 Tinker v. Des Moines School District, 393 U.S. 503 (1969).

100 376 U.S. 254 (1964).

101 395 U.S. 444 (1969).

102 *Id.* at 447.

103 *Id.* at 447-49.

104 I say »virtually« as the *New York Times* case itself allowed placing purely commercial advertising beyond the constitutional shield. Since then, even this speech has received constitutional protection. *See* Virginia State Bd. of Pharmacists v. Virginia State Consumers Union, 425 U.S. 748 (1976). *See also* Attanasio, *Lawyer Advertising in England and the United States*, 32 AM. J. COMP. L. 493 (1984).

105 376 U.S. at 269 (citations omitted). *See also* Kalven, *The New York Times Case: A Note on ›The Central Meaning of the First Amendment,‹* 1964 SUP. CT. REV. 191.

106 *New York Times*, 376 U.S. at 273 (speech defaming government officials in their official capacity only actionable if made »with knowledge that it was false or with reckless disregard of whether it was false or not«).

107 Besides the protection against criminal sanctions offered by *Brandenburg*, *New York Times* declared unconstitutional a long since repealed congressional statute that had imposed criminal penalties for criticizing the government or governmental officials. *Id.* at 280.

108 *See* New York Times v. United States, 403 U.S. 713 (1971).

109 *See* Larson v. Valente, 456 U.S. 228 (1982).

110 The Court states the basic test for the Establishment Clause in *Lemon v. Kurtzman:*
>First, the statute must have a secular legislative purpose; second, its principal or primary effect must be one that neither advances nor inhibits religion; finally, the statute must not foster »an excessive government entanglement with religion.«

403 U.S. 602, 612 (1971).

111 *See* Sherbert v. Verner, 374 U.S. 398 (1963); Thomas v. Rev. Bd. of the Ind. Employment Security Div., 450 U.S. 707 (1981).

112 Some have complained that the courts have not vigorously enforced the Free Exercise Clause. *See, e.g.,* Equal Employment Opportunity Comm'n v. Townley Engineering and Manufacturing Co., 859 F.2d 610, 624 (1988) (Noonan, J., dissenting).

113 U.S. CONSTI. amend. XIV. While the Fourteenth Amendment only applies against the states, the Court has incorporated the Equal Protection Clause into the Due Process Clause of the Fifth Amendment that does apply against the federal government. *See* Bolling v. Sharpe, 347 U.S. 497 (1954).

114 *See, e.g.,* Palmore v. Sidoti, 466 U.S. 429 (1984).

115 *See, e.g.,* Bernal v. Fainter, 467 U.S. 216 (1984).

116 *See, e.g.,* Lalli v. Lalli, 439 U.S. 259 (1978).

117 *See, e.g.,* Mississippi Univ. for Women v. Hogan, 458 U.S. 718 (1982).

118 *Id.* at 744.

119 *See, e.g.,* San Antonio Ind. School Dist. v. Rodriguez, 411 U.S. 1 (1973).

120 *See, e.g.,* Reynolds v. Sims, 377 U.S. 533 (1964); Harper v. Virginia State Bd. Election, 383 U.S. 663 (1966).

121 *See* Shapiro v. Thompson, 394 U.S. 618 (1969).

122 *See, e.g.,* Ake v. Oklahoma, 470 U.S. 68 (1985).

123 *See, e.g.,* Cleburne v. Cleburne Living Center Inc., 473 U.S. 432 (1985) (rights of the mentally retarded).

124 Although the substantive due process cases decided in the first third of this century primarily involved freedom of contract, a few cases did implicate what today would be called personal rights. In *Pierce v. Society of Sisters,* 268 U.S. 510 (1925), the Court guaranteed a right to send one's children to parochial school. *Meyer v. Nebraska,* 262 U.S. 390 (1923), struck down a state law that prohibited teaching German to public school children. While these cases could today rest on First Amendment grounds, the Court that decided them utilized substantive due process analysis. *See* G. Gunther, Constitutional Law 502-03 (11th ed. 1985).

125 *See* G. Gunther, *supra* note 124, at 514.

126 For example, *Griswold v. Connecticut,* 381 U.S. 479 (1965), included several concurring opinions that explicitly engaged in substantive due process analysis.

127 410 U.S. 113 (1973).

128 *See* J. Nowak, R. Rotunda & J. Young, *supra* note 88, at 697-711.

129 109 U.S. 3040 (1989).

130 For cases involving the family, see N. Redlich, B. Schwartz & J. Attanasio, *supra* note 17, at 523-33.

131 Bowers v. Hardwick, 478 U.S. 186 (1986).

132 *See* N. Redlich, B. Schwartz & J. Attanasio, *supra* note 17, at 488-89.

133 *See id.* at 489-90.

134 *See supra* text accompanying notes 70-74.

135 *See* Hawaii Hous. Auth. v. Midkiff, 467 U.S. 229 (1984).

136 *See* Andrus v. Allard, 444 U.S. 51 (1979); Ruckelshaus v. Monsanto Co., 467 U.S. 986 (1984).

137 *See, e.g.,* Keystone Bituminous Coal Ass'n v. De Bendictis, 480 U.S. 470 (1987) (surface support requirement that a certain amount of coal not be mined); Penn Central Trans. Co. v. New York City, 438 U.S. 104 (1978) (restricting development of an historic landmark); Duquense Light Co. v. Barasch, – U.S. –, 109 S. Ct. 609 (1989) (utility rate regulations).

138 *See, e.g.,* Nollan v. California Coastal Comm'n, 483 U.S. 825 (1987) (conditioning a building permit on a easement constitutes a taking); First English Evangelical Lutheran Church of Glendale v. County of Los Angeles, 482 U.S. 304 (1987) (requiring compensation for a temporary taking).

139 *See, e.g.,* cases cited at note 136 *supra. See also* Pennell v. City of San Jose, 458 U.S. 1 (1988) (rejecting a challenge of rent control law partly on ripeness grounds).

140 U.S. CONSTI. art. I, § 10, cl. 1.

141 *See* United States Trust Co. v. New Jersey, 431 U.S. 1 (1977); Allied Structural Steel v. Spannaus, 438 U.S. 234 (1978).

142 *See* Energy Reserves Group, Inc. v. Kansas Power and Light Co., 459 U.S. 400 (1983); Exxon Corp. v. Eagerton, 462 U.S. 176 (1983).

143 Shapiro v. Thompson, 394 U.S. 618 (1969).

144 *See supra* text accompanying notes 119-23.

145 Harper v. Virginia St. Bd. of Elections, 383 U.S. 663 (1966) (invalidating poll tax).

146 Shapiro, *supra* note 143.

147 *See, e.g.,* Ake v. Oklahoma, 470 U.S. 68 (1985) (indigent defendant right to free psychological examination).

148 *See, e.g.,* Snaidach v. Family Finance Corp., 395 U.S. 337 (1969) (garnishment of wages); Fuentes v. Shevin, 407 U.S. 67 (1972) (seizure of stove and stereo pending suit on installment sales contract).

149 Goldberg v. Kelly, 397 U.S. 254 (1970).

150 Matthews v. Eldridge, 424 U.S. 319 (1976).

151 Cleveland Bd. of Educ. v. Loudermill, 470 U.S. 532 (1985).

152 *See* R. Batra, The Great Depression of 1990, 118 (1987).

153 Goldstein, *The End of the American Dream?*, 236 INDUSTRY WEEK 76, 80 (Apr. 14, 1988).

154 *See generally* J. Keynes, The Economic Consequences of the Peace 18-22 (1919), noted in J. RAWLS, A THEORY OF JUSTICE 298-99 (1971).

155 In 1929, 36.3 % of America's wealth was concentrated in 1 % of the population. R. Batra, *supra* note 152, at 118. In 1969, only 24.9 % of the wealth was so concentrated and in 1973 approximately 27 % of the wealth was so concentrated. *Id.*; Goldstein, *supra* note 153, at 80. By 1983, 34.3 % of America's wealth was concentrated in 1 % of the population. R. Batra, *supra*, at 118. By 1987, the figure approached 36 %. Goldstein, *supra*, at 80.

156 *See, e.g.*, J. Rawls, *supra* note 154, at 298-303.
157 *See, e.g.*, Goldstein, *supra* note 153; Gordon, *The Myth of Upward Mobility*, Washington Post, Jun. 14, 1987, at H3.
158 *See* J. Rawls, Liberty, Equality, and the Law (1987); Dorsen & Gora, *Free Speech, Property and the Burger Court: Old Values, New Balances*, 1982 SUP. CT. REV. 195; *see also* Fiss, *Free Speech and Social Structure*, 71 IOWA L. REV. 1405 (1986).
159 *See, e.g.*, J. Rawls, *supra* note 154.
160 424 U.S. 1 (1976).
161 *See, e.g.*, Dorsen & Gora, *supra* note 158. *See also* Farber & Nowak, *The Misleading Nature of Public Forum Analysis: Content and Context in First Amendment Adjudication*, 70 VA. L. REV. 1219 (1984).
162 460 U.S. 37 (1983).
163 466 U.S. 789 (1984).
164 468 U.S. 288 (1984).
165 Hudgens v. N.L.R.B., 424 U.S. 507 (1976).
166 C.B.S. v. Democratic National Committee, 412 U.S. 94 (1973).
167 *See* Attanasio, *supra*, note 104, at 515-17; Jackson & Jefferies, *Commercial Speech: Economic Due Process and the First Amendment*, 65 VA. L. REV. 1, 14-18 (1979). Of late, the Court has in some degree relaxed protection for commercial speech. *See* Board of Trustees of the State University of New York v. Fox, U.S. , 109 S. Ct. 3028 (1989); Posadas de Puerto Rico Associates v. Tourism CO., 478 U.S. 328 (1986).
168 First Nat'l Bank v. Bellotti, 435 U.S. 765 (1978).
169 *See generally id.* at 807 (White, J., dissenting).
170 *See* Goldstein, *supra* note 153, at 80.
171 *See* R. Batra, *supra* note 152, at 118. Similarly, wealth was comparatively concentrated in 1922 at 31.6 %.
172 *See id.* at 105-25 (claiming that extreme concentrations of wealth cause economic depressions).

Fritz Ossenbühl

Economic and Occupational Rights

I. *Principles*

1. *Economic Constitution and Economic Freedoms*

German Public Law has made repeated attempts to combine the economic freedoms of the Basic Law in order to achieve an overall fundamental decision in favor of an economic constitution rooted in constitutional law.[1] From the outset the Federal Constitutional Court has opposed this on the basis of the »economic neutrality of the Basic Law.«[2] As is often the case, the truth lies somewhere in between. On the one hand, it is indeed ahistoric to wish to derive from basic rights fundamental system decisions of the constitution for individual areas. Basic rights are the results of historic struggles against threats to the individual, often varying from nation to nation, and have arisen separately one by one. This is also true of the various elements and aspects of the freedoms of business and commercial trade. On the other hand, the Basic Law guarantees both the protection of free earnings and the protection of what is earned.[3] Consequently, the master plan of a competitive economy has come about as a result of a variety of guarantees of basic rights, albeit from different sources in history and intellectual history, and as such is certainly conceivable in many variations. Irrespective of the legislator's freedom to shape the economy, the essence is probably conveyed by the Federal Constitutional Court's observation that »the existing economic constitution contains as one of its basic principles the fundamentally free competition of entrepreneurs entering the market place as supplier and buyer.«[4] The economic freedoms of the Basic Law do not constitute a developed economic constitution, but mold the economic system.[5] Although they are, like all basic rights, based primarily on the protection of the individual, they also have crucial repercussions on the structure and functional efficiency of the entire economic system.

251

2. Constitutional Position of the Freedom of the Entrepreneur

In the opinion of the organizers of the Constitutional Council, the basic rights of professional and economic activity were not to be represented in their entirety, but should be concentrated under the heading of freedom of the entrepreneur and enterprise.

The Basic Law does not contain a basic right which expressly and specifically guarantees the »freedom of the entrepreneur.«[6] Rather, the different forms and contents of business activities are covered thematically by several guarantees of basic rights which are independent of one another.[7] The main ones are freedom of trade and freedom of occupation as provided by Article 12 (1) and the guarantee of ownership as provided by Article 14 (1). The freedom of trade and freedom of occupation protect business initiative (freedom of will and disposal), while the guarantee of ownership protects the existence of the enterprise (trading firm) as the material basis of commerce. The specific basic right of freedom to move (Article 11 [1]) ensures the free choice of a business location in the Federal Republic. The basic right of freedom of association (Article 9 [1]) guarantees the right to form trading and limited companies and company amalgamations (groups, holding companies).[8] Finally, the guarantee of general freedom of action (Article 2 [1]) also protects freedom in commercial trade and the freedom of contracts, if they are not already covered by special basic rights provisions.[9] The question of who may have the aforementioned basic rights guaranteeing economic freedom can be answered in a variety of ways. Some basic rights (freedom of occupation, freedom of association, freedom of movement) are only granted to Germans, whereas in the case of freedom of ownership and general freedom of action, foreigners are also included under the protection of the basic right. Foreigners are not entitled to freedom of occupation, freedom of association and freedom of movement; nor may these freedoms be granted to them through the circuitous route of the »catch-all basic right« of Article 2 (1) of the Basic Law (general freedom of action).[10]

Both natural and legal persons are entitled to economic freedoms, insofar as they are applicable by their nature to the latter (Article 19 [3]). The latter not only enjoy freedom of movement[11] and the constitutional protection of property, but they also have the right to form associations[12] and practice a trade, insofar as the nature of the activity allows it to be practiced in the same way by a legal or natural person.[13]

Foreign legal persons are not entitled to basic rights protection (Article 19, [3]).[14]

252

II. The Federal Constitutional Court's Conception of Basic Rights

Essentially the Federal Constitutional Court does not monitor laws in terms of basic rights using the model of subsumption, which may be modeled on fairly clearly outlined premises. Rather, the basic rights guarantees of the Basic Law often provide only a vague concept which in turn must be defined more precisely[15] and can offer no more than criteria for a plausibility check, which is based on the sound findings and judgments of legislative facts.[16] Before this is illustrated by concrete examples, it is absolutely essential to establish which argument the Federal Constitutional Court uses in its jurisprudence.

1. The Basic Right of Freedom of Occupation as Provided by Article 12 (1) of the Basic Law as a Specimen Case

The basic right of freedom of occupation as provided by Article 12 (1) may serve as a specimen case in this respect. It is more or less the main basic right of free economic activity. The jurisprudence on this basic right[17] is therefore particularly extensive, varied, equivocal, and informative. It contains all the important forms of thought, principles of interpretation, topoi of argument, and methods of weighing the pros and cons, which are also used for the other basic rights, in particular for the second mainstay of economic freedom, namely the basic right of ownership. These include in particular a basic personal view of freedom rights, the graduated weighing of freedom rights against public welfare interests, the social benefit of basic rights, the dominant role of the principle of relativity in assessing interference with basic rights, and the importance of the freedom of the democratic legislator who shapes the area of economic matters. All these elements and components in arriving at the law are combined in a scheme of argumentation which serves to give constitutional monitoring of government decisions, namely of laws, the rationality required for jurisprudence.

2. Article 12 (1) of the Basic Law as »Basic Right of Small Firms«

a) In the basic pharmacy judgment of 1958, the Federal Constitutional Court stressed the freedom of occupation as a key basic right for ensuring the personal development of the individual. It summed up this emphasis by

253

saying, with a note of pathos, »that the basic right [thus] gains in importance for all social strata; work as an ›occupation‹ has the same value and rank for everyone«.[18] This »personal principle« of freedom of occupation, stressed from the outset, has been emphasized again and again in later decisions.[19] »In name, the personal basic right doctrine of the Federal Constitutional Court points to the ideas of freedom in German idealism, and in subject matter it entertains an opening up, in terms of social welfare, of economic basic rights as opposed to legislative determination.«[20]

b) The social welfare orientation of the freedom of occupation, applied in the »individual-right approach,«[21] has, however, had virtually no effect in practice. Efforts to bring into effect and develop Article 12 (1) as a »basic right of the employee« too[22] have also not found expression in the jurisprudence of the Federal Constitutional Court[23]. However, the reason for this is found not in the Court's indifference towards paid work, but in the logic of the legal construction of the basic right guarantee and its sanctioning, which primarily develops its direction of defense against the state, if need be indirectly against fellow citizens, and specifically against the employer.[24]

c) In the practice of jurisprudence, the basic right of the freedom of occupation has remained primarily a »basic right of the small firm.«[25] This is not a criticism, because the Court does not select the cases and conflicts which it decides. However, the majority of cases decided by the Federal Constitutional Court involve government regulations and interventions in the area of »medium-sized firms« and the so-called liberal professions (e.g. doctors, pharmacists, naturopaths, lawyers, accountants, tax consultants, test engineers for architectural statics and architects).[26] Large firms (e.g. petroleum importers, firms with over 2,000 employees, department stores, large bakeries, bread factories, tobacco producers, and large mills) have hitherto used jurisprudence less. Under these circumstances, it is quite natural that the major guiding decisions of the Federal Constitutional Court involve primarily conflicts in the small-firm sector.[27]

3. The Problems of the »Intervention« Perspective

A description of economic freedoms with the aid of the jurisprudence of the Federal Constitutional Court inevitably suffers from a certain bias and distortion, indeed from a lack of reality. The reason for this can be found in the system of basic rights protection. The Federal Constitutional Court adjudicates only on interferences with basic rights which are brought to the court. Hence, only a section of reality is represented, one moreover which concerns only the areas of conflict, the »pathology of state power.« All laws which restrict freedom and regulate activities, but are not even brought before the court because of expediency, resignation or other reasons, remain unnoticed. Those countless laws and ordinances,[28] which in their passion for regulation satisfy the German yearning for a professional career, a preordained job description, a state examination, and subsequent awarding of a title, also remain unnoticed. However, it cannot be expected that an outline of the basic rights conception of the Federal Constitutional Court should also give a comprehensive picture of the complete reality of economic freedom.

Moreover, because of the one-dimensional approach of the basic rights conflict applied to it, the »intervention« perspective often offers only a problem-curtailing and therefore distorting picture. Over the years, German administrative law has developed a distinct conception of the administrative act with third-party effect, which favors one and penalizes another.[29] By contrast, although the ambivalence of legislative acts which interfere with economic freedoms is recognized, it has remained undeveloped inconceptional terms. It is clear that the problems of the special position of economic freedoms can hardly be conveyed in full with the customary ideas on the third-party effect of basic rights. The basic right of the freedom of occupation, unlike any other basic right, is entwined in communicative relationships with the present society based on division of labor.[30] For example, the regulation of shop opening times may be considered not only from the aspect of state intervention in the freedom of the trader to choose an occupation, but also, the rights of the worker, and particularly the position of the buyer and consumer – that is, the population as a whole – which in Germany is virtually ignored, are fundamentally affected. In reality, the one-dimensional, state/trader intervention affects the polygonal relationship between state, trader, worker, and buyer. Each would like his interests to be taken into account and to exercise his (basic) right, but that is not enough. Shop opening regulations, discount laws, self-service bans, advertising bans, and other regulations have an ambivalent effect within the same sector of the economy or between different sectors. Frequently, they consciously serve to »protect the small firm« from competition from large firms[31] or »protect a sector« from undesirable or unfair competition.[32] The State carries all this out under the banner of protection of public welfare. This is certainly correct, but the fact that economic freedoms are not (only) unilaterally restricted by the state, but are »measured out,« »apportioned on a restricted basis« to promote public welfare, should not be ignored. The state protects freedoms by distributing them »fairly.« The closer people live and work together, the less freedom there is and the more freedom becomes a problem of distribution and the more the liberal idea of freedom must submit to and open up to change from a welfare state point of view.

4. The Scheme of Argumentation of the Federal Constitutional Court

The Federal Constitutional Court developed a scheme of argumentation in the aforementioned basic pharmacy judgment of 1958 for the application of the basic right of freedom of occupation as provided by Article 12 (1) of the Basic Law. According to this scheme, the freedom of occupation and the public welfare are brought into a relationship with one another by a graduated and sophisticated system of consideration of the degree of intervention and the ranking of community interests to be protected (the so-called three-stage theory).[33] The essence of this scheme is still retained today, although individual points have been improved.[34]

Using the scheme and the text of Article 12 (1)[35] as a basis, the Court distinguishes between three different stages of regulation of the (standard) basic right of the freedom of occupation:[36] stage 1 deals with the practice of one's occupation; stage 2 deals with the choice of an occupation and terms of admission to that occupation (e.g. age, knowledge); and stage 3 deals with occupational choice and the practical terms of admission (e.g. monopolization of activities by the state, numerus clausus). Interference with freedom of occupation must comply with the principle of relativity. It may only occur at stages 2 and 3 if the regulations at stage 1 (regulations concerning the practice of an occupation) are not sufficient to achieve the purposes of the public welfare sought by the intervention. The requirements for justification of interference in freedom of occupation become more stringent from stage to stage. Interference in the practice of an occupation (stage 1) is justified if it is supported by »reasonable grounds based on the public welfare.« It is not difficult to find such grounds. Hence it is difficult to attack the regulations of the practice of an occupation from the point of view of Article 12 (1). The terms of admission of an individual for choice of occupation must be justified by »particularly important (paramount, high-value) community goods.« Practical terms of admission to an occupation, which are external to the person of the applicant and which he cannot personally meet, are only admissible for »protection against ascertainable and serious dangers for a community good of paramount importance.«

The above scheme of argumentation reflects only some of the text of Article 12 (1). After having proved its worth in current decision-making[37] for 30 years, it has established itself as a great praetorian achievement of the Federal Constitutional Court, which has improved legally on the barren text of Article 12 (1) of the Basic Law by creating an applicable constitutional monitoring yardstick. Nevertheless, the three-stage doctrine also has weaknesses. One must be aware of these weaknesses in order to understand the value and limitations of the three-stage theory as a monitoring system.

5. »Switchinq Points« and »Weak Points« of the Three-Stage Theory

As in any legal deduction, the three-stage theory contains »switching points,« (*i.e.* Elements which set the terms under which decisions are to be taken.) It also contains »weak points,« elements in which the legal argument loses rational verifiability and slides into political judgments and voluntary decisions. Some »switching points« also are simultaneously »weak points.«

a) The Stage Qualification

The admissibility of a regulation on occupation is prejudiced by the stage qualification, because the establishment of the intervention stage is a determining factor in the strength and importance of the grounds for justification which must support the intervention. However, considerable difficulties arise here, which result from the fact that the practice of an occupation (stage 1) and the choice of an occupation (stages 2 and 3) cannot always be clearly delineated. Regulations of a practice may, because of their actual effects, achieve a degree of intervention which intrudes upon the choice of an occupation.[38] In such a case, the intervention can no longer be justified by any reasonable consideration of public welfare, but only with interests of public welfare which carry so much weight that they have precedence over the freedom of occupation of the entrepreneurs.

A far more serious problem is the prejudicing of the stage qualification by the setting of so-called job descriptions and the delimitation of occupations. Traditionally, distinct occupations as well as atypical activities are protected per se by the freedom of occupation.[39] However, the practice of an occupation and the choice of occupation may only be differentiated if there is a fixed concept of the particular occupation. If »worker leasing in the building trade« is not an independent occupation, but only part of the more comprehensive occupation of »worker leasing,« the ban on »worker leasing in the building trade« does not affect the choice of an occupation,[40] but only the practice of an occupation, with the result that this ban may be justified relatively easily.

Accordingly, the legislator may narrow down the free choice of an occupation by setting job descriptions.[41] The extent of the legislator's power to define jobs is a much debated question.[42]

b) Legitimizing Interests of Public Welfare

In order to justify interference in the free choice of an occupation, the legislator's regulation of an occupation must aim to protect qualified »community goods.«[43] These »community goods« may be used as constitutional decision-making criteria only if they can be established in the Basic Law. However, this is not the case in the jurisprudence of the Federal Constitutional Court.[44] In practice, the Court only examines the plausibility of the legislator's motives, without seeking textual support in the Basic Law. Some »community goods« are considered so abstract and are formulated in such a way that it is virtually impossible to explain them rationally by the legislative intervention at issue. Examples of legitimizing grounds are maintenance of a high standard of performance of craft work,[45] protection against health-damaging nightwork,[46] security of energy supply,[47] security of food for the nation,[48] maintenance of efficient national wine growing,[49] protection of the population and its rights,[50] security of financial stability of the providers of social insurance,[51] security of an ordered labor market and a stable labor and social insurance situation of dependent workers,[52] health of the people,[53] the fastest and most reliable recovery of the insured,[54] maintenance of an efficient tax law system,[55] security of financial stability of the statutory health insurance,[56] and protection of wild animals,[57] particularly those threatened with extinction.

c) Weighing of pros and cons

The three-stage theory is no more than a scheme of argumentation. The reference points of this scheme and the decision-making criteria are vague. Furthermore, there are no precise yardsticks for using the relativity principle to weigh the pros and cons of interference in the freedom of occupation against the purpose pursued by the legislator. This lack of a reliable legal method is at least to some extent compensated for by a form of argument which is heavily oriented towards tradition, convention and custom and is based on legislative facts which have to be explained more thoroughly and carefully. In this way, the tightrope walk of constitutional jurisdiction between law and politics is achieved.

III. *Individual Areas of the Protection of the Freedom of the Entrepreneur and the Possibilities of Restricting Them*

1. *Freedom to Establish an Enterprise and Freedom to Enter the Market Place*

a) *Principle*

In principle, Article 12 (1) also protects »freedom of the entrepreneur« in the sense of free establishment and management of enterprises.[58] In principle, there is no difference here between small- and medium-sized firms on the one hand and large firms and groups on the other. However, the individual-right component of freedom of occupation in the case of large firms is to a great extent lost. The social benefit and social function of the freedom of the entrepreneur stands out clearly in large firms. This is important to the extent of the legislator's power of regulation.[59]

b) *Practical Barriers to Entry*

Practical barriers to entry with the effect of a total block on an occupation are rare. Frequently, practical terms of admission also do not constitute impenetrable barriers, but only hurdles which are difficult to overcome.

aa) An absolute barrier to an occupation is triggered by a state-ordered monopoly, which may occur in various forms.[60] A monopoly of this type declared permissible by the Federal Constitutional Court exists in the area of recruitment of workers, and, to be precise, not only for the »recruitment of the traditional and average worker,« but also for the »management staff of industry.«[61] However, the Court has declared the extension of the monopoly to worker leasing agreements (staff leasing) to be unconstitutional.[62] The Federal Constitutional Court finds it difficult to justify as constitutional that conventional building insurance monopoly maintained in some states.[63] As early as 1871, the transport monopoly of the Deutsche Bundespost (German Federal Post Office) ceased to include conveyance of parcels.[64] The state telecommunications monopoly has recently been restricted by law to a network monopoly and a telephone service monopoly.[65] The remaining telecommunications services have been opened to the market. The prevailing opinion in the academic world and jurisprudence is to regard monopolies in the industrial sector with an altogether critical eye.

bb)   By contrast, protection of the freedom of the entrepreneur against the *competitive economy of the state* is virtually ineffective.[66] »Article 12 (1) does not protect against competition, not even against the competition of the public authorities; the Basic Law does not guarantee private industry exclusivity of economic trade.«[67] However, »intervention by competition« by the authorities is conceivable,[68] because even the »nationalized firm is not a firm, but the state.«[69] Not only is »destruction competition,« by means of which the state creates an actual monopoly by excluding private industry,[70] a contravention of basic rights, but also state »supplantation competition,« where typically whole groups of occupations are expelled from the market without a legitimizing public purpose.[71]

cc)   The state frequently steers the economy by examining the requirements for individual sectors and providing for quota restrictions. This is particularly true of passenger transportation and long-distance goods haulage. Approval of a regular transport service in commercial passenger transportation depends on the existence of a corresponding transportation requirement. Such an examination of requirements is intended to ensure »the reliable and permanent functioning of this transportation« both »for government policy and for economic and social policy reasons«.[72] It is hence justified vis-a-vis Article 12 (1) of the Basic Law. This protection against competition is the legitimizing ground for establishing maximum figures (quota restrictions) in the transportation of goods, because the »functional efficiency and profitability of the Deutsche Bundesbahn« is a »community good of paramount importance.«[73] The Mill Law of 1957 laid down a barrier to entry limited in time by banning the further establishment of mills.[74] The purpose of the ban was to reduce a structural surplus capacity in order to prevent a concentration of large mills in a few locations, in the interests of security of supply even in times of crisis and war. In the much-quoted pharmacy judgment of 1957,[75] the Federal Constitutional Court rejected a necessity test as unconstitutional. Its prognosis at the time – that the dangers to public health of which the

260

government complained at the time did not exist - proved to be correct.[76] On the same lines there are even earlier judgments by the Federal Constitutional Court examining the requirements laid down in the law on restaurant businesses.[77]

c) Terms of Admission for the Individual

Terms of admission for the individual (*e.g.*, knowledge, reliability, minimum or maximum age, credit worthiness, or assets) are rooted in the individual sphere of life and risk of the entrepreneur.[78] It is noteworthy that regulation of terms of admission for the individual constitutes an element of the legal regulation of a job description which in its turn is set by the legislator.[79] In the words of the Federal Constitutional Court, those community values »which arise only from special economic, communal and social conceptions and aims of the legislator« may also be protected by terms of admission for the individual.[80] In this manner, the legislator himself lays down in advance the examination criteria (»protection of community goods« as a ground for legitimizing interference in freedom of occupation), which are used as a constitutional yardstick for verifying laws.

It is the monitored legislation and not only any longer the Basic Law that determines the extent and result of the check by the Federal Constitutional Court. This much-criticized[81] consequence has resulted in much debated decisions. For instance, the Federal Constitutional Court regards as constitutionally acceptable the »high level of proof of ability« in craft work provided by law (requirement of the master's diploma), because it serves to »maintain the standard of performance and efficiency of craft work and to ensure that there are new recruits for the commercial economy as a whole.«[82] However, the Court declared unconstitutional the statutory proof of knowledge for the retail trade, because it was intended »primarily to serve the interests of the occupation itself, maintenance of its efficiency and its social status.«[83] It is difficult to understand why craft work should be protected and retail not. In the final analysis, the »old legal tradition« of craft work has played a decisive role in maintaining the master's diploma.[84]

d) Protection of Confidence

Statutory interference in the freedom of an occupation affects those already gainfully employed more than those who are only about to start on a particular economic activity (job candidates). Hence, the legislator is obliged to introduce an appropriate transition regulation because of the

261

constitutional principle of relativity and from the point of view of protection of confidence.[85]

2. Freedom of Organization of the Entrepreneur

A component of freedom of the entrepreneur is freedom of organization.[86] It gains special importance in so far as the organization of an enterprise is at least a determining, if not a crucial, factor in its economic success.

a) Company Name and Choice of Location

The entrepreneur gives the enterprise its name, which provides the enterprise with its identity and is an important advertising medium. A component of the personal right guaranteed in Article 2 (1) in conjunction with Article 1 (1) of the Basic Law is the power to practice a commercial activity under one's own name.[87] In principle, even free choice of the location of the enterprise or trading branch falls within freedom of the entrepreneur. In some cases statutory obligations of residence are provided for the so-called liberal professions,[88] which as regulations on practice of occupation do not have a high constitutional hurdle to overcome.[89] However, it is also possible to indirectly influence the location of enterprises. For example, the aforementioned 1957 ban on the establishment and extension of mills was intended to prevent the concentration of large mills in a few locations.[90]

b) Form of Organization of the Enterprise

There is no »law on a specific internal organization of an enterprise.«[91] The legislator may standardize the forms of organization.[92] However, the freedom of the entrepreneur directs and limits his power of standardization. The forms of enterprise must allow entrepreneurial trade sufficient space to develop.
Within the forms of enterprise available, there exists the freedom to amalgamate enterprises (groups, holding companies) and the choice of a »group-independent«, or »small-firm« form of enterprise.[93] The group is also entitled to the freedom of the entrepreneur. »The entrepreneurial freedom of group management includes accordingly the fact that it may determine the structure of the group, give it its organization and hence ordain the field of its economic activity in accordance with its plans.«[94]

262

As far as the so-called liberal professions are concerned, restrictions of freedom of organization result in particular from partnership bans.[95]

c) *Formation and Composition of the Enterprise's Executive Bodies*

The internal constitution of enterprises, in particular the determination of number, structure and staff of executive bodies which make the crucial decisions of the enterprise, is of special importance. This problem played a central role in the codetermination judgment of the Federal Constitutional Court.[96] The constitutional admissibility of supervisory boards with an equal number of employers and managers within large firms is regarded from the point of view of freedom of occupation (Article 12 [1]) and the guarantee of ownership (Article 14 [1]). It was declared admissible in the codetermination judgment because the decision-making mechanism to be judged and to which the codetermination was subject found slight advantages on the employer's side. The Court stressed that the shareholders must not lose »control over selection of the management in the enterprise« and must retain »the right of ultimate decision.«[97]

It is also conceivable that the particular image of the profession influences the composition of the executive bodies of the enterprise.[98]

d) *Centralization and Decentralization*

The enterprise organization must be able to find a happy medium between centralization and decentralization. This is also an essential element of freedom of the entrepreneur. Hence, special taxation of branches (subsidiaries) of an enterprise is not permissible in principle, even if the underlying thought of »protection of the small firm« may be legitimate *per se.*[99] On the other hand, the special taxation of interworks long-distance traffic[100] has been justified as an economy-controlling measure using the argument that it is necessary to »protect the whole traffic system.«[101]

3. *Freedom of the Management of an Enterprise*

Freedom of the entrepreneur also includes freedom to manage and develop the freely established and organized enterprise using his own ideas, plans, assessments, and decisions. In this respect, mention should be made of the following freedoms:

a)   Freedom of Disposal

The main elements of the freedom of disposal are free economic planning, staffing policy and disposal of operating resources. In this respect, from a constitutional viewpoint, statutory restrictions on the power to dispose of operating resources, and staff in particular, have played a part.[102] A considerable part of social policy, control of the economy and the redistribution associated with both policies is not accomplished by the state budget, but is realized by statutory appropriations of benefits and corresponding penalties directly among employers and employees,[103] among the various sectors of the economy[104] or among »rich« and »poor« firms.[105] These redistribution actions are generally associated with interference in the enterprise management of a more or less large group of enterprises. This is true in the area of labor deployment as regards the statutory granting of an annual training break for employees of 5 days.[106] However, the resulting penalization of entrepreneurs is probably rather marginal compared with other commitments (*e.g.,* protection against employee dismissal) which neverless have not yet become part of the constitutional process. On the other hand, the jurisprudence offers a rich and colorful picture concerning economy-controlling taxes and special levies.[107] They fall under a consideration of freedom of the entrepreneur because not only selective statutory interventions but also indirect actual effects of laws on basic rights are measured.

Another type of commitment of operating resources is the commissioning of the enterprise by the state, such as its engagement in the process of tax collection[108] or the imposition of stockpiling obligations to secure the national energy supply.[109] In both cases, government regulation trims the power of the enterprise to dispose of the labor input, and particularly the capital input. Since such regulations involve the practice of on occupation, the degree of justification is not high.

b)   Freedom of Production

Freedom of production may be curtailed by bans on production, restrictions on production or production requirements. Production bans are issued only rarely as so-called repressive bans, whose intent is usually to suppress behavior which is harmful to society.[110] More often they entail preventive bans which place a specific economic activity under the proviso of state approval, in order to control the economy and occupation by granting permits and to prevent dangers.[111] Restrictions of production in time serve *inter alia* to protect the health of the employee[112] and other public interests, such as transportation requirements.[113] The function of practical production restrictions in the form of upper limits (quota restrictions),[114] maximum numbers in long-distance goods haulage,[115] minimum stocks of certain operating resources,[116] production ceilings,[117] etc., is to control the economy and relieve the state. Production requirements in the areas of industrial safety, protection of the environment and health, as well as of technical safety, which exist on the basis of production standards by means of pragmatic and action-related obligations for the entrepreneur, are widespread in statute law, but hardly appear in constitutional law.

c) *Freedom of Investment and Development*

Freedom of investment can be restricted by compulsion to invest[118] and by bans on investment.[119] Both occur, but rarely.[120] Freedom of development concerns free decision on the future shape of the enterprise. It may, in the sense of freedom of growth,[121] be directed towards internal and external extension or amalgamation with other enterprises, but also may involve the freedom to concentrate groups, »to make oneself smaller,« and »healthily to shrink« the firm (freedom to shrink). Freedom of development is a subject of freedom of occupation (Article 12 [1]), of the guarantee of ownership (Article 14 [1]) and of freedom of association (Article 9 [1]).[122] Freedom of growth may be narrowed from the outset by the job description defined by law[123] and may be subject to restrictions limited in time[124] as a result of structural policy considerations. It finds its absolute upper limit in the legislation on cartel law. On the other hand, the freedom to shrink comes up against social policy hurdles (security of jobs, interim and compensation payments for laid-off workers).[125]

4. *Freedom of Market Activity*

a) *Freedom of Price*

Free pricing as an essential catalyst for the market economy may be restricted by government price setting and price controls.[126] Price changes in the energy sector, the transportation sector and certain liberal professions are particularly subject to compulsory government approval. The general provisions of the price laws serve only to protect against abuse. They may not be used for purposes of control.[127] However, the obligation of price marking does not serve to protect against serious interferences threatening the overall pricing situation, but is there for a purpose »which the normal situation of price shaping determined by the functions of the market and competition already provides.«[128]

Compulsory price marking, price setting and price regulation may be constitutionally significant from the point of view of freedom of occupation (Article 12 [1]),[129] the guarantee of ownership (Article 14 [1]),[130] the general freedom of action (Article 2 [1]),[131] and of the general clause on equality Article 3 [1]).[132] Generally they contain permissible regulations of the practice of an occupation and ownership commitments.[133]

b) *Freedom to Market and Sell*

Effective forms of marketing and efficient selling methods are essential for the success of an enterprise. In this respect it may be necessary to ban certain forms of marketing or to block certain methods of selling in order to protect important community goods. The existing jurisprudence on this subject is not extensive. It mainly relates to the mail-order business and marketing of drugs. Drugs for human medicine are subject to the pharmacy monopoly. Marketing is not allowed by traveling salesmen, yet veterinary drugs may be marketed by soliciting orders from forestry and agricultural businesses.[134] For the purposes of protection of an orderly drug supply, a pharmacist may also not enter into an agreement with a particular dealer or a group of dealers.[135] Leaflets harmful to the young are not allowed in the mail-order business in order to protect the young.[136] On the other hand, the Federal Constitutional Court has declared as unconstitutional an indiscriminate ban on the dispatch of live animals to be paid for on delivery, issued for the purposes of animal protection, since it was acknowledged that it was acceptable to dispatch mealworms as invertebrates, for example, even C.O.D.[137]

c) *Freedom to Compete and Advertise*

The main feature of the market place is competition, in which advertising plays a determining role.[138] Freedom to compete and freedom to advertise are therefore central topics of constitutional jurisprudence.

In the area of competition and advertising the state has a dual task. On the one hand, it must guarantee competition by providing the framework conditions and normative regulations for fair and transparent competition; on the other hand, it must be able to eliminate in part the mechanism of

266

competition from certain areas of the economy and sectors or products for reasons of public welfare. The main task is to protect the entrepreneur in his competitive struggle from abuse of freedom of competition. This is usually achieved by cartel law regulations[139] and special regulations against dishonest competition.[140] »The freedom of economic activity must not result in individuals obtaining advantages in competition by prohibited practices.«[141]

Price marking, which is intended to promote clarity of pricing and correct pricing, serves to »intensify competition.«[142] Hence, government publication of transparency lists using price, efficiency, and quality assurance data for drugs is also allowed, but needs to be regulated through formal law.[143] From the point of view of freedom of competition, government measures which are intended to control the economy in individual cases are a problem. These include, for instance, exemptions from statutory bans for individual entrepreneurs[144] or one-sided subsidizing of a competitor which distorts the competition situation and damages the unsubsidized entrepreneur's economic position unreasonably and to an unacceptable extent.[145] General regulations on shop closing times are ambivalent. They affect enterprises differently depending on size, location and particular structure, so that, in the interests of maintaining equality of competition as provided by Article 3 (1), exemption regulations may be offered,[146] or extensions of shop closing times for large firms, not legitimized in practice, may be justified.[147]

The central constitutional position of freedom of competition lies in Article 12 (1) of the Basic Law. The behavior of the entrepreneur in competition is a part of the practice of occupation.[148] This does not mean that individual facts relevant to competition are not (also) covered by other guarantees of basic rights, such as Article 14 (1),[149] Article 2 (1)[150] and Article 3 (1) of the Basic Law (equality of competition).[151] Advertising bans also represent government restrictions of competition. These advertising bans may relate to individual products, to certain occupations or to certain advertising forms. The ban on advertising to the layman of radium-containing products is justified in the interests of protection of health.[152] There are extensive general advertising bans for doctors,[153] lawyers,[154] pharmacists[155] and tax consultants.[156] These bans are based on laws governing professional ethics which find expression in independently issued vocational regulations of professional bodies. The advertising ban for the liberal professions is justified on the basis of the consideration that it is intended to »prevent misrepresentation of the job description by use of advertising methods, as are customary in the commercial sector.«[157] The particular occupational activity should »follow the course of decency, uprightness and good manners supported by the conviction of the members of the profession.«[158] The consideration that inaccurate expectations may arise due to advertising value statements which cannot be verified and should be prevented by advertising bans seems more straightforward and plausible.[159] It seems doubtful whether the advertising ban, observed almost pedantically in practice, can be maintained so stringently.[160]

Certain forms of advertising have only occasionally been constitutionally rejected. An example is the ban on unsolicited doorstep selling of gravestones which was issued in the interests of »protection of privacy of the individual.«[161] The Federal Constitutional Court has not yet dealt with the modern problems of »junk mail« and the blocking of telefaxes with advertising information.

d) *Freedom to Contract*

Freedom to contract concerns the freedom to enter into a joint agreement with a contracting party of one's choice. In terms of subject matter, it is included in the special guarantees of freedom and is protected as an element of the freedom of occupation in Article 12 (1).[162] The exercise of the freedom of contract is therefore subject to the graduated and differentiated limits of Article 12 (1). Where freedom to contract is not covered by special basic rights, it is part of the general freedom of action as provided by Article 2 (1) of the Basic Law.[163]

5. *Protection of the Existence of an Enterprise*

a) *Freedom of Occupation and Guarantee of Ownership*

Freedom of occupation and guarantee of ownership are the two pillars of economic freedom. Freedom of occupation protects earnings while the guarantee of ownership protects what is earned.[164] This catchy formula, however, conceals the fact that freedom of occupation and guarantee of ownership are not only »related to one another in functional terms,«[165] but that the areas of protection of the two guarantees of freedom overlap in practice.[166] This is because Article 14 protects both the existence and assets of property as well as its use and disposal.[167] Hence, occupational activity and use of property may be identical, legally speaking being in a relationship of ideal competition with one another.[168] Compulsion to make costly investments restricts the entrepreneur not only in the practice of his occupation, but also in his use of property.[169] The codetermination judgment expressly acknowledges the coexistence of freedom of occupation and the guarantee of ownership, but also rejects it, often hastily and without closer examination. Whether the basic right protection of the entrepreneur is enhanced with ideal competition depends on how ownership and freedom of occupation are defined. In its codetermination judgment, the Federal Constitutional Court states that the constitutional view of codetermination from the point of view of Article 12 (1) may »in principle« not be different from the point of view of Article 14 (1).[170] The fact that this is not true is shown by the glaringly wrong decision of a preliminary examination board of the Federal Constitutional Court, in which the codetermination of employees in determining shop opening times in the retail sector is treated solely as a subject of freedom of occupation; it is declared as acceptable as a regulation of the practice of the occupation.[171] Contrary to the terms of the codetermination judgment, the applicability of Article 14 (1) is expressly rejected,[172] clearly because the problem of equality of codetermination would have come up for decision again, this time with even more clarity. All in all, it is apparent that jurisprudence must fundamentally reorient its position with respect to competition in Article 14 (1) and Article 12, (1).

b) *Bases of the Constitutional Guarantee of Ownership*

The guarantee of ownership in Article 14 (1) has microeconomic and macroeconomic system functions.[173] As a result of the »macroeconomic system function of the basic right of guarantee of ownership . . ., the principle of private ownership of production sources necessarily requires and sets an economic system which organizes the real economic process according to the structural laws of private-sector autonomy, actual competition, that is not laid down by regulative policy or theory, and decentralized self-regulation.«[174] The value judgment in favor of efficient private ownership includes a decision in favor of an economic system which recognizes as essential the individual initiative and responsibility of the entrepreneur in the market economy system.[175]

The microeconomic system function of the guarantee of ownership consists in allowing the individual as a person engaged in economic activity economically usable space. The guarantee of ownership is »an elementary basic right which is closely and intimately associated with personal freedom.«[176] It is intended to provide the individual with space in the area of property law. »The main features of the legal content of the constitutionally protected right of ownership are individual usefulness, (*i.e.,* appropriation to a legal entity in the hands of which it should be »of use« as a basis for individual initiative and in the individual's interests, for which he is solely responsible, and the power to dispose of the property which is not always clearly delimited from this use.«)[177] The guarantee of ownership is not merely a guarantee of the value of property, but also a guarantee of its existence and the legal entity. Above all, it grants the power to counter any unjustified interference with the existence of the protected goods.[178]

The Basic Law does not provide a set of individual rights; it provides a standard ownership.[179] It does not differentiate between »large« and »small« property,[180] property earned by achievement or unearned or between ownership for use, consumption or supply, ownership of land, ownership of production resources, or ownership of an enterprise, etc. The ownership protection it affords is not graded and differentiated by type of ownership; it is merely a standard ownership.[181] However, ownership restrictions varying in degree may arise from the social commitment of ownership. »The legislator has set narrow limits where the function of ownership as an element in the securing of private freedom of the individual is concerned. On the other hand, the greater the power of the legislator to determine the content and limits of property, the greater the social benefit and social function of the article of property.«[182] Consequently, degrees of ownership protection which are oriented towards the function of ownership and the social benefit arise from the social commitment.[183] In this manner, the associated structure of the constitutional monitoring of laws from the point of view of guarantee of ownership is similar to the three-stage examination in the freedom of occupation.

c) *Protected Existence of the Enterprise*

Article 14 of the Basic Law also protects ownership of an enterprise.[184] Conventionally, this is the »right to the established and operated trading firm« as a protected property right.[185] The »property and right in its entirety«[186] of the firm is guaranteed in its »substance,« (*i.e.,* the undisturbed functioning of the firm), interference with which prevents the entrepreneur from making lawful use of the organization embodied in the form of personal and material resources. Accordingly, the enterprise is protected as a functioning economic unit,[187] just as individual elements of this unit are already subject *per se* to the constitutional protection of ownership as independent rights (*e.g.* patent rights,[188] trade mark rights[189] and copyrights[190]). However, the whole is greater than the sum of its parts, which becomes immediately apparent in practice when an enterprise is not reconstructed by means of composition but is divided up in bankruptcy.[191] Only already existing assets, rights and owned articles are protected, not mere (sales and profits) opportunities, expectations or actual circumstances.[192] The entrepreneur cannot rely on the maintenance of the legal situation[193] or the existing framework.[194]

Guarantee of ownership also includes the ownership of a share in the larger firms.[195] The Federal Constitutional Court recognizes the macroeconomic system-wide functions of share ownership which are the »prerequisite for accumulation of the capital required to run a modern firm, of a differentiated organization under private law of limited companies and which are of crucial importance for the efficiency of an economic system based on decentralization and distribution of power, opportunity, risk, and supremacy.«[196] However, these »objective, legal, systemwide functions« can be compared (only) on a secondary basis with the prime importance of the guarantee of ownership as a human right. The share owner is different from the owner manager who interacts directly with his property and bears full responsibility, in that the former does not have the element of personal entrepreneurial activity. Share ownership is typically more a capital investment than a basis for entrepreneurial initiative.[197] This special nature of share ownership is crucial to the extent of legislative power in determining the content and limits of share ownership.

d) *Protection of Business and Operating Secrets*

Business and operating secrets are part of the economic basis of an enterprise. They are protected as property just like patent rights, copyrights, etc., by virtue of Article 14 (1).[198] Protection of secrecy has become virulent, particularly in the area of preventive supervision of the economy and government product controls. In the approval of drugs, licensing of technical installations, and the investigation of chemicals, the state can carry out its task of protection of health and the environment appropriately and effectively only if the entrepreneur provides all the necessary information. The disclosure of operating and business secrets necessary for this is regulated through a number of special laws and has only been fully identified as a problem in the last decade. The problem is intensified by the fact that participation of the public is provided for through a number of administrative procedures.

There is no concept for a standard solution, nor is there likely to be one. Solutions to conflicts can only be achieved in an area-specific manner and by graduated considerations in which the public interest in control of a product or plant is weighed against the basic right of protection of secrecy of the entrepreneur.[199]

IV. *General Assessment and Outlook*

The above survey of economic freedoms as reflected in the jurisprudence of the Federal Constitutional Court provides an extremely varied and colorful picture, although it cannot in any way claim to be complete. Solutions to conflicts involving basic rights are being oriented less towards catch phrases and more towards a painstaking processing of the legislative facts on which they are based. The solution grows more out of circumstances and the concrete system than out of written rules because the constitutional rules in the form of a guarantee of basic rights as a yardstick for verification and assessment are vague, often providing no more than a topos of argumentation, at best a scheme of argumentation. The problem of applicability of basic rights and the effectiveness of economic freedoms consists in the realization of the basic rights, which requires a minimum consensus on their content and, moreover, authorities which promote and guarantee their realization. The legislature and the Federal Constitutional Court have to fulfill this task of being guardian and promoter of basic rights in a variety of roles. Although basic rights should protect against state intervention in the autonomous sphere of the individual, effective guarantees of basic rights cannot be achieved without the state. This is so not only because the freedoms represented in the basic rights, and in the case of economic freedoms in particular, are threatened by fellow citizens and competitors, but also because, according to the understanding of a democratic state, it is a fundamental task of the state to ensure human freedom. Basic rights are therefore not only a limit to, but also a source and justification of the power of the state.[200] Legislation not only restricts basic rights, but also develops and realizes them. In this respect, the Federal Constitutional Court examines whether the legislature falls short of or exceeds the subject matter of the basic right. Since the content of the basic right is not defined precisely and unchangingly, legislation with respect to basic rights policy is an expression of predetermined contents of basic rights. The definition of job descriptions by the legislature which uses the »old legal tradition« as a basis and continues it in accordance with the modern requirements of

272

occupational life clearly illustrates this. Hence, interpretation and definition of the substance of basic rights is not a monopoly of the Federal Constitutional Court, but a joint task of the legislature and the Court. Both authorities fulfill this task from different points of view, using different methods. The legislature follows political opportunity; it argues politically and in some respects irrationally by absorbing society's opinions, trends and desires. The Federal Constitutional Court approaches the same problem using legal methods and is subject, in its decision-making process, to completely different conditions.[201] When reviewing a law constitutionally, two different decision-making processes are reconciled with one another and hence rationalized. The Federal Constitutional Court must in many respects give precedence to the legislature. It does this in the case of freedom of occupation, for example, by conceding and respecting job descriptions set by law or by granting the legislature room for forecasting in assessing general facts and future developments. However, in the final analysis, this is not unconditional and always depends on the case in question. The Federal Constitutional Court does not deny itself the power to correct the job description laid down by law or to reject the legislative prognosis as implausible.[202] Finally, in all matters, it reserves the right to determine the competence of the legislature.

However, its justification is not its rightfully wide and deeply based authority, but rationality, force of conviction, and the correctness of its decisions, which in turn once again justify the authority of the court. The scheme of argumentation developed for freedom of occupation, which is also used in the guarantee of ownership by virtue of its structure, has proven successful. In this respect, the Pharmacy Judgment of 1958 was purely and simply a stroke of luck for the development of jurisprudence and basic rights.[203]

It would be wrong to criticize particular decisions as unsuccessful within an overall evaluation. Two general remarks should be added. In my opinion, basic rights protection of economic freedoms is rooted too dominantly in terms of subject matter in Article 12 (1). In infringements against enterprises, the Federal Constitutional Court frequently declares very quickly and too apodictically that the protected area of guarantee of ownership is not affected. In this respect, it must be repeated that freedom of occupation and guarantee of ownership overlap in their subject matter, and jointly strengthen the protection of basic rights. Also, the third active component in economic freedoms is conceptually underdeveloped. Economic freedom is often endangered to a greater extent by unfair competition or by biased background conditions than by government

273

intervention. This is a focal point of the guaranteeing of basic rights. The state as guarantor, rather than opponent, of economic freedoms is a topic which must receive fair consideration in a free economic system.

The economic freedoms guaranteed in the Basic Law cannot be considered at present without casting a glance at developments in Europe. The legal regulations of the European Economic Community have precedence over the national law of the member states, including national constitutional law with its guarantees of basic rights. National economic law is increasingly being replaced by European Community law. The conflicts between the German legislation in economic matters and businessmen subject to German economic law will therefore of necessity decrease. Once the Federal Constitutional Court has given up its brief to assess European regulations as related to the basic rights of the Basic Law, the task of protecting basic rights in the economic field will have fallen decisively on the European Court. But the European Court has a different structure and motivation than the Federal Constitutional Court.[204] It is understood as the integrating element of European unification. Its jurisprudence is affected by this. However, the European Court must above all integrate a multiplicity of different national regulations and give expression to these in its jurisprudence. It reasons and works in different categories and schematics and with other phraseology than the Federal Constitutional Court. What will come of this, in spite of the increasing tendency to guarantee basic rights in Europe in writing,[205] remains to be seen. From the German point of view, it is possible to predict that for economic freedoms, an era of national jurisprudence is coming to an end.

Notes:

1 Cf. Hans-Jürgen Papier, »Grundgesetz und Wirtschaftsordnung« in Handbuch des Verfassungsrechts, 1983, p. 609 *et seq.;* Ulrich Karpen, Wirtschaftsordnung und Grundgesetz, 1979; Hans D. Jarass, Wirtschaftsverwaltungsrecht und Wirtschaftsverfassungsrecht, 2nd ed., 1984, p. 77 *et seq.;* Peter Badura, Grundprobleme des Wirtschaftsverfassungsrechts, JuS 1976, p. 205 *et seq.*
2 Cf. BVerfGE 4, 7 (17 and 18); 7, 377 (400); 14, 19 (23); 30, 292 (315); 50, 290 (336 and 337).
3 Cf. BVerfGE 30, 292 (335) concerning the delimitation of the areas of protection of freedom of occupation (Article 12 I of the Basic Law) and of the guarantee of ownership (Article 14 I of the Basic Law).
4 Cf. BVerfGE 32, 311 (317).

5 Cf. for example the explanations of Rupert Scholz, Entflechtung und Verfassung, 1981, p. 85 *et seq;* ditto in Maunz-Dürig-Herzog-Scholz, Grundgesetz-Kommentar Article 12 marginal note 78 *et seq.* (as of September 1981); Hans Heinrich Rupp, Grundgesetz und »Wirtschaftsverfassung«, 1974, pp. 35 and 36; Walter Leisner, Sozialbindung des Eigentümers, 1972, p. 224 *et seq.;* also Gerd Rinck-Eberhard Schwark, Wirtschaftsrecht 6th ed., 1986, marginal note 62; Breuer, »Freiheit des Berufs« in Isensee-Kirchhof (eds.), Handbuch des Staatsrechts VI 1989, p. 147, marginal notes 19 and 20 and BVerfGE 11, 168 (184).

6 The concept »freedom of the entrepreneur« is used only occasionally by the BVerfGE, e.g. BVerfGE 50, 290 (363).

7 Cf. Scholz loc. cit. (No. 5), marginal notes 123 *et seq.;* E.R. Huber, Wirtschaftsverwaltungsrecht, 2nd ed., 1953, p. 646, mentions 6 elements of »freedom of private economic activity«: freedom of trade, commercial freedom to move, commercial freedom of association, commercial freedom of ownership, commercial freedom of contract and freedom of competition.

8 Cf. Scholz *loc. cit.* (No. 5), Article 9 marginal note 39 (situation August 1979); Pieroth-Schlink, Grundrechte, Staatsrecht II 4th ed., 1988, marginal note 814; Detlef Merten, Vereinsfreiheit in Isensee-Kirchhof (eds.), Handbuch des Staatsrechts, VI, 1989, Paragraph 144 marginal note 39 et seq.

9 Cf. BVerfGE 74, 129 (151 and 152) on the matter of basic right concurrence in the area of economic freedoms. See Tettinger, Das Grundrecht der Berufsfreiheit in der Rechtsprechung des Bundesverfassungsgerichts, AöR 108 (1983), p. 92 *et seq.,* (129 *et seq.*); Breuer *op. cit.* (No. 5), marginal note 96 *et seq.*

10 Although foreigners are entitled in the same way as Germans to the basic right of general freedom of action (Article 2, Para. 1 of the Basic Law), this basic right does not entitle them to a basic right position which evens out the differences between the basic rights of Germans and the basic rights of anyone; cf. Stern, Das Staatsrecht der Bundesrepublik Deutschland III/1, 1988, pp. 1040 and 1041; Pieroth/Schlink *loc. cit.* (No. 8), marginal note 135 *et seq.;* on the basic right protection of EC foreigner; see Breuer, *loc. cit.* (No. 5), marginal note 21.

11 Cf. Dürig, in Maunz-Dürig-Herzog-Scholz, Grundgesetz, Kommentar, Article 11 marginal note 42 (situation September 1970).

12 Cf. No. 8.

13 BVerfGE 21, 261 (266); 22, 380 (383); 30, 292 (312); 50, 290 (363); 74, 129 (148 and 149).

14 See Stern *loc. cit.* (No. 10), p. 1136.

15 Cf. Hans Huber, in Gedächtnisschrift fur Imboden, 1971, p. 191 et seq.

16 Cf. Ossenbühl, »Die Kontrolle von Tatsachenfeststellungen und Prognoseentscheidungen durch das Bundesverfassungsgericht« in Bundesverfassungsgericht und Grundgesetz, 1976, p. 449 *et seq.* (483 *et seq.*).

17 Cf. the reports of Hans Heinrich Rupp, Das Grundrecht der Berufsfreiheit in der Rechtsprechung des Bundesverfassungsgerichts AöR 92 (1967), p. 212 *et seq.;* Peter J. Tettinger, AöR 108 (1983), p. 92 *et seq.;* Breuer loc. cit. (No. 5).

18 BVerfGE 7, 377 (397).

19 Particularly in BVerfGE 50, 290 (362 and 363).

20 Peter Badura, »Arbeit als Beruf (Art. 12 Abs. 1 GG)«, in Festschrift für Herschel, 1982, p. 21 *et seq.* (27).

21 BVerfGE 50, 290 (363).

22 Cf. in this regard Hans-Peter Schneider, »Artikel 12 GG Freiheit des Berufs und Grundrecht der Arbeit«, VVDStRL 43 (1985), p. 7 *et seq.* (14 *et seq.*).

23 The careful reference to freedom of occupation of the employee in the codetermination Judgment is an exception, BVerfGE 50, 290 (363).

24 Cf. Jost Pietzcker, »Artikel 12 Grundgesetz-Freiheit des Berufs und Grundrecht der Arbeit«, NVwZ 1984, 550 (554).

25 Cf. Breuer *loc. cit.* (No. 5), marginal note 29 with evidence.

26 See BVerfGE 10, 354 (364). On the concept of a liberal profession see 33, 125 (specialist doctors); 71, 162 (Doctors); 7, 377; 17, 232; 38, 373; 50, 265; 75, 166 (Pharmacists); 57, 121; 72, 26; 76, 171; 76, 196 (Lawyers); 78, 155; 78, 179 (Non-medical practitioners); 64, 72 (Test engineers); 58, 282 (Architects).

27 Cf. Ludwig Frohler-Georg Mortel, Die Berufsbildfixierung im Handwerksrecht und die Frage ihrer verfassungsrechtlichen Problematik, 1978, p. 97 *et seq.* The codetermination judgment is an example of an exception, BVerfGE 50, 290.

28 See, for instance, the 127 legal orders on job training (Deutsche Bundesrecht, as of August 1988, Survey III B 70 x a p. 1).

29 Cf. Erichsen-Martens, Allgemeines Verwaltungsrecht, 8th ed., 1988, page 214 *et seq.*

30 Cf. Breuer, *loc. cit.* (No. 5), marginal note 26 *et seq.*; Rainer Pitschas, Berufsfreiheit und Berufslenkung, 1983, p. 32 et seq.

31 BVerfGE 23, 50 (60) (Night baking ban I); 21, 292 (299) (Discount Law); 19, 101 (184) (conc.: branch tax).

32 Cf. BVerfGE 65, 237 (Protection of taxi business against car rental firms).

33 BVerfGE 7, 377.

34 Cf. Bernhard Schlink, Abwägung im Verfassungsrecht, 1976, p. 57 *et seq.*

35 Article 12, Paragraph 1 of the Basic Law reads as follows: »All Germans are entitled freely to choose their occupation, place of work and choice of education. Practice of an occupation may be regulated by law or on the basis of a law«.

36 On further differentiations see Schlink *loc. cit.* (No. 34).

37 See, for instance, Breuer *loc. cit.* (No. 5), S 148 marginal note 8; Hans-Jürgen Papier, »Art. 12 GG Freiheit des Berufs und Grundrecht der Arbeit«, DVBl, 1984, 801 (804).

38 Cf. BVerfGE 11, 30 (42 and 43); 16, 147 (167); 61, 291 (311); 77, 84 (106).

39 BVerfGE 7, 377 (397).

40 BVerfGE 77, 84 (105).

41 BVerfGE 13, 97 (98).

42 Cf. Frohler-Mortel *loc. cit.* (No. 27).

43 With regard to the qualifying of »community goods« the Federal Constitutional Court uses the following attributes for example: »especially important community good;« »prominent community good;« »high-value community good;« »good of paramount importance;« cf. BVerfGE 54, 301 (315); 75, 246 (267); 77, 84 (107).

44 Cf. Schlink *loc. cit.* (No. 34), p. 52.

45 BVerfGE 13 97 (113).

46 BVerfGE 23, 50 (57); 41, 360.

47 BVerfGE 30, 292 (323).

48 BVerfGe 25, 1 (16).

49 BVerfGE 37, 1 (22); 51, 193 (210).

50 BVerfGE 75, 246 (267).
51 BVerfGE 70, 1 (26, 30); 77, 84 (107).
52 BVerfGE 77, 84 (107).
53 BVerfGE 78, 179 (192).
54 BVerfGE 78, 155 (162).
55 BVerfGE 21, 173 (179); 54, 301 (315); 69, 209 (218).
56 BVerfGE 69, 193 (218); 70, 1 (29).
57 BVerfGE 61, 291 (312 and 313).
58 BVerfGE 50, 290 (363).
59 BVerfGE 50, 290 (363).
60 *E.g.,* as a finance monopoly (*e.g.,* spirits monopoly, ignitor goods monopoly), as an administrative monopoly (*e.g.,* finding employment, building insurance), as compulsion of connection and use vis-a-vis public companies and services (*e.g.,* with communal services), as private monopolies (*e.g.,* sweeping monopoly of the district sweep or examination monopoly of the Technical Supervision Unions).
61 BVerfGE 21, 245.
62 BVerfGE 21, 261.
63 BVerfGE 41, 205.
64 In this respect, see Peter Badura, Der Paketdienst der Deutschen Bundespost, Jahrbuch der Deutschen Bundespost 1977, p. 76 *et seq.* (102 *et seq.*).
65 Cf. Article 3, Poststrukturgesetz (Federal Law Gazette) I, 1989, 1026.
66 See Breuer *loc. cit.* (No. 5), p. 148 marginal note 57 *et seq.* and Papier *loc. cit.* (No. 1), pp. 625 and 626.
67 BVerwGE 39, 329 (336).
68 Cf. Ossenbühl, Bestand und Erweiterung des Wirkungskreises der Deutschen Bundespost, 1980, p. 118.
69 Herbert Krüger »Das Staatsunternehmen – Ort und Rolle in der Marktwirtschaft«, ZBR 1979, 157.
70 Cf. Ossenbühl *loc. cit.* (No. 68), page 117 and Papier, *loc. cit.* (No. 1), p. 626.
71 Cf. Ossenbühl *loc. cit.* (No. 68), p. 120 and 121.
72 BVerfGE 11, 168 (184); the same does not apply to casual traffic using cabs and rented vehicles (p. 185 *et seq.*).
73 BVerfGE 40, 196 (218). A further »community good« which may be mentioned is the »improvement of traffic safety« (p. 221).
74 BVerfGE 25, 1 (15).
75 BVerfGE 7, 177.
76 For an evaluation of the decisions of the Federal constitutional Court, see Klaus Jürgen Philippi, Tatsachenfeststellungen des Bundesverfassungsgerichts, 1971.
77 See BVerwGE 1, 48 (49 *et seq.*); 1, 269 (270 *et seq.*); 3, 304 (305 and 306).
78 Cf. Breuer *loc. cit.* (No. 5), p. 148 marginal note 38.
79 BVerfGE 7, 377 (406).
80 BVerfGE 13, 97 (107).
81 Cf. *e.g.,* Rupp, AöR 92 (1967), pp. 221, 234 and 235; Peter Haberle, »Gemeinwohl Judikatur« und Bundesverfassungsgericht, AöR 95 (1970), p. 86 (101 and 102); Helmut Lecheler, Art. 12 GG Freiheit des Berufs und Grundrecht der Arbeit, VVDStRL 43 (1985), p. 48 (53 and 54).
82 BVerfGE 13, 97 (107 *et seq.*).
83 BVerfGE 19, 330 (339).

84 BVerfGE 19, 330 (341). With regard to the argument on legal tradition see also BVerfGE 17, 232 (243) Also worthy of mention is BVerfGE 21, 150 (158): »Erhaltung und Sicherung eines gesunden Winzerstandes als Rechtfertigungsgrund für Anbaubeschränkungen (Maintenance and security of a healthy wine growing industry« as a ground for justifying cultivation restrictions).

85 BVerfGE 21, 173 (183) (Tax attorneys); 22, 275 (276) (Tax consultants); 25, 236 (248) (Dentists); 31, 275 (284, 289 and 290) (Copyright); 32, 1 (22 and 23) (Preliminary examinees); 36, 281 (293) (Patent law); 43, 242 (288 and 289) (Hamburg University Law); 44, 1 (21 and 22) (Illegitimacy Law); 50, 265 (274 and 275) (Pharmacist's assistant); 59, 1 (29 et seq.) (Geriatric nurses); 71, 137 (144) (Fishing lease); 75, 246 (278 and 279) (Legal adviser).

86 See Scholz loc. cit. (No. 5), Article 12, marginal note 124, 185.

87 BVerfGE 71, 183 (201) (The advertising ban for doctors does not contain any compulsion to withold the name of a doctor as an owner of a sanatorium).

88 *E.g.* for lawyers, patent attorneys.

89 See BVerfGE 65, 116 (126) (Patent attorneys). It is sufficient that the orderly business between those seeking the law and the courts and authorities with the patent attorney should be guaranteed in the interests of the legal system.

90 BVerfGE 25, 1.

91 Herbert Wiedemann, Gesellschaftsrecht, I, 1980, p. 698.

92 Cf. Breuer *loc. cit.* (No. 5), S 147 marginal note 62.

93 BVerfGE 30, 292 (312 and 313).

94 BVerfGE 14, 263 (282).

95 See BVerfGE 54, 237 (249 and 250) (Ban on partnerships between notaries and auditors); BVerfGE 60, 215 (229 and 230) (Ban on partnerships between tax consultants and persons not belonging to the profession [*e.g.,* actuaries]. The question of supralocal partnerships of lawyers is debated and controversial in practice; on this subject, *e.g.,* BGH, NJW 1981, 2477; Hanns-Christian Salger, NJW 1988, 186; Wilhelm Feuerich, Die überortliche Anwaltssozietät, AnwBl 1989, 360.

96 BVerfGE 50, 290.

97 BVerfGE 50, 290 (350).

98 See BVerfGE 21, 227 (232). A tax consultant must head and be responsible for a tax consultancy firm organized as a GmbH (limited company) or AG (public company). Tax attorneys are exempted.

99 BVerfGE 19, 101 (114 *et seq.*). The Federal Constitutional Court finds an infringement against Article 3 I of the Basic Law, because retail chains and large retail firms have not been properly differentiated and hints that this type of differentiation is probably unlikely.

100 »Interworks long-distance traffic« is any conveyance of goods for a company's own purposes outside the so-called proximity zone (50 kilometers from the location).

101 BVerfGE 16, 147; on the special taxation of goods haulage by road generally: BVerfGE 38, 61.

102 BVerfGE 22, 380 (Coupon tax deduction by the banks); BVerfGE 30, 292 (petroleum supply by petroleum importers).

103 BVerfGE 77, 308 (employee training break).

104 See BVerfGE 4, 7 (Investment aid by the commercial sector for coal mining, the iron and steel producing industry and energy supply).
105 BVerfGE 18, 315 (Equalizing levy on the dairy industry).
106 BVerfGE 77, 308.
107 Cf. BVerfGE 4, 7; 16, 147; 18, 315; 37, 1; 38, 61; 67, 256.
108 E.g. banks (BVerfGE 22, 380).
109 BVerfGE 30, 292.
110 BVerfGE 61, 291 (ban on possession, use or sale relating to protected species of dead or living birds).
111 BVerfGE 9, 83 (87 and 88) (ban on the production of medical finished products); BVerfGE 8, 71; 21, 150 (ban on wine growing), (primarily concerning guarantee of ownership as provided by Article 14, Paragraph 1 of the Basic Law); § 21 of the Medicines Law (compulsory licence); § 4 of the Chemicals Act (compulsory notification).
112 BVerfGE 22, 1 (20 and 21) (working hours system); 23, 50 (56); 41, 360 (370) (ban on night baking).
113 BVerfGE 26, 259 (263 and 264) (ban on weekend travel for trucks).
114 BVerfGE 9, 63 (70 et seq.), 40, 196 (218 et seq.).
115 BVerfGE 40, 196.
116 BVerfGE 30, 292 (312 et seq.) (petroleum supplies); 41, 334 (358) (compulsory minimum reserve of banks).
117 BVerfGE 39, 210 (225 et seq.).
118 BVerfGE 30, 292 (petroleum supplies [creation of expensive storage space]).
119 BVerfGE 25, 1 (ban on establishment and extension for mills).
120 Cf. No. 118 and 119.
121 Cf. Scholz loc. cit. (No. 5), Article 12, marginal note 186 et seq.; ditto, Entflechtung und Verfassung, 1981.
122 Cf. Scholz loc. cit. (No. 5), Article 12, marginal notes 187 and 188.
123 BVerfGE 17, 232 (241 et seq.) (ban on multiple business in pharmacy law [the legislator's example: the »pharmacist in his pharmacy«]).
124 BVerfGE 25, 1 (ban on establishment and extension for mills).
125 See §§ 111 et seq. law on enterprise constitution.
126 Cf. the survey of economic sectors having government price regulations in Rinck-Schwark loc. cit. (No. 5), marginal note 869.
127 BVerfGE 53, 1 (16 and 17) (pricing law).
128 BVerfGE 65, 248 (261).
129 BVerfGE 33, 171 (182 and 183); 47, 285 (325); 58, 283; 65, 248 (258); 68, 193 (216); 68, 237 (255); 68, 373 (378). See also Hans Peter Ipsen, Kartellrechtliche Preiskontrolle als Verfassungsfrage, 1976, p. 45, 79 et seq.
130 BVerfGE 8, 274 (330); Ipsen loc. cit. (No. 129), p. 85.
131 BVerfGE 8, 274 (328); 70, 1 (28).
132 BVerfGE 21, 292 (discrimination against department stores by § 6 of the discount law).
133 BVerfGE 8, 274 (330); on the basic right limits of price control see Ipsen loc. cit. (No. 129), p. 85 et seq.
134 BVerfGE 17, 269 (276 and 277).
135 BVerfGE 17, 232 (251).

136 BVerfGE 30, 336 (350 and 351).
137 BVerfGE 36, 47 (62).
138 See Peter Lerche, Werbung und Verfassung, 1967.
139 Law against competition restrictions (Cartel Law) in the version of 24 September 1980 (Federal Law Gazette I page 1761).
140 Law against unfair competition of 7th June 1909 (RGBl. p. 499).
141 BVerfGE 32, 311 (316).
142 BVerfGE 65, 218 (260).
143 BVerfGE 71, 183.
144 See., *e.g.,* BVerwGE 65, 167 (dispensation as provided by the shop closing law).
145 See BVerwGE 30, 191 (197 *et seq.*); 60, 154 (161); 65, 167 (174); 71, 183 (191); see also Breuer *loc cit.* (No. 5), § 148 marginal note 70 *et seq.*
146 Cf. No. 144.
147 Cf. No. 31.
148 BVerfGE 32, 311 (316).
149 Cf. BVerfGE 51, 93 (216) (Trademarks).
150 BVerfGE 17, 306 (309); 30, 191 (198); 60, 154 (159); 65, 167 (174).
151 Cf. No. 132.
152 BVerfGE 9, 213 (221 *et seq.*).
153 BVerfGE 71, 162; 71, 183.
154 BVerfGE 36, 212 (219 *et seq.*); 57, 121 (133 and 134); 6, 196 (205 *et seq.*).
155 BVerfGE 53, 96 (97 *et seq.*).
156 BVerfGE 60, 215 (229 and 230).
157 BVerfGE 33, 125 (170); 60, 215 (232); 71, 162 (173 and 174).
158 BVerfGE 60, 215 (232).
159 BVerfGE 76, 196 (208).
160 See also BVerfGE 71, 162 (198).
161 BVerfGE 32, 311.
162 See Breuer, *loc. cit.* (No. 5), § 147 marginal note 97.
163 BVerfGE 8, 274 (328); 70, 1 (28); 74, 129 (151 and 152).
164 BVerfGE 30, 292 (334 and 335).
165 BVerfGE 50, 290 (365).
166 See Breuer, *loc. cit.* (No. 5), S 147 marginal note 100 and Scholz, *loc. cit.* (No. 5), Article 12 marginal note 124.
167 See Leisner, »Eigentum« Isensee-Kirchhof, Handbuch des Staatsrechts III, 1989, § 149 marginal note 52; Rudolf Wendt, Eigentum und Gesetzgebung, 1985, p. 264, 270.
168 See Breuer, *loc. cit.* (No. 5), § 147 marginal note 100.
169 BVerfGE 30, 292 (334 and 335) is therefore already a problem. On the »dual« protection of investment freedom see also Scholz, Entflechtung und Verfassung, 1981, p. 108.
170 BVerfGE 50, 290 (365).
171 BVerfGE, NJW 1986, 1601 (Judges Simon, Heussner, and Niemeyer); more remarkably this decision against more recent practice is not documented in the official register of the Federal Constitutional Court.
172 On the subject of criticism, see Rupert Scholz, »Verdeckt Verfassungsneues zur Mitbestimmung?,« NJW 1986, 1587.

173 See Rupert Scholz, Entflechtung und Verfassung, 1981, p. 87 *et seq.* On the macroeconomic functions of share ownership, see BVerfGE 50, 290 (344).

174 Rupert Scholz, »Grenzen staatlicher Aktivität unter der grundgesetzlichen Wirtschaftsverfassung« in Duwendag (ed.), Der Staatssektor in der sozialen Marktwirtschaft, 1976, p. 113 *et seq.* (124).

175 Karl Heinrich Friauf and Rudolf Wendt, Eigentum am Unternehmen, 1977, p. 66.

176 BVerfGE 50, 290 (339).

177 BVerfGE 50, 290 (339).

178 BVerfGE 24, 367 (400).

179 See Leisner *loc. cit.* (No. 167), § 149 marginal note 46 *et seq.*

180 Issing and Leisner, »Kleineres Eigentum,« 1976.

181 Leisner *loc. cit.* (No. 167), § 149 marginal note 46 *et seq.*

182 BVerfGE 53, 257 (292).

183 See Ossenbühl, »Der Eigentumsschutz sozialrechtlicher Positionen in der Rechtsprechung des Bundesverfassungsgerichts« in Festschrift für Wolfgang Zeidler, 1, 1987, p. 625 *et seq.* (640).

184 See Leisner *loc. cit.* (No. 167), § 149 marginal note 108 *et seq., Papier, ins Maunz-Dürig-Herzog-Scholz, Grundgesetz-Kommentar, Article 14, marginal note 96 *et seq.* (September 1983).

185 BVerfGE 1, 264 (277); 13, 225 (229); 18, 85 (90); 22, 380 (386 and 387); 45, 142 (173); 77, 84 (118).

186 BVerfGE 1, 264; 13, 225 (229) or the question raised in BVerfGE 51, 193 (222 and 223) of »whether the trading firm as such has the constituent features of the constitutional concept of ownership« see Scholz, Entflechtung und Verfassung (1981, p. 91) is probably no longer up to date (cf. BVerfGE 77, 84) (118).

187 See Rudolf Wendt, Eigentum und Gesetzgebung, 1985, p. 273 and 274.

188 BVerfGE 36, 281 (290).

189 BVerfGE 51, 193 (216).

190 BVerfGE 31, 229 (239).

191 Papier, *loc. cit.* (No. 184), Article 14 marginal note.

192 Here, BVerfGE 77, 84 (118) considers the existing business relations, the customer base obtained and market position.

193 Therefore no protection against a change in customs tariffs (BGHE 45, 83), stricter regulations of industrial safety law which force production changes.

194 *E.g.,* positional advantages as a result of a specific road network.

195 BVerfGE 14, 263 (276); 25, 371 (407); 50, 290 (342); Leisner, *loc. cit.* (No. 167), § 149 marginal note 112 *et seq.*

196 BVerfGE 50, 290 (344).

197 Papier *loc. cit.* (No. 184), Article 14 marginal note 185.

198 See Martin Bullinger, »Wettbewerbsaufsicht bei präventiver Wirtschaftsaufsicht,« NJW 1978, 2173 *et seq.;* Werner Hahn, Offenbarungspflichten im Umweltschutzrecht, 1984, p. 170 *et seq.;* Meinhard Schröder, »Der Schutz von Betriebs- und Geschäftsgeheimnissen im Umweltschutzrecht,« UPR 1985, 394 *et seq.;* Rudiger Breuer, »Schutz von Betriebs- und Geschäftsgeheimnissen im Umweltrecht,« NVwZ 1986, 171; *ditto, loc. cit.* (No. 5), § 148 marginal note 6 *et seq.*

199 See Breuer, *loc. cit.* (No. 5), § 148 marginal note 27.
200 Kupp, AöR 92 (1967), 227.
201 See Ossenbühl, »Die Interpretation von Grundrechten in der Rechtsprechung des Bundesverfassungsgerichts«, NJW 1976, 2100 *et seq.* (2106).
202 See BVerfGE 50, 290 (332 and 333). Ossenbühl, »Die Kontrolle von Tatsachenfeststellungen und Prognoseentscheidungen durch das Bundesverfassungsgericht«, in Festschrift BVerfG, 1, 1976, p. 458 *et seq.*
203 See also Kupp, AöR 92 (1967), 214 and 215.
204 BVerfGE 73, 339 (Solange II). On this subject, see Hilf, 1987, 1 and Rupp, JZ 1987, 241.
205 See the explanation of basic rights and basic freedoms by the European Parliament of 12 April 1989 in EuGRZ 1989, p. 204; see also Beutler, *ibid.* p. 185.

Mary Ann Glendon

Comments on Part 4

A superficial comparison of legal developments in the area of basic rights and liberties in the United States and the Federal Republic over the past 40 years would suggest that in both countries the legal protection of personal liberties has increased, while that accorded to economic liberties and property rights has diminished. All three papers addressed to this subject, however, reveal how difficult it is to make a sharp distinction between economic and personal rights. And, so far as the United States is concerned, Professor Attanasio convincingly argues that (contrary to appearances) legal protection of some property interests is not weaker, but merely less direct.

Since the panelists have confined themselves primarily to describing and analyzing legal developments in their respective countries, my commentator's role can perhaps be most usefully performed by offering some comparative observations and by making some connections between the subjects of this panel and those treated elsewhere on the program. In so doing, I will concentrate on two major subjects discussed in the papers: the image of the welfare state in each country's constitutional jurisprudence and the current status of constitutional protection of property rights.

At first glance, the contrast could not be greater between the affirmative commitment to a social state (*Sozialstaat*) in Article 20 of the West German Basic Law and the American constitutional regime of negative liberties as described by Chief Justice Rehnquist in an important recent decision that affords a revealing glimpse of the kind of government the current Supreme Court believes that we have in the United States.[1] According to Professor Sontheimer, the proclamation of Article 20 (1) that »The Federal Republic of Germany is a democratic and social federal state« is understood by the *Bundesverfassungsgericht* to mean not only that the state is under an obligation to offer minimum subsistence to those citizens who need it, but that it is also obliged to create social conditions enabling or empowering individuals to protect their own human dignity. How different this notion of the state sounds from that set forth in *DeShaney v. Winnebago County Department of Social Services* where our Chief Justice stated that »our cases have recognized that the Due Process Clauses generally confer no affirmative right to governmental aid, even where such aid may be necessary to secure life, liberty, or property interests of which the government itself may not deprive the individual.«[2]

The contrast diminishes somewhat, however, if we take account of the fact that in the *DeShaney* case the Supreme Court was merely confirming that an individual has no *constitutional* right to affirmative governmental assistance. Under our constitutional regime, the Chief Justice pointed out, it is up to ordinary democratic political processes to determine what relief should be available to someone like the young plaintiff in *DeShaney* (who was left in the custody of his violent father even after state social workers were aware that he was in serious danger). As the Chief Justice put it:

> The people of Wisconsin may well prefer a system of liability which would place upon the State and its officials the responsibility for failure to act in situations such as the present one. They may create such a system, if they do not have it already, by changing the tort law of the State in accordance with the regular law-making process. But they should not have it thrust upon them by this Court's expansion of the Due Process Clause of the Fourteenth Amendment.[3]

As a practical matter, such matters are left to the political process in West Germany, too. There, as in the United States, the actual work of constructing the welfare state has been carried out by legislation, not by court decisions and constitutions. Thus, the crucial question in both countries is how well the political process works to meet the needs of the poorest and most vulnerable members of society. Nevertheless, one cannot discount the effect that a highly visible constitutional commitment to a social state (such as that contained in Article 20) may have on the formation of popular opinion and on the operation of the political process. In light of the discussion of representative democracy in the preceding panel, it would be interesting to explore further with our West German colleagues the question of which regime in theory and in practice is in a better position to work out (and constantly reexamine) the optimal mix in each country's mixed economy as well as to establish priorities in the allocation of national resources.

Turning from the welfare state to the narrower, but related, subject of the protection of property rights treated by Professors Attanasio and Ossenbühl, one notes that there are some quite striking similarities in the accounts given by both authors. Like the United States Supreme Court, the *Bundesverfassungsgericht* gives extensive deference to legislative decision-making in this area, and does not seem to assign a particularly high value to the protection of many types of ownership rights. The two panelists differ in their reactions to this state of affairs, however. Professor Ossenbühl expresses the concern that these trends may have gone too far in the Federal Republic, whereas Professor Attanasio believes that the United States Supreme Court has indirectly privileged certain property interests by giving them advantages in the political process through its free speech decisions. If Professor Attanasio is correct, we may be in the presence of a real difference here. Again one is reminded of the discussion of party politics and finance in the panel on representative government. As in that session, important questions have been raised concerning the extent to which, in each country, distortions in the political process may affect the balance between private property rights and the general welfare.

Professor Ossenbühl's elaborate description of the approach to protection of property rights worked out by the West German Constitutional Court suggests to my mind a possible interpretation of the recent group of takings decisions by the United States Supreme Court that have so puzzled American commentators. On the basis of Basic Law Article 14 (2), which provides that the »use« of property »should also serve the public weal«, the *Bundesverfassungsgericht* has found it appropriate to differentiate among various types of property according to the social function that they perform. Thus, the legislature may legitimately define the content and limits of ownership rights in shares of stock somewhat differently from a person's ownership of, say, his own dwelling place. Professor Attanasio describes with approval a strain in American scholarly writing that urges a move in this direction.

It may be, however, that a more differentiated approach to constitutional property protection is also beginning to appear in American case law. In the recent takings cases of the United States Supreme Court, most court watchers seem to agree that there has been some kind of shift in approach. But interpretations of precisely what kind of change has taken place differ drastically, and most commentators find the recent decisions difficult to reconcile with one another.[4] Some of the recent cases seem to authorize unprecedented uncompensated takings of property, whereas in others the Court seems to be engaging in a more stringent review of legislative interference with private property rights than has been seen since the era before the New Deal. Where one scholar discerns and deplores a return to formalism,[5] another sees the opposite: an alarming trend toward »ad hoc balancing.«[6]

If one examines the *types* of property involved in each of the recent cases, however, the possibility arises that there is at work in these decisions a concept similar to that which has shaped the West German Court's interpretation of Article 14. In the three recent cases where the Supreme Court protected ownership rights from legislative interference, the property involved was, respectively, a single family home,[7] a church-run camp for handicapped children,[8] and inheritance rights of individual members of an Indian tribe.[9] The two recent cases where the court found that rather extensive legislative regulation did *not* amount to a taking involved extensive coal mining operations[10] and investments in rent-controlled residential property.[11] Is it fanciful to think that what may be emerging, but not yet articulated in these cases, is a coherent, differentiated approach to takings that would give considerable weight to the social function of the property involved?

I would like to conclude these observations by trying to relate them to a theme sounded by Professor Durham at the outset of our conference. As mentioned above, any attempt at comparative examination of the West German and American welfare states and of the protection accorded to economic interests in each country necessarily involves us in comparison of political processes. Such a comparison requires us to confront an increasingly serious problem faced by both systems. Representative government, in order to function well, requires a citizenry that is capable of participating in democratic processes. A welfare state, in order to function well, needs a citizenry that possesses a sense of fellow-feeling, as well as a sense of individual responsibility. But where in our modern societies can the skills of self-government be acquired and practiced? And where can the capacity for compassion and self-restraint be formed?

A traditional answer to these questions would be that these skills and virtues are acquired and formed in the institutions that comprise the fine texture of civil society in families, neighborhoods, churches, workers' associations and real political parties. Such institutions are what Professor Durham had in mind, I believe, when he said that we need to attend to the »seedbeds« of civic virtue where succeeding generations learn anew to appreciate the benefits and sacrifices necessary for a constitutional order.

But here we encounter a problem and a paradox. The problem is that the intermediate structures that may be essential to modern representative governments and welfare states are themselves threatened by the expansion of the state and, to some extent, by the expansion of individual rights against the group. The paradox is that these endangered, small, social environments that are somehow necessary to modern liberal states are not necessarily liberal or egalitarian or democratic themselves. Nevertheless, I would suggest that these fragile social environments are in as much need of protection from deliberate or inadvertent destruction as is our natural environment. The problem of how to revitalize them – or even of how to avoid harming them – is one of extraordinary difficulty and complexity.

Our discussions at this conference have concentrated primarily on the individual and the state. Neither in West Germany or in the United States, it seems, do we have an adequate vocabulary or conceptual apparatus to deal with the small mediating structures that lie between the two. In our scholarly exchanges of ideas we have benefitted greatly from interdisciplinary cooperation with economists and political scientists, the former with their great knowledge of the market, the latter with their sophisticated understanding of the state. As we continue our studies of constitutionalism, it is to be hoped that we will also hear more from those whose special knowledge concerns the structures of civil society.

Notes:

1 *DeShaney v. Winnebago County Department of Social Services,* 109 S. Ct. 998 (1989).
2 Id. at 1003.
3 Id. at 1007.
4 See the various conflicting interpretations in the articles in the symposium on takings in the December 1988 Columbia Law Review.
5 Michelman, *Takings 1987,* 88 Columbia L. Rev. 1600, 1621-22 (1988).
6 Rose-Ackerman, *Against Ad Hocery: A Comment on Michelman,* 88 Col. L. Rev. 1697, 1711 (1988).
7 *Nollan v. California Coastal Commission,* 107 S. Ct. 3141 (1987).
8 *First English Evangelical Lutheran Church v. County of Los Angeles,* 107 S. Ct. 2378 (1987).
9 *Hodel v. Irving,* 107 S. Ct. 2076 (1987).
10 *Keystone Bituminous Coal Association v. DeBenedictis,* 107 S. Ct. 1232 (1987).
11 *Pennell v. City of San Jose,* 108 S. Ct. 849 (1988).

Part 5:
The Basic Law and the Economic System

Horst Siebert*

Principles of the Economic System in the Federal Republic - An Economist's View

Germany's »social market economy« has its roots both in historical experience and in a value orientation centered around the individual. The immediate historical background is to be found in the years of an Orwellian dictatorship repressing individual tastes and individual behavior. Another aspect of the German experience was the interventionism of the state and the central planning mechanism that slowly developed in the late 19th century and became dominant in the war economies and in the thirties. The inflation of 1923, the repressed inflation of 1936-1948, the problem of the alienation of the worker in the 19th century, and the endogenous erosion of competition through large firms also formed part of this historical background. The consensus of the founding fathers of the Basic Law was a value orientation stressing individual freedom, human dignity, and the principle of subsidiarity in the organization of society.

1. Basic Principles

In this paper, we shall not study in detail the founding fathers' concept of the social market economy and the system introduced in 1948.[1] We shall focus instead on the social market economy in actual practice (»Verfassungswirklichkeit«). Moreover, we are interested in the challenges the future holds.

Individual Liberty

Due to the experience of having been ruled by a dictator, and in accordance with constitutional history in Europe, the first articles of the Basic Law define the rights of the individual. The »dignity of man« (Art. 1), »inviolable

291

and inalienable human rights« (Art. 1), »the right to the free development of one's personality« (Art. 2), »the right freely to express and to publish one's opinion by speech« (Art. 5), »freedom of movement« (Art. 11), the »rights of ownership and inheritance« (Art. 14) and many other provisions show that the cornerstone of the Basic Law is to respect the choices of the individual. In terms of economics, the basic presumption of the Basic Law is that individual preferences should count, that it is for the individual to decide. One is free to choose what to consume, whether to consume or save, whether to work or enjoy leisure, which job to take, where to live, where to travel, and what to produce for someone else.

Basing the decisions on individual preferences implies confidence in the sovereignty of the individual. The individual is the best judge of his own affairs; he will weigh the benefits and costs of a preference, evaluate the risk associated with it, and will have a strong incentive to obtain the relevant information for his choice.

The Competitive Order

A system that is ultimately geared towards the preferences of the individual must have an institutional mechanism by which the individual can voice his preferences. The institutional vehicle is the market or a set of markets – i.e., the competitive order. If a market economy is established by an adequate institutional framework, the individual can vote with his purse and with his feet. By giving up income and spending money on specific products, the individual clearly signals his opportunity costs and marginal willingness to pay. In choosing one place to live, and not another, he indicates his willingness to pay for a specific location. By deciding how many hours to work or not to work, he indicates his evaluation of work and leisure. When these individual evaluations are summed up by the market, the value of a good from the point of view of the demand side is specified.

Economic decentralization not only refers to revealing the marginal willingness to pay. Markets also allow a decentralized autonomy of decisions on production and investment; they signal the incentives to produce. By expressing opportunity costs (the costs of an opportunity foregone) the market economy prevents inefficiency. Firms making a loss have to exit because their opportunity costs are too high. Resources could be better used elsewhere.

Information on economic and technical conditions is not ubiquitous in an economy, but is distributed asymmetrically among the subsystems. Decentralization allows the utilization of comparative advantages in the generation and processing of information. It is an incentive to collect and reveal information.

The competitive order satisfies the conditions for static efficiency and provides for dynamic efficiency as well. Firms search for new technical knowledge and new possibilities for investments. Thus, markets are not only a mechanism to disseminate a given set of information; they are an exploratory device in the sense of Hayek (1968), generating new knowledge. The competitive order is not explicitly written down in the constitution. One may question whether it is a principle in its own right as stated by Eucken, who regards it as the only basic principle,[2] or one may take the view that the competitive order is instrumental in allowing individual liberties. Decentralization allows personal choice and provides options; thus, it is part of an open society.[3] Still, other writers may link the competitive order to the overall target of efficiency (the economic principle).

Equity

Besides giving freedom to the individual, the constitution also protects the individual. No one is permitted to violate the rights of others (Art. 2) or the right to property (Art. 14), and the Federal Republic is a »social federal state« (»Sozialer Bundesstaat,« Art. 20). Equity dictates other provisions in the constitution, such as preventing regional disparities in living conditions (Art. 72). *De facto*, there is a strong material protection of the individual, especially through a net of mandatory social insurance systems including unemployment, disability, and old age insurance. The market as an allocation mechanism is corrected in order to attain socially acceptable results.

2. *The Social Market Economy as an Economic Order*

The principles of individual liberty, competitive order and equity do not yet fully specify the Federal Republic's economic system. The »social market economy« must be understood as an institutional arrangement defining the rules for the decision-making of households, firms, and politicians, including restraints as well as incentives.

The social market economy (*Soziale Marktwirtschaft*) has to be interpreted as a specific form of an economic order (*Wirtschaftsordnung*). It is an »ensemble,« a frame of reference, a self-regulating system with its target being individual freedom and choice, efficiency through decentralized autonomy in a competitive order and equity. A »social market economy may be described as a permanent search for an economic and social framework, designed to encourage both an efficient production of the means of material well-being and personal freedom in a socially-balanced order.«[4]

An important strand has developed in the literature of institutional economics – that of the principal-agent paradigm, where the principal sets rules that influence the agent's behavior, where the principal cannot fully observe the agent's behavior, yet where the agent's behavior determines the result of the activities. In a way, *Wirtschaftsordnung* is a super principal-agent contract. The principals are (i) the fathers of the constitution and (ii) the legislature when it has the appropriate majority for constitutional changes and the normal majority for other legislative alterations. To some extent, the judiciary plays the role of the principal when the rules are interpreted anew. The individuals (the households and the firms) are the agents that may behave according to the incentive structure and the institutional framework developed by the principal. The principal wants to reach its maximum in its targets, of freedom, efficiency and equity, for instance, by maximizing one target subject to restraints from others. In an optimal solution, the principal will devise rules so that the optimal conditions of the agent are satisfied.

The description of the *Wirtschaftsordnung* as a super principal-agent problem is not yet complete. To some extent, the voter becomes the principal when he is discontent with prevailing institutional conditions and wants change. However, in contrast to specific policy areas, the rules of the game require constancy and ought to change only under rare circumstances. This is especially true for constitutional change.

»Denken in Ordnungen«

»Denken in Ordnungen« – to think in terms of an order – was a central demand of the founding fathers of West Germany's social market economy. They were concerned with the question of how a small institutional change affects the overall system after all the households, all the firms and other agents such as policy makers have reacted. In a cybernetic context, it is the question of how the system changes if the rules are slightly altered. This is analogous to the general equilibrium analysis for an institutional arrangement (see the concept of »market conformity« below). It seems to me that this concept of »Denken in Ordnungen« is not understood by many economists in the United States.

Hutchison[5] may come closest to the concept of *Wirtschaftsordnung* by distinguishing between a Ricardian and Smithian mode of the competitive market economy.[6] The Ricardian concept stresses »an abstract, purely economic model of competitive equilibrium« presented as achieving some kind of Utopian »maximum« or »optimum,« while the Smithian concept is »formulated in much broader terms, comprehending the political and social order.«[7]

Economic policy in a social market economy has two crucially distinct roles: to establish and preserve the economic order (*Ordnungspolitik*) and to influence economic processes (*Prozeßpolitik*). *Prozeßpolitik* attempts to modify the business cycle, growth, and allocation in day-to-day, year-to-year or longer-term operations, for instance, in providing social overhead capital. *Ordnungspolitik* refers to the establishment of property rights, of the incentive system, of institutional arrangements and of the rules, including constitutional procedures. The Ordo-liberals who laid down the intellectual foundations of West Germany's economic order also argue that the main policy task is *Ordnungspolitik, i.e.,* the establishment of institutional arrangements for a market economy. *Prozeßpolitik* should be limited to special cases.

Eucken developed the constituting principles of the competitive order.[8] Open markets, presently the most important ingredient of the concept of contestable markets,[9] are a prerequisite for competition. Private ownership is both a guarantee of individual liberty and an incentive to minimize costs and reveal truly economic information. Freedom of contract is conducive to competition. Liability ensures that social costs are internalized. The constancy of economic policy helps prevent the intertemporal misallocation of resources, and price level stability (see below) is *a sine qua non* for the price mechanism to operate.

An economic order for the economy as a whole may be interpreted as consisting of separate, partial orders for specific functional areas (order for the competitive process, monetary system, social order, and labor market) or for specific policy areas (trade policy, business-cycle policy, agricultural policy). A basic issue is how these partial orders can be made consistent with each other.[10] A related problem is how macro policies can be integrated into the order of a social market economy.[11]

The social market economy as an institutional framework must satisfy a set of important requirements for the institutional framework to function. These conditions[12] are the system (market) conformity of policy measures, the defense of competition, price-level stability, and the social order. The historical experience of Germany prior to 1945 is vital in understanding these elements.[13]

Interventionism, Market Conformity and the Role of the State

The German population in general and particularly the intellectual fathers of the social market economy had experienced an interventionist state, especially in the thirties and during the war. It was clear to the majority that a controlled economy - »une economie dirigee« - »had produced an appalling amount of inefficiency.«[14] Therefore, decentralization and a competitive order was called for.

The interventionist experience of the twenties and thirties showed that one intervention quickly leads to another. This is especially true for price regulation. For example, regulating the price of a standard loaf of bread would quickly spread like a cancer to all types of bread, including bagels and croissants, to the labor costs of the baker, to flour, to the milling process, to wheat, and all other inputs as well as product substitutes.[15] As we know from the present European agricultural policy, intervention cannot be partially confined to one specific product, but tends to have side effects which are seldom recognized *prima vista*.

A specific intervention may not only affect other markets (via the interdependence of markets by the potential for substitution and by complementarity), but may also have an impact on the market system itself, changing the basic properties of the allocation mechanism. Therefore, the intellectual founding fathers of the *Soziale Marktwirtschaft* demanded that policy actions should be compatible with the market economy (*»Marktkonform«*), narrowly interpreted,[16] and that a policy decision should not induce such a change or disequilibrium in another market so that a new intervention becomes necessary. In a broader sense, a policy measure should not change the property of the overall system.

It has proven extremely difficult to pinpoint the concept of market conformity. In a static view, one can quickly see how the regulation of one market shifts demand or supply to another. In intertemporal decisions, however, such as the choice of a location, capital accumulation and the depletion of resources, it takes a long time to see impacts. Moreover, the concept of market conformity is extremely difficult to define with respect to the impact on the system as a whole (system conformity). Finally, the concept »does not provide a conclusive answer to the question as to what activities the state should fulfill in a free society and what decisions are reserved to the market.«[17]

A specific aspect of interventionism is the issue of the nationalization of basic industries. This was a prominent topic in the early days of West Germany. Although it occasionally flares up, it is no longer an issue, partly due to the severe inefficiencies of German firms which were supposed to have been oriented towards the common weal (*Gemeinwirtschaft*) in the last twenty years, partly due to the experience in Eastern Europe.

Apart from the issue of interventionism, the state as a »*Rechtsstaat*« is restrained in its activities by a set of rules and procedures. It has been assigned the role of protecting individual liberty and of guaranteeing the institutional arrangement of the competitive order, for instance, by competition policy (see below). Eucken and Miksch required a strong government that could defend the competitive order and suppress specific interests.[18] The state »is assigned a crucial role in monitoring the proper functioning of the competitive process, which, if left alone, is believed to degenerate due to monopolistic tendencies and growing disproportions of private power.«[19]

According to Buchanan,[20] the state has the role of providing public goods (or rules for public goods, as in environmental quality management). Moreover, the West German state has taken over a dominant role with respect to the equity targets, *e.g.*, in the attempt to produce fairness. With respect to the proper productive role of the state, such as with public goods, market aggregation of individual preferences is not possible (free rider). A political aggregation mechanism has to substitute for the market process through voting . Voting is also applied when merit goods, such as policy targets, are involved. In deciding on public and merit goods, a federal structure based on the subsidiary principle allows the expression of regional preferences. Thus, economic decentralization is to some extent accompanied by political decentralization.

Endogenous Tendencies to Monopolies and a Framework for Competition

Competition is a necessary condition for effective decentralization, but the spontaneity of the market may be endangered endogenously by the behavior of firms. Profit-maximizing firms can improve their position by reducing competition. They can form cartels and engage in other forms of cooperation in order to reduce competition; they can strive for a monopolistic position by internal growth or can attain it by mergers. This was the experience in Germany in the three decades preceding World War I and at the time of the Weimar republic, reflected in the debate in the late 1920s and early 1930s.[21] These potentially endogenous tendencies would severely affect the institutional setting of a market economy. At the same time, firms could engage in rent seeking and attempts to influence the institutional arrangements under which they operated. Historically, the result was an industrial complex interlinked with the state (»Vermachtung« der Wirtschaft).[22]

Competition policy is therefore an important framework of a social market economy's institutional arrangement. Its role is to guarantee that competition is not eroded endogenously by principally ruling out cartels, by controlling mergers, and by monitoring the abuse of a monopolistic position. But other important aspects include free market entry to keep markets contestable and an open economy to allow competition from abroad.

Inflationary Experience and the Independence of the Bundesbank

Germany has experienced two major inflations: the hyperinflation of 1923 and the repressed inflation from 1936-1948. Inflation generates severe repercussions from distorting allocation and especially from hurting individuals with a fixed nominal income, such as wage earners. Inflation can therefore be a danger to an economic system. It can lead to a political destabilization of society, and it violates the condition of constancy of economic policy. For these reasons, price-level stability is an important target of economic policy; the Bundesbank was institutionalized as an independent central bank. The government cannot monetize its budget deficit by taking recourse to the central bank.

These provisions are not part of the constitution, but of the Federal Bank Law, (*Bundesbankgesetz*). It is interesting to note that the actual position of the Bundesbank is not only defined by the legal rules, but by a consensus in the population. This more or less holds for other aspects of the institutional system as well. If the consensus changes, the institutional setting may vary.

The late 19th and the early 20th centuries in Europe were dominated by the social question. Industrialization, new forms of production, and the migration from the countryside to industrial locations gave rise to social problems. Socialist movements claimed to have found an answer to how economic efficiency, progress and personal freedom could be obtained by public ownership of the means of production and central planning. The social ethics of the Catholic church centered on improving the conditions of human life. From this historical perspective, any economic system must provide an answer to the social question, both from an ethical point of view and from a practical one. There must be some consensus on the economic system.

The experience with a central collectivist planning system in Europe was that such a system did not deliver the promises it made. It did not protect the worker as an individual but rather required an Orwellian-type control of the individual worker; for instance, in limiting his choice of work place or controlling what type of work he did in order to allocate food stamps in a rationing system. Thus, introducing the market economy in 1948 was in itself a social reform. The system provided economic opportunities and choices.

Besides stressing this positive property of the market economy, the attribute »social« market economy refers to the basic position of some Ordo-liberals that the allocation process by markets may lead to an income and wealth distribution that warrants correction.[23] An important aspect of this can be found in the social insurance schemes which were started in the 1880s and developed further in the 40 years of the Federal Republic. The »productive state«[24] has gained a more important role. Moreover, the worker participated in economic growth – to wit the wage drift in the fifties and sixties – and he was integrated in economic terms by his ability to acquire real property (houses) and financial wealth. Finally, the issue of the workman's position of the last century had changed. With 54.9 percent of the work force in service activities (including 20.1 percent in government) and only 40.1 percent in industry (*Statistisches Bundesamt* 1989), the social question of the 19th century has disappeared from center stage.

3. Trends and Challenges: How do the Principles Work?

How has the social market economy performed in 40 years? Can we recognize trends? Is there a slow erosion of the »social market order.«[25] Is the German economy still a social market economy?[26] And what will be the challenges of the future?

Economic Policy Targets

From a historical perspective, the social market economy has done well in generating products, in stimulating technical change and providing high rates of economic growth. At eight percent, the growth rate of real GNP was high in the early fifties. It has come down to three percent in the late eighties (four percent in the sixties, three point five percent in the seventies and a slump in the early eighties). The unemployment rate was originally high, but it was quickly reduced in the fifties and remained very low up to 1974, rising steadily thereafter to a high level of nearly nine percent. Inflation was nonexistent in the fifties (except in 1951) and sixties, but increased in the seventies and early eighties.

External Shocks

A tremendous initial challenge was the inflow of 12 million refugees. The nation had to provide employment and housing, supply an infrastructure, and integrate the refugees into society. Overall, the system fared quite well. The two oil crises of the seventies provided another shock, and though some voices mistrusted the market, the market mechanism did well in adjusting to this scarcity shock. Essentially, the Federal Republic underwent a stark change in its sectoral structure by strongly reducing employment in agriculture, by a continuous rise of the service activities and, since 1970, by a relative decline in manufacturing.[27] The overall consensus is that the German economy, being heavily dependent on foreign trade, has to adjust to the changes in the world economy.

Table 1 - Macroeconomic Variables, Federal Republic of Germany (five-year average)

Period	Real Growth-Rates	Unemployment Rate	Rate of Inflation
1950-1954[a]	8,7	8,5	2,0
1955-1959[a]	6,0	3,8	1,9
1960-1964	4,6	0,9	2,7
1965-1969	4,0	1,2	2,1
1970-1974	3,0	1,3	6,1
1975-1979	3,9	4,4	3,7
1980-1984	1,0	7,0	4,3
1985-1989	2,8	8,8	1,0

[a] except for the Saarland

Source: Deutsche Bundesbank (1975); Sachverständigenrat zur Begutachtung der gesamtwirtschaftlichen Entwicklung (1988). Monatsberichte der Deutschen Bundesbank (1990).

The Conflict between the Principles

There is a broad range of problems where the effort is to bring the basic principles of personal liberty, the competitive order, and equity into harmony. The competitive order is instrumental in allowing personal freedom and in contributing towards a solution to the social question. There are, however, problems where the basic principles are in conflict and where a balance between efficiency and equity has to be found. The problem of finding a balance is a continuous process, and the opportunity costs of solutions will only become apparent over time. Since it is an important issue, the overall features of the social market economy should not be destroyed. There are five areas where these overall features are challenged; namely, through subsidies and distortions, the size of the government, regulation, rent seeking, and specifically through social regulation.

Subsidies and Distortions. Subsidies for ailing industries like coal, shipbuilding, and steel have dampened sectorial adjustments. Subsidized sectors are

301

typically characterized by a small number of firms, low growth, strong import penetration, and a historically high level of protection. Most subsidized or protected sectors once had a large number of employees (and voters), but today they are quite capital intensive (mining, steel, shipbuilding, and even parts of textiles and clothing). Shielding workers from too-strong structural adjustments is a specific motive, and rent-seeking is a good explanation.

In the coal industry, a work place is subsidized by 35,000 DM per annum (1986), which amounts to 57 percent of the average total labor costs per person employed in this industry (calculated by the Kiel Institute of World Economics). Subsidies have severely changed the position of individual firms. For instance, subsidizing Arbed has severely affected the private producer Korf. They have distorted the sectoral structure and retarded the adjustment of sectors and whole regions. Their most detrimental impact has been to ward off the location of new industries, for instance, by preventing lower wages in regions with ailing industries and by their impact on the planning of land use.[28] Politicians have not been at all courageous in reducing subsidies, and a sunset law for subsidies has never been tried.

A defensive sectoral policy for ailing sectors is not the only case of distortion. Industrial targeting may become the more relevant area. Politicians do not trust the market to develop new sectors, and they claim to know better in which sectors to place capital, including public funds. This appeal of strategic trade policy extends beyond subsidies. In the eyes of the European Commission, competition policy can be more generous vis-a-vis larger units if they fit into the strategic trade policy concepts.

Experience with promoting new sectors in Germany artificially, such as subsidizing the development of nuclear plants and larger computers, is disappointing. Cycles of interventionism have been observed in government activities, for instance, in town planning.[29] There is no doubt that strategic trade policy is a threat to the market economy because decentralized private decisions are substituted by a political process. Strategic trade theory seems to be so fascinating for the political area that the concept of »Wirtschaftsordnung« tends to move into the background.

The experience with subsidies is disillusioning. The amount of subsidies is high, being estimated at 133 billion DM for 1989; that is, 5.9 percent of GNP (Kiel Institute of World Economics) and not too far from the wage income tax receipts (182 billion DM, 1989), the most important single tax in Germany. The risk of the system as a whole is that specific interest groups may be able to dominate the state. An institutional check on subsidies and distortions would consist of clearly defining the role of government in a market economy, especially its allocative function to provide social overhead capital (technical infrastructure) and other public goods (basic research), as well as financing (taxation schemes). A compulsory depreciation rule for subsidies may be a powerful tool.

Privatization and the Role of Government. The share of government expenditures in GNP may be considered to be an indicator of the government's role in a market economy. For the Federal Republic, it has moved around 48 percent in the last 15 years, with a peak of 50 percent in 1982. In the late 1980s, there was a small decline. A large part (18.5 percentage points) is made up of the social security system with an increasingly upward trend.

Public enterprises are mainly engaged in electricity, gas, water, local and urban transportation services, railways, communication, residential construction, and some areas of manufacturing. They account for seven percent of employment and roughly 15 percent of gross investment in the Federal Republic of Germany.[30] The privatization of public firms has been rather timid. Constitutional checks on the size of government, on governmental expenditures, or on financing may be the appropriate answer to the government's tendency to assume a larger role in a market economy.

Regulation. Regulation of industry and services has occurred in many areas, namely in all sectors that have received exemptions from the German antitrust law (*Gesetz gegen Wettbewerbsbeschränkungen*), agriculture, the coal and the iron industry, banking and insurance, transportation, communication (including the postal service), and public electric, gas and water utilities. Moreover, regulations apply to environmental protection and to many other aspects, such as the health system and information media.[31]

The basic feature of regulation is to exclude competition and to limit market access. It has been estimated that, measured in terms of value added, roughly 50 percent of the German economy is severely regulated. In order to prevent excessive profits from being gained out of the monopolistic position created by regulation, in some important cases the setting of prices is also controlled. Often, however, the right of a restricted market entry is given away for free, for instance, when limited emission rights are *de facto* granted at a zero price.

Arguments for regulation are made in light of the growth of natural monopolies, the need for consumer protection, and the internalization of externalities. The basic question is to what extent these arguments are valid and to what extent regulation really is in the interest of the individual. Besides the primary effects of higher prices due to reduced competition, regulation tends to have side effects that may not be immediately apparent. The German regulation of trucking, for example, has increased the comparative

303

advantage of Dutch truckers and has shifted locational advantage away from the North German ports. Moreover, regulation of trucking – for example, forbidding market entry to the trucking division of producing firms or cabotage rules for foreign truckers – generates excess traffic which is inconsistent with energy conservation and environmental protection.

One way out would be to auction off access rights whenever these rights can be linked to quantities, for instance, auctioning off emission rights, the right to participate in a stock exchange, and the right to provide a transportation service. The other way is to explicitly allow market access. This is especially important in the light of new concepts of competition such as contestable markets. Europe '92 may be a way to improve market access.

A challenge for the market economy will be to revise the exemptions from the German antitrust law. In banking and insurance, protection of the customer (*Anlegerschutz, Gläubigerschutz*) should not be attained by limiting market access. Stock exchanges should be opened to more competition. In the case of the postal service we see a modest structural change including a more open market in final products. In electricity, new property rights for common carriers will have to be developed to allow competition. Finally, in the transportation sector, deregulation is possible in trucking and in airlines.[32] In all these areas and in other regulated fields (coal, steel, crafts), a huge potential for deregulation exists.

Rent-seeking. Subsidies may be controlled by sunset laws and excessive government expenditures may be checked by rules of financing. Competition policy is the answer to an endogenous tendency to encroach upon competition by establishing noncompetitive market positions. What is the institutional response to rent-seeking, by which the frame of reference for private decisions is altered and by which partial orders are politicized? Linked to this issue of rent-seeking are the problems of economic power and vested interests.[33] Apparently, a systematic institutional check on rent-seeking does not exist. Competition policy of the traditional type – relating to positions in the relevant market – is not an adequate answer. Guaranteeing free market access in order to keep markets contestable is an important step against rent-seeking. But it does not seem to be a sufficient institutional safeguard because rents are determined by many factors, including favorable institutional (legal) conditions of operation. To think in terms of an economic order – »Denken in Ordnungen« – may be a guarantee against special interests of subgroups of society and against rent-seeking, but there may be some indications that this philosophy is losing ground.[34]

Protection of the Individual versus Flexibility. The regulation of the labor market has its roots in the intention to protect the individual. Labor market regulation consists of three basic aspects: (i) governmental insurance schemes if people are unemployed, ill, disabled or retired, (ii) lay-off restraints, and (iii) the delegation of bargaining for the wage contract to employer and employee organizations, with the bargaining solution de facto becoming law and being mandatory for all employees, including trade union non-members (*»Allgemeinverbindlichkeit«*).

This system of regulation implicitly defines the incentives to supply and demand labor. The incentives work to reduce the demand for labor and uncouple employment and growth as well as investment and employment. This is a deficiency of the system.[35] As is the case for any insurance, social insurance gives rise to moral hazard behavior of those insured. Lay-off restraints explicitly define exit conditions and implicitly stipulate entry conditions by influencing the demand for labor. Generalized wage bargaining allowing an organizational integration of the employees prevents a differentiation of wages according to occupation, sectors and regions. Moreover, the three types of regulation interact with each other. For instance, social security and lay-off regulations define the bargaining position of trade unions.

Besides problems of moral hazard behavior, a regulating system protecting the individual may also lead to different attitudes among individuals: they would expect individual protection from the government and the regulatory system, and they would tend to think in terms of aspirations against the government. There is a trade-off between the insider and the outsider; but more importantly, there is a trade-off between individual protection and the open society characterized by Popper as »competition for status among its members.«[36] There is definitely a conflict between individual protection and the efficiency or flexibility of the system. This is possibly best documented in the discussion on the closing hours of stores (*Ladenschlußgesetz*). On the whole, politicians have not been courageous in allowing or initiating more flexibility.

Erosion of the Market Mechanism. Subsidies for ailing and new industries, some forms of regulation, rent-seeking, and the reduced flexibility in the labor market point out that the market mechanism is being endogenously eroded in a slow process. Hindsight tells us that such a process may have been checked better if the market economy had been explicitly laid down in the Basic Law. Not having such a constitutional anchor, the legal system has been indifferent to the problem of »*Marktkonformität*« with respect to the system as a whole. Here is an open question: »Denken in Ordnungen« may not be sufficient as a defense.[37]

Institutional Competition versus European Centralization

The institutional framework of Germany's social market economy will be affected by European integration, especially by the Single Market. There is a consensus to enter the Single market, but there is also some awareness that European integration may change the rules of the game. Reminiscent of the discussion in the 1960s on the role of »planification« is the debate on whether the institutional setting for Europe has to be defined centrally in Brussels or whether it can be delegated to a process of institutional competition.

Institutional competition means that different national institutional arrangements can exist simultaneously in a single market, and that the rules of the country of origin (for a product or a service) are mutually recognized. The implication of institutional competition is the arbitrage of consumers and firms. Consumers vote with their purses and their feet while firms take advantage of differentials in national regulations. Countries compete for the mobile factors of production, and the emerging institutional setting is the result of an open-ended process. The most important impact of institutional competition will be to open up markets that so far have been closed due to national regulation.

The conflict between the strategies of institutional competition versus prior harmonization is an expression of a deeper conflict of orientation. On a constitutional level, it is the conflict of federalism versus centralization. On a philosophical level, the conflict is between liberalism in the classical or British sense versus a more planning-oriented approach. Here we have diverging views on such issues as confidence in the functioning of markets or any type of interventionism, sovereignty of the consumer, or the need for his or her »protection,« the role and the size of the government, spontaneity of autonomous decision making, and decentralized processes versus constructivism, or the English case law versus the logic of the Roman law. Europe is in search of its institutions, and the showdown between the British and the French concept of Europe is still to come.

Nature and Environment

A fascinating issue is how the institutional system has dealt with the challenge of environmental disruption which was not recognized until the early 1970s. The economist came to perceive the environment as a scarce good, used for the competitive purposes of consumption and of receiving wastes.

306

For our analysis it is irrelevant whether preferences for environmental quality have changed or whether the demand for the assimilative services of the environment has increased. There was a shock to the system, not exogenous as in the oil crisis, but endogenous.

Institutionally, the system reacted by attempting to create new property rights for the use of the environment as a waste receptacle and by signaling environmental scarcity to the subsystems of the economy. New laws for air quality management (*Bundesimmissionsschutzgesetz, Abwasserabgabengesetz*, etc.) were introduced in the early 1970s and revised in the mid-1980s. Admittedly, these laws predominantly used the regulatory (licensing) approach to the environmental issue, but a debate has been going on in 1989 on institutional arrangements for environmental incentives. A new institutional arrangement has to be developed which puts a greater emphasis on price instruments. There is also the issue of a constitutional amendment with respect to the environment. I think one can be confident that the institutional arrangement can be changed to accommodate the environmental problem.

A challenge for an institutional setting is how it accommodates the vital interests of future generations.[38] In the case of capital accumulation this issue can be left to private decisions. The generation retiring from production can sell the value of a capital good to the next generation. For the environment, new property rights have to be found that take the interest of future generations into account. The accumulation of pollutants in the environment over a ten or twenty year span has to be reflected in the price system. It will be a special challenge to the social market economy how strict irreversibilities will be incorporated into an institutional framework allowing a preventive environmental policy.

4. *Conclusions*

Looking back over forty years of *Soziale Marktwirtschaft*, the system has fared quite well. It has allowed economic well-being, individual autonomy and an ample net of social security. It was not questioned by public opinion in Germany after having been accepted by the major parties. In a time of an Orwellian crisis of socialist planning in Eastern Europe, the relative merit of the social market economy is apparent. The concept of the social market economy with its principles may in fact provide an orientation for the east

European countries in their search for a better institutional setting for their economies. Institutional competition in Europe, if it is allowed to come into being, will be an invigorating stimulus for the system.

The social market economy has reacted as well to external shocks such as to the inflow of refugees and the energy crises, and one can be confident that the environmental issue can also be integrated into the system. What is now of concern is that the system will be slowly eroded endogenously by subsidies for ailing industries and by strategic trade and industry policy, by regulations favoring specific interests, by rent-seeking, by the inflexibilities in the labor market, and by the conflict between a political demand to be secured by government and the overall necessity to have an open society allowing individual liberty.

Notes:

* I would like to thank Klaus-Werner Schatz, Karl-Heinz Paque and Holger Schmieding for their comments on an earlier draft of this paper.

1 A. Müller-Armack, Wirtschaftsordnung und Wirtschaftspolitik, 1966; W. Ropke, Ein Jahrzehnt Sozialer Marktwirtschaft in Deutschland und seine Lehren, 1958; *idem.,* Economics of the Free Society, 1963; and H. Giersch, Allgemeine Wirtschaftspolitik, 1960.

2 W. Eucken, Grundsätze der Wirtschaftspolitik, 1952, p. 254.

3 K. Popper, The Open Society and its Enemies, 1944.

4 C. Watrin, »Principles of the Social Market Economy – It's Origins and Early History« in Zeitschrift für die gesamte Staatswissenschaft 135 (1979), p. 419.

5 T. Hutchison, »Walter Eucken and the German Social-Market Economy« in The Politics and Philosophy of Economies – Marxians, Keynesians and Austrians, 1981, p. 162.

6 V. Vanberg, »›Ordnungstheorie‹ as Constitutional Economics – The German Conception of a Social Market Economy« in Ordo, 1988, p. 16 *et seq.*

7 T. Hutschison, »Notes on the Effects of Economic Ideas on Policy: The Example of the German Social Market Economy« in Zeitschrift für die gesamte Staatswissenschaft, 139 (1979), pp. 426-41.

8 See Eucken, *supra* note 2.

9 W. Baumol, J. Panzar, and R. Willig, Contestable Markets and the Theory of Industry Structure, 1982.

10 See Eucken, *supra* note 2, at 304 and N. Kloten, 40 Jahre Soziale Marktwirtschaft, Deutsche Bundesbank, Auszüge aus Presseartikeln, Nr. 50, June 22, 1989, pp. 10-16.

11 See the discussion in the 1960s in Kloten, *supra* note 10 at pp. 12-13.

12 I do not quite follow Eucken's four regulating principles. His fourth problem, namely inverse supply reaction, is not a major issue. His third problem that prices correctly reflect scarcity is a dominating issue. See the section on Nature and Environment, *Ibid.* at 22.

13 In the early years of the Federal Republic strong political forces favored a centralization and some type of central planning.

14 Watrin, *supra* note 4, at 411.

15 If you do not like the old-fashioned example, look for natural gas price regulations in the United States in the 1970s and 1980s and some phenomena in trade policy such as upgrading or local content rules as a consequence of quantitative restrictions.

16 See Eucken, *supra* note 2; A. Müller-Armack, Genealogie der Wirtschaftsstile, 1944 and Wirtschaftsordnung und Wirtschaftspolitik, 1966; and W. Ropke, Die Gesellschaftskrisis der Gegenwart, 1942.

17 Watrin, *supra* note 4, at 421.

18 »Es erwies sich, daß die Gewährung von Freiheit eine Gefahr für die Freiheit werden kann, wenn sie die Bildung privater Macht ermöglicht, daß zwar außerordentliche Energien durch sie geweckt werden, aber daß diese Energien auch freiheitszerstörend wirken können.« Eucken, *supra* note 2, at 53. See also L. Miksch, Wettbewerb als Aufgabe, 1937.

19 Vanberg, *supra* note 6, at 19.

20 J. Buchanan, The Limits of Liberty, 1975, p. 68.

21 See L. Mises, Kritik des Interventionismus, 1926; F. Hayek, The Road to Serfdom, 1944; and A. Rustow, untitled paper in Deutschland und die Weltkrise, Schriften des Vereins für Sozialpolitik 187 (1932), pp. 62-69.

22 See Kloten, *supra* note 10, at 11. The problem of political power (Macht) was a central issue for the Ordo-liberals. See Eucken, *supra* note 2, at 169.

23 Vanberg, *supra* note 6, at 20.

24 Buchanan, *supra* note 20, at 68.

25 See P. Bernholz, »Freedom and Constitutional Economic Order« in Zeitschrift für die gesamte Staatswissenschaft 135 (1979), pp. 520-532; R. Klump, Wirtschaftsgeschichte der Bundesrepublik Deutschland, 1985; Vanberg, *supra* note 6; and H. Willgerodt, »Die Krise der Wirtschaftspolitik« in Zeitschrift für Wirtschaftspolitik 37 (1988), at 5-12.

26 See Kolten, *supra* note 10, at 14.

27 H. Siebert, »Anpassungsprobleme in einer offenen Volkswirtschaft« in B. Gahlen *et al.* (eds.), Wirtschaftswachstum, Strukturwandel und dynamischer Wettbewerb, E. Helmstadter zum 65. Geburtstag, 1989a, pp. 187-199.

28 *Id.*

29 H. Siebert, »Allokation zwischen Generationen« in D. Duvendag and H. Siebert (eds.), Politik und Markt, 1980, pp. 353-370.

30 See Europäischer Zentralverband der öffentlichen Wirtschaft 1987, pp 35 and 37.

31 J. Donges and K.W. Schatz, Staatliche Interventionen in der Bundesrepublik Deutschland: Umfang, Struktur, Wirkungen, 1986, no. 119/120, p. 26 *et seq.*

32 *Id.* See also R. Soltwedel *et al.,* Deregulierungspotentiale in der Bundesrepublik, 1986.

33 Kloten, *supra* note 10, at 15.
34 *Id.*
35 »In der Sozialordnung gibt es zahlreiche, damals unterschätzte, sich später als schwerwiegend erweisende konstruktive Mängel« *Id.,* at 12.
36 See Popper, *supra* note 3, at 174.
37 Possibly, fiscal federalism both in a spatial and a functional interpretation is an answer. By linking taxation and government financing to the supply of public goods the voter can see what the government is providing. This relates to the regional dimension of public goods (and financing) where regions decide on their public goods and the financing. It refers to the splitting up of some government services (railroads, postal services) into an infrastructure company owning the tracks or telephone lines and operating companies which can be private. And it also implies a financing through user charges wherever possible.
38 See Siebert, *supra* note 29.

Reiner Schmidt

Principles of the Economic System in the Federal Republic of Germany - A Legal View*

I. *The Basic Law and the Economic System*

1. *The State and the Economic System in the Federal Republic Since 1945*

In the post-war history of the Federal Republic,[1] four essential stages of development can be distinguished in relations between state and economy.
First, a new economic order had to be established immediately after 1945. During the discussion of the Basic Law within the parties, and the dealings between the various parties, the Third Way proposed by the neoliberals proved the most successful. It trod a middle ground between a discarded historical liberalism and a threatening collectivism. The »night watchman state« of old liberalism was to be replaced by a strong state which would be in a position to ensure a truly free economy. The CDU's Ahlen Program had called for the socialization of primary industries, the dismantling of monopolies and cartels, a state economic plan, and new opportunities for employee codetermination in major companies. By contrast, Müller-Armack's formula of the »social market economy« placed clearer emphasis on the principles of competition and private ownership of the means of production. When the Federal Constitutional Court eventually ruled, in 1954, that the economic and social order of the social market economy was a possible system under the Basic Law, but was not the only possibility, the debate concluded for the time being.
The second phase, which moved on from the fundamental question of the economic system, established the limits for government intervention in the economic sector - in particular, the limits established by the basic rights.
A new note was struck when, against the background of the severe recession of 1966/67, the planning debate resulted, in terms of economic theory, in the concept of global control, the new version of Art. 109 and in the passage of the Stability and Growth Act. This assisted the breakthrough, in legal terms, of the idea of necessary state interference in the economy.

Today, the Keynesianism of the Stability and Growth Act tends to be viewed critically in the Federal Republic. It is not that any new legal instruments have replaced it; merely that economic policy prefers to rely on control of the money supply by the German Federal Bank, which is supposed to make, or at least tend to make, discretionary isolated interventions in the economic process unnecessary.[2]

2. The Economic System in Constitutional Jurisprudence

The dispute about the economic system under the Basic Law is principally explained by the »openness« of its economic articles. This, in turn, is the result of its origins. As we have seen, the authors of the constitution were unable to agree on any particular program of economic policy. In addition, the Parliamentary Council understood the Basic Law to be a provisional measure which was not intended to anticipate the social process. Lack of clarity in defining concepts was a further problem. The definitions used in economics for »economic order« often say nothing different from those used in jurisprudence to define the »economic constitution.« In what follows, the terms »economic constitution« refers to those constitutional provisions relating to the organization of the economy.

In the constitutional organization of the economy, the economic constitution may seek to standardize a particular economic system or go no further than to lay down the basic outline for the organization of the economic order, without having a particular economic system in view. A distinction must be made between two main cases representing ideal types: central control by the state (centrally administered economy) and decentralized control by competition (market economy).[3]

a) The Economic Constitution and the Economic System

In the early history of the Federal Republic, the concept of the economic constitution was essentially linked to the idea of a particular economic system as a normative institution. Nipperdey, in particular, who regarded the Basic Law as an institutional guarantee of the social market economy,[4] believed that the constitution was identified with a particular economic system. By way of justification, he relied on an economy-oriented interpretation of basic personal rights guaranteed in Art. 2 (1) (right to the free development of personality) and the principle of the social state. The

312

critical point of his thesis was his elevation of the social market economy to an independent yardstick of constitutional law.[5] Certainly it was never Nipperdy's intention to guarantee a statically immutable model of the social market economy. For him, all that remained between a centrally administered economy and unfettered liberalism was the possibility of the »social market economy.« Since he deliberately based his arguments on what was then the valid and essential conception of economic policy, his thesis was generally interpreted as a normative guarantee of the social market economy; an economic system had become a constitutional yardstick. The capacity of a governmental measure to alter competitive opportunities should in itself be sufficient to be a distortion of competition in breach of Art. 2 (1).[6]

The conception of the social market economy as a constitutionally guaranteed system could not become generally accepted: First, the economic articles of the Basic Law were the product of compromise; second, they did not embody a clear concept of the social market economy. This concept is admittedly able to describe a certain economic style, but as a legal system, it leaves many essential questions unanswered. Thus, there is often no clear way of distinguishing between interventions which are in conformity with market conditions and those which are not.[7] Finally, and most importantly, the consequence which would have been involved in adopting an economic system into the constitutional order was apparent: the surrender of the supreme law to the uncertainties of a social order and its theory.

Huber's theory of the institutional guarantee of a mixed economic constitution is open to objections similar to Nipperdy's[8] to the extent that it is understood as a guarantee of an economic system. It is true that Art. 2 (1) provides for freedom of competition, contract, production, sale, purchase, and consumption. It is unconvincing, however, if the principles of subsidiarity and proportionality are invoked in support of a system where interventions in economic freedom are only accepted when the primary requirements of the public good »cannot be fulfilled by the self-regulation of the market through a competitive economy.«[9] The protected principle is not the self-regulation of the market but the individual basic economic law as such. For its curtailment, however, an exception-and-rule relationship applies. The criterion here is the particular fundamental law affected. Its status and limitations as a fundamental law have to be determined, the greatest difficulties being caused by the general freedom of action guaranteed by Art. 2 (1) because its scope is not specifically outlined.

If we discount Huber's elaboration, and his »mixed guarantee« and its consequences, his work contains important descriptions of the tensions in the economic constitution between the guarantee of freedom on the one hand and the social guarantee on the other.

Even the revival of the debate about the economic constitution, which began with the amendment to Art. 109 in 1967,[10] produced no new findings regarding the relationship between the Basic Law and the economic system. The newly created link between the budget management of the Federal Government and the Länder, the requirements of overall economic equilibrium, and the creation of machinery for that link in the form of a long-term finance plan, compulsory anticyclical reserves and credit limit regulations, together with other tools provided by the Stability and Growth Act, resulted in a significant increase in the number of standards relating to the field of economics. Despite these moves towards a globally controlled market economy incorporating planning elements,[11] it was only the economic style that had changed. This style, understood as global control, aimed to continue using competition to regulate the microeconomic parameters, while the macroeconomic parameters were to be made more easily manageable for the state.

b) *A Functional Guarantee of the Market Economy?*

Even more successful than the literary endeavors to convert the »politico-economic neutrality« of the Basic Law into a system guarantee were those approaches which placed the basic rights in the effective and organizational context of the economy, hence arriving at certain functional guarantees for decentralized economic activity.[12] The constitutional guarantees of private ownership (including its economic utility [Art. 14]), the vocational, trading and entrepreneurial freedoms guaranteed in Art. 1 (2), the opportunities for free selection of workplace and training location, the right created by Art. 9 to form trading companies, and finally Art. 2 (1), believed to enshrine the guarantee of competitive and contractual freedom, form the premise for considering the Basic Law as *not* being neutral towards the economy. The centrally administered economy as a form of coordination was intended to be excluded. According to this prevalent opinion, the share in the economic and social organization guaranteed to the individual through basic rights prevents the political system from obtaining absolute control over the economy. This angle of interpretation, which cannot seriously be disputed, is also not questioned by the power of socialization set out in Art. 15, since the latter, if only because of the compulsory compensation aspect, makes it

314

legally and not just practically impossible to institute a form of socialization which would replace the ownership guarantee.[13]

The interpretation of the economic provisions based on the individual basic right and its functional conditions moves in the context of conventional basic rights theory. For example, the guarantee of private ownership of the means of production compels an economic order that assumes a private enterprise market. The generally accepted hermeneutic approach is abandoned, however, when the criterion[14] is no longer the individual standard, but rather a »system relationship« constructed as a major premise. Put differently, according to functional theory, the market and competition as such are not institutions guaranteed by the basic rights. But their elimination is prevented by the ownership guarantee in Art. 14.[15]

3. *The Economic Constitution in the Decisions of the Federal Constitutional Court*

a) *The Thesis of »Politico-economic Neutrality«*

In the view of the Federal Constitutional Court, the politico-economic program is subject to the principle of the »neutrality of the Basic Law.« The constitutional authority did not expressly decide on a specific economic system; this enables the legislator to pursue whatever economic policy he may see fit in a particular case, provided he conforms to the Basic Law in doing so.[16] This principle, formulated as long ago as 1954 in the investment grant case,[17] underwent only insignificant refinements up to the codetermination judgment.[18] In summary, the Court deems it to be constitutionally irrelevant:

- whether an act is in harmony with the existing economic and social order;
- whether the means used »conform to market conditions« in the sense of the »social market economy;«
- whether a measure is in harmony with a received economic opinion on which particular economic policy is based;
- whether a politico-economic opinion revealed in the act is approved by the judge;
- whether an act has been passed in the interests of one group;
- whether an act is neutral with regard to competition.[19]

In the Court's view there is also no compulsion to provide equal competitive opportunities.[20] Against these freedoms, the Court sets obligations which form part of the essential basis of every constitutional state and contain little that is not taken for granted. In fact, the legislator is bound by the Basic Law, and particularly by basic rights. Any measure taken to control the economy intervenes in the process of social life so as to shape its course, thus adjusting the free interplay of forces. The public interest requires such laws, laws that do not wilfully disregard the interests of others who are deserving of protection.[21] The emphasis on the fundamental politico-economical freedom of organization enjoyed by the legislator has met with widespread agreement, not least because of the absence in the Basic Law of any explicit statements on the economic system.[22] This should by no means be misinterpreted as a failure of the Basic Law to deal, and deal decisively, with the economy. The Basic Law is merely »relatively open;« the normative force of the constitution must not be put at risk.[23]

b) *Individual Basic Rights as a Yardstick*

The controversy about the »economic constitution,« often declared extinct, reappears in modified form in the question of a special criterion for the assessment of the politico-economic legislator. Here we see the extent to which his »extensive freedom of organization«[24] is restricted in the economic sector. The actual benefit of the controversy over economic constitutional law is therefore also to be found in thinking back to the problem of interpretation. Characteristically, the most important, relevant later decision, the codetermination judgment,[25] employs the criteria of examination under constitutional law, whereas the fundamental question of economic constitutional law is treated somewhat casually and routinely.[26]
Contrary to the »Cologne Report,« which refers to the »institutional protective and organizational connection between the constitutional freedoms, rights and guarantees relating to the economy and those relating to labor,«[27] the Federal Constitutional Court applies, as the criterion for constitutional scrutiny, »those individual fundamental rights which mark the constitutional framework conditions and limits of organizational freedom which the legislator has in introducing an extended codetermination.«[28] This statement highlights the significance of the factual theme in question as a guiding aspect for interpretation by referring to the Codetermination Act. Yet additionally, and most especially, those efforts are rejected which link the concept of the »economic constitution« to a systemic concept which transcends fundamental rights. On the other hand, the Court was unable to set aside the principle which it had itself sometimes applied: every

316

provision of the constitution is linked, in terms of meaning, with other provisions of the constitution, representing an internal unity.[29] Without expressly referring to its own judgment, the Court emphasizes in the codetermination judgment that individual fundamental rights »cannot be interpreted without taking into account the overlaps, additions and relationships between their field of protection and that of other basic rights, nor can they be interpreted without reference to the principles which support the Basic Law.«[30] With this choice of words, the Court came so close to the approach of the »Cologne Report,« which it had itself several times decisively rejected, that it was barely possible to distinguish between them. The »Cologne Report« had brought out the »interdependence of the economic context and its legal regulations.«[31] The distinction, far from clear, lies in the Court's emphasis on the individual basic rights as personal defensive rights, the Court seeing their function as objective principles, referring back to its earlier judgment,[32] and only »as reinforcing their validity in principle.«[33] The freedom of the individual citizen and the protective scope of the individual basic right against the legislator ordering the economy has hence been substituted by the Federal Constitutional Court for the phantom »economic constitution.«

The significance of the codetermination judgment in terms of economic constitutional law is therefore found not in the repeated refusal to incorporate an economic system into the constitution, but in giving concrete form to the binding effect of the Basic Law, only vaguely referred to in the investment grant judgment. In fact, this binding nature is not only based more clearly on the basic rights, but also and at the same time on a particular theory of basic rights – a mixed theory. It emphasizes the basic rights as defensive rights, while reducing the importance of their institutional, or objective law, content;[34] Thus the Federal Constitutional Court referred the disagreement over the »economic constitution« back to the interpretation of the individual basic economic rights. What remains is to pursue the question of whether it can, after all, be inferred from the individual observations on basic rights relevant to the economy that the Court regards a minimum of private market economic activity as guaranteed for economic operations under the Basic Law.

c)   *The Necessity of Justifying Market Intervention*

For the Federal Constitutional Court, the economy of the Federal Republic is in principle a free economy. Restriction of the freedom of economic action by means of market regulations, for example, is only permissible

317

where it is required for overriding considerations of the public good.[35] Laws imposing measures to control the economy, which become necessary as a result of immediate crisis situations, are to be rescinded once they have accomplished their purpose. »Then, in principle, the freedom of economic activity must again prevail.«[36]

Although the Court has repeatedly refused to see the Basic Law as a system guarantee for the economy, it does not balk at referring to the »existing economic constitution« which, as a basis, contains the »fundamentally free competition between the commercial forces of supply and demand in the market place as one of its fundamental principles.«[37] However, the context in which these more general remarks are made must not be overlooked. It is in each case the specifically relevant right of liberty, such as the freedom to follow an occupation (Art. 12 [1]), whose scope of freedom is widened and whose circumscription is subject to compulsory justification. How the Court arrives at systemic statements on economic constitutional law is not a matter of indifference; for example, whether it does so through an overall view of the constitution or inductively from a single basic right. What is important is whether the basic right applies within the terms of a particular economic system, or whether, while producing certain systemic effects, it is nonetheless to be interpreted primarily from its specific field of protection. The Court decided in favor of referring to the individual basic right. At the same time it has not only accepted that the legislators have ordered the economy »in principle as a market economy,«[38] but it finds even in the constitution a priority for freedom of economic activity.[39] This priority, however, must not be reinterpreted as a systemic guarantee for a free market.[40] Rather, the Court elaborates in each case only in the field of protection of the individual basic right, whereby Art. 12 (1) and 14 (1) are more significant in their protection of freedom because of their more closely circumscribed scope for restriction, than in the freedom of activity in the economic area guaranteed by Art. 2 (1), which is subject to restrictions imposed by the legislators, particularly in the context of »constitutional order.« Nevertheless, the Court maintains that »appropriate freedom of action for the development of commercial initiatives« is inviolable even here.[41] The result, therefore, is that every legislative activity in the economic field is considered an intervention in an intrinsically free market and subject to pressure for justification. Even if the requirements to be satisfied by the legislator are not set unreasonably high, and even if a »justifiable and constitutionally acceptable politico-economic aim«[42] in view of the absence of a normative doctrine governing the functions of government can easily be advanced in each case, the exception-and-rule relationship thus justified provides additional security for private economic activity free of government influence.

The judgments of the Federal Constitutional Court on the question of the economic constitution should not be credited with more consistency than they actually contain. The global rejection of a guarantee of a specific economic system stands in contrast to a commitment to the free market and the insight into the functional conditions and mode of functioning of basic economic rights. The Court, however, has hitherto taken little advantage of the opportunity to pursue this aspect in more depth. Also, contrary to other legal practice, basic economic rights coexist in a largely unconnected ' manner. This is probably more a matter of verbal declaration (as a defense against attempts to introduce global constructions of economic constitutional law as a whole) than one of actual practice.

Overall, the Court has spoken with notable clarity on the fundamentally private nature of economic activity, but has otherwise consistently followed its flexible line between normatively guided, problem-oriented and topical procedures.[43]

II. *Responsibility for and Instruments of Economic Organization*

1. *The Objective of »Overall Economic Equilibrium«*

Among the many acts passed by the Federal Government to organize and control the economy, of particular interest are those which clearly show the decision in favor of the market economy and which orient economic policy towards a specific goal. Examples include the Act against Restraints on Competition of 1957, the Stability and Growth Act of 1967, and the Act relating to the Formation of a Council of Experts, dating from 1963. These acts make particular reference to the free market economy, and they attempt to safeguard it.

Particularly interesting is § 1 StabG [Stability and Growth Act], which brings more detailed clarification to Art. 109 (2). According to this regulation, the Federal Government and the Länder must consider the requirements of the overall economic equilibrium in managing their budget. Section 1 of the StabG generalizes this governmental objective in relation to budget management, requiring that it should apply to measures taken by the Federal Government and the Länder not only in the field of financial policy, but economic policy as well. The Stability Act also clarifies the concept of overall economic equilibrium, without interpreting it in a binding manner, by ruling that those measures must contribute, given constant and appropriate economic growth, to price stability, a high level of employment, and foreign trade equilibrium. The effect is a normative obligation on economic policy as a whole.[44]

The principle of overall economic equilibrium, founded in Art. 109 and clarified in § 1 of the StabG, is directed at the Federal Government and the Länder (and hence, through the latter, at municipalities too), but offers no foundation for individual entitlements. The absence of a binding legislative definition does not mean that infringement of the principle of overall economic equilibrium within the government will entail no consequences; rather it is the subject of the auditing and release procedure set out in Art. 114 of the Basic Law. Ultimately, the obligation of the Federal Government and the Länder for overall economic equilibrium is controlled by the Federal Constitutional Court, to which one could appeal under Art. 93 (1) [1-3], if a legal dispute were to arise between the Federal Government and one or more Länder as to whether a certain measure on economic policy was constitutional. The correct legal classification of the »overall economic equilibrium« in the typology of terms of normative authorization doctrine[45] is not crucial here, so long as the fundamental liability to legal recourse is endorsed.[46]

2. *The Machinery of Economic Policy*

a) *General*

The provision of machinery for economic policy by the Stability and Growth Act is based on the concept of global control which aims to leave the microparameters to free competition, but endeavors to control the macroparameters (national income, imports and exports, and investment rates) principally through the budget.[47] Whereas in the previous theory of the free market economy the line of separation ran between the market organization policy and the procedural policy, this shift in emphasis focuses on the ability of counter-cyclical financial policy to guarantee a high level of employment and overall economic equilibrium. By contrast, procedural policy had referred both to the microeconomic (prices, production volumes) and to the macroeconomic (national income, employment) ratios. The concept of global control is based on the two fundamental preconditions of stable growth and stable economic climate. It was not adequate for the new phenomenon of stagflation (simultaneous occurrence of high inflation rates and high unemployment), and came under pressure from monetarism.[48] This counter-revolution against the Keynesian revolution expects fiscal policy to produce not a global but merely an allocative effect, and relies on monetary policy, or more precisely on a fixed and specific rate of an overall monetary parameter geared to the growth rate.[49]

In addition to global control and monetarism, discussion in the Federal Republic also centers on the possibility of a supply-oriented stability policy.[50] The machinery of a supply-oriented policy, which is determined less by a self-contained concept than by the pragmatics of the »policy mix,« cannot be presently described. We shall deal here only with those elements of the machinery which refer to fiscal policy and monetarism, since these are covered by standards, which is not the case for supply-oriented policy, with the exception of the structural policy employed to implement it.[51]

b)   *The Instruments of Financial Policy*

aa)   *Opportunities for Use and Obstacles to Use*

Since economic policy and the legislators (§ 1 StabG) underscore the fact that »overall economic equilibrium« is to be the guiding aim of any economic policy, Art. 109 (2) can be seen as the normative consequence of a trend during which the demand-fulfillment function of budget policy has been increasingly overshadowed by its politico-economic function. As a result of budget law acquiring this politico-economic use, it runs the risk of overtaking its capacity for control.[52] The practical and legal limits to a politico-economic use of the budget are manifold. Some of these limits arise from the fact that more than 80% of the budget volume is substantially bound by law.[53] Even so, the amount remaining for maneuver seems adequately large, when we consider the fact that almost 1/5 of overall economic demand for goods and services is determined by the state.

Legal impediments exist primarily because of the fundamental independence of the budget management of the Federal Government, the Länder and the municipalities. As the Federal Government accounts for only about 15% of public investment, it has to rely on the cooperation of the municipalities and the Länder.

Constitutional limits to a counter-cyclical deployment of budget funds exist as a result of the Federal Government's right of approval of increased expenditure (Art. 113), and the restriction on financing by way of credit imposed by Art. 115. However, this provision, which links borrowing to capital expenditures, has been weakened by the fact that exceptions are possible to prevent disturbance of the overall economic equilibrium – conditional on circumstances whose existence can easily be demonstrated in view of the fundamental liability of any politico-economic situation.[54]

bb)   *Counter-cyclical Expenditure Policy*

The constitution provides a broad basis for the Federal Goverment and Länder to manage their budgets to suit the economic situation, while legislation provides them with extensive machinery for doing so. Thus, Art. 109 (3) broke through the principle of separate budget management (Art. 109 [1]), enabling the legislator to establish principles which apply equally to budget law, to budget management oriented to the economic climate, and to long-term financial planning by the Federal Government and the Länder. The new paragraph 3 of Art. 109 made possible, in 1969, the passage of the Budgetary Principles Act, which, together with the machinery of the Stability and Growth Act passed two years earlier, allows for compensatory organization of the public budgets. In addition, paragraph 4 of Art. 109 permits the Federal Government to influence the budget arrangements of the public sector as a whole through credit restrictions and compulsory anti-cyclical reserves in order to prevent disruption of economic equilibrium. Finally, Art. 115, also amended in 1969, makes it possible to circumvent the rule in which income from credits must not exceed the total expenditure on investments estimated in the budget. The intention behind the authorization of additional borrowing, however, is to provide protection against transitory disturbances of the equilibrium, not general coverage of budget shortfalls.[55] However, the extent and rate of borrowing evident since the beginning of the 1970s is less attributable to utilization of the expanded version of Art. 115 (1) [2] – in other words increasing investment expenditure for politico-economic purposes – than to the general, excessively expansive budgetary policy.[56] The conception of an increase or reduction in public spending to stimulate or suppress demand is provided with more detailed machinery in the Stability and Growth Act. The principal elements of this machinery, apart from budget freezes imposed by the Federal Finance Minister (§ 6, Para. 1, StabG, 5 41 BHO), are compulsory anticyclical reserves and credit limit regulations by the Federal Government (§§ 15 *et seq.*, §§ 19 *et seq.* StabG).

cc)   *The Use of Taxes*

Among the fiscal instruments for controlling the economic cycle, the most powerful is the Federal Government's power to increase or reduce the income, wage and corporation taxes by a maximum of 10% for not more than one year by means of a decree to be approved by the Federal Council (§§ 26 No. 3b, 27 No. 1 StabG, § 51 par. 3 EStG [Income Tax Act], § 19c KStG [Corporation Tax Act]). In this case the legislators have gone to the limits of what is constitutionally permissible, since the right of the Federal Government to vary such important taxes infringes on the historical budgetary of Parliament.[57]

c)   *Instruments of Information*

The non-binding but nevertheless effective machinery of the Stability Act includes the *Annual Economic Report of the Federal Government*, which, pursuant to § 2, par. 1 StabG, must be presented to the Bundestag and the Federal Council in January of each year. The Annual Economic Report must contain comments on the annual appraisal by the Council of Experts, a presentation of the aims being pursued in economic and financial policy (annual projection) and the measures planned for the current year in economic and financial policy (§ 2, par. 1, Clause 2, StabG). The special significance of the annual appraisals lies in the fact that the package of politico-economic objectives referred to in § 1 StabG is not quantified, whereas this cannot be avoided in the case of the Annual Economic Reports. As a result of the comparison between the current annual projection and the actual values of the target indicators (price index for private consumption, unemployment rate, net visible and invisible exports as a percentage of the gross national product, and growth rate in percent), the Federal Government comes under pressure to succeed. However, the Annual Economic Report is intended not so much to permit monitoring by the public as to serve principally as an instrument of information, orientation and coordination for the public institutions responsible for economic policy and for the corporate groups. Fears that the Annual Economic Report would promote a change in the nature of global control to mere planning[58] have proven unfounded.

A further important instrument of information, aimed at curbing subsidies, is the *Subsidies Report*, which according to § 12, pars. 2 to 4, StabG is to be produced every two years. The report, which contains a statistical survey of financial subsidies, including tax benefits, must also include the reductions planned by the Federal Government, with specific time limits, for ending this financial aid (§ 12, Para. 4, Clauses 3 and 4, StabG). Following the appearance of 11 *Subsidies Reports,*[59] it must be said that the reports have remained virtually ineffective as far as curbing subsidies is concerned.[60]

According to § 12, Para. 1, StabG, the Federal Government is under obligation, beyond the character of the report, to grant subsidies in such a manner that they do not conflict with the goal of overall economic equilibrium. Despite the binding nature of this regulation, it appears to produce no practical effect.

d)   *Instruments of Coordination*

The aim of *Concerted Action* – a group consisting of political bodies, trade unions, and industrial associations whose mission it is to adopt a common policy in order to achieve the aims of overall economic equilibrium (§ 3 StabG) – was to influence consensus formation within the autonomous groups without infringing upon the autonomy of collective bargaining under Art. 9 (3). As a paragon of »cooperative pluralism,«[61] it was intended to replace the egotistical and utilitarian competitive principle and open the way to a form of cooperation committed to the common good.

The discussions held several times yearly from 1966 to 1973, under the chairmanship of the Federal Minister of Economie, were initially attended by representatives of the central associations of the employers' organizations (DIHT, BDI, BDA), representatives of commerce and handicrafts, and of the trade unions (DGB, DAG). These were later joined by the Council of Experts and the Federal Bank. Representatives of other associations, such as agriculture, were invited on a continuous or case by case basis.

The vehement legal controversy surrounding *Concerted Action,* which was attacked by its critics as being either a »socialization of the nation« or a »nationalization of society,« was in many cases conducted without reference to the heart of constitutional law represented by Art. 9 (3) and by Art. 20 (2).[62] Fears that this cooperation at the »table of social reason« (Karl Schiller) was a constitutionally dubious general treaty between state and coalitions have proven unfounded. There was no threat to the internal sovereignity of the state, because the cooperation in accordance with § 3 StabG never went beyond a non-binding clearing house of interests.

Other instruments of coordination with an advisory function are the *Business Cycle Council* (§ 18 StabG) and the *Financial Planning Council* (§ 51, Para. 1, HGRG). Both committees, made up of representatives of the

324

Federal Government, the Länder and the municipalities, serve to coordinate their financial planning and steer the budgets in the direction of the overall economic equilibrium.

A final instrument of financial policy which must be mentioned is the *middle-term financial plan* (§§ 6, 9, 10, 14, 17 StabG), the function, aims and constitutional admissibility of which are still subject to disagreement.[63] This five-year financial plan introduced by the legislators for the Federal Government and the Länder requires both, each on their own behalf, to relate the scope and structure of their expenditure and income to the potential performance of the economy as a whole, or if appropriate, in alternative global economic calculations. The finance plan, which is approved by the Federal Government and is to be submitted to Parliament together with the budget, is adapted and updated annually in line with developments (§ 9, par. 2, StabG).

The financial plan, designed as a non-binding government plan, has yet to produce the anticipated unwelcome effect of imposing *de facto* obligations on Parliament. In the opinion of the Council of Experts, it has degenerated »into a lamentable state,« becoming a »tedious duty.«[64] Models of a parliamentary financial plan, possibly based on the American Committee on the Budget,[65] would be discussed only if the virtually unanimous judgment of practical experience that the middle-term finance plan is a »residue from the preparation of the budget«[66] was refuted.

e) Critique of the Stability and Growth Act

The »toolbox« of the Stability and Growth Act is virtually complete. Even so, one might consider raising the maximum limits set (tax variation by not more than 10%, reduction of the credit volume in the last 5 years by a maximum of 20 or 30%). One might also think of finding statutory ways of eliminating possible evasions in organization of the obligatory anticyclical reserves (dissolution of voluntary reserves, utilization of cash credits, etc.). The problems of the act, however, are found less in the normatively inadequate nature of its instruments than in Keynesian theory and in a general failure of (economic) policy.

3. Structural Policy

Structural policy is intended to implement overall economic or sector-related aims through direct or indirect influence exerted on the economic structure. In addition to promoting future-oriented products, regions or sizes of enterprises, the intention is to produce an appropriate income ratio for these things. Adaptation to structural change (*e.g.*, protection by the imposition of import quotas) is facilitated for reasons of social and security policy.[67]

Sectoral structural policy - that part of economic policy aimed at changing the share in the overall economic figures accounted for by one industrial sector - is closely interrelated to general economic policy and regional structural policy. The instruments available cannot be systematized. They range from financial incentives to provide further vocational training, through measures to improve the infrastructure, tax relief and subsidies, to the regulation of markets and capital expenditures for whole economic or production sectors. *Investment control* typically solidifies sectoral structural policy.[68] It has been discussed from various aspects in the Federal Republic, as indirect investment control or as direct investment control which aims to replace private enterprise investment decisions with a global government investment plan. This discussion of investment control has largely died down. To the extent that investment control models aimed to introduce a general obligation for approval of private investment, they were ruled out by the freedoms provided by Art. 12 (freedom of occupation) and Art. 14 (freedom of ownership). Art. 15 permitted related socialization measures only with compensation. Also, service operations such as banks and insurance companies could not be socialized.

In the same way as sectoral structural policy, *regional policy* is intended to have only a supplementary and corrective effect in the market economy system. As a territorially oriented form of structural policy, it aims to make a selective contribution to increased efficiency of general economic policy and/or to the reduction of variations in interregional prosperity. The constitution provides a regulatory framework for this in Arts. 72 (2) [No. 3], 91a (1) [No. 2] and 104a (1).[69] Although no great disparities have arisen in the Federal Republic, as compared with other countries, between the center and periphery,[70] there are still problem areas in the rural regions, usually near frontiers. They are namely traditional development areas with the community task of »improving the regional economic structure« and, since the mid-1970s, the old industrial centers (mining areas on the Ruhr and Saar, and the shipbuilding sites on the coast) where the Federal Government, the Länder and even municipalities apply policy on a regional level for reasons of growth policy or to equalize differences between regions.

The most important instrument of regional structural policy is the community task of »improving the regional economic structure,« which was incorporated into the Basic Law in 1969 by Art. 91a (1).

An important administrative element of the community task is the outline plan of the Federal Government and the Länder envisaged in the Community Tasks Act. The plan is prepared for regional economic structure by a committee whose members include the Federal Minister of Economics as Chairman, and the Federal Finance Minister and the economic ministers (senators) of the Länder. The number of votes held by the Federal Government equals those held by the Länder; resolutions by the planning committee require a majority of 3/4 of the votes (§ 6, Para. 1, 2 Joint Tasks Act).

The planning section of the joint committee set up under Art. 91 (3) is a new constitutional institution restricted to general planning by the Federal Government and Länder. Its primary purpose is one of coordination; therefore, it can only act indirectly, through the Länder or the municipalities.[71]

Along with unsolved economic problems relating principally to defining the development areas and to possible ways of monitoring success, legal questions arising out of the federalistic organization and the incorporation of the Federal Republic into the European Community have caused difficulties in the context of the community task of »promoting the regional economic structure.«

The Community Tasks Act provides aid as well as the Investment Subsidies Act,[72] according to which »projects particularly deserving of assistance in the interests of the national economy« are to be supported by the granting of investment subsidies of 10% (in the strip bordering East Germany) and 8.5% (in the other areas requiring development aid) (§ 1, Para. 4, Investment Subsidies Act). There are also a number of other laws at the federal level whose purpose is to promote regional economies. Particularly noteworthy is the Border Strip Development Act, the Act relating to the European Recovery Program Special Fund[73] and the Berlin Development Act, whereas financial aid granted by the Federal Government under Art. 104a (4) for important investments by the Länder and municipalities has no specific impact on regional policy.

The federalistic and supranational problems, particularly the EC's difficulty in monitoring national aid to the regions under Arts. 92 to 94 of the EEC Treaty, plus the lack of definition of the regulations on regional aid especially, pose virtually insurmountable problems of interpretation. In many cases even the operational aims are not adequately defined. The interpreter of standards must provide a »functionally adequate interpretation specific to the standard,« in order to harmonize »the special structural situation of the particular region and its sectoral problems«[74] with those in the economy as a whole, a task whose definition is ultimately political even if the intention is to grant very extensive administrative powers of final decision.

4. Monetary Policy

a) Position, Tasks and Instruments of the Federal Bank

The Federal Bank's importance in organizing the overall monetary and currency system in the Federal Republic is undisputed. This is made clear by the constitutional emphasis in Art. 88 (»The Federal Government shall establish an issuing bank as a Federal Bank«), a novelty in German constitutional history. Further details of the status and organization of the Federal Bank are found in the Federal Bank Act of 1957.[75] According to § 2, Clause 1, Federal Bank Act, the Federal Bank is an agency of the Federal Government and a legal person under public law, an institution which enjoys a special position because it is not subject to instructions in exercising its powers under § 12, Clause 2, Federal Bank Act.[76] The Federal Bank is principally the custodian of the currency and the bank for other banks; it also acts as the bank for the state. According to § 3 of the Federal Bank Act, it is charged with »safeguarding the currency.« The simultaneous obligation to meet the general economic policy of the Federal Government (§ 12, Clause 1, Federal Bank Act) and the retrospective obligation, imposed by § 13, Para. 3, StabG, and framed as a directory provision, to fulfill the aims of stability of the price level, high employment and external equilibrium, given constant and appropriate economic growth (§ 1 StabG), cannot overshadow the aim of safeguarding the currency specifically imposed on the Federal Bank by § 3 of the Federal Bank Act. In the conflict with the Federal Government over which monetary and economic policies to pursue, the bank may, in case of doubt, plead a threat to the stability of the value of money, which must be dealt with as a priority. The legal regulation of the politico-economic aims in § 1 StabG has given the Federal Bank additional room for maneuver, because the Bank's duty of allegiance to the general economic policy ends if, in the Bank's opinion, the Federal Government is departing from the framework of overall economic equilibrium. However, the primary aim of safeguarding the currency, meaning the domestic purchasing power and the external value of the currency, does not devolve upon the Federal Bank alone. Responsibility for this is shared, within the framework of economic, financial and social policy, by the Federal Government, which decides on the important fixing of the currency parity,[77] and by the legislators. Because of its monopoly on the issuing of notes, however, and more particularly because of its power to regulate monetary wealth through bank credits, the Bank has virtually sole responsibility for controlling the quantities of money and credit in circulation.

Since 1974 the Federal Bank has pursued the primary aim of safeguarding currency by controlling the amount of money in circulation. In other words, it controls the money creation process by using its machinery of monetary policy in such a way that the growth in the volume of money in circulation remains within the Bank's chosen limits. In this manner, there is a tendency to replace individual politico-economic attempts at government control. The opportunity for this change in concept arose when, in 1973, the unrestricted obligation to intervene in the currency markets was lifted. The capacity to control the creation of money rules out both pressure on the issuing bank to pursue particular credit transactions and extensive obligation to intervene in favor of foreign currencies. In the opinion of the Federal Bank itself, the obligation to intervene within the terms of the European Monetary System (EMS) remains »at a low level of magnitude.«[78] As regards safeguarding the currency, § 3 of the Federal Bank Act provides that regulating the circulation of money, supplying credit to industry and handling payment transactions are the principal tasks of the Federal Bank. Whereas the circulation of money and the provision of credit primarily represent an objective of monetary policy, the handling of payment transactions in Germany and with foreign countries is a technical operation of banking; the two areas of operation are interrelated.

What is not expressly regulated is the Federal Bank's activity as the state bank to the Federal Government. This is not a genuine function of an issuing bank. As the bank to the state, the Federal Bank acts as a provider of credit (so-called cash credits to compensate temporary shortfalls). Because of unfortunate experiences with the financing of government deficits by issuing banks, the level of these cash credits yielded to Federal Government, Länder, railroads, post office, the Equalization of Burdens Fund, and the ERP Special Fund is strictly limited to about DM 10 billion (§ 20 Federal Bank Act).

The intention of the legislator was that the Federal Bank should be granted all powers »which, in accordance with modern monetary theory and practice, are appropriate and necessary for the manipulation of the volume of money in circulation.«[79] Therefore, virtually no additions to the generously scaled machinery have since been necessary. One exception is the so-called cash deposit (6a, Para. 1, Foreign Trade Payment Act), which, from 1971 to 1974, obliged non-banks to maintain interest-free deposits with the Federal Bank in the case of capital imports.

With its powers to implement discount, credit, open market, minimum reserve, investment and foreign currency policies, the Federal Bank can call on a substantial arsenal, which is further supplemented by the use of »moral suasion.« Since the introduction of money supply control, the machinery has increasingly been used in the form of silent, globally effective measures (in particular security transactions under repurchase agreements), while the minimum reserve policy has become less important and the foreign exchange control has been abandoned.

b)   The Independence of the Federal Bank

There are several legal bases for the independence of the Federal Bank. The general economic policy imposed by § 12, Clause 1, Federal Bank Act and by § 13, Para. 3, StabG states that the Bank must follow only the basic line taken by the Federal Government, and not every individual measure. Hence, the Bank's obligation to the policy contains room for maneuver. Despite this obligation, however, the *lex specialis* regulation provides that the Federal Bank must give priority to its most essential function of safeguarding the currency. Finally, the predetermined objective of »overall economic equilibrium« pursuant to § 1 StabG has imposed a *legal obligation* on the general economic policy. In conflicts between the Federal Government and the Federal Bank over the correct economic policy, the Federal Bank can now refuse to give its support by citing a breach of law by the Federal Government (§ 1 StabG).

Only a minority regards the independence of the Federal Bank as being guaranteed by Art. 88 BL. Prevalent opinion in the literature and judicial practice finds that no constitutional guarantee of independence can be inferred either from the wording, sense and intention of Art. 88 BL or from its origins.[80]

The admissibility of the independence granted by the legislators can be disputed from the standpoint of the fundamental prohibition of areas beyond ministerial or government influence.[81] Such a prohibition can be inferred from the Federal Government's responsibility to parliament to the extent that functions with »political implications may not in general be removed from governmental responsibility and transferred to bodies which are independent of the government and parliament.«[82] In justification of the

330

Federal Bank's independence, reference is made to its links to a system of dependencies of a factual or personal nature, or to a general authority in the Basic Law, according to which typically pluralistic undesirable developments could only be prevented by an independent bank.[83]

None of the attempts at justification have proven sufficient enough to incorporate the Federal Bank's autonomy into the parliamentary government system in a constitutionally sound manner. The most convincing argument remains the concept that the constitution (Art. 88 BL) grants (not guarantees) the Federal Bank a special function in protecting its monetary policy.[84] The independence of the Federal Bank is, in any case, consistent with the constitution and is politically desirable, even if it may not be constitutionally required. In view of the fear of inflation felt by the population of the Federal Republic, based on historical experience, there seems for the present to be a guaranteed democratic concensus in favor of Federal Bank autonomy, which is mentioned by the Federal Constitutional Court.[85]

III.   *The Federal Republic of Germany in the International Economic and Monetary Community*

1.   *The Economic Community*

More than any other political area, currency and the economy are interwoven in economic terms.[86] The Basic Law endeavors to bring national and international legal systems into harmony essentially by means of three constitutional provisions. Art. 25 BL pronounces a general system of validity for »the general rules of international law;« according to Art. 59, Para. 2, BL, the law of international agreements is transformed into the internal legal system in that the bodies responsible for Federal legislation must cooperate in the form of a Federal act; but particularly important is Art. 24, Para. 1, BL, according to which the Federal Government may, by simple act, assign its own rights of sovereignty and those of the Länder to international institutions, hence effecting a material amendment to the constitution.[87]

The instruction that the law be applied by an official act, as required in Art. 24 BL, can be seen, so far as the Federal Republic of Germany is concerned, in the acts ratifying the treaties establishing the European Communities.[88]

Limitation to the transfer of sovereign rights according to Art. 24, Para. 1, BL is seen in cases where intervention into the characteristic, fundamental structure of the constitution takes place as a result of EC legislation without a formal amendment of the constitution.[89] This is currently being debated with particular regard to the federalist state organization of the Federal Republic, specifically because the Länder, unlike the Federal Government, have no direct access to Community decision-making processes, but merely cooperate either informally or through the Federal Council in shaping the intention of the Federal Government in relation to the EC.[90]

The European Communities influence the legal system of the Federal Republic directly through the treaties (primary law) or through the law established by them (secondary law). The question of the economic system of European treaties converging with that of the Federal Republic is therefore of particular interest.

The EEC treaty, which assumes the existence of private enterprise, has rightly been described as »an ordered or regulated competitive economy.«[91] The assignment of a specific economic control system remains disputed. The treaties have subjected the sectors of agriculture (Art. 38 to 47 EEC Treaty), coal and steel (ESC Treaty), and – far less drastically – transport (Art. 74 to 84 EEC Treaty) to a separate, interventionist regime. The machinery available for this, such as price fixing (Art. 61 ESC Treaty) and investment control (Art. 54, Para. 5, ESC Treaty), is statist.

The Community as a whole is characterized by different principles, among which the system of the free market economy is dominant. The Common Market is in essential agreement with the free market economy, as practiced under the Basic Law, under the following conditions: it is used as a principle of political integration; it is characterized by equal conditions of competition, the four basic freedoms and the prohibition of discriminatory practices by Art. 7 EEC Treaty as a specific expression of the general equality clause,[92] only partially broken by market organizations. Both the economic constitution of the EC and that of the Basic Law allow the Community institutions and the legislators extensive freedom, but exclude the type of coordination that characterizes the centrally controlled economy. The primary law of the EC has expressed this more clearly than the Basic Law in Art. 2 and 3 EEC Treaty and in Art. 1 and 2 ECSC Treaty, since in the case of the Basic Law the principle may only be found in individual basic rights, organizational regulations and general constitutional principles.

2. The International Monetary Community

The level of international integration in monetary matters is by no means less than that in the economic sector. The Federal Republic ratified the agreement on the International Monetary Fund (IMF) as early as 1952. Important international monetary institutions or forms of cooperation in which the Federal Republic participates include the Bank for International Settlement (BIS), the regular conferences of the EEC Economics and Finance Ministers (ECOFIN) and the EEC Monetary Committee in the EEC sector, and within the OECD »Working Group 3,« which runs a continuous analysis of trends in the balance of payments relations between important countries.

Even more important for the Federal Republic's autonomy in monetary policy than its membership in the IMF and the World Bank group is its involvement in the European Monetary System (EMS).[93] This binds the currencies of nine EC states in a system of fixed, unchangeable exchange rates, provides for obligatory intervention by its members with reference to a deviation indicator, and operates on the basis of efficient assistance mechanisms in the event of balance of payment problems among member states. The EMS introduced the European Currency Unit (»ECU«) and created the basis for a European currency. The Federal Bank, which was initially skeptical of the tendencies to strengthen the currency character of the ECU, has now made possible its private use to the same extent as that of foreign currencies.[94]

The proposed complete removal of restrictions on the free movement of capital within the European Community, which is connected with the implementation of a single European market, set for 1992, will further constrict the room for maneuver in national monetary policy. The cooperation which is becoming increasingly necessary within the EMS will only be able to safeguard its principal elements - stable value of money, free movement of capital and fixed, nominal exchange rates - if they are placed not in the hands of governments but in those of an independent European central banking system. Arranging the independence of this distantly perceived European system is currently one of the most contentious questions in European economic and monetary policy.

IV. *Prospects*

In view of the increasing network of international and supra-national economic ties, the Federal Republic must make greater efforts to safeguard the basic principles of its free economic system. Structural changes such as the reduction of parliamentary influence, shifts in emphasis in favor of the central governments, diminishing importance of the federal Länder, transfer of government responsibility to the Federal Bank, and in quite general terms, the weakening of the principles of the constitutional state are obvious. Yet it is not only increasing international ties which pose a threat to the free economic system of the constitutional state. Rather, in the Federal Republic, the principles of political order have largely been forgotten in the course of the expansion of the social state. The level of subsidies in the Federal Republic speaks for itself. In an international comparison of fourteen major industrialized states, the Federal Republic ranks ninth with a subsidy quota of 2.1% (based on the gross domestic product), while the USA ranks lowest insubsidies, at 0.6%.[95] Another reason to reconsider the principles of the free market economy is that the important new national task of environmental protection will inevitably require more extensive intervention in the economic process.[96] The Basic Law will in the future supply the (expanded) legal framework for this by incorporating the »state objective of environmental protection« into the text of the constitution.

Notes:

* Several sections of this paper are based on published and unpublished studies, in particular my two articles in Isensee and Kirchhof, *Handbuch des Staatsrechts,* Vol. III, 1988. See especially »Money and Currency,« pp. 1121 *et seq.* and »Government Reponsibility for the Economy,« pp. 1141 *et seq.* See also my »Öffentliches Wirtschaftsrecht,« to be published shortly by Springer, Heidelberg, and others.

1 For a discussion of the first plans for a new economic order, see Reiner Schmidt, Öffentliche Wirtschaft, 1989, p. 7 *et seq.*

2 Cf. on the subject as a whole U. Scheuner, Die staatliche Einwirkung auf die Wirtschaft, 1971, pp. 9 *et seq.;* U. Scheuner, A. Schule, »Die staatliche Intervention im Bereich der Wirtschaft« VVDStRL 11 (1954), pp. 1 *et seq.;* Reiner Schmidt, »Staatliche Verantwortung für die Wirtschaft« in J. Isensee and P. Kirchhof (eds.), HdbStR III, 1988, pp. 1141 *et seq.* with subsequent references.

3 On the dispute about the economic constitution, see among the numerous references H.F. Zacher, »Aufgaben einer Theorie der Wirtschaftsverfassung« in Festschrift für Franz Bohm, 1965, pp. 63 *et seq.;* P.C. Müller-Graff, Unternehmensinvestitionen und Investitionssteuerung im Marktrecht, 1984, pp. 246 *et seq.* and Reiner Schmidt (Fn 1), pp. 1148 *et seq.*

4 Soziale Marktwirtschaft und Grundgesetz 2nd ed., 1961, p. 44.

5 Cf. P.C. Müller-Graff (FN 2), p. 254.

6 Cf. in more detail Reiner Schmidt, Wirtschaftspolitik und Verfassung, 1971, pp. 128 *et seq.*

7 Cf. R. Blum, Article »Marktwirtschaft, soziale« in Handwörterbuch der Wirtschaftswissenschaften 5, 1980, pp. 153 *et seq.*

8 E.R. Huber, Wirtschaftsverwaltungsrecht 1, 2nd ed., 1953, pp. 18 *et seq., 30 and 31.*

9 See, however, E.R. Huber, DöV 1956, pp. 200 *et seq.* (205).

10 Fifteenth Act amending the Basic Law, June 8th, 1967 (BGBl [Federal Law Gazette] I, p. 5180).

11 Cf. E. Stachels, Das Stabilitätsgesetz im System des Regierungshandelns, 1970, pp. 204 *et seq.*

12 Cf., as one example among many, H.J. Papier, Grundgesetz und Wirtschaftsordnung in Handbuch des Verfassungsrechts, 1983, pp. 609 *et seq.* and subsequent references, and R. Scholz in Der Staatssektor in der sozialen Marktwirtschaft, 1976, pp. 113 *et seq.* (123 *et seq.*).

13 Relevant is W. Leisner, Privateigentum ohne privaten Markt?, BB 1975, pp. 1 *et seq.* (4 and 5.).

14 *E.g.* R. Scholz, Entflechtung und Verfassung, 1981, pp. 91 and 92.

15 *Ibid.*, p. 125, n. 13.

16 BVerGE 4, 7 (17); 7, 377 (400); 50, 290 (338).

17 BVerfGE 4, 7.

18 BVerfGE 50, 290.

19 BVerfGE 12, 341 (347).

20 BVerfGE 14, 19 (23); 20 BVerfGE 4, 7 (8 and 9).

21 BVerfGE 4, 7 (1 *et seq.*).

22 Cf. *inter alia* P. Badura, F. Rittner, B. Ruthers, Mitbestimmungsgesetz 1976 und Grundgesetz, 1977, p. 249, and further comment in Fn 225.

23 BVerfGE 50, 290 (338).

24 BVerfGE 7, 377 (400); 25, 1 (19 and 20); 30, 292 (317, 319); 50, 290 (338).

25 BVerfGE 50, 290.

26 *Id.* pp. 336 *et seq.;* for further details on the codetermination judgement, see Reiner Schmidt, Das Mitbestimmungsgesetz auf dem verfassungsrechtlichen Prüfstand, Der Staat 19 (1980), pp. 235 and 236.

27 According to P. Badura, F. Rittner B. Ruthers (fn 21) in particular pp. 186 *et seq., 190 et seq., 246 et seq., 296 and 297.*

28 BVerfGE 50, 290 (336).

29 BVerfGE 1, 14 (32); 34, 165 (183); 39, 234 (368).

30 BVerfGE 50, 290 (336).

31 Cf. P. Badura, F. Rittner, B. Ruthers (fn 21), p. 248.

32 BVerfGE 7, 198 (205).

33 BVerfGE 50, 290 (337).

34 On the identity of the »institutional« function of the basic rights with their objective law function, see J. Schwabe, Probleme der Grundrechtsdogmatik 1977, p. 286.

35 BVerfGE 18, 315, (327).

36 BVerfGE 25, 1 (23).

37 BVerfGE 32, 305 (317).

38 BVerfGE 30, 292 (312); 38, 348 (361).

39 BVerfGE 25, 1 (23); 50, 290 (366).

40 See also M. Schmidt-Preuss, Verfassungsrechtliche Zentralfragen staatlicher Lohn-und Preisdirigismen 1977, pp. 99 and 100.

41 BVerfGE 29, 260 (267); 50, 290 (366).

42 BVerfGE 19, 101 (114-115) and 21, 292 (299).

43 On the interpretation of the constitution as a whole, cf. R. Hesse, Grundzüge des Verfassungsrechts der Bundesrepublik Deutschland 16th ed., 1988, pp. 19 et seq.

44 See R. Stern in Stern, Münch, Hansmayer, Kommentar zum StabG, 2nd ed., 1972, pp. 144 et seq., and other references.

45 For further details on this see E. Schmidt-Assmann, in Maunz-Dürig, Grundgesetz-Kommentar, II, November 1988, notes 188 et seq. to Art. 19, Para. 4, Basic Law.

46 Ibid. IV, November 1988, notes 38 et seq. to Art. 109 and other references; cf. recently BVerfG, DVBl, 1989, pp. 610 et seq., which uses Art. 109, Para. 2, in combination with Art. 115, Para. 1, p. 2, as a constitutional criterion.

47 On global control, see R. Schiller, »Wirtschaftspolitik« in HdSW, 12, 1965, pp. 210 et seq. and J. Starbatty, Theorie und Praxis der Globalsteuerung, 1974.

48 On this basic concept, see W. Ehrlicher, »Geldtheorie und Geldpolitik« in HdWW, 3, 1981, pp. 423 et seq. (436 et seq.).

49 Cf. M. Friedman, »Die Rolle der Geldpolitik« in Brunner et al. (eds.), Geldtheorie, 1974, pp. 314 et seq. (329).

50 On supply-side policy, see. P.J. J. Welfens, Theorie und Praxis angebotsorientierter Stabilitätspolitik 1985, pp. 13 et seq.; M. Feldstein et al., Economic report of the President. Annual Report of the Council of Economic Advisers, 1983 and A.B. Laffer, Supply-side Economics, Financial Analysts Journal 37 (1981), pp. 29 et seq.; cf. also (Expert Committee) on the reporting of overall economic trends, 1981/82 Annual Report, FT publication 9/1061, p. 143.

51 On the connection between encouraging supply and a dirigistic and conserving sectoral structural policy, cf. 1976-77 annual report of the Expert Committee on the reporting of the overall economic trend, FT publication 7/5902, pp. 133 and 134.

52 For details see A. von Mutius, and G.F. Schuppert, Die Steuerung des Verwaltungshandelns durch Haushaltsrecht und Haushaltskontrolle VVDStRL 42 (1984), pp. 147 et seq.; pp. 216 et seq.

53 Estimates range from 80% to 95%; see H. Koller, Der öffentliche Haushalt als Instrument der Staats- und Wirtschaftslenkung 1983, p. 201.

54 The Federal Constitutional Court is trying to prevent devaluation of Art. 115, Para. 1, Clause 2, by emphasizing its exceptional character and ruling that it believes increased borrowing to be justified only in the event of a serious and lasting or immediately impending disruption. See BVerfG, DVBl. 1989, pp. 610 et seq. (614).

55 Cf. H. Fischer-Menshausen, in I. v. Münch (ed.), Grundgesetz-Kommentar 3, 2nd ed., 1983, Note 14a to Art. 115.
56 See Monatsberichte der Deutschen Bundesbank, July 1979, pp. 15 *et seq.*
57 For further details cf. Reiner Schmidt, Wirtschaftspolitik, 1971, p. 213.
58 See written Reports of the Economic Committee on BT publication V/1678, p. 4.
59 Cf. the last 11th Subsidies Report dated November 25th, 1987, BT publication 11/1338.
60 Cf. H. Zimmermann, FinArch, N.F. 35 (1976/77), pp. 451 *et seq.* (467).
61 E. Denninger, Staatsrecht 1, 1973, pp. 44 *et seq.*
62 For an overall view, see the articles in E. Hoppmann (ed.), Konzertierte Aktion, 1971.
63 Among the copious references, see H.H. Nachtkamp, Mehrjährige Finanzplanungen und mittelfristige Zielprojektionen der Bundesregierung, 1976.
64 Council of Experts on the appraisal of overall economic development 1976/77 Annual Report, BT publication 7/5902, p. 141-2.
65 In this context, see E. Moeser, Die Beteiligung des Bundestages an der staatlichen Haushaltsgewalt, 1978, pp. 194 *et seq.*
66 E.H. Ritter, »Theorie und Praxis parlamentarischer Planungsbeteiligung«, Der Staat 19 (1980), pp. 413 *et seq.* (428).
67 In many cases a rather different terminology is used, with references to, for example, adjustment, maintenance and organizational interventions. Cf. P. Klemmer, Regionalpolitik auf dem Prüfungstand, 1986, pp. 23-24.
68 Among the many references, see H. Baumler, Staatliche Investitionsplanung unter dem Grundgesetz, 1980 and P.C. Müller-Graff, Unternehmensinvestitionen und Investitionssteuerung im Marktrecht, 1984.
69 See among the references H. Neupert, Regionale Strukturpolitik als Aufgabe der Länder, 1986 and the articles by P. Klemmer. W. Möller, H. Neupert, M. Pfeifer, G. Puttner, P. Waldchen, G. Frhr. v.Waldenfels and H. Zimmermann in Reiner Schmidt (ed.), Aktuelle Fragen der regionalen Strukturpolitik, 1989.
70 The point correctly made by the Council of Experts in the appraisal of the overall economic development in the 1984/85 Annual Appraisal, BT publication 10/2541, p. 199.
71 Cf. BVerfGE 39, 96 (109).
72 Of January 28th, 1986 (BGBl. I, p. 231) (in the version of July 25th, 1988 (BGBl. I, p. 1093).
73 Cf. E. Pauker, Das ERP-Sondervermögen, 1987.
74 P.J. Tettinger, Rechtsanwendung und gerichtliche Kontrolle im Wirtschaftsverwaltungsrecht, 1980, p. 221.
75 Act of July 26th, 1957 (BGBL. I, p. 745).
76 Further details in Reiner Schmidt, »Geld und Währung,« in HdbStR, III, 1988, pp. 1121 *et seq.* (1133).
77 Cf. W.P. Hoffmann (Riem), Rechtsfragen der Währungsparität, 1969; C. Tomuschat, Die Aufwertung der deutschen Mark, 1970.
78 German Federal Bank (eds.), Die Deutsche Bundesbank: Geldpolitische Aufgaben und Instrumente. 3rd ed., 1985, p. 13.
79 Federal Government legislative intent regarding the draft of an act relating to the German Federal Bank, BT publication II/2781, annex 1, p. 27.
80 See the careful comments in BVerwGE 41, 334 (354 *et seq.*).

81 Cf. in this context BVerfGE 55, 144 (149); 68, 1 (109).

82 BVerfGE 9, 268 (282); 22, 106 (113). See also BVerwGE 7, 66 (73); 12, 20.

83 See, for example, H.H. v.Arnim, Staatslehre der Bundesrepublik Deutschland 1984, p. 342.

84 See, for example F. Ossenbühl, Satzung, in HdbStP, III, 1988, pp. 463 et seq. (483).

85 BVerfGE 62, 169 (183).

86 See, in general, C. Tomuschat, Reiner Schmidt, Der Verfassungsstaat im Geflecht internationaler Beziehungen, VVDStRL 36 (1978), pp. 7 *et seq.;* pp. 65 *et seq.*

87 BVerfGE 58, 1 (36).

88 BVerfGE 52, 187; 31, 145.

89 Cf. C. Tomuschat, in Bonner-Kommentar, 2nd ed., June 1985, note 49 to Art. 24 BL.

90 See Art. 2 of the Act of Consent to the EEA (BGBl. II/1986, p. 1102).

91 Cf. P. Badura, Bewahrung und Veränderung demokratischer und rechtsstaatlicher Verfassungsstruktur in den internationalen Gemeinschaften, VVDStRL 23 (1966), pp. 34 *et seq.* (78 and other references).

92 Cf. EuGH Slg. 1977, 1753 (1770).

93 Set up by resolution of the European Council of December 5th, 1978, reprinted in M. Schweitzer and W. Hummer, Textbuch zum Europarecht, 2nd ed., 1984, pp. 390-393.

94 Cf. Annual Report of the German Federal Bank, 1983, pp. 73 ff.

95 Cf. the 11th Subsidies Report of the Federal Government, BT publication of 11/1338, p. 19.

96 On the legal bases for a uniform and comprehensive European environment policy, cf. Art. 130r to 130t EEC Treaty.

Christopher S. Allen

Principles of the Economic System - An American View

Introduction

Several years ago, at the height of the »Eurosclerosis« and »Europessimism«
period, I visited the German Industry Association (BDI - Bundesverband
der deutschen Industrie) to conduct interviews on economic adaptation in
the West German economy. At the time, I had a post-doctoral research
fellowship at the Harvard Business School and was working on a project
that examined the relationship between ideology and national competitiveness. At one of the interviews with a high ranking official - which we
conducted in German - I asked what he thought would be the most appropriate set of economic policies for the Federal Republic to pursue. He
immediately mentioned the apparent success of the »Reagan revolution« in
producing high job growth, new start-ups, venture capital, and an unfettered
climate of deregulation. I responded that, while this model might possibly
be suitable for the United States, it seemed to me that the German economy
had a very different tradition. Namely, German economic strength had been
built on a more »organized« capitalist footing, with close links between
manufacturing and finance, a pattern of creating jobs measured in quality
not just in quantity, and a broad regulatory »framework« that avoided the
wide swings between the uncertainties of total laissez faire, on the one hand,
and over-specific, over-detailed regulation, on the other. Thus the American
model might prove quite inappropriate for the Federal Republic. My
interviewee then smiled and said: »It seems, Herr Dr. Allen, that you know
more about the German economy than I thought you did.« We then
proceeded to have a fruitful discussion that surrounded the second set of
assumptions about the German economy.
After leaving the interview, I began to wonder why this BDI official had
begun to tell me one story and then so quickly had changed his tune. My
first guess was that the last three Americans with whom he had spoken were
all editorial page writers for the *Wall Street Journal,* so he was merely

telling one more American what he thought I wanted to hear. Upon further reflection, however, I thought that something deeper might be involved. While there has been close cooperation and understanding between the United States and West Germany in the forty years since the founding of the Federal Republic, in the area of economic policy the »American view« of the West German economy has been most inconsistent. When economic performance has been particularly strong during the postwar period in the Federal Republic, Americans have been quick to praise the West German commitment to the »free market.« However, when economic performance has lagged, as was the case in the early 1980s, many Americans have identified the reason as a too ponderous and over-generous »welfare state«. Yet a glance at the percentage of GDP going to the public sector has not shown wide swings. In fact, the period of the sharpest rise in public spending – the late 1960s and early 1970s, the reform years of the SPD-FDP coalition – was also a period of fast economic growth and full employment.

Why is the Federal Republic's economy so difficult for Americans to understand? This article argues ultimately that the »American view« of the West German economy immediately looks for evidence of »laissez faire« when it hears the phrase »market economy.« The problem is that economic policy has never been based on a primary reliance upon »laissez faire,« either during the forty years of the Federal Republic, or before. Rather, the foundations of West German economic policy are based on three concepts that prove especially difficult for Americans to understand. These concepts are: *Ordnungspolitik* (the politics of industrial order, or in Andrew Shonfield's terms »organized capitalism«; *Rahmenbedingungen* (an overlapping and coordinated set of general – not specific – framework regulatory policies); and the labor-market institutions of *Mitbestimmung* (co-determination, or union participation on firms' supervisory board of directors) and *Betriebsräte* (works councils of employees in virtually all West German firms) which provide both a steady source of skilled, unionized labor and generally insure labor market peace. The following three sections will analyze why these three concepts are so difficult to understand. The conclusion will suggest that, as the United States economy continues to experience international competitive pressures similar to those of the Federal Republic, application of »American versions« of these concepts may prove increasingly appropriate.

340

I. *Ordnungspolitik*

Pure laissez faire is not relevant for the Federal Republic as the primary foundation for its market economy both because of the lack of this tradition in the 19th century as well as of the breakdown of the economic order several times in this century. Yet a strong role for the central state in economic policy is also proscribed due to the abuse of the central state by the Nazis during the Third Reich. Therefore, German public law has evolved a tradition in which an overlapping network of public, private, and para-public institutions have developed the ability to act strategically and via their interaction, produce economic flexibility and political stability.[1] It has also meant that changes in major policy issues, such as economic policy from one government to another, remain incremental.[2] But what has been the foundation of this organized capitalist institutional pattern?

The first issue to mention in this context is that the West German banking system is a universal one.[3] It can perform all banking functions and it is not limited by the provisions of a U.S.-style Glass-Steagall act in which individual banks have been barred from engaging in equities transactions. The banks were the instrument of choice for directing and allocating investment during 19th century Germany's late industrialization, since there was not sufficient finance capital from other sources.[4] Consequently, this historical pattern has given the banks an elevated position and has allowed them to stand above the (microeconomic) fray and understand how particular industries can best be shaped. The banks clearly see themselves as having a major role in shaping the patterns of innovation and change in German industry. When asked what role the Deutsche Bank had played in long term patterns of German innovation, an aide to former Bank Chairman Wilfried Guth stated, »The Deutsche Bank was founded in 1870. Or, in other words, one year before there was a Germany there was a Deutsche Bank.« He paused and continued, »Regimes come and regimes go, but we will always be here.«[5] This suggests that patterns which were established at the turn of the century have not substantially altered.[6]

Since the founding of the Federal Republic in 1949, however, how have both democratic politics and a greater sensitivity to concentration of economic power affected the banks' role in the economy? The short answer is very little. One analyst has described the postwar power of financial capital as follows:

The big banks and insurance companies (have) had an important role in this system . . . they function effectively as private ›structure and investment steering institutions‹ for the entire economy – as far as a planned steering of capitalism is at all possible – and they do so by accumulating credits, securing direct and indirect participation (depot proxy voting rights), personnel penetration of supervisory and executive boards and, lastly, by a system of pooled information on the development of business and profitability in all enterprises and sectors.[7]

The banks have been active both in rescuing failing firms and sectors as well as pushing new products and forms of innovation. In dealing with corporate crisis, the banks have used their powerful – and legally legitimate – institutional position to impose major adjustment strategies on failing firms. The most notable examples of this »bank-led rescue« (in addition to VW) have been AEG-Telefunken, the electronics firm, and HapagLloyd, the shipping firm.[8] This process has been aided by West German cultural attitudes toward quasi-public authority, and how the »›forced‹ collectivist responses within the industrial culture . . . also forced inter-organizational linkages (within) a supportive structure of political power.[9]

But the criticism during the early 1980s – the ›Eurosclerosis‹ period – has argued that the large and powerful banks have been too slow and cumbersome in responding to the internationalization and deregulation of financial institutions and equities markets. The banks have also taken note of the criticism of the supposed lack of venture capital in Germany. The response of the Deutsche Bank, for example, was to found five »in house« venture capital operations, allow each to compete with one another, and then mobilize the bank's ample resources around the most successful possibilities.[10] More generally, however, this trend indicates that the banks – as collective and private institutions – are very much aware of the importance of innovation and that their politically sanctioned position allows them to play an important role in shaping sectoral change.

Thus, the role of the German banking system during the 1980s goes beyond Schonfield's comprehensive – if now partially dated – study. The danger in relying on Schonfield for studying the postwar banking system in West Germany, is that one may miss some of the many, if subtle, changes that have taken place since the 1960s. Recent scholarship suggests that within a larger framework of stability, a multitude of smaller changes have occurred under the roof of the universal banking system.[11] The major thrust of the Baethge and Oberbeck argument is that the West German banks have been very adaptive institutions, especially given the changes that have been taking place gradually in the sector since the 1960s. The universal banks have sought continual growth via new markets as the German laws did not restrict banking activity. With respect to their employees, there has not been much dequalification of workforce skills, but a systematic rationalization of the lower skilled workers. A good example of this phenomenon has been the centralization of back office functions in West German banking since the 1970s. Specifically, the percentage of back office workers has dropped steadily since the early 1970s; from 33 % in 1972; to 20 percent in 1976; to only 10 % in 1986. Despite the decline in low skilled workers, the key issue is not quantitative change as it is qualitative change in the personnel structure. While Baethge and Oberbeck are concerned due to the job loss among the low skilled workers, they do note that those workers with higher basic skills were able to get retrained. The thrust of their argument, in this context, is that the West German banks adaptive structure – much small-scale change within the context of the flexible universal bank structure – placed them in good shape for the more competitive 1980s. But this is evidence of internal flexibility, what of external flexibility and the banks' role in a global financial »supermarket« where the banks careful »organization« might prove too slow to respond?

As a sign that the German financial system has been misread by Anglo-American observers, one has only to cite a single example. Some of the people who were most condescending toward a »Sclerotic« Europe in the mid-1980s, were most fearful of the strength of a post-1992 »Fortress« Europe. The recent criticism in West Germany of the socalled *Macht der Banken* issue is interesting in the context of the earlier ›Eurosclerosis‹ context, because the supposedly slow and non-responsive German banks now possessed the economies of scope and scale[12] to become major players in the single European market of the 1990s.[13] In essence, the German banks have been able to deflect both laissez faire and left populist critiques within the Federal Republic by pointing to Europe 1992 to deflect criticism. They acknowledge that they have some power in the German economy, but that they use it responsibly. However, they also simultaneously argue that they are acting in the interests of Germany in the Europe of the 1990s.[14] The main domestic line of response by the banks has been that the banks maintain only minority positions on various firms and that they do not involve themselves in investment decisions (although it is interesting that the personal connections issue is not asserted to be a problem for their concentration). Also, the banks also use the *Mitbestimmung* issue to show that unions have their own form of personal connections and *Aufsichtsrat* (supervisory board of directors) influence. Internationally, the German banks' share of the world market is used as a defense too, especially as a

343

precursor to the German position in Europe after the single market decision.

What will regulation of the financial markets look like in Germany (and Europe) in the context of the banks' ability to influence private investment. The outcome is uncertain, however much of what passed for conventional wisdom in the mid 1980s seems most unlikely in the 1990s. Many observers – among them the Eurosclerosis crowd – saw West Germany's (and Europe's) financial market system becoming more like the US or British system in which equities markets would become more influential than banks in financing investment. This paper argues that the opposite is more likely, in that the German banks have solidified their position in Europe (and tend to dominate stock trading themselves anyway). What seems a more likely outcome, is that the US is lurching toward a universal-style banking system without realizing it.

II. *Rahmenbedingungen*

The second element of American misunderstanding of the West German economy is a close cousin of ›organized capitalism‹ and is called *Rahmenbedingungen,* which is loosely translated here as an overlapping and coordinated set of general – not specific – framework regulatory policies. In this context, the industry and employer organizations play a crucial role in shaping the framework within which an industry's firms can adapt.[15]

If practiced in the United States, this shaping of the competitive *Rahmenbedingungen* by the industry and employer organizations would be likely be illegal under anti-trust laws. Yet the concept is an integral foundation of the Federal Republic's economic structure and is used frequently by all major actors in the economy. More specifically, this paper argues that the practice of *Rahmenbedingungen* is one of the primary reasons for the simultaneous stability *and* flexibility of the West Germany to retain a leading competitive position in the world economy of the late 1980s. In fact, the frequency of this articulation and practice in the Federal Republic, combined with an inability for a precise translation into English, suggests an important distinction between American and German versions of these organizations and their role in a national institutional framework. In the U.S., industry organizations are often conceived as »special interest groups« or »lobbying organizations,« the main function of which is to defensively

344

»limit the damage« of public sector policies or to protect against »unfair« competition from comparable industries in other countries. In West Germany, on the other hand, these institutions envision a much more strategic relationship for themselves. A key distinction which the industry and employer groups make is between »Strukturpolitik« (industrial policy) and »Ordnungspolitik«.[16] To the industry organizations, the former is to be avoided because in this case the public sector is »too much« involved with the direction of the industry. As a form of selfregulation, the latter is far more preferable since under Ordnungspolitik the firms and the industry organizations play the dominant role.[17] It is significant that Ordnungspolitik is also difficult to translate precisely, as »policies of order« is the closest approximation. But this linguistic distinction only confirms the difference between the strategic role of these institutions in Germany – setting the »framework« for industrial »order« – and the merely defensive role of their counterparts in the U.S.

But what of the American argument that the ability of the large West German firms and their powerful encompassing organizations creates powerful anti-trust problems? In other words, how does the Federal Republic avoid the economic inefficiencies of oligopoly power among a few powerful firms and organizations? An interesting lesson can be drawn from the early years of the Federal Republic and American attempts to introduce a more individualistic, laissez faire ideology after the Third Reich. In seeking to resuscitate the destroyed German economy, the American economic advisers first moved, as they did in Japan, to break up some of the large economic units.[18] American occupation authorities used individualistic and small-firm conceptions of how a national economy was to function and who were to be the dominant actors as they attempted to apply strict anti-trust guidelines. Yet German industrial development was scarcely the mirror image of the U.S. For the Germans, large firms were the norm and not the exception, and to expect them to adopt an unfamiliar pattern of reindustrialization was unlikely. Anti-trust has its deepest resonance in countries that are either economically isolated or have large and powerful domestic markets upon which to rely. Both of these conditions applied to the United States (at least until the early 1970s) yet neither applied to the Federal Republic. Since West Germany had to export to survive, competition was not defined primarily as *domestic* competition between individual firms within the domestic market, but as *international* competition between specific industries in other countries. Under the latter set of circumstances, anti-trust becomes almost irrelevant.

Yet in the mid 1950s, when U.S. policy makers wanted to see an econom-

345

ically strong West Germany, they were quick to forgive West German industrialists for returning to familiar patterns of framework regulations. West Germany does have a symbolic anti-trust law (the Kartellgesetz of 1957), but there are enough loopholes to drive a Mercedes through.[19] This reference is hardly frivolous or irrelevant, especially given the recent Daimler-MBB merger. Yet in praising the West German »Economic Miracle« of the 1950s, these American observers saw laissez faire and not a regulatory framework. Anti-trust regulations are one of the most telling examples of individualistic ideological conceptions of the economy, because they assume that a nation of atomized entrepreneurs represents the »natural order« and is always and irreparably damaged by »unnatural« and predatory large firms. More seriously here, however, the anti-trust advocates failed to realize that the process of firm growth in a capitalist economy almost guarantees »imperfect« competition. In postwar West Germany for example, the allies broke up the notorious IG Farben chemicals cartel into four »smaller« firms. The three major surviving »offspring« (BASF, Bayer and Hoechst) are today *each* larger than was IG Farben at its zenith.

But what is the intellectual and legal foundation for this pattern of *Rahmenbedingungen?* Because inflation and economic chaos had characterized much of the Weimar period, the Federal Republic's leading economists – from the Freiburg School – wanted to ensure that an effective and »organized framework« policy would protect the resuscitation of the economy from undue public interference and all inflationary tendencies.[20] They put a premium on policy that was designed to foster a stable set of expectations in the private sector. Public policy was to be aimed at four major goals:

1. They upheld the primacy of monetary policy, on the grounds that a stable money supply would make anti-cyclical policy unnecessary. Hence, a strong central bank (Bundesbank) was to be the guardian against any misuse of power by the political authorities.

2. They sought an open international economic system, in reaction to the Nazi policy of autarky. Hence, these economists supported greater economic contacts with the United States and Western Europe, and they saw exports as the key to German growth.

3. They favored increased market competition, but within the context, described above, of an ›orderly market framework‹. The latter could be provided by banks and industry associations in conjunction with limited

action by the state. In a sense, Freiburg economists like Walter Eucken saw the whole nation as a unit within a setting of international competition. Hence, some cooperation among firms was quite acceptable in that it would lead to a positive sum outcome for the German economy.

4.   They wanted a limited measure of state intervention. The role of the state was to provide a stable legal and social order, including an important measure of social security, as well as infrastructural measures to aid in the establishment of a higher market equilibrium.

Perhaps the best words to summarize the ›framework‹ philosophy of this school come from the economist Wilhelm Röpke:

> . . . (our program) consists of measures and institutions which impart to competition the framework, rules, and machinery of impartial supervision which a competitive system needs as much as any game or match if it is not to degenerate into a vulgar brawl. A genuine, equitable, and smoothly functioning competitive system can not in fact survive without a judicious moral and legal framework and without regular supervision of the conditions under which competition can take place pursuant to real efficiency principles. This presupposes mature economic discernment on the part of all responsible bodies and individuals and a strong impartial state . . .[21]

Rather than the anti-statism of traditional Anglo-Saxon laissez faire, the Freiburg School saw the state performing a crucial and positive role in enhancing investment-led economic growth.

III.   *Mitbestimmung and the Betriebsräte*

Few Americans realize the institutionally strong position that the trade unions enjoy in the Federal Republic. Stereotypes about cooperative workers and engineering skills abound, but few are aware of the specifics of the unions' presence. The labor movement's strong role in the Federal Republic has been enhanced by its creation and maintenance of such important institutions as the Works Councils and Codetermination. The labor movement has also enjoyed minimal inter-union conflict. The one union-one industry and one union-one plant policy effected by the industry unions was an important improvement for the postwar labor movement after the divisiveness of the Weimar years.[22]

Although the most radical of their immediate postwar demands – owing to nationalization and worker control of factories with the deepest complicity with the Nazi regime – were deflected by the Adenauer governments of the 1950s, the trade unions still retained symbolic power and considerable real influence in German society. They were able to create several elaborate systems for worker participation. In 1951, they obtained provisions for *Mitbestimmung* (codetermination) in which workers and union members from the coal and steel industries made up just under 50 % of the members of the boards of directors of firms in these industries. In 1952, codetermination was extended to all other large firms in other industries, but union membership on the company boards amounted to only 33 %. In 1976, under the SPD-FDP coalition government, the codetermination law was expanded to stop just short of the virtual full-parity codetermination which coal and steel workers had enjoyed since 1951. A third institution which benefited workers was a system of *Betriebsräte* (works councils) in all firms – union and non-union – with 20 or more employees. These works councils, their name and spirit taken from the Weimar legislation, tended to deal with only social and personnel matters only because collective bargaining responsibilities remained with the unions themselves. The unions were suspicious of these councils because, as parallel organizations, they could potentially undermine the trade unions' influence. In 1972, however, the SPD-FDP coalition government also extended the provision of this law to provide more rights for trade unions inside the workplace and, thereby, inside the works councils.

· Unions were particularly sensitive to competing organizations inside the workplace due to their experiences during Weimar. In the 1920s, the presence of trade unions affiliated with the Social Democratic, Communist and non-socialist movements, caused fragmentation and prevented the labor movement as a whole from effectively resisting the Nazis. The German Trade Union Confederation, DGB, established in 1949 and headed by Hans Böckler, insisted on a system of union organization that was unified (i.e. no confederations explicitly affiliated with political parties) and industry-specific (i.e. one industry-one union and, more importantly, one plant-one union).

Despite weaknesses in the unions during the early years of the Federal Republic, they were able to build on their organized structure and on the institutions of worker participation discussed above to become major actors in German society by the 1960s and 1970s. And once the SPD came to

348

power in the late 1960s, the unions became even more influential. Not only were SPD policies much closer to the unions' than were those of the CDU, almost all DGB leaders were also SPD members.

The strength of the West German unions goes beyond the fact that they represent some 35%–40% of the country's workforce. They have maintained a strong social presence in the Federal Republic as well, evidenced by their informal influence both in the works councils – which exist for all workers and are found in plants of 20 or more employees – and in other para-public institutions such as those dealing with vocational education. Together with national and regional governments, as well as employer groups, the trade unions play an active role in shaping the vocational education system on which high quality export goods depend.

The West German unions' system of collective bargaining is both strong and flexible due to its short term and long term perspective on issues. Prevailing practice among unions since the late 1960s has been to bargain on wage issues on a yearly basis. The union in the strongest position, usually IG Metall, bargains with the employers first, with less powerful unions following IG Metall's attempted »pattern setting.« The unions engage in »framework bargaining« (Manteltarifverhandlungen) only once every five years on larger and more fundamental issues, for example, working conditions, the structure of the workplace, and working hours. IG Metall's attempt to set a 35 hour work week in 1984 took place during these latter contract negotiations. This dual system allows the unions to focus on wages without getting locked into unfavorable long-term contracts, and provides the »framework« round to address more qualitative, basic issues. The short-term wage focus never allows wages to get out of line with inflation. While the long term focus on a general framework gives unions and employers a firm foundation to create internationally competitive products.

West Germany has relied heavily on its skilled blue collar workers throughout the postwar period. Unlike the massive job loss in manufacturing industries in the United States, there has been little decomposition of this segment of the West German working class. They are simply too important for the economic health of the flexible system production processes of such »fulcrum« or bellweather industries as machine tools, automobiles, chemicals, and industrial electronics. Although there has been some evidence of partial decomposition in weaker industries such as steel and shipbuilding, where there have been major job losses, working class decomposition is far less pronounced than in either Britain or the U.S. West Germany has seen only a small growth of service sector jobs, unlike the United States, where a large proportion of the new jobs are in services.

The right wing in West Germany has argued that the country should emulate the U.S. by creating new jobs in this area. The left wing has countered with the assertion that most service sector jobs in the U.S. are low paying jobs at fast-food restaurants with few benefits. They argue that the strains placed on society by this plan for employment growth, in the form of inadequate economic demand (due to low wages) and increased social spending (due to lack of fringe benefits), would represent a net loss for West German society. The plan for high productivity, high-wage unionized employment has sustained the economy for many years. The American »solution,« they believe, is the wrong choice.

A key component of the innovative economic adaptation in internationally competitive industries is the skill base of the West German working class. Long a crucial factor in Germany's economic strength, the role which these workers play has often been overlooked in the Federal Republic's industrial adaptation. Through the organs of worker participation – the Betriebsräte and Mitbestimmung[23] – as well as the elaborate labor court system for conflict resolution,[24] the West German labor movement is institutionally well-placed to play a positive role in industrial adjustment. These are powerful reasons why West German employers and regional governments – if not the Kohl government – have refrained from embarking on the strong »union bashing« trajectory of Britain and the U.S. The majority of German conservatives realize that unionized workers are skilled workers, and that they are needed if Germany's fulcrum sectors are to adapt and remain internationally competitive.[25] And when the shortage of worker skills in the U.S. is juxtaposed to the German reliance on an institutionally vibrant system of recruiting and training skilled workers in flexible system manufacturing, the question of which country has the more successful model of adaptation may have to remain open. Since German unions are organized on an industry rather than a craft basis, they can respond more easily to changes which go beyond one firm. Social scientists have argued that the role of these workers is the primary reason for innovation and adaptation in the chemical, automobile and machine tool sectors.[26] More importantly – and unlike Piore and Sabel who stop short of speculation – Kern and Schumann argue that these changes represent an opportunity for the German labor movement to build a »producer consciousness« to shape progressive economic and social change.

The ability of unions as collective institutions to play this role in industrial adjustment can often encounter various kinds of obstacles. One has been the push for increased flexibility on the part of West German employers. The unions are not opposed to flexibility in theory, however in practice the employers have often acted to undercut union attempts to develop industry-wide strategies for their membership.[27] The experiences of IG Chemie and IG Metall have shown that each has been partially frustrated in developing industry-specific strategies but for different reasons.[28] Thus, conflict does remain inside the West German workplace, but it is not on opposition to technological change, but on what kind of change – and what kind of flexibility – will take place. At a time when Americans are wondering where the needed skilled workers will come from, the West German approach may merit more increased American scrutiny.

IV. *Conclusion*

The Federal Republic and the United States have had a close relationship on many issues: political, military, cultural, and scientific, among many others. The United States has rightly considered its West German relationship to be the prime foundation for its relationship with Europe. In one sense, the above examples of divergence between the United States and the Federal Republic on economic policy are not particularly surprising. Different countries do embrace different policy styles when addressing domestic and international economic issues. What is surprising, however, is that there has been so little understanding by the Americans of how the Federal Republic's economy actually works.

This paper has argued that the dominant »American view« of the West German economy immediately looks for evidence of a nonexistent »laissez faire« when it hears the phrase »market economy«. Because *Ordnungspolitik, Rahmenbedingungen,* and the institutions of *Mitbestimmung* and *Betriebsräte* have been so difficult conceptually for Americans to understand, the more »orderly framework« of economic relationships in the Federal Republic is overlooked. Yet if the issue were just a matter of different approaches by each country, which were successful in their different respective contexts, then the differences would have little larger significance. However, that is not the case. As the United States economy continues to experience international competitive pressures similar to those that the Federal Republic has faced throughout the postwar period, Americans may have more to learn from this German complex of economic institutions than they now believe.

For much of the postwar period, many policy makers believed that the West

351

German economy was becoming more »Americanized«. To that end, whenever the West German economy faced any kind of economic difficulty - such as the »Eurosclerosis« period - then American »solutions« such as deregulation, increased venture capital, and weakening of the trade unions were proposed. This paper argues that the borrowing of economic policy styles should be going in the other direction. At a time when Americans lament the short term focus of most firms, the close relationship between manufacturing and finance may have something to offer rather than continually touting more deregulation of financial markets which only serves to intensify the short-term American focus. That is, an American-style »Ordnungspolitik« might provide a better long term investment climate than do the hypermobile American financial markets. At a time when Americans lament the ability of their firms to gain access to foreign markets, a scrapping of old fashioned »anti-trust« policies geared to a time when the US faced little international competition and could rely on a secure domestic economy might be appropriate. In other words, the United States could learn much from the West Germans about providing an effective »framework« for international competitiveness. Lastly, at a time when Americans wonder whether there will be enough skilled workers to make internationally competitive products, the West German system that can produce ever more skilled workers in internationally competitive manufacturing industries looks far less »sclerotic« than Americans once thought.

Notes:

1 Peter Katzenstein, Policy and Politics in West Germany: The Growth of a Semi-Sovereign State (Philadelphia: Temple University Press, 1987).
2 Edgar Grande, »Neoconservatism and Conservative-Liberal Economic Policy in West Germany,« European Journal of Political Research, 15 (1987), pp. 281-296.
3 Andrew Shonfield, Modern Capitalism (New York: Harper, 1965); and Hans Hermann Francke and Michael Hudson, eds., Banking and Finance in West Germany (New York: St. Martin's, 1984).
4 Richard Tilly, »Germany: 1815-1970,« in Rondo Cameron, ed., Banking in the Early Stages of Industrialization (New York: Oxford University Press, 1967), pp. 151-182; and Rainer Fremdling and Tilly, »German Banks, German Growth, and Econometric History,« Journal of Economic History, 36 2, (June 1976), pp. 416-424.
5 Interview with Jochen Degkwitz, Deutsche Bank, Frankfurt, June 26, 1985.

6   For the major critical reference work on the banks' historical legacy of power, see: Rudolf Hilferding, Finance Capital (London: Routledge and Keegan Paul, 1981).

7   Josef Esser, »State, Business and Trade Unions in West Germany after the ›Political Wende‹,« West European Politics, 9 2, (April 1986), pp. 198-214.

8   Kenneth Dyson, »The Politics of Corporate Crisis in West Germany,« West European Politics, 7 1, (January 1984), pp. 24-46.

9   Dyson, »The Politics of Corporate Crisis,« p. 44.

10 For a specific analysis of the role of the Deutsche Bank, see »Markt und Herrlichkeit der Deutschen Bank,« Der Spiegel, February 11, 1985.

11 Herbert Oberbeck and Martin Baethge, »Computers and Pin-stripes: German Financial Institutions between Dominant Market Control and Conservative Business Policy,« in Peter J. Katzenstein, ed., Industry and Political Change: Toward the Third West German Republic. (Ithaca: Cornell University Press, 1989). pp. 275-303.

12 Alfred Chandler, The Visible Hand (Cambridge = Belknap, 1977).

13 Wolfgang Roller speech, Frankfurt, 2/89.

14 Arndt, Franz-Josef, »»Macht der Banken‹ gegen Macht der Fakten: Anmerkungen zu einer DGB-Publikation,« Die Bank, No. 12 (1986), pp. 641-643; and Deutsche Bank, »Von der Macht der Banken,« Geschäftsbericht, (Frankfurt 1986), pp. 3-8.

15 Here is made a distinction between organizations of ›collective capital‹ in the macroeconomic sense, namely those (such as the BDI in West Germany) which represent the interests of all industry, and those which represent the interests of specific industries in the meso-economic sense. The former have been analyzed by Gerard Braunthal in the 1960s. See The Federation of German Industry in Politics (Ithaca: Cornell University Press, 1965), and more recently by Ulrich von Alemann and Rolf G. Heinze, eds., Verbande und Staat (Opladen: Westdeutscher Verlag, 1980); Wolfgang Streeck, »Neo-Corporatist Industrial Relations and the Economic Crisis in West Germany.« European University Institute Working Paper # 97,1984; and Philippe Schmitter, »Democratic Theory and Neo-Corporatist Practice, »Social Research, 50 4 (Winter 1983), 885-928. The latter have been analyzed by Schmitter and Streeck, eds., Private Interest Government (Beverly Hills: Sage, 1985) as they examined the role of organized capital at the industry level. Portions of this argument have been drawn from: Allen, »Germany: Competing Communitarianisms,« in George C. Lodge and Ezra Vogel, eds., Ideology and National Competitiveness (Boston: Harvard Business School Press, 1987), pp. 79-102; and Allen, »Regional Governments and Economic Policies in West Germany: The ›Meso‹ Politics of Industrial Adjustment.« Publius, XX 3 (Fall 1989), pp. 147-164.

16 For a distinction which one industry association makes between the two terms, see: Verband der Chemischen Industrie, »Die Rolle der Verbände im Wirtschafts- und Gesellschaftsystem der Bundesrepublik Deutschland,« January 14, 1985.

17 In dealing with a declining sector, the industry associations and the public sector will allow and/or encourage the formation of a »crisis cartel« to undertake strategic adjustment. See: Dyson, »The Politics of Corporate Crisis in West

Germany.« For a more theoretical treatment of the tension between the private and public sector on approaches to industrial adjustment, see: Bob Jessop, »The Capitalist State and the Role of Capital: Problems in the Analysis of Business Associations,« West European Politics, 6 2, (April 1983), pp. 139-162; and Douglas Webber, »A Relationship of ›Critical Partnership‹? Capital and the Social-Liberal Coalition in West Germany,« West European Politics, 6 2, (April 1983), pp. 61-86.

18 Joseph Auerbach, »Interview on original design of Morgenthau Plan,« Harvard Business School, 1986.

19 See Gerard Braunthal, The Federation of German Industry in Politics (Ithaca: Cornell University Press, 1965) for an excellent account of the evolution of the law.

20 Portions of the following argument are drawn from Allen, »The Underdevelopment of Keynesianism in the Federal Republic of Germany,« in Peter A. Hall, ed., The Power of Economic Ideas: Keynesianism Across Nations (Princeton: Princeton University Press, 1989).

21 Wilhelm Röpke, ›The Guiding Principles of the Liberal Programme,« in Horst Friedrich Wunche, ed., Standard Texts on the Social Market Economy (Stuttgart and New York: Gustav Fischer Verlag, 1982), pp. 361-365.

22 For a more extensive discussion of the labor movement, see: Andrei S. Markovits and Christopher S. Allen, »Germany,« in Peter Gourevitch, et al., Unions and Economic Crisis; Britain, West Germany and Sweden (London: George Allen and Unwin, 1984).

23 Andrei S. Markovits, The Politics of the West German Trade Unions (Cambridge: Cambridge University Press, 1986).

24 Ralf Rogowski, »Meso-Corporatism and Labour Conflict Resolution: The Theory and its Application to the Analysis of Labour Judiciaries in France, The Federal Republic of Germany, Great Britain and the United States,« International Journal of Comparative Labour Law and Industrial Relations, 1 2, (Summer 1985), pp. 143-169.

25 Wolfgang Streeck, Josef Hilbert, Karl-Heinz van Kevelaer, Frederike Maier, and Hajo Weber, The Role of the Social Partners in Vocational Training and Further Training in the Federal Republic of Germany, unpublished ms.

26 Michael Piore and Charles Sabel, The Second Industrial Divide (New York: Basic, 1984; and Horst Kern and Michael Schumann, Das Ende der Arbeitsteilung? (Munich: C.H. Beck Verlag, 1984).

27 Esser, »State, Business, and Trade Unions in West Germany after the ›Political Wende‹;« and Marion Alexis, »Neo-Corporatism and Industrial Relations: The Case of the German Trade Unions,« West European Politics, 6 1, (January 1983), pp. 75-92.

28 Portions of the following account have been drawn from: Allen, »Trade Unions, Worker Participation, and Flexibility: Linking the Micro to the Macro.« Comparative Politics, (April, 1990), pp. 253-272.

354

Ellen Kennedy

Comments on Part 5

We think of constitutions as higher than the laws of their system, or to use the language of the *Grundgesetz*, more fundamental. When they work, constitutions are wonderful things. They give us a picture of the world that is clear enough to allow for distinctions in its image, but not so sharp that the focus is fixed for all time. We can see ourselves and our forebears in its reflection, but we can also see our children and their childrens' children in it too. A constitution articulates our political identity authoritatively; we exist as individuals with rights and as citizens with duties. In defining its members as more than subjects of the civil and criminal law, constitutions demarcate the boundaries of a public sphere. None of that can be said of the ordinary laws.

What gives a constitution this special status in the polity? Its existence at the nexus of politics and law.

I.

The constitution of the United States and the *Grundgesetz* of the Federal Republic of Germany carry a particular political issue at their core, the issue of property. Our contributors in this panel present different views of the development of liberal democracy in Germany after 1949, but their analyses all focus on property rights as the central problematic of the Basic Law. All three papers address a common subject, the »Principles of the Economic System in the Federal Republic of Germany«, from different perspectives. The German contributors, Professor Reiner Schmidt (Augsburg) and Professor Horst Siebert (Kiel), offer the views of a lawyer and an economist respectively. Professor Christopher Allen (Georgia) adds the perspective of an American political scientist.

The main theme of Reiner Schmidt's analysis of the legal aspect of the principles of the economic system is the tension between »the guarantee of

freedom on the one hand and the social guarantees on the other.«[1] The Basic
Law sets up that tension because it is fundamentally a liberal document:
neutral with respect to the economic organization of society, it gives priority
to individual rights including the right of property. While he considers the
impact of three pieces of legislation which make up the principal elements
of »organized capitalism«,[2] these do not limit the liberal constitution for
Professor Schmidt. Rejecting an interpretation of the Basic Law that it guarantees a social market economy in the Federal Republic, Professor Schmidt
argues that its economic system is basically free. Although attempts were
made to secure social principles institutionally within constitutional
jurisprudence, »the conception of the social market economy as a constitutionally guaranteed system could not become generally accepted«.[3]
Reviewing the courts' decisions, Professor Schmidt finds that an economic
vision close to that of classical liberalism – a marketplace of individual
buyers and sellers – informs the decisions of Germany's Constitutional
Court.[4] Since the late 1970s, the Federal Constitutional Court has reaffirmed the primacy of private property (Art. 14) via its interpretation of
»economic basic rights«. The implication of Reiner Schmidt's analysis is
that constitutional mediation of individual liberty and social guarantees in
the United States and the Federal Republic has created legally similar
systems in both countries.

Horst Siebert presents a similar view from the economist's perspective but
introduces a significantly different normative perspective that links individualism as a value to the institutions of a social market. Judged solely on
economic criteria, markets work better than planned economies, producing
more goods more efficiently and predictably. At best, Professor Siebert
argues, central planning squanders the productive energies of society
through the inefficiencies of a large and costly state. At worst central planning appears as a symptom of dictatorship »repressing individual tastes and
individual behavior.«[5] The liberalism of Basic Law asserts »the sovereignty
of the individual« as a constitutional principle, but market competition,
whose institutions are not guaranteed by the constitution, gives effect to
individual choices.[6]

For Professor Siebert, the principles of the German economy are not
neutral, as they are for Professor Schmidt, but originate in historical experience and consciously affirmed values. »The consensus of the founding
fathers (sic) of the Grundgesetz was a value orientation stressing individual
freedom, human dignity and the subsidiarity of societal organization.«[7] The
constitutive values of the Basic Law anchor individual freedom, the first
principle of classical liberalism, in a social context where equity is ensured

356

through the network of protective legislation. »The market as an allocation mechanism«, Professor Siebert writes, »is corrected in order to attain results which are socially acceptable.«[8]

How are theoretically conflicting principles of individualism and equity to be balanced? Not through laissez-faire, but by replacing classical economic theories of markets as individual actors making rational choices with a theory of the social market economy as »an institutional arrangement defining the rules for the decision-making of households, firms, and politicians, including the restraints as well as the incentives.«[9]

Christopher Allen agrees with Horst Siebert that Germany's »social market economy« successfully combines theoretically incompatible principles, but »Principles of the Economic System: An American View« shifts to a more political account of its origins and functioning. His is the Germany of Hilferding's »Finanzkapital«, with a continuous tradition of organizing economic competition around the necessities of international competitiveness. The Anglo-American model of laissez-faire capitalism based on individualist ideology doesn't fit Germany's circumstances now any more than it did a hundred years ago. It is neither economically isolated nor does it have a large domestic market.[10] Germany's economic miracle was produced by institutionalizing social needs in the politics of order (Ordnungspolitik) frameworks (Rahmenbedingungen) and codetermination (Mitbestimmung). These have allowed German political culture to establish an economy more equitable and more competitive than laissez-faire liberalism. Its style of making policy has been so successful, Professor Allen's analysis suggests, that it should be adopted by the United States. While American observers offer American-style solutions to »Eurosclerosis«, more borrowing in the other direction would be appropriate.[11]

Such brief summaries can hardly do justice to the articles that precede, or to their discussion at the Washington conference. But simplifying their lines of argument allows the central constitutional issue to emerge clearly: What is the constitutional status of Germany's social market economy? Is it protected by the Basic Law, or is the web of government policy and social insurance which we identify as »the social market economy« better understood as a product of political compromise that could be changed just like any particular policy or legislated act? Which view of Germany's economic constitution is more accurate – one that sees it as similar if not identical to the American organization of state and society, or the interpretation of the Basic Law as a framework for a new kind of social democracy, an alternative to liberalism and collectivism?

I am going to argue that Professor Schmidt is closer to the truth, and that many of the differences between the United States and the Federal Republic pointed out by Christopher Allen – a better educated and skilled work force, higher standards of living for its workers, the maintenance of manufacturing industry's competitiveness – are the result of characteristically German norms that lack comparable legitimacy in this country. These norms constitute a concept of the rule of law beyond individual rights and private property.

German legal theorists first advanced this idea of a *sozialer Rechtsstaat* in response to the political and economic turmoil of the 1920s, but it found insufficient support under the Weimar Republic's regime of antagonistic pluralism. A generation later the authors of the Basic Law turned broad public consensus on the inadequacies of liberalism and the dangers of authoritarianism into a partial institution of the *sozialer Rechtsstaat*. But this dimension of German democracy is under pressure today. Constitutional jurisprudence now aims at limiting the principles of social equity to the advantage of a more liberal market.[12] This applies particularly to the element of labor representation in the economic constitution.

II.

The articles above refer to a case that is particularly revealing of the political dimensions of the Federal German constitution, the Federal Constitutional Court's 1979 decision on the Co-determination Law of 1976. (BVerfGE 50, 290) the main question before the Court concerned the extent to which the 1976 law expanding trade union rights of co-determination *(Mitbestimmung)* in their firms could be said to constrain those firms' freedom of choice and thus impinge on the property rights guaranteed by Art. 14 of the Basic Law. The case revived a longstanding controversy on whether the Basic Law contained an »economic constitution«. Viewed from the perspective of a political science of constitutional law, the question of an economic order within the Basic Law becomes somewhat different: Are there any limits to the legislative power of the people's elected representatives? In that form it is familiar to students of Weimar's constitutional history as the question of the social meaning of fundamental rights.[13] In this respect Germany's constitutional history is one example of a continuous debate on liberal institutions in the democratic state.

It is a political commonplace that conservatives tend to champion liberal (individual) rights when the issue of social legislation is raised. Their opponents see precisely those features of the constitution that guarantee subjective rights as a dialectic in which the rights guaranteed move further away from persons toward the protection of property. This question from the last year of the Weimar Republic reappeared during the 1960s in West Germany. The controversy »*Rechtsstaatlichkeit*« vs. »*Sozialstaatlichkeit*«[14] that flared up when the Social Democratic Party formed a Grand Coalition with the Christian Democrats in 1967 focused on the dilemma of liberal principles of law in the welfare state: How far could the state go in guaranteeing social rights without infringing on the individual's liberties? The issue was framed in the long discussion in Germany over an economic constitution. Reiner Schmidt correctly sees the Constitutional Court's 1979 case on *Mitbestimmung* as its most important decision on this issue.[15]

The key to the case was its subsumption of corporations as legal persons under the guarantees of the Basic Law which protect individual choice of professional education (Art. 12, § 1) and the use of private property (Art. 14, § 1). The Court assumed that for the purposes of Art. 14 there is no difference between having »a property in labor« (*Arbeitsvermögen*) and labor power. Both are equally protected because the Basic Law protects the relationship between an owner and his/her property whether that is the »property« of labor or the means of production. Moreover the Federal Constitutional Court emphasized the subjective (*privatrechtlichen*) aspect of Art. 14, § 1 and gave an essentially economic interpretation to the notion of »general freedom of action« (*allgemeine Handlungsfreiheit*) in Art. 2, § 1.

Neither Horst Siebert nor Christopher Allen gave due weight in their papers to the fact that the notion of private property embedded in the constitutional jurisprudence on the German economy rests on a fiction – the fiction of the private person as owner. This assumption is as essential to the legitimacy of the liberal constitution as the notion of a popular sovereign is to the democratic constitution. The problematic of each is that they *are* fictions, at best representations, which must be constantly reproduced in the political culture of constitutional law. The Constitutional Court is a vital instrument of that reproduction. So long as it is accepted as the final interpreter of constitutional meaning, the Basic Law will remain the fundamentally liberal document of Reiner Schmidt's description.

III.

No constitution is fixed in meaning for all times. Precisely in the openness of its texture or what Ronald Dworkin calls the »fuzziness« of law we can uncover the nexus of law and politics characteristic of constitutional interpretation. An interpretative move, construing a particular argument, resolves the tension between right and might contained in the idea of the state. A constitutional case orders relations between the positive law and particular principles of justice enunciated in a constitution by subsuming a particular case under a general principle, or reviewing the constitutionality of laws and governmental acts. In the hierarchy of legal forms, constitutional cases come closest to those fundamental political decisions that express the general will of the sovereign because an interpretation specifies the concrete form of an original intention. Constitutional cases are never wholly unpolitical but some interpretations are more legitimate than others. The greater the political tension within a constitutional culture, the more constitutional claims and social reality diverge, the more likely decisions of a constitutional court are to appear as illegitimate »political« decisions.[16]

Professor Schmidt indicates this in his reference to the »interpretation problem« at the heart of persistent debate in Germany on the economic constitution. When their articles were originally written Reiner Schmidt and Christopher Allen all appeared relatively sanguine about the stability of Germany's legal consensus although each interpreted the jurisprudential status of property in the Basic Law differently, and both based their arguments on a positivist view of the constitution. But if we attend to the »problem of interpretation« the echoes of politics are never far away. The continuing political debate surrounding the assertion of those basic liberal values articulated in Horst Siebert's analysis of the principles of the German economy has intensified since the articles below were first written. With the coming unification of east and west Germany, high constitutional politics have shaken the optimistic assumptions of legal positivism. Constitutions are, as Otto Kirchheimer remarked many years earlier, »always books of possibilities«. In that book I find many questions that make me feel less than sanguine about the future of the Basic Law:

1.   What are the boundaries of an interpretative scheme – individual rights, or the internal coherence of the constitutional document?

2.   If the latter, how secure is the Constitutional Court's liberal interpretation?

3. At a time when the German question is being raised by international developments in the European Community and the collapse of the Soviet order in the east, will the balance of a social market economy be maintained in a newly-constituted Federal Republic? Or will the Court's interpretation of the primacy of individual rights in the Basic Law become an endorsement of laissez-faire liberalism in a new political system?

Notes:

1 Reiner Schmidt, »Principles of the Economic System in the Federal Republic - the Legal Aspect«, MS (English translation), p. 7.
2 See Andrew Shonfield, *Modern Capitalism* (New York: Harper, 1965). Christopher Allen uses the term synonymously with »the politics of industrial order« and as an equivalent to the German *»Ordnungspolitik«* in »Principles of the Economic System in the Federal Republic of Germany - An American View«, MS, p.3.
3 Schmidt notes that Nipperday's thesis (*Soziale Marktwirtschaft und Grundgesetz* (1961) has been understood as »a normative guarantee of the social market economy; an economic system had become a constitutional yardstick«. Schmidt, »Principles of the Economic System in the Federal Republic - A Legal View«, MS (English), p.6.
4 Schmidt, *op cit*, MS (English), p.17.
5 Horst Siebert, »Principles of the Economic System in the Federal Republic - An Economist's View«, p. 1.
6 Siebert expresses some worry that market mechanisms are being endogenously eroded through subsidies and regulation and exogenously through European (and now German) unification. »From hindsight such a process may have been checked better if the market economy had been explicitly laid down in the Basic Law.« Without a constitutional anchor, he sees the market side of the social market economy inadequately defended by »denken in Ordnungen«. Siebert, *op. cit.*
7 *Ibid.*
8 *Op. cit.*
9 *Ibid.*
10 Christopher Allen, »Principles of the Economic system: An American View«, pp. 11-22.
11 *Op. cit.*
12 Reiner Schmidt, *Der Staat*, 19 (1980), pp. 235ff.
13 Franz Neumann, »Die soziale Bedeutung der Grundrechte in der Weimarer Verfassung« (1930); »Über die Voraussetzungen und den Rechtsbegriff einer Wirtschaftsverfassung« (1931) in Alfons Sollner (ed.), *Franz L. Neuman. Wirtschaft. Staat. Demokratie. Aufsätze 1930-1954* (Frankfurt: Suhrkamp, 1978) (English translation in Keith Tribe (ed.) *Social Democracy and the Rule of Law. Otto Kirchheimer and Franz Neumann* (London: Allen & Unwin, 1987).

14 Ernst Forsthoff, *Rechtsstaatlichkeit oder Sozialstaatlichkeit* (Darmstadt, 1968). The question is a definitive preoccupation of German constitutional law in this century. From among the large literature on this subject, see Carl Schmitt, *Verfassungslehre* (1928); Rudolf Smend, *Verfassung und Verfassungsrecht* (1928); Hermann Heller, *Staatslehre* (1934); Ernst Forsthoff, *Der Staat der Industriegesellschaft* (1971) and E.W. Böckenförde (ed.) *Staat und Gesellschaft* (1976).

15 Schmidt, *op cit.*

16 In this context, it is hardly surprising that one of the most frequent interpretative moves begins with a reference to the framers' intentions.

Part 6:
Special Contributions

Rudolf Dolzer

The Path to German Unity: The Constitutional, Legal and International Framework

1. *Policy Perspectives for Germany*

Seen from the vantage point of the early months of 1990, the opening on November 9,1989, of the Wall dividing Berlin appears as the first and the decisive step of self-determination by the German people after four decades of separation in the wake of World War II.

The Basic Law *(Grundgesetz)* of the Federal Republic of Germany (FRG), which was passed in May 1949, states in its preamble that the establishment of German unity in peace and freedom is a mandatory objective of German policy. But until November 1989 this objective was a task rather than reality. The dictatorial foundations of the German Democratic Republic (GDR) denied its citizens the exercise of their right of self-determination.

In the months since November 1989, the people of the GDR have indicated clearly and unhesitatingly that the constitutional demand for German unity as laid down in the Basic Law put into written form and expressed the political will not only of those living in the Federal Republic, but of all Germans. Four decades of political indoctrination in schools, factories, organizations and at all other levels in the GDR with a view toward making permanent the division of Germany could not alter or bend this will. The results of the first free elections in the GDR in March 1990 formalized and confirmed the formation of the will of the Germans in the GDR in favor of unity.

Prospects for the realization of German unity based on the right of self-determination and within the framework of specific and freely made agreements between Germany and the victorious powers of World War II gradually began to appear in April 1990. The historic changes ushered in by the events of November 1989 should, however, not make us lose sight of the fact that the steps on the road to unity were complex and difficult at various levels. They can only be partly anticipated today.

Moreover, the question of the legal framework within which unity is to be established remains open. The Basic Law provides not only for the establishment of unity according to Article 23[1] through the accession of the GDR (or of its *Länder,* or states), it also makes the creation of a new constitution possible according to Article 146.[2] Good reasons argue for establishing unity constitutionally and according to international law in a single step, but implementing its practical realization step by step in keeping with the special characteristics and requirements of the various areas of the legal system. Economic and monetary policies, social policy, environmental policy, and transportation policy might, for instance, be dealt with differently from foreign policy and defense policy.[3] Basic questions about the security and foreign policy of a future Germany also are still open today and can only be determined during impending international negotiations. One cannot say now whether these talks will conclude with joint declarations, bilateral agreements, the traditional kind of peace treaty, or with other legal equivalents.

2. *The Collapse of the German Democratic Republic*

Analyses and statements made during the political celebrations and the academic conferences on the occasion of the 40th anniversary of the Basic Law in May 1989 were to a large extent identical in their essentials.[4] On the one hand they emphasized that the Basic Law, with all the inadequacies of any living constitution, has on the whole turned out to be an extraordinarily stable foundation for the national, economic and societal development of the Federal Republic of Germany. On the other hand, it was also recognized that even after four decades, this constitution has standing in one part of Germany only. Since the war, about 17 million Germans have had to live under the rule of a constitution which might have deserved that name in the formal sense, but which actually, according to the precepts of a free and democratic state based on the rule of law, in no way represented the norm for establishing or limiting state power.

After 1945, the physical border between the two parts of Germany was drawn in a fatefully arbitrary manner within the framework of agreements by the four victorious powers of World War II, the United States, Britain, France and the Soviet Union. When this essay was presented in its original version in October 1989, the Wall between the two German states showed no cracks to the outside world. Even then, however, the decision by Hungary in the summer of 1989 to open its border with Austria had already had consequences for German-German relations by publicly raising questions about the legitimacy of the Communist government in East Berlin. How else was one to explain the flood of those seeking to emigrate, who used the first opportunity since the erection of the Wall in 1961 to leave the GDR, even though they were violating the GDR's laws on »Flight from the Republic.« Yet it still seemed in October 1989 that there was no hope in the short run to overcome the partition of Germany, and that only utopians could offer easy solutions for the German question. A few months later, this cautious outlook for German unity had been overtaken by history. During these months, the authority of the state bodies of the GDR has teetered on the brink of collapse. Against this background, the political groupings and regroupings within the GDR, which have developed within the period of a few months, have indicated unanimously that German unity can be achieved very soon.[5]

Only the concept of revolution is adequate for comprehending the precipitous events in the German-German relationship of recent months. The driving force of this revolution was a negative one: rejection of the political, economic and social conditions of life as perceived by a majority of the GDR population after four decades under communism.

The prospect of liberal reforms immediately deprived the Communist state of its basis without presenting a readily apparent alternative to a political and social order patterned after that of the Federal Republic of Germany. As late as February 1990 the GDR's prime minister of the day, Modrow, had spoken about the bitter experience of the defeat of »real socialism« as if a still noble ideal of a political system had failed because of fateful fortunes in Germany's postwar history. But 1989 will enter German history not primarily as a year of bitter defeat, but as the year of communism's bankruptcy declaration and of a new beginning toward a free system of government based on respect for human dignity.

And from the vantage point of the Federal Republic of Germany, the movement for freedom in the GDR in 1989 also represented a special kind of point of crystallization. *Ostpolitik* (Eastern policy),[6] introduced in 1972 with the conclusion of the Basic Treaty between East and West Germany, has many levels of political motivation which cannot be easily depicted. Its result was, in any case, that the goal of German unity gradually began to recede more rapidly than had been the case during the period immediately after 1949. In 1985, a minister of justice of the Federal Republic called for the elimination of the reunification precept from the Basic Law; during the

367

period just after that the concept of »reunification as a living lie« of the Federal Republic was not at all an uncharacteristic description among important political groups in the country.

But the coalition government in office since 1982 refused to let itself be influenced by this renunciation of the goal of German unity, even though the visit of Erich Honecker, chief of the East German state, to Bonn in 1987 might have given the outward appearance of a new orientation in intra-German policy. When the political explosiveness of the movement for freedom in the GDR became apparent at the end of 1989, Chancellor Kohl – in a first act of self-determination – without prior consultation with West Germany's allies, reiterated the goal of German unity and in his Ten-Point program of November 28 presented a practical concept for a road toward establishing it.[7]

Political reaction in West and East to the efforts to establish unity was as diverse and rapid as were developments within the Federal Republic. The Soviet Union, for instance, had pointed out year after year for decades that the division of Germany was one of the realities governing the situation in Europe in the aftermath of Nazism and the world war which the Nazis had started. There is no simple explanation for the change in the Soviet viewpoint toward the end of 1989, particularly with regard to the partition of Germany. The decisive political and economic factors will require further research. The Soviet terminology, used on a number of occasions also by Gorbachev, which made it possible to abandon previous positions, is that »history itself decides about processes and destinies.«[8]

That also applies to the variegated position taken by the Western allies toward the problem of a divided Germany. Until President Bush took a positive stand on the German question, Secretary of State Baker preferred as late as November 1989 to talk about »reconciliation« and not about »reunification« of the two parts of Germany. And remarks by other leading politicians among the Federal Republic's Western allies, frequently just barely concealed by diplomatic language, expressed concern about the eventual consequences of the establishment of German unity. In the end, the decisive thing was apparently less the view of the German past under Nazism than the political concept of freedom and the principle of self-determination under international law. The limited historical experience of four decades ago could not prevail against such fundamental and universal concepts relating to the justness of the German desire for the establishment of unity.

A reunited Germany poses questions for the European Community, particularly for its plans for the quick creation of an economic and monetary union. These questions go far beyond special economic ones. It is significant in this regard that the federal government has stressed repeatedly that it sees no contradiction between the establishment of German unity and Germany's integration into a European Community that develops further. Nothing indicates that the citizens of the GDR would in any way oppose integration into the Community.

The Ten-Point program of the Kohl government of November 1989[9] still sketched out the road toward German unity as leading from a contractual partnership between the Federal Republic and the GDR via a confederation of the two parts of Germany. The joint communique by the heads of government of the two German states after their meeting of December 20 even contains a reference to that prerequisite of good neighborliness which was expressed in the Basic Treaty of 1972 when it gave precedence to the mutual recognition of the existence of two German states.[10] In a short period of time, however, things have moved beyond the prospect of a lengthy process bringing the two German states closer together. This happened not because of conceptual factors, but rather as a practical result of the rapid deterioration of the authority of the GDR.

3.   *Origin of the Basic Law and its Reunification Mandate*

Parallel with the evolution of a GDR regime inimical to freedom and human welfare, there developed in Germany after 1945 a political, legal and economic system which, after turning away from totalitarianism, reestablished connections with liberal Western traditions.[11] The question arose early whether to aim for the founding of a new state, to wait for improved chances for reunification, to conduct a neutral foreign policy or to opt unambiguously for integration into Western organizations.

After the surrender of the German armed forces in May 1945, the Allies took over supreme authority in Germany. Germany was divided into four occupation zones, and the Germans exercised governmental authority only to a limited extent and at a lower level. At first there was no central authority by Germans. That was exercised by the Allied Control Council. In 1948, the Western Powers agreed to set up a constituent part in their occupation zones in the form of a federal state. The representatives of German state authority, the prime ministers of the *Länder*, realized immediately that establishment of a constituent part must avoid giving the wrong impression of abandonment of German unity. What settled the matter in favor of a new organization of statehood were, first, pragmatic considerations concerning the Germans' own perception about the task of rebuilding the German economy and, secondly, the gradual replacement of occupational rule. At that time there was little hope for reestablishment of German unity in the short term. During the preceding months blockaded Berlin had survived only with the help of the American armed forces and of the airbridge. The Cold War was well under way by 1949.

Against this background the Germans, then responsible for the conduct of affairs, decided to set up the Federal Republic of Germany on the territory of the German *Reich*,[12] but at the same time also to draft a new constitution as an expression of a transition state looking to the reestablishment of a single Germany. The prime ministers of the *Länder* therefore insisted that it be made clear that the structure to be created was »only provisional, an institution which owes its existence solely to present circumstances related to the current occupation of Germany.«[13] The new state came into being on this basis in 1949 with the agreement of the Allies. Its provisional nature is mentioned in numerous places in the Basic Law *(Grundgesetz)*, the document that was approved in 1949. Its preamble states that the people are called upon »to achieve the unity and freedom of Germany in free self-determination.« The term »constitution« was avoided because of its possible appearance of finality. Instead, the more neutral title of »Basic Law« was chosen in order to underline its transitional character.

The provisions of the Basic Law show that its Founding Fathers put the constitutional state at the service of Germany's reunification by making it mandatory in the preamble for all organs of the Federal Republic of Germany to observe the precept of safeguarding German unity and working to attain it. The Federal Constitutional Court *(Bundesverfassungsgericht)* has repeatedly ruled that the directives of the Basic Law pertaining to Germany are not merely of a non-binding or programmatic nature, but constitutionally oblige the state organs to take action in a practical sense. »The preamble of the Basic Law has primarily a political, but also a legal significance. All political organs of the state are legally obliged to work with all their power for the unity of Germany; they must direct their actions toward this goal, and they must above all refrain from doing anything that legally impedes reunification or makes it in practical terms impossible to achieve.«[14] This is not the place to discuss how the Constitutional Court could enforce this obligation, or the leeway that was left for political judgement to find the appropriate way to achieve reunification in light of the existing political situation.[15]

This inclusion of reunification policy in the constitution, together with its monitoring by the Constitutional Court, sometimes met with ignorance or misunderstanding outside Germany. One hears it occasionally said abroad that it is unrealistic to make the division of Germany, and consequently the division of Europe, the subject of a domestic constitutional norm. In this context it was also pointed out that any great power which controls Germany could at the same time dominate Europe.

The division of Germany in its origins was not a national constitutional problem, but rather an expression of East-West rivalry. It preserved this fundamental characteristic until the recent dramatic changes. For this reason overcoming the division has been and remained in the first instance also a question of the shifting or the development of geopolitical constellations. Nevertheless, it is not at all incongruous or meaningless that the Basic Law postulated a reunification mandate. Establishment of German unity requires a practical and active policy, which naturally must be conceived and implemented first and foremost by German state organs. Hegelian faith in the automatic progress of history toward reestablishment of German unity would have been naive and ahistorical.[16]

While the process of the division of Germany was virtually politically completed during the past decades, that process could not divide the nation in its larger sense, that of a cultural entity. German unity remained a legal reality as well as a trust imposed on the government bodies of the Federal Republic.

4.   *The Idea of the Nation-State in the Basic Law*

The constitutional mandate of the Basic Law was based on the belief in the possibility of reunification and in the desirability of reestablishing the unity of the German nation on German territory as it has developed historically. This view occasionally met with the objection that the idea of unity of state, nation and sovereignty expresses a 19th century model of philosophy and state theory, and that this idea should be considered obsolete under present-day circumstances. This is a correct view inasmuch as a return to a 19th century national pattern of thought is in fact neither possible nor desirable today. Imperialism and militarism, which were common all over Europe at that time and which reached a uniquely low point in Nazi Germany in the 20th century, certainly have no basis in German society and politics. Rather, risks are greater today from an apolitical understanding of the state and society and, parallel with it, from neutralism in foreign policy.

The openness of the Basic Law on the necessity and opportunity toward all forms of modern international cooperation appears most clearly in Articles 24 and 25. According to Article 24, it is constitutionally possible to transfer sovereign rights to international institutions; and Article 25 stipulates that the general rules of international law are not only components of federal law but also have precedence over domestic norms in every case.

A central function of the limitations of international law on *Deutschlandpolitik*, the Federal Republic's policy toward the GDR, is apparent from a look at the ways in which that policy may be implemented. The Basic Law explicitly forbids any war of aggression (Article 26). It also prescribes that with the precedence accorded the rules of international law, the prohibition of the use of force has precedence over all legislation passed by the legislature (Article 25). It thus is readily apparent that the Basic Law has drawn consequences from the Nazis' illegal and nationalistic policies not only for the Federal Republic's domestic system, but also for its conduct of foreign relations.

The basic need for the individual's identification with his community remains unchanged today, even under present circumstances. The idea of a world government on the one hand or of the abolition of any kind of ruling structure on the other is illusory and cannot replace the need and the desire for a state organization within the framework of a community that has »developed historically« - in any case not a present.[17] Against this background the Federal Republic's constitutional mandate to restore national unity proves to be not anachronistic, even today.

At the general level, there will be no objections from the United States in any case. Germans never cease to be amazed when they discover that it is a matter of course that in everyday life American school children pledge their allegiance to the flag or spectators sing the national anthem at the start of a game in a university stadium. It will be a central task of practical German politics in coming years to find a healthy balance between the overemphasis on the national during the Nazi period, and its downplaying in the decades after 1945.

5. The Basis of Reunification Policy in International Law

Besides the constitutional situation, it is important to understand the international law framework of Bonn's *Deutschlandpolitik* up to now. The feature to be stressed in this regard is the close mutual relationship between politics and law. The Federal Republic's *Deutschlandpolitik* has had a firm basis in general international law and in international treaties. The *Grundgesetz* made the commitment to reunification a legal duty. The Federal Republic used its treaties with the victorious Western Powers of World War II (the United States, France and Britain) as an instrument for the realization of this obligation. In Article 7, Paragraph 2 of the »German Treaty« of 1955 the victorious Western Powers made a binding commitment to support the aim of German reunification. On the other hand, Article 2 of the »German Treaty« makes it clear that reunification is possible only with the agreement of the four allies (the Western three plus the Soviet Union). As in past centuries, so after 1945 too the German question still did not »belong to the Germans.« After World War II all four allied occupation powers granted themselves the right to veto any change in the situation. The peculiarity of allied rights for Germany consisted of the fact that these rights incorporated both the common voice in the affairs of central Europe as well as the conflict over that common voice. The continuing responsibility of the Four Powers, the three Western allies plus the Soviet Union, for »Germany as a whole« has been confirmed many times by the Allies.[18] That responsibility was, moreover, the essential basis for the continuing legal existence of the German *Reich.*

If the Federal Republic's international treaty policy has assumed a positive function in West Germany, the constitution's reunification mandate assumed the function of limiting cooperation in *Ostpolitik.* The treaties signed with the Soviet Union in 1971, with the German Democratic Republic in 1972 and with Poland in 1974 do not contain any clauses or formulations which impede Bonn's active reunification policy. In particular, the national question has been expressly set aside in the extremely carefully formulated treaty with the GDR.

Limiting implementation of *Deutschlandpolitik* to peaceful means fits in a positive sense with the concept of more recent international law which has found its expression in the demand for the right of national self-determination. After President Wilson called for the recognition of this right in his famous speech in 1917, it took up to 1945 until the international community recognized the right to self-determination as valid. Today it is anchored in the most prominent place in all human rights agreements.

The universal grounding of the right of self-determination in human rights shows that this right cannot be limited either geographically or historically and that it is indivisible. It is at this point that the consonance of the constitutional demand for reunification of the German nation with the foundations of international law becomes clear. The argument about the anachronism of this constitutional precept in the *Grundgesetz* is refuted by valid international law when measured against the explosiveness with which the right of self-determination has established itself as a legal concept since 1945 and with which it also has changed reality in the community of nations. This basic concept of international law thus does not take into consideration reunification of Germany. Rather, it calls for reunification's realization.

It should not be concealed here that the reunification mandate could come into conflict with the right of self-determination if account is taken of the post-World War II expulsion of Germans from Germany's eastern territories, which lie in present-day Poland and in the Soviet Union. Today these eastern territories are only sparsely populated by Germans. In contrast to the GDR, if a vote were taken today among the inhabitants of these territories there would be no majority in favor of a Germany reorganized within its former, pre-World War II frontiers. There is no real constitutional conflict in this case, however, because the Basic Law does not under all circumstances require the complete territorial reestablishment of the *Reich*. It is significant in this context that in its more recent statements and comments the federal government has put more emphasis on the right of self-determination, on the idea of freedom and on human rights, than on the idea of territorial unity.[19] It should also be noted here that the people of the GDR have their own right of self-determination. They cannot be outvoted by the people of the Federal Republic. The reason for this is that the Federal Republic has recognized the GDR as a state in the Basic Treaty of 1972.

Clear from these considerations is the surpassing importance of the idea of the law for grounding but also for limiting and for implementing reunification policy, as laid down in the Basic Law. In particular the basic organizational principle of the right to self-determination has demonstrated its autonomous value in shaping international relations in a special way during the upheaval in intra-German relations after the events of November 1989. In the final instance, the variety and many levels of the emotive international reaction to the positive steps toward German unity could be articulated only to a limited extent because they faced the force of the right of self-determination, a recognized principle of the international order. Invoking this right prevailed also against tendencies toward a strictly political and emotional assessment of the division of Germany.

6. *Integration into the West - The Priority after 1949*

Although the question of German unity was hardly on the international agenda explicitly between 1945 and 1989, questions of a German identity and of the meaning of German nationality were in the foreground implicitly. Reflection - but also silence - about the historical course and meaning of German national unity, which so far has only existed for 74 years (between 1871 and 1945), was pronounced in the Federal Republic after World War II. Often it was so pronounced on both a private and on an official level that development of future perspectives was - despite the constitutional mandate to take action - dismissed as a trivial pastime unrelated to the times or to reality. Even for a German observer it is not always easy to decide to what extent Germany's refraining from burdening the European Community, the Western Alliance, or the United Nations with the German question constituted a dimension of practical policy relating in the sense of a silent integration and of a strengthening of Germany's reputation as a necessary first phase of *Deutschlandpolitik*. It should not be overlooked, however, that paradoxically a feature of *Deutschlandpolitik* was that it could only achieve success if based on the reality of the division. To overcome the *status quo* after the early consolidation of the GDR on the international level in the early 1970s it became necessary to a considerable extent to respect the *status quo*.

A neutral state in the center of Europe is an impossibility. To balance a world power like the Soviet Union in Europe will always require corresponding political and military weight. As far as economic importance and geographic situation are concerned, the entire situation of Germany has to be judged completely differently than that of Switzerland or Austria, for example. In such circumstances the main priority in the foreign policy of the Federal Republic after 1949 was integration into the West and its community of values. Only smaller groups playing no major role in official policy, which are to be found moreover on the right and the left of the political spectrum, are tempted to blur this clear concept and, instead, to make reunification on the basis of neutralization the central and direct objective of German policy in the West and in the East. The fear of Germany as a »wanderer between two worlds« comes up repeatedly in the media, including the American media. But this fear has no foundation if one analyzes practical German foreign policy as it is determined by the political and geographical situation in Europe.[20]

At the current stage of dynamic progress in the European Community toward a single market it cannot be denied that until 1989 the prospects and successes already achieved in European integration policy attracted public attention to a much greater extent than did the subject of reunification, a policy which until 1989 had at most brought only the so-called »small steps« which resulted in assistance to individuals. However, the mass exodus of GDR citizens in 1989 refocused the attention of the German and the international public on the consequences of the division of Germany in a unique fashion. But at no time did the Federal Republic allow any doubts to arise about its will to continue to support the EC integration process. Over half the inhabitants of the GDR have close relatives in the Federal Republic of Germany, and one-quarter of those living in the Federal Republic have relatives in the GDR. It was no coincidence that the Communist regime in East Berlin adopted a decidedly defensive attitude toward the reform process in 1989, since the GDR state was based on Marxist ideology only and not on political or cultural unity that had grown historically. A GDR constituted in freedom would have had no meaningful legitimacy next door to the free Federal Republic. As both the weaknesses of the Communist system in East Germany and Western humanitarian solidarity became apparent, the idea of brotherhood following the partial collapse of state authority in the GDR became linked in a new way to the idea of freedom and equality, particularly in the thinking of the younger German generation.

7. *Foundations of Deutschlandpolitik within the Framework of European Integration*

The preamble to the Basic Law states that German unity is to be achieved in a united Europe. The model for the new constitutional organization of the German state is thus not the isolated national state with strict emphasis on its own sovereignty. On the contrary, the aim is the existence of the German state in close cooperation with neighboring European countries. The Basic Law does not contain the express mandate for integration into the West.

376

Thus there has been a difference since 1949 from the mandate for reunification.

When the Basic Law was passed in 1949 the European Community (EC) did not yet exist. There were only vague contours at that time of the »united Europe« foreseen in the Basic Law. This explains why the Basic Law does not make any reference to Western European integration. »Europe« as described in the Basic Law has no limits to the East. The task of the Basic Law is to define the geographical framework of a »united Europe« as broadly as possible. The Basic Law does not provide for a limitation to Western Europe. The Basic Law does not address in detail the form and structure of the Europe of the future. The only requirement is that the individual states must continue to exist in a new Europe. Article 237 of the European Economic Community Treaty shows, as does the preamble of the Basic Law, that the individual peoples of Europe will also constitute the basis of European unity in the future. In the Single Europe Act, which in 1987 partially put the EC on a new treaty basis, there was agreement on a reformulation of the objective of an increasingly closer union.

When the Rome Treaty, signed in 1957, came into force in 1958, the Federal Republic expressly drew the attention of its EC partners to the existence of the German question in connection with integration in the West. It made the following declaration to the other EC member states: »The federal government assumes the possibility that in the event of the reunification of Germany there will be a reexamination of the treaties relating to the Common Market and to Euratom.« This declaration is in line with the statement of the Federal Constitutional Court, according to which all bodies of the state are required »to work with all their power for the unity of Germany; they must direct their actions toward this goal, and always use the appropriateness of this aim as a yardstick of their political actions«[21] and »refrain from doing anything that legally impedes unification.«[22]

Apart from this formal announcement of the 1950s, which is still valid, when the Treaty came into effect the Federal Republic drew an eminently practical consequence from its legal views on the continued existence of the German *Reich* and the reunification mandate. Since 1957, trade between the two parts of Germany has not been treated as foreign trade within the framework of the EC, but rather as domestic trade. The GDR gained considerable benefit from this legal situation, which gave it advantages which the states in Eastern Europe did not have.

The partners of the Federal Republic in the EC formally agreed from the outset to this practice of intra-German trade. They also acknowledged German efforts for reunification on other levels. For example, they recognized in their own jurisprudence the continuing existence of a single citizenship for all Germans. This is expressed in the practice that citizens of the GDR have not been treated as foreigners in the Federal Republic - a practice that has also existed since the EC Treaty came into force.

Thus the Federal Republic has consistently, and pursuant to its constitutional mandate, introduced the goal of reunification into the new legal system during the building of the European Community and also into the framework of EC practices. The partners to the Rome Treaty have not only acknowledged the goal of reunification, but have also kept their practices in line with it. This preservation of its legal position by means of the Federal Republic's policy on treaties has, from the outset, prevented a legal conflict arising out of an incompatibility between the question of reunification and of EC integration.

The Federal Constitutional Court has made it clear that although Article 24 of the Basic Law permits rights of sovereignty to be transferred to international organizations, in particular to the EC, such transferral authority has its limits where the identity of the constitutional system of the Federal Republic of Germany is altered in its structure. The preamble of the *Grundgesetz* shows clearly that the reunification mandate also belongs to the foundations of the constitution within the meaning of this interpretation of the Basic Law. It would thus be inadmissible under constitutional law to undermine the reunification mandate through reference to the possibility of the transferral of sovereign rights to international organizations under Article 24 of the Basic Law.

Harmonizing integration policy with *Deutschlandpolitik* has presented no difficulties in practice either for the Federal Republic or for its Rome Treaty partners.[23] This can be explained by the internal development of the Community during its first three decades. The EC's internal development has been determined largely by the dominance of the member states, expressed in practical terms particularly in the effort to achieve unanimity in the Council of Ministers and to represent national interests there at the same time. The concept of supranationality, in the sense of an inherent dynamic of Community interests, has been developed by the European Court of Justice in Luxembourg through establishment and development of the legal system of Community law.

In practice, member states have not been willing to accept a general renunciation of sovereignty by means of strengthening either the supranationally-oriented Commission or even of the European Parliament in Strasbourg. This basic attitude was, of course, bound to lead to a stagnation of integration, then to dissatisfaction, and then to efforts to achieve further progress. The result of these efforts was the modification of the Rome Treaty by the Single Europe Act of 1987.

The preamble of this Act states for the first time that the EC's aim is an increasingly closer union. So-called European Political Cooperation (EPC), which is institutionalized by the Act, is the first attempt at a harmonizing of foreign policy in substance among the member states, even if this does not occur, in strict legal terms, within the framework of the EC Treaty. According to the Single Europe Act, a single market is to be achieved by 1992. Since 1987 the Community has had new jurisdiction in environmental and research policies.

When German reunification takes place, these two policy areas will require considerable efforts because of the actual situation in the GDR. In these two areas the distribution of costs between European Community regional policy and German federal fiscal policy is bound to be the subject of difficult and intensive discussions.

New procedural regulations in force since 1987 expressly permit majority decisions in important areas of authority. As a result, the principle of taking vital national interests into consideration – as such interests are defined by individual member states – thus moves legally, if not politically, into the background. These and other important developments relating to the Rome Treaty that move Western Europe toward a uniform system have since 1987 gained a momentum that affects virtually all areas of politics and have also led to a tendency to a far-reaching definition of the concept of »the economy,« for example in areas such as regulation of professional training and of the mass media. The entry of all East Germany into the EC will consequently lead to many practical questions at the Community level.

Currently the European Community does not have the authority, as the Federal Constitutional Court has stressed, to develop in an evolutionary manner beyond its existing powers without the agreement of the member states. That is, the will of the member states is decisive for the overall development of the Community and for progress of European unity. The member states, as the Federal Constitutional Court has emphasized, remain »masters of the Community treaties.« The Community is not a sovereign state under international law. Neither territorial nor personal sovereignty of the member states have been transferred to it. The legal situation was expressed clearly when the Treaty of Rome was amended in 1987 by the Single Europe Act in regard to foreign policy. On the one hand it was significant that this amendment was not made without the express agreement of the member states. On the other hand, it is worth noting that »European Political Cooperation« was not incorporated legally into the framework of the European Community, but forms an additional level of cooperation among member states. If the Community had the legal power to further develop without limits in an evolutionary manner even without approval of the member states, such an amendment would not be understandable.

The existence of the European Community and the inclusion of the Federal Republic within its structure has turned out to be an essential – and perhaps even the decisive – element in the formation of the political will of the Western allies and of Germany's neighbor in the East in favor of the German unification process. Over the past few months it has repeatedly, often daily, been emphasized by one and all, including the Federal Republic, that a reunited Germany must be integrated into the »architecture of Europe.« In that regard, security interests are as important as economic considerations.[24]

Realization of a single EC market by 1992 as well as plans for an EC monetary and economic union in the near future have without a doubt contributed to the economic consequences of reunification being viewed by Germany's European neighbors not as a threat but potentially as an integral part of an extension of the European market.

Although the European Community has accumulated considerable experience over the decades in integrating different economic systems, integration of the GDR with its history as a planned economy will nevertheless pose a new challenge for the Community. The Community as well as the other former East Bloc states will pay very close attention to experiences arising out of this process. Integration of East Germany into the EC could become a model if other East European states, which formerly had planned economies, decide to enter the Community. Obviously this prospect could also exert considerable influence in determining the future weight of the Community in international economic policy.

The chances for such a development are reinforced by the fact that the forms and obligations of cooperation within the EC permit and even require distinct separation of the levels for economic policy, for foreign policy and for security policy. The pressure for economic cooperation among member states is matched by their freedom in the conduct of national security policy. Between these two extremes can be found cooperation in foreign policy which, in the framework of »European Political Cooperation,« so far is not wholly integrated because the Community is not the only instrument by which member states can conduct foreign policy. One may speculate now as to what degree a further European integration will sooner or later either blur or possibly completely eliminate these distinct separations of levels. When the Community was established in the 1950s, its economic theory was based on the assumption that a functional approach to cooperation would ultimately have to lead from economic to political union. This idea has been neither refuted nor comprehensively validated by empirical developments over the past decades.

8. *Legal Steps Toward Reunification*

The Basic Law not only adheres to the principle of Germany unity, it also points to the constitutionally possible forms of reunification. If, as is to be hoped and wished for, reunification will occur on the basis of Article 23 of the Basic Law, two constitutional steps are required: first, an application to accede by the GDR (by its states *[Länder]* or by its districts *[Bezirke]*);[25] and second, by a legal act on the part of the Federal Republic which defines the expansion of the jurisdiction of the Basic Law. Conceivably a plebiscite on reunification would follow this two-step process. It would be in line with the democratic principle of the people as the *pouvoir constituent* that the establishment of German unity take place in this manner although, or precisely because, the people took no such action when the Basic Law came into force – at that time only the *Länder* assented. It is true that at present the Basic Law contains no provision for such a step and it would therefore have to be amended.

To a certain extent the entry of the Saarland into the Federal Republic in 1956 gives us some clues about the procedures for the constitutional steps toward accession by the GDR. The Saarland applied for accession on December 14,1956. On the same day the *Bundestag* passed an incor- poration law, which the *Bundesrat* (Federal Council) approved a week later. The territorial extension of the jurisdiction of the Basic Law occurred on January 1, 1957. It occurred in conjunction with the coming into force of the incorporation law, which provided for a step-by-step transition period of three years for implementing the Saarland accession. In the case of the Saarland this procedure was preceded by an agreement between the Federal Republic and the former sovereign power in the Saarland, France. Because of the special situation of the Saarland created by the Coal and Steel Treaty, Luxembourg and the European Coal and Steel Community also participated in the negotiations on this agreement. The result of the negotiations, the

Saar Treaty, was a treaty document of 250 pages which, in addition to basic issues, regulated a mass of details, among them an amnesty for criminal acts committed during the political struggle for the Saarland.[26]

In the case of reunification it can be assumed that there will be negotiations between the Federal Republic and the GDR which will culminate in a treaty under international law constituting the basis for an application by the GDR under Article 23 of the Basic Law. And that would be followed by passage of an incorporation law by the Federal Republic. The parties involved, West and East Germany, will themselves have to determine which areas of jurisdiction are to be subject of the treaty. It is, for instance, conceivable that regulation of the question of property ownership connected with the many expropriations in the GDR since 1945, the question of integration of GDR civil servants into the Federal Republic's administration, and basic regulations for retirement insurance for GDR residents will be included in such a treaty. All three of these areas raise sensitive political questions, solutions for which can probably best be found in a prior bilateral agreement between the GDR and the Federal Republic and not later through unilateral legislation by an all-German parliament. It would also be advisable to consider an amnesty for certain political crimes, as was the case with the Saarland.

Special questions will arise during negotiations between the Federal Republic and the GDR, because accession under Article 23 of the Basic Law will, according to prevalent opinion, result in the automatic incorporation of the GDR into the European Community without the need for new EC negotiations over the Treaty of Rome. Because the GDR has been organized along centralized economic lines, and because its economic strength and competitiveness are currently not comparable with those of the other EC member states, it will be necessary to apply secondary law promulgated on the basis of EC treaties to the GDR in stages.

Transitional regulations will have to be provided for the GDR ranging from agricultural markets to regional development funds, from the right of competition to trade policy and environmental protection. Regulations of coal subsidies will also have to be clarified.[27]

Currently it is assumed that there will be no institutional changes in the Community. Germany will continue to have two Commissioner positions and ten Council votes for the immediate future. How reunification will affect the number of deputies from Germany in the Strasbourg Parliament remains an open question. Working agreements between the Federal Republic, the GDR and the EC will be necessary not only on a time-sequential application of the European Community's secondary right to the territory of the GDR. In certain areas - in environmental protection, for instance - the Federal Republic no longer makes the rules. EC member states have transferred jurisdiction to Brussels. Negotiations will be needed to clarify what forms the transition to a new system of law will take.

Elimination of the GDR's commitments toward third states outside the EC will raise special questions. This is because in important areas, particularly that of commercial law, the Community has jurisdiction. Consequently there must be careful coordination between the Federal Republic and the Community. There will also have to be negotiations on conforming international treaties which the GDR has concluded with third countries. Under international law it can be assumed that the GDR will cease being subject to international law once it accedes to the Federal Republic under Article 23 of the Basic Law, and that therefore treaties concluded by the GDR will no longer be valid. But this latter assumption is not exclusively true and cannot apply to agreements »territorially rooted,« those which give third states special rights (such as, for instance, easement and riparian rights). Moreover, it is up to the agencies of the Federal Republic which have jurisdiction to decide which GDR treaties they will take over and which they will renegotiate.

No question about the continuing validity of international treaties concluded by the Federal Republic arise after accession by the GDR under Article 23 because the legal subject will remain (even if its name changes). The legal situation would be different if unification came about under Article 146. In that case there would be no previous determination of the relationship of the new state to the Federal Republic. If it came to the creation of a new entity under international law which in the end differed from the Federal Republic, all international treaties concluded by the former Federal Republic would have to be renegotiated, including the NATO Treaty and the Treaty of Rome on the EC. This would create considerable instability about the basis of the new German state within the Western alliance. This too is an argument in favor of GDR accession according to Article 23.

Germany has recognized too that accession under Article 23 cannot take place, as far as its timing is concerned, without due regard for the interests of the community of nations. According to the »doctrine of moving treaty borders,« recognized in international law, treaties concluded by a state cease to exist once that state is incorporated into another existing state. In the security policy area, for instance, NATO membership of the GDR without prior discussion with the NATO partners and with the Warsaw Pact would therefore mean that the FRG would be establishing unilaterally a situation leading to the non-existence of commitments of GDR obligations to the Warsaw Pact. In order to avoid such a unilateral change and to accommodate the interests of the Soviet Union, in particular, the GDR's request for accession must be preceded not only by negotiations between the two German states as well as by discussions with the EC, but also by talks with the Western and Eastern treaty partners of the two existing German states.

It will also be necessary as well in this connection to clarify the modalities for eliminating the still existing rights of the victorious powers of World War II which, after 1945, resulted from the occupation of Germany and later treaties under international law. A »peace treaty« is not required. Such peace treaties were concluded in the past shortly after the end of a war. Forty-five years have now passed since World War II, a period during which the Federal Republic has gained its rightful place in the community of nations on the basis of a foreign policy of peace and of law. Consequently there is no longer any need to formalize peace on the basis of international law. And four decades after the end of the war, the question of reparations is no longer the same as it would have been in the framework of a classical peace treaty. Agreements within the Conference on Security and Cooperation in Europe (CSCE) framework and arrangements with the four victorious powers on the basis of developments since 1945 can take the place of a peace treaty.

Presumably, the powers of the four victorious allies of World War II which have been established in relation to German territory will also be terminated on the basis of a treaty to be concluded between these powers and the two German states. As of June 1945, the Allied Powers assumed rights and responsibilities relating to »Germany as a whole.« The general regime of occupation lasted in West Germany and in East Germany until 1955. West Germany formally recognized in 1954 that the rights and responsibilities of the Western Powers with regard to Berlin and Germany as a whole were retained.

The substance of these rights was never clearly defined, but it is clear that they concerned the external modalities of reunification and the question of the German borders. The right to station troops on German territory also belonged to the rights retained. As in a magnifying glass, the status of the four victorious powers came to be sharply seen in Berlin after 1945. The four have had the right to move their military personnel to and within the entire city of Berlin, to exclusive landing rights in the city for their aircraft, to civilian and military control over the organization of air security in and around Berlin. After forty-five years all these rights are likely to come to an end on the basis of agreed terms with resulting full and unqualified sovereignty of Germany in the sense of termination of all war-related rights of the four victorious powers.[28]

9. Outlook

Half a century after World War II began, the foreign rule established after that war in the countries of Central and Eastern Europe is coming to an end. Germany's partition was one consequence of a war which Hitler's state spread over large parts of the globe in flagrant disregard for international law. Despite this special political and moral background to Germany's partition, the arbitrary drawing of the border must have appeared especially intolerable to Germans in the eastern part of the country. Poverty and affluence, lack of freedom and freedom, were directly and comparatively experienced; the immediate proximity of the two systems in Germany made this experience particularly painful. The idea of national unity was never weakened or destroyed, despite, or perhaps even because of, the difference of two national systems in the two states. At the first opportunity for this unity to manifest itself to the outside world, it did so in an unusually humane way in spite of the political forces arrayed against it. German unity, which had been protected by the Basic Law without any break, turned out not to be a legally empty shell, but rather a substratum in law of an historical, linguistic and cultural reality which had for a time been buried in the years after the second World War.

The achievement of renewed national unity will constitute a unique challenge for Europe and for Germany in the coming months and years. It is still an open question today whether the road to unity can run completely straight. In economic policy particularly, the question will be which measures to establish a free market system should be taken all at once and for which measures a gradual approach over a period of time seems appropriate. Energy policy as a central component of economic policy will have to take account of the very extensive destruction of the environment which the Communist leadership of the GDR evidently wanted to conceal from the outside world but which it was prepared to tolerate at home as the necessary price of its inefficient economic policy. The costs of cleaning up this environmental damage cannot yet be estimated. Fundamental reforms are required in social and transportation policies, as well as in primary and higher education. The legal system of the GDR, which had ceased developing a few years ago at the level of the 18th century,[29] must be completely rebuilt. A liberal concept of basic rights and an effective system of separation of powers have been unknown in GDR law.

To cope with such tasks, the traditional federal structure of Germany's political system, which was taken over into the Basic Law, will make a significant political contribution. It will provide a common denominator for the need to differentiate on the one hand and to integrate into a legal unity on the other.

Still open is the question whether the Basic Law in its present structure and form will also become the future constitution of an all-German state. If the GDR accedes on the basis of Article 23, that would indeed be the case initially. If unity comes about as the result of decisions of a constituent assembly of both parts of Germany, then the decision on a new constitutional system – and thus also on the Basic Law – would be at the disposition of such a constituent power.

As developments are now, there are many reasons for letting the Basic Law serve for the time being as the constitution of a new Germany (with modifications that may be necessary).[30] The extraordinary esteem which the Basic Law has gained, even in international comparison, in its development in recent years reflects the stable and just order of the community which has arisen on the foundation of the Basic Law. It is extremely questionable whether a constituent assembly could, after what would be a relatively brief debate, under existing circumstances create a better or a more just constitutional system.

Also currently still unresolved is the international legal framework within which Germany's unity can be accomplished. The conference of the four victorious powers of World War II and the two German states served to establish the basis for German unity. The CSCE, with its much larger circle of participants, will escort the reunification process with accompanying measures. Still to be clarified is whether a conventional peace treaty will be concluded within this CSCE framework or whether a multilateral treaty that is differently structured will serve as the functional equivalent of a peace treaty.

Certainly these negotiations will fix the border of a future Germany with its neighbor Poland. A number of states, among them the Soviet Union and Poland, have already in earlier contractual agreements given up their pecuniary claims from Germany. Future security systems for Germany, and consequently also for Europe, will surely be a central point in all the negotiations and agreements. This will involve finding a common denominator for the security concerns of the Soviet Union and of NATO, as well as for the legitimate interests of the Federal Republic of Germany. Elimination of the rights of the victorious powers in Germany will be accomplished in this framework. After that the question can be answered about the unified military status or the introduction of different levels of permissible military activity on German territory. The Federal Republic in 1954 already unilaterally renounced its right to possess, produce and transfer nuclear, biological and chemical weapons; it can be assumed that this renunciation will be confirmed for all of Germany during negotiations on establishing German unity.

Apparent in the end result is a picture in law of the future of Germany which will be significantly modified in many areas and on many levels compared with the classic ideal of state sovereignty. The supranational legal forms of the European Community, Germany's renunciation of the right to possess nuclear, biological and chemical weapons, as well as absolute and territorial limits for the future conventional armed forces of a united Germany – all are based on further development of conventional international law of coordination toward the cooperative elements of international collaboration. It is obvious that the form of a reunited Germany that is to be created under international law is not of an accidental nature but represents a prerequisite for international acceptance of the reestablishment of German unity.

Limitations of national sovereignty which are established in this fashion, when seen from the historical perspective of international law, take the place of formerly well-established forms of safeguarding peace in politically and militarily sensitive geographic regions and particularly take the place of the classic concept of neutrality. In the long run a united but neutral Germany could not have found a place in that central area of political forces which is the heart of Europe. The basis for establishing German unity is to be found in the differentiated development of modern forms of cooperation under international law – forms which will limit national sovereignty in the global areas of security policy and which will constitute and organize national sovereignty anew within this modern framework of international law.

Notes:

1 Article 23: »For the time being, this Basic Law shall apply in the territory of the States *(Länder)* of Baden, Bavaria, Greater Berlin, Hamburg, Hesse, Lower Saxony, North Rhine-Westphalia, Rhineland-Palatinate, Schleswig-Holstein, Württemberg-Baden, and Württemberg-Hohenzollern. In other parts of Germany it shall be put in force on their accession.«

2 Article 146: »This Basic Law shall cease to be in force on the day on which a constitution adopted by a free decision of the German people comes into force.«

3 Transitional regulations might be required for the civil service, the financial system, the military organization and for other sectors. It might well be that during this transitional period existing GDR law will continue to apply even though this does not accord with the principles of the Basic Law. In the medium-term at least, changes in the Basic Law will be necessary with regard to the way the preamble is formulated, and to the national goals contained in it, and also with regard to the stipulations of Articles 23 and 146. Adjustments will also have to be made with regard to certain institutions.

4 Kirchhof, »Gegenwartsfragen an das Grundgesetz,« *Juristen Zeitung* vol. 44 (1989); p. 453 *et seq.;* Schenke, »40 Jahre Grundgesetz,« *Juristen Zeitung* vol. 44 (1989); p. 653 *et seq.:* Grimm, »Das Grundgesetz nach 40 Jahren,« *Neue Juristische Wochenschrift* vol. 42 (1989: p. 1305 *et seq.;* W. Bethge, »Staatszwecke im Verfassungsstaat,« *Deutsches Verwaltungsblatt* vol. 104 (1989): p. 841 *et seq.*

5 See Daniel Hamilton, »After the Revolution: The Political Landscape of East Germany,« *German Issues No. 7,* American Institute for Contemporary German Studies, May 1990.

6 *Ostpolitik,* policy toward the East, is the term customarily applied to the Federal Republic's policy toward the Warsaw Pact countries, usually including the Soviet Union and sometimes meant to include policy toward the GDR also. *Deutschlandpolitik* policy relating to Germany is the term more usually employed for West Germany's intra- or inner- German policy toward the GDR.

7 *Bulletin der Bundesregierung,* November 29,1989, No. 134, p. 1141 *et seq.*

8 As expressed in the text of an interview in the *Frankfurter Allgemeine Zeitung* of March 8,1989: »We believe that the process of the reunification of the two German states is a natural process. That can be seen in the view which I have always held. History has bequeathed us this question as a legacy. History will show us how to solve this question. And just now history has suddenly begun to move at great speed.«

9 See fn 4.

10 See Dolzer in Kirchhof and Isensee, eds., *Handbuch zum Staatsrecht,* vol. 1, pp. 547, 567.

11 See Hans Maier, »Die Deutschen und die Freiheit,« *Zeitschrift für Politik,* vol. 36 (1982) p. 1.

12 The territorial holdings of Germany as of December 31, 1937, before absorption of territory from other states.

13 Mussgnug, in *Handbuch zum Staatsrecht,* pp. 219, 228. Kirchhof/Isensee.

14 *Bundesverfassungsgerichtsentscheidung* (BVerfGE) 5, 85 *(Leitsatz),* 128.

15 See BVerfGE 5, 85; see also 36, 1, 17, 77, 137, 149.

16 A debate in the *Bundestag* in June 1989 still indicated that there was no complete unanimity among the large German parties as to whether the goal of the reestablishment of German unity should be adhered to. Jürgen Schmude, an SPD *Bundestag* member, once proposed to strike the reunification precept from the Basic Law. See »Deutsch-deutsches Verhältnis« in *Informationen der Sozial-demokratischen Bundestagsfraktion*, May 17, 1985. Repealing the reunification precept through a change of the constitution would have created a general problem of constitutional theory, namely whether there are basic decisions relating to the formation of a state which are beyond any constitutional change.

17 This point will be treated below in connection with the trends in more recent international law and in particular the more recent political developments in Western Europe.

18 To this extent it is worth noting that the pertinent treaties between the GDR and the Soviet Union of 1955, 1964 and 1975 refer to the rights of the victorious powers.

19 See the address of the chancellor on July 11, 1989 *(Presse und Informationsamt Bulletin)*, July 13, 1989: »Freedom, human rights and selfdetermination are the core of the German Question. During the past few months the discussion about Poland's western border became unreal because everyone knew that the victorious powers are united on this issue.

20 The widespread idea of the victorious powers that Germany is only a land of obedience and not of freedom has no historical foundation. See Hans Maier, *op. cit.*

21 BVerfGE 5, 85, 127.

22 BVerfGE 5, 85, 128.

23 Discussion of the relationship between the reunification mandate and integration into the West has so far taken place in three stages. In the first stage, in the 1950s, it centered primarily on whether integration into the West was not in fundamental conflict with the aim of reunification and should therefore give way to a neutralist policy. In the following decades this discussion almost ceased because the public had come to accept the existence of the EC. The third stage began in the mid-1980s, when the intensification of cooperation within the EC and the Community goal of political union focused attention again on the relationship between EC integration and German reunification.

24 The verification question will also play a special role in connection with security agreements after the dissolution of Four Power rights. Article 24 of the Basic Law permits the transfer of sovereign powers to international institutions. From the German viewpoint, it is certainly important whether the results of such Four Power agreements create a special status for Germany, something that is bound to be intolerable in the long run. This has led to the question of whether the frequently cited new »cooperative security structures« in Europe will also include agreements for other European states, including corresponding stipulations concerning verification. The question of a special status for Germany could also arise in connection with a Four Power guarantee for Poland's Western border. In such a case as well a permanent departure from the principle of equal rights for all states would not be acceptable from a German viewpoint. It is, however, conceivable that as far as its borders are concerned, Germany would subject itself in a binding fashion for the future to the jurisdiction of an international court.

25 See the interpretation of Article 23 in BVerfGE, 36,1, 28 *et seq.*

26 The law on the incorporation of the Saarland took up four pages of the Federal Law Bulletin *(Bundesgesetzblatt)* and consisted of only 20 paragraphs. Corresponding rules on the incorporation of the GDR will certainly be considerably more extensive.

27 The German-German »Unification Treaty« was signed on August 31,1990. It provides the constitutional and legal framework for unification. After approval by the parliaments of the two states, the Treaty will go into effect on October 3. It also provides that all European Community laws will apply to the former GDR, with certain exceptions for transitional periods.

28 In Moscow, on September 12, 1990, the two Germanys and the World War II victorious powers, the United Stated, Soviet Union, Britain, and France, signed the »Treaty on the Final Settlement with Respect to Germany,« concluding the so-called Two-Plus-Four talks started in Bonn on March 14. In this Treaty the four powers give up their occupation rights in Berlin and in German territory which they had established at the Potsdam Conference in 1945.

29 For more detail, see Dolzer, »Die administrative Durchsetzbarkeit öffentlich-rechtlicher Positionen – Verwaltungsinterne Rechtsschutzverfahren in der DDR,« *Die Verwaltung,* 1985, p. 461.

30 In discussions about the legal form of establishing German unity by means of Article 23 or Article 146 of the Basic Law it should not be overlooked that constituent assemblies usually act by majority decision. Based on the number of inhabitants of the Federal Republic and of the GDR, members of such an assembly would come mainly from the Federal Republic of Germany. It is therefore quite conceivable that they would outvote the GDR representation according to the principles of majority decision.

Roman Herzog

The Separation and Concentration of Power in the Basic Law

The subject which I have chosen and would now like to discuss requires –
especially before an audience which does not deal with the German constitution every day – two things: first, one must examine the text of the constitution itself to see where it provides opportunities for the separation of
power on the one hand and the concentration of power on the other.
Second, it is necessary to discuss how matters have actually developed in
the 40 years since the Basic Law came into force, and where they hang in
the balance today.

In the next half hour, I intend to do both as honestly as I possibly can. I will
have to ask my German colleagues for their understanding if I often only
repeat what I have already stated in print (although, admittedly, I am not
sure whether they always read everything that I publish). I must also ask my
American listeners in advance to bear with me if, on my tour through the
constitutional situation of the Federal Republic, I sometimes stride ahead
too quickly; but, given the short time available to me, this cannot always be
avoided.

I.

The subject requires that I should start with the idea of the separation of
powers, which is said to have been discovered more than two thousand
years ago by the Greek philosopher Aristotle, and which certainly played a
significant role in the writings of the French state philosopher Charles de
Montesquieu and in the Federalist Papers. I don't wish to bore you with
more details on this. Suffice it to say that this theory of the separation of
powers requires the separation of the legislative, executive and judicial
powers, and above all that they should be exercised by different state
bodies. It has naturally also been incorporated in the Basic Law of Bonn, in

391

a provision which, according to Article 79, Paragraph 3 of the Basic Law, may not be changed, let alone annulled, by anyone under any circumstances. Therefore, in the Federal Republic of Germany, too, laws are passed by the parliament - the Bundestag - the executive power is entrusted to the government and the judicial power to the judges, of which we have between 15,000 and 20,000 serving a population of 60 million.

This figure alone shows that there must have been major changes, at least in the judiciary, since the days of Hamilton, Madison and Jay, and even more so since the days of Montesquieu. I would only like to mention this briefly.

When these worthy gentlemen spoke of judicial power they were certainly not thinking of all the matters which our judges have to decide upon at the close of the 20th century, but were thinking more of that which today is carried out by the ordinary courts, that is to say civil and criminal jurisdiction. The fact that in Germany especially any sovereign act by a state authority can be examined by a judge must have been far beyond their powers of imagination. To a great extent the administration, with whose emanations the administrative, social and tax courts are concerned today, did not even exist. There has, therefore, been a significant change in this respect. Jurisdiction is no longer, as Montesquieu was able to state, »more or less nothing,« but has become a powerful state authority which, although it cannot pursue its own conscious policies, can apply considerable restraints on the policies of government and administration.

The legislature has, of course, not escaped this fate either, which brings me - as you will have noticed - to constitutional jurisdiction, which is established in Germany. The fact that I am its highest representative is probably the reason I have been invited to talk here.

In Germany, separate courts for disputes between the empire and its territories, between the subjects of various sovereign rights and, at times, between the individual citizen and his ruler, have been in existence for hundreds of years. This is also one of the reasons why the Federal Republic of Germany does not have a single Supreme Court to decide both questions of simple law and questions of constitutional law. Rather, it has no less than five supreme courts which monitor the correct application of the law. Above these five courts there is a separate Federal Constitutional Court which monitors all state bodies, including the supreme Federal courts themselves, to ensure adherence to the constitution, the Basic Law.

However, this is, if I am correct, the only serious differende between our two supreme courts. Any citizen may turn to the Federal Constitutional Court, as to the Supreme Court, if he believes that the constitution has been violated as far as he is concerned, and, in particular, the Federal Constitutional Court, like the Supreme Court, can also examine any laws regarding their conformity with the constitution. More than 180 years ago the Supreme Court, presided over by Chief Justice John Marshall, availed itself of this right. In 1925 the German supreme court at the time (the Reichsgericht) followed suit. The Basic Law has developed this, with certain procedural corrections, into a constitutional institution. Thus the new emphasis which has been given in both countries to the idea of the separation of powers is so tangible that I feel there is no need to add anything more on this point. I personally feel, therefore, that I am, effectively, a successor of John Marshall and his colleagues.

In the United States, as well as in Germany, there has always been a second form of separation of powers, which we in Germany call vertical separation and which is connected to the phenomenon of the federal system. There is no reference to this, naturally, by the Frenchman Montesquieu and his English colleagues. We know, of course, that when both the American and German federal states were founded they were based not on separation of powers, but on political feasibility. Nevertheless, the idea of the vertical separation of powers played a role right from the start, and this idea prevails today in every German debate, whenever the question of the viability of the federal system is raised yet again. Here, too, the Germans rely far more on the Americans than they are even aware. Admittedly, the co-existence of a central state and several member states was originally established in Germany in order to avoid putting the non-Prussian princes and their dynasties out of a job in the unification of the empire under Bismarck, but that is obviously no longer a reason for the German federal state. Above all, when those concerned with constitutional law in Germany began to organize themselves after 1867 or 1871 in the newly created federal state, they took their most important ideas from the United States, which by then had almost a hundred years of experience. The Southern Germans, by the way, adopted more from the southern states of America and the Northern Germans more from the crown lawyers of the Union. This is no longer the case. Today, the southern statesman Calhoun, to whom the Bavarians in particular referred at that time, has, of course, also been forgotten in Germany.

Apart from this, the German federal state is based on the system of the separation of powers in two ways: by the distribution of state power between the Federal Government and its »Länder,« and by the fact that the Bundesrat, which is composed not of senators elected by the people, but of members of the regional governments, plays a role in the federal legislature next to the parliament. For several reasons, this provides a genuine counterbalance to the political parties, which, in Germany, dominate not only the parliament but also the executive. I will come back to this point later.

II.

If we return for the time being to the so-called classical separation of powers, we must stress that the parliamentary system of government, which the Federal Republic of Germany copied from Great Britain, naturally represents exactly the opposite of separation of powers. If the government as a whole, or at least the head of government, is dependent on the parliament in such a way that he has to be elected by it and can also be voted out of office again at any time, then he is not – at least theoretically – of equal status with the parliament, but is subordinate to it. If, however, in political reality he is the one who rallies a fixed parliamentary majority around him and who represents the figurehead in parliamentary elections, then it is also he who in turn dominates the parliament, and there can be no question of both powers having equal status. This is, therefore, one of the processes of concentration of power which is the subject of my lecture. I do not wish to say any more on this for the moment; I will come back to the specific shape that this phenomenon takes in Germany, namely, the so-called chancellor democracy.

Let us keep, for the moment, to the subject of the processes of concentration of power which are not so clearly defined in the Basic Law as those of the parliamentary system of government, but which are also not prohibited by it. At this point I would like to remind you of the undermining of the distribution of federal state authority that has taken place in the last 40 years in the sector of legislation. If you read the text of the German constitution, your first impression will be that the majority of responsibilities for legislation are distributed equally among the Federal Government and the »Länder.« But this impression is deceptive. On the one hand, newly introduced responsibilities – air transport, defense legislation, nuclear energy, cleanliness of waterways, etc. – have been transferred to the Federal Government and not to the »Länder,« and further amendments to the constitution have given further responsibilities to the Federal Government at the expense of the »Länder.« Apart from this, the Federal Government – to this extent with the full support of the Federal Constitutional Court – has interpreted, not to say extended, its responsibilities to such a degree that it has left the »Länder« with only an extremely marginal area of legislation. An American will probably find it impossible to imagine what this means in a country in which anything may only take place as the result of a law, or with legal approval. The fact that the »Länder« are still politically independent despite this is due to their position in the Bundesrat, and to the fact that even in Germany not everything can be achieved by laws. Tasks such as regional planning, distribution of infrastructure and educational establishments, preservation of old cultural monuments, and restoration of historic areas cannot be regulated simply by laws, and at present the »Länder« are profiting from this.

Overall, however, there has been a considerable concentration of power in Germany which, even if it cannot be considered directly unconstitutional, is in any case counterproductive in the sense of the concept of separation of powers. The single European market which is being created will play a significant role in this respect.

The supreme courts of the Federal Government are, moreover, playing a very enthusiastic part in further restricting the legislative scope of the »Länder« through their rulings. As you are probably aware, the Federal Government and the »Länder« play an almost equal part in the administration of justice in Germany. The first and second instances are in the hands of judges who are appointed by the »Länder.« They monitor both federal authorities and those of the »Land,« and they apply to their cases all the applicable laws, whether federal or »Land« laws. If, however, a case passes to the third instance, the so-called appeal stage, judges of the Federal Government, who normally only examine legal questions – questions of federal law – decide upon it. This means that they develop federal law; that is to say, they produce federal laws even in cases where the federal legislature has not thought of it and, since understandably none of the subordinate »Land« judges would wish to be the subject of a complaint by his supreme federal court in a later trial, the result is that these legal rulings produced by the federal judges are applied no less strictly than in the countries which use case law, to which Germany does not really belong.

The Federal Constitutional Court, of which I am the President, pursues this beneficent course of action with great dedication, and although strictly speaking it is only authorized to interpret the Basic Law, its output has been considerable – almost 80 volumes of decisions. Let me put it this way: In 1949, when the Basic Law came into force, German constitutional law was composed of 146 articles. Today, 40 years later, it consists of approximately 15,000 to 16,000 printed pages of rulings related to constitutional law. No one can claim that that is not also the exercise of power, even if it is power exercised by independent judges who are often not properly aware of their power.

The few examples of continuing legislation by the »Länder« make one suspect that the development which I have just outlined was virtually inevitable for practical reasons. In fact, the »Länder« have, almost without exception, issued concurrent provisions in all the areas for which they are still responsible for legislation. I realize, of course, that there are exceptions. For example, almost every »Land« has a different school system, a somewhat different relationship between the mayor and the council in its communities, and a few peculiarities in police law. On the whole, however, the laws correspond to each other and one has to ask oneself why there are such intense arguments about responsibilities for legislation or, to be more precise, why their loss is so lamented.

The reason for this development is easily recognizable. Germany is, at least from a territorial point of view, a small country in which almost every interested citizen is familiar with the situation in several, if not all, of the »Länder« in which cultural, technological, economic, and social development is extremely homogeneous, and in which, at least among the more aware and more powerful social groups, there is considerable mobility. Taking myself as an example, I would like to tell you that in the course of three decades, out of the eleven »Länder« which make up the Federal Republic of Germany, I have already enriched four of them by working in their civil service, and if I have counted correctly, the same will be more or less true of my colleagues who are with us today.

In a state of this kind it is no surprise if the majority of the population demands, and finally achieves, as great a degree of legal uniformity as possible. The consequence of this is that the federal state's function of separating powers has become increasingly weaker during the last four decades. In fact, the eleven federal »Länder« voluntarily ensure that their legal systems are essentially the same in the course of regular meetings of their chief ministers and their ministers who are responsible for particular areas. There is even a specialist's term for this: the cooperative federal state.

However, this development has gone hand in hand with a continuous enhancement of the status of the Bundesrat, in which delegates elected not by the people, as in the US Senate, but by the members of their regional governments represent all the »Länder.« The Bundesrat has gained importance to the extent that the separation of powers between the federal government and the federal parliament no longer works, and also to the extent that the delegates of the Bundestag can no longer cope with the concentrated expertise of the federal ministries.

396

The members of the Bundesrat, in turn, can have the support of bureaucracies of the »Länder,« which are in any event an equal match to the federal civil servants. This means that there are two opposing bureaucratic complexes, similar to the bureaucracy of the President and that of the Congress in the United States. The effect that this has on separation of powers cannot be denied.

III.

So far I have only spoken of those effects of concentrated power which have arisen as the result of inevitabilities of either constitutional law or society. But in the 40 years since 1949, concentration effects have also arisen, more or less as a result of historic coincidences and can, therefore, also disappear again, although the Germans have become so used to them in the meantime that the majority of the population considers them part of the constitution.

The most significant example is the so-called »chancellor democracy.« We associate its creation with the name and political achievements of Konrad Adenauer. Chancellor democracy is a short term for a parliamentary system of government in which the head of government rules to a certain extent both the parliament *and* the government, with rather less influence over the government than the President of the United States has, for example, but consequently with more influence over the parliament.

Even today there are constitutional lawyers in Germany who assume that this system of government, with which the Federal Republic has managed to live well for more than thirty years, is anchored in the Basic Law itself. It is correct that the Basic Law has made great efforts to create stable conditions of government, and that it has used every trick in the book to deprive the Federal President of power in comparison with his predecessor, the Reich President of the Weimar constitution. Nevertheless, it still doesn't add up. It has not yet been put to the test, thank goodness. Such a test is extremely unlikely, whether or not stable conditions of government - and in a parliamentary system that means stable majorities in parliament - can be legally safeguarded at all, as long as we retain the system of proportional representation and we do not change to majority representation. However, the rights which at one time made the Reich President so powerful have either been completely removed (such as the right to pass emergency decrees) or have been mutilated beyond recognition (such as the right to dissolve parliament and the supreme command of the military, which has actually been passed to the government). In any case they have not given more power to the Federal Chancellor, if we do not take into account the fact that his side of the balance has been lowered because that of the President has become lighter. The creation of the chancellor democracy, however, certainly cannot be attributed to the chancellor's competence for issuing guidelines, which is quoted so frequently. After all, he had such authority even under the Weimar constitution, and, as everyone knows, it wasn't a great deal of help to him at the time.

I don't believe that I generalize too much if I once again put forward the theory that the main reason for the creation of the German chancellor democracy lies in the peculiarities of the German party system, which emerged in the years since 1951/52, but which may also disappear again at any time. It is not to be ruled out that this system has currently reached a turning point. I am talking about the following facts:

1. The German parties are organized and run in a much tighter and much more centralized manner than those in the United States. On almost every political question, there is - granted often not until discussions have been held within the party - an official opinion of the party, or at least of the ministers and delegates belonging to it. The more the chancellor proves to be the party's »source of hope,« that is to say an election vehicle, the more likely he is to form the opinion of his party in an autonomous way, and there will be hardly a holder of an office or seat who will dare to oppose him.

2. For more than thirty years the German party system has been virtually a two-party system - although there are no majority elections - because there were really only two major parties. The third, the F.D.P., was always engaged in long-term coalitions with one of them. This actual situation has had consequences of its own, and though the German public at present may tend to see mostly the negative consequences, it is my view that the positive ones have far outweighed them.

At one time, the leader of whichever party alliance won the election automatically became Federal Chancellor as well, because the delegates who supported him already had the absolute majority in the Bundestag on mathematical grounds. This is how, in effect, the people became convinced - in contrast to the text of the constitution - that they, and not the parliament, would elect the Federal Chancellor, and in 1982, when the F.D.P. changed its coalition partner and thus the chancellor during the current election term, there were opinion polls in which countless citizens complained that this had denied them their right to elect the chancellor. A Federal Chancellor who in the end, however, owed his seat to the people would be almost in a better position than the President of the United States, who may similarly have the emotional advantage of having been elected by the people, but in general does not have control of the Congress.

The second consequence of the effective change of system was that the two major parties, at least, had to look for voters in almost every class of society. They were, contrary to European tradition, no longer able to appear as class parties for the workers, farmers, businessmen, etc. They had to be able to offer something tangible to every level of society in their manifestos. This led, admittedly, to the party manifestos being made basically similar, and, according to European opinion, to their becoming colorless and boring. However, it was - alongside the economic prosperity - the main reason for the balance, the basic fairness and above all the stability of the social system in the Federal Republic of Germany. Anyone who has ever given thought to the stabilizing effect of this system on the state created by the Basic Law, which is by no means inwardly strong, cannot estimate this achievement of the party system highly enough. You probably know as well as I that there have been significant changes in the German party system recently. Several years ago the Greens established themselves on the left of the political spectrum, and for the past year the Republicans have become active on the right. The number of voters which they attracted was by no means insignificant. The problem these new forces pose is not primarily that of extremism; after all, not all Greens are Communists, nor are all Republicans Nazis. In any case, the parties supporting the state will be able to deal with these groups politically in the long run. However, the transformation of the system of government, which would inevitably be the consequence of a four or five-party system, is not to be ignored. The Federal Chancellor would once again be chosen behind closed doors in coalition negotiations, no longer in an open public election. The democratic parties would again face the choice, as during the Weimar Republic, as to whether they wished to control their extreme rivals by cooperation or form a major coalition with them, which would again be subjected to the risk of being torn apart from the left and right. Above all, we would lose the opportunity to balance conflicting social interests in the party manifestos instead of later in the government program.

These are the major questions to be faced in the system of government of the Federal Republic of Germany, questions which the voters must decide. No one knows how the situation will eventually develop - whether it will be possible for the well-tried party system to re-establish itself after a period of confusion and clarification, or whether a situation will arise such as that which we have seen in Italy or France before de Gaulle. The options have been laid out and with them the imponderables, which even a democratic constitution cannot escape.

IV.

To deal with the question of the separation and concentration of powers seriously, it cannot be limited to aspects of classical and federalistic separation of powers. We must instead remind ourselves that in free constitutional systems there is also a division of functions between the state and free society, especially between the state and the economy. From the point of view of constitutional law, it is usually based on basic rights, primarily the rights which secure freedom not only for the individual citizen, but for society as a whole. In this sense the rulings by the Federal Constitutional Court in Germany in favor of basic rights have the effect not only of limiting power, but also of dividing it.

In the short time left it is not possible for me to give a proper account of this phenomenon, even in outline form. I will therefore limit myself to pointing out some of the most important aspects. First of all, even in the freest of societies there is no guarantee against the accumulation of power. If an area of responsibility is left to self-regulation by society, it represses state power, and therefore has the effect of curbing power. However, this usually cannot prevent other »social« forces from coming into play in this area: groups and mass associations, media kings and multinationals, fashion dictators and literary gods. Their power can, if things go wrong, be far more unpleasant for the individual than that of a state committed to law and the constitution. The response of the constitutional state to such a problem lies in attempts to have a power-limiting and power-separating influence here, as well. I would remind you of the forms of cartel and antitrust legislation, which in Germany are admittedly only of a constitutional nature where the electronic mass media are concerned. These are laws which impose a minimum amount of internal democracy and separation of powers on clubs, associations and societies, and attempts, which have not been very successful so far, to allow certain basic rights to be effective not only against

400

the state, but also against the holders of power in society. No more need be said on this point.

Another point is that the state in Germany has assumed far more responsibilities than in the United States, for example. This may be the most significant difference between our constitutional and social systems. I would like to point out that in the Federal Republic of Germany, the school and university system is state-run to a great extent, that state operators run rail and air traffic, that companies whose shares are held by the state or the communities run the power supply organizations, that so far there are hardly any private radio and television stations and only a few private hospitals, that public institutions provide the overwhelming majority of citizens with social security - health insurance, pensions, accident and unemployment insurance - and that even housing is repeatedly pointed out to be the responsibility of the state, even more so since the flood of refugees from East Germany in recent weeks.

This means that state laws and regulations, state control and planning, for the most part state businesses and state employees, and every improvement that is demanded by someone somewhere means more of the same: more bureaucracy and ever-increasing state influence on the lives of the people. In Europe we have talked of the law of growing public expenditure for many years, but this only gives a name to the symptom. In reality the law states that it is not only public spending but state responsibilities which are currently growing unchecked.

The citizens of our country clearly feel that this is not a good development and that the state is becoming too powerful in Germany. They are therefore unanimous in demanding a reduction in public spending. They demand fewer regulations, fewer forms, and less bureaucracy. As they are not, however, prepared at the same time to renounce the benefits of all these fine things, they are in the final analysis demanding the squaring of the circle. In fact, they are deceiving themselves as far as the constitution is concerned. And that is not all. Many of them go to court for the very last state benefit to which they believe they are entitled, and if gaps or even errors appear in the entire complicated system, they are - if surveys are to be believed - deeply disappointed (the current specialist term for this is »Betroffenheit« or consternation). They reject the state - and here, too, there is a fashionable expression, namely »Staatsverdrossenheit« or state weariness.

It may be that I see the situation too bitterly. It is also possible that I have expressed it too drastically today. In the close confines of Europe, given its complicated social conditions, it is probably quite impossible to classify the subjects which I have just mentioned in any other way than in a state system, and the awful power which a state supply, education and health system could exercise over people is certainly not abused in the Federal Republic of Germany. The constitutional and administrative courts would prevent that from happening. But the citizen's awareness of his dependence remains, as does the lack of willingness among many people to understand minor omissions and mistakes. Thus, in its 40th year of existence, the Basic Law of Bonn, strictly speaking, constitutes a highly heterogeneous state:

- a state which can easily hold its own in the community of democratic nations with its constitution and constitutional jurisdiction, with its basic rights, its separation of powers and its social justice,
- a state where the system of government may be under examination again but which has so far functioned excellently and has produced outstanding achievements, both nationally and internationally,
- but also a state which may give the impression that in some cases it has taken on too much, and in some cases it is not loved as much as it deserves, simply because it occasionally tries to do too much for the sake of welfare.

No one knows how this will all turn out in the next 40 years, least of all myself. However, recognizing a problem is the first step in solving it, and we are already on the way in the Federal Republic of Germany. In my opinion, this means that the future will continue to be exciting - and that, I believe, is the best thing that we can say about any future.

Annemarie Renger

The Role of the Plebiscite in Representative Democracy

I am pleased to be here in your country to express a few thoughts on the relationship between representative democracy and so-called plebiscitary instruments such as initiatives and referenda.

Your country was the first to translate representative democracy into practice. The Declaration of Independence drawn up by your Founding Fathers in 1776 includes the statement that the people have the right to alter or abolish a government which disregards their basic human rights and institute a new government. This is the shortest definition I know of representative democracy.

It is not the citizens themselves who pass laws and govern, but their elected representatives, and at the next election the citizens decide whether these representatives have lived up to their expectations and are worthy of their confidence.

In the Federalist Papers, Alexander Hamilton and James Madison made a clear distinction between a »republic,« in which the people govern and administer the affairs of state through representatives and officials, and »democracy«, in which citizens themselves meet and govern.

In Europe, developments since the French Revolution have not been uniform. Of the numerous theories of the state which have been developed since then, the ideal of so-called direct democracy, which I consider to be misconceived, remains attractive to the present day. Representative democracy is understood to be merely a compromise, a worse form of government, as it were, than »genuine« democracy, in which no one exercises power over people and they jointly settle their affairs themselves. Reference is sometimes made to Switzerland, where referenda decide important issues.

In the Federal Republic of Germany, demands have been made for some years now for representative democracy to be supplemented by plebiscitary elements. It is assumed that the fundamental decision-making process, which takes place through parties, elections, parliaments, and their legislation, could be geared more closely toward the interests and concerns of the population if, in addition, referenda were permitted on certain subjects. The Green Party and the Social Democratic Party are discussing such demands. I doubt whether the two models – majority decisions taken by parliaments on the one hand and referenda on the other – can complement each other or are even compatible, as is the case, for instance, with the principle of majority rule, basic rights and minority rights, which are combined in all Western-style democracies.

In my view there are, as regards their history and the way they function, two different and even diametrically opposed models of the political process which are ultimately not mutually compatible under the prevailing political conditions in a state such as the Federal Republic of Germany, where we are generally concerned with complex developments with extremely far-reaching consequences. Let me mention, for example, the introduction of new weapons systems, the legal provisions governing health insurance and old-age pensions, and the granting of credits running into billions to other countries.

It is thus impossible to combine various components of both systems at will and hope that they will complement each other in a positive way.

To avoid any misunderstanding, let me point out that a considerable number of plebiscitary elements already exist in our democracy. The mere fact that citizens may cast their votes in so many elections – from the elections to the Bundestag and to the Land parliaments and to local elections – shows that they are frequently given an opportunity to express their views at all levels.

The possibility of participating in the activities of parties, in citizens' action groups and associations, the right to petition as well as the right to express one's opinion through demonstrations (to mention just a few) broaden the wide range of plebiscitary instruments which already exist.

When I said that the basic instruments of direct democracy cannot be combined with representative government, this only applies to plebiscites in the real sense of the word, from referenda to initiatives, and it only applies to the policies of the Federation, for which the Bundestag, the Federal Government and the Bundesrat are responsible to the people.

In this connection, we should consider the following questions:

- In what way would general parliamentary elections still be important if major decisions were not taken by the elected representatives, but by asking the voters' opinion on individual issues?

- How can a government still be held responsible for its performance if it can point out that it has not taken important decisions, but has instead submitted them to a referendum?

- What importance would parties with their political programs and plat-

404

forms still have, and would it matter whether one or the other party obtained a majority in parliament?

- What about the notion of »representative government,« according to which a government is responsible to the voters, if the government can, in difficult cases, evade this responsibility and ask the voters themselves to take a decision on the controversial issues concerned in a referendum?

- In the event of referenda being held, what about the protection of minorities: Would the interests and concerns of those who failed to assert themselves in a referendum still be taken into account in any way through compromise, as is the case with the decisions adopted by a majority of the elected representatives in parliament, or would they fall completely by the wayside, at least for a long time?

- Conversely, how can the majority be protected against abuse by minorities: Would it not also be possible for a minority to tyrannize the majority by repeatedly calling for referenda so as to delay or prevent parliament from taking decisions of which the minority does not approve?

- Can the results of referenda still be revised to some extent, and, in the event of a change in public opinion, how quickly can an issue be put on the ballot again?

- How can the policies pursued by a large country still show any consistency in substantive terms if individual issues are submitted to a referendum?

- Assuming that referenda are to be ruled out on certain subjects, such as tax legislation, who would decide what subject areas these would be?

- What political issues could be put on the ballot - social policy, economic policy, defense policy, agricultural policy, foreign aid or even foreign policy? Would questions of criminal law or the execution of sentences be submitted to a referendum? Or the granting of credits to other countries? Or the federal budget?

- Fellow citizens, colleagues, neighbors, and even members of the same family would be continually obliged to vote on controversial issues, which would inevitably lead to an endless series of disputes. What would be the effect on society?

The time available is too short for me to elaborate or even touch on all the complex problems which are described in detail in the extensive literature on the subject of public and constitutional law. Of all the arguments advanced in this connection, I consider the erosion of political responsibility to be the main problem. Plebiscites in pure and unadulteraded form would remove this very responsibility, because the people cannot call themselves to account. In fact, this would mean translating the totalitarian core of Rousseau's teaching into practice.

Once the barriers erected for the protection of minorities had been destroyed through referenda, the arbitrary rule of the majority over the minority would sooner or later be given free reign. Such arbitrariness could have just as disastrous consequences as the totalitarian rule of any power clique. Wherever arbitrariness is given free reign, there is no longer any room for politics, either. People would not only fall victim to repression or be deprived of their political rights; they would also be deprived of the elixir of life which politics represents for them.

Even if I leave these extremes aside, I still have the impression that, on balance, we would raise more questions and problems than we would solve by introducing plebiscitary forms of decision-making. Parties, the electoral process and parliaments would be weakened, and the close link that exists between the decision taken at the polls and government action would be destroyed.

In light of the experience of the Weimar Republic, we had very serious historical reasons in Germany for virtually excluding referenda from our present constitution, a constitution which has worked well for the last 40 years. I think this is also due to the fact that we adopted the political structures of Western-style democracies. We learned a great deal from the American Constitution in particular, which strictly adheres to the notion of representative government and is based on the separation of powers.

In light of all these considerations, it is my wish that we in the Federal Republic will continue to adhere to this order which can look back on 200 years of proven democratic tradition. There is no reason why the Federal Republic should experiment with mixed forms which have no positive historical experience to recommend them. Thank you for your attention.

Warren E. Burger

200 Years of American Constitutionalism

The Berlin Wall is crumbling, not physically at the moment, but politically, psychologically and with enormous potential economic consequences. Just how great will be the impact on the economics of Europe remains to be seen, but that wall has been too long a symbol conflicting with the concept of the European Community and the Common Market – and the ideas of freedom. History shows that when nations built walls it was usually to keep enemies out; the Berlin Wall was to keep people in, and, from the day it was built, it was as surely doomed as Hitler's thousand year Reich; all history teaches us that people cannot be kept in very long by walls. At one time in our earliest years people were forbidden to migrate beyond the Appalachian Mountains – but the people ignored that barrier.

The impact on the future of commerce and trade in political Europe takes on new significance with Hungary's announcement this week that it is a democracy. Today, Moscow confesses serious treaty violations and a »moral« mistake in making war on Afghanistan. All this follows the changes in Poland and demands for democracy within the Soviet Republics and the Baltic States – and in East Germany.

All of this recalls to the American mind some events of 200 years ago – and earlier. Alexander Hamilton, that great economist and statesman, and others of the early leaders including Madison and, of course, George Washington, were profoundly concerned about the economic as well as the political barriers that came into sharp focus once the War of Revolution was over. They believed that if the commercial and economic problems were settled the political problems would be well on their way toward solution and, in 1786, they invited all of our 13 sovereign states to a meeting in Annapolis, Maryland, to resolve economic, commercial, and trade problems. At that time our 13 states were functioning under the Articles of Confederation which constituted hardly more than a multilateral treaty of friendly cooperation.

By the very terms of the Articles of Confederation each of the 13 states retained its sovereignty and its independence. Each state had its own currency. Each of the states was free to have its own army and navy and each state could put up trade and travel barriers with respect to its own borders. Of course, in that day with travel and the movement of goods and merchandise so difficult except by sea, the trade problems did not loom as large or complex as in Europe in 1957 when similar problems were being considered in the Treaty of Rome. But Hamilton and the others were looking into the future and thinking of the day when travel and communication would be improved. And they knew that a unity of commercial interests would lead to greater political unity and that economic unity - a common market - would, in due course, resolve many of the state to state conflicts.

We remember also that, although 13 states were invited to attend the Annapolis Convention in 1786 to consider trade problems, only five states were represented. It has been called the most successful failure in our history because it produced a unanimous resolution asking the Continental Congress to invite delegates from all of the 13 states to Philadelphia in the summer of 1787. The stated objective of the leaders of these five states at the Annapolis Conference was to resolve commercial problems but there was an unspoken desire to change the loose, unworkable structure of the Articles of Confederation because the commercial problems could not be settled until the political problems with a stronger central government were solved.

The Continental Congress was very cautious, however, and when the invitations went to the 13 states to send delegates to Philadelphia it was carefully circumscribed: »for the sole and express purpose of revising the Articles of Confederation.« In short, it was not a constitutional convention at the beginning but it became our Constitutional Convention by what the delegates did. One particular provision of that Constitution has a bearing on what is going on in the European Community and the objectives that are sought to be achieved by 1992.

We must constantly keep in mind that in 1787 there were 13 sovereign, independent states each with the power to regulate and defend its own borders, to issue its own currency, and otherwise to regulate its own commercial as well as its own political affairs.

In eleven simple words in the Constitution a gigantic step was taken that created the Common Market for our country in 1789. It was in this setting that those eleven words were written - long before the idea was described as a »Common Market.«

What happened after our War for independence was resolved at the Battle of Yorktown, with Cornwallis' surrender, is what has happened to every victorious wartime alliance in history: the victorious allies began to fall out and quarrel. Our thirteen allied states followed that pattern. They had been »united« by the necessities of war under what today we would call a multi-lateral treat - »a firm league of friendship,« as the Articles of Confederation described the relationship. It was essentially a wartime alliance.

They called themselves the United States of America then, but they might have been more accurate to say »States United,« for, under the Articles of Confederation, which were not ratified until 1781, each retained its own sovereignty. This is a significant factor in our story. When the delegates met in Philadelphia in May, 1787, except for a common language, each state was almost as independent as the states in Europe in that era.

In 1786 Washington, Hamilton, and Madison despaired. They were fearful that, unless we created a strong, unified system with an effective central government in place of the feeble Confederation, the great powers, including our recent ally, France, would be competing to divide and devour out thirteen states.

These leaders knew that the war for independence was the glue that held us together and without that adhesive there would be no real future if thirteen separate states remained separate and sovereign as a confederation, not truly a nation.

It is difficult today to grasp those state and regional attitudes, even though my generation is closer to the Civil War than anyone here. My grandfather, who had come from Austria, fought in the Union Army, so something of those attitudes was known to us as we were growing up. The mindset of people of that day is illustrated in several episodes. When New Jersey troops reported to George Washington at Valley Forge they did the usual thing that those of you in the military would remember; a sergeant major went out and asked the men to raise their right hands to swear allegiance to the United States. They refused and then one man stepped forward and said, »Our country is New Jersey.« Virginians felt that way about it; for New Yorkers and for the men of Massachusetts Bay - for all of them - that was the attitude. No constitution can change attitudes overnight, and this attitude did not change for more than a century. The states of Eastern Europe - and indeed the people of some of the Soviet Republics - are facing similar problems in the months and years ahead.

The separation of powers is a key part of our system, but it hardly needs any demonstration that our Constitution does not necessarily produce a tidy system of government. To have a really tidy system of government with everything always in order is not always compatible with freedom. To make our system work there must be a responsible sharing of power. Adolf Hitler produced a »tidy« system of order for a brief period, but at a terrible price.

409

As Mr. Gorbachev tries to open his system just a tiny bit, problems arise; the Communists are finding that giving people a little freedom is dangerous; people always want more.

The sixteen words of the Commerce Clause gave Congress the power to control commerce between states and with foreign nations, which meant that our states could not impose protectionist tariffs against one another. Those few words gave our country the common market in 1789. New York could no longer add a tariff or tax on all goods flowing through its port to other states. We know from our reading of history that many wars have been started in the world over less than the differences on commercial matters and boundaries that existed between some of our states between 1781 and 1787.

The Commerce Clause of our Constitution, aided by the coinage clause and the provision of the patent clause inviting development and rewarding performance, explains how a small country on the edge of a wilderness, as we were in 1789, with a population of barely three and a half million people, could become a world power by the end of World War I. Of course, other factors entered into that result, but that clause was the key that unleashed the talents and energies of a whole people in a way never before witnessed in all history.

Now, today, we see signs that the talents and energies of people all over Europe are being unleashed by the urge for freedom. This week the genie of freedom has been let out of the iron box of Communism in the year when we celebrate two hundred years of freedom under our Constitution. And it can never be put back.

William Rehnquist

Constitutional Courts - Comparative Remarks

It is a pleasure for me to join the distinguished scholars and jurists who have gathered here to celebrate the fortieth anniversary of the Basic Law of the Federal Republic of Germany. It has been my pleasure during the past few months to meet one member of the German Constitutional Court - Professor Grimm - at Aix-en-Provence, France, another one - Professor Kirchhof - in Ann Arbor, Michigan, and to have had the pleasure of meeting and talking with Chief Justice Herzog and former judge, Professor Steinberger in my chambers yesterday.

Those who believe in constitutional government basically put their trust in the idea that political power should be constrained by law. This idea is well-expressed I know in the Latin expression used by the early English legal writer Bracton: *»Non sub homine, sed sub deo et lege.«* This maxim is carved in stone on one of the buildings of the Harvard Law School in the United States, and epitomizes this belief in the rule of law.

Two centuries ago, when the United States had just begun to operate under its constitution, the idea of a written constitution such as we had was a novel one. Almost at the beginning of this era, our Supreme Court decided that this written constitution gave the courts the authority to declare legislative acts invalid or unconstitutional. This was a remarkable innovation at the time it happened, and for the next century and a half the United States, almost alone among nations, operated under this system of judicial review. But within the past half century, after the Second World War, numerous other nations have adopted written constitutions or Basic Laws and entrusted their courts with the power of judicial review: West Germany, Italy, France, to name but a few. Hungary and more recently Spain are newcomers to this scene, and both have patterned their constitutional courts on the West German model. The provisions of the constitutions vary, the structure of the court systems may differ, but the underlying idea is the same.

Even in the countries which do not have a written constitution, and therefore have no judicial review - such as Great Britain - or in those countries which have a written constitution which in theory grants judicial review, but in which that power is unexercised – such as Sweden – there is considerable discussion about the desirability of granting this authority to the courts. President Mitterand suggested last summer that the authority of the French Constitutional Council be broadened. And of course the European Human Rights Court sitting in Strasbourg is already providing a form of international judicial review for those countries adhering to the Treaty of Rome.

These European constitutional courts have not hesitated to enforce constitutional guarantees. In this country we are familiar with the decision of the Constitutional Court of the Federal Republic of Germany upholding the rights of political participation under Article Twenty-One of the Basic Law. In this decision, we understand that your court sought to ensure that major political parties could not use their power to establish party funding or election financing schemes that unconstitutionally discriminate against small or unpopular parties.

For nearly a century and a half, courts in the United States exercising the power of judicial review had no precedents to look to save their own, because our courts alone exercised this sort of authority. When many new constitutional courts were created after the Second World War, these courts naturally looked to decisions of the Supreme Court of the United States, among other sources, for developing their own law. But now that constitutional law is solidly grounded in so many countries, it is time that the United States courts begin looking to the decisions of other constitutional courts to aid in their own deliberative process. The United States courts, and legal scholarship in our country generally, have been somewhat laggard in relying on comparative law and decisions of other countries. But I predict that with so many thriving constitutional courts in the world today – of which the Constitutional Court of the Federal Republic of Germany is an outstanding model – that approach will be changed in the near future.

Summary

In these closing comments we would like once again to thank the Dräger Foundation and the American Institute for Contemporary German Studies for sponsoring this conference on the Basic Law of the Federal Republic of Germany. Our decision to hold the conference in Washington, D.C is a notable affirmation of the enduring friendship between our two countries. In these last few days we - Germans and Americans - have celebrated a harmony of interest rooted in and nourished by our shared commitment to constitutional values and political democracy. In a way, we have been celebrating each other's constitution, for the 40th anniversary of the Basic Law happens to coincide with the last year of the bicentennial of the United States Constitution. The keynote address of Professor Roman Herzog, President of Germany's Federal Constitutional Court, and the closing remarks of William H. Rehnquist, Chief Justice of the United States, were eventful moments in our proceedings, fully emblematic of the symbiotic relationship between our two constitutions.

Our purpose in holding this conference was to consider various features of the political and economic system created under the Basic Law and to compare these features with American constitutional practice. We asked our participants not only to examine and assess the past but also to explore the likely shape of constitutional and political change in the years ahead. In this respect, the papers yielded a wide variety of views and perspectives. Apart from the papers dealing with the Basic Law generally, the major presentations focused on the topics of federalism, separation of powers, basic rights, political representation and democracy, the structure and principles of the social market economy, and the problem of German unity. These presentations, along with the formal remarks of our featured speakers - Roman Herzog, Annemarie Renger, Warren Burger, and William H. Rehnquist - produced insightful commentaries by our distinguished moderators and considerable argument among conference participants.

The opening panel set the tone for the rest of the conference. Even as he acknowledged the gap between constitutional ideal and reality in Germany - a gap, incidentally, that exists in all constitutional democracies - Klaus Stern's criticism of recent German developments nevertheless proceeded

413

on the assumption, one shared by all of our participants, that the Basic Law has been firmly woven into the fabric of German society and politics.

According to Cole Durham, the Basic Law offers the world a vision of freedom as appealing as the very different vision projected by the United States Constitution. And now, with German unity a reality, the Basic Law will extend its sway, probably in perpetuity, over the whole territory of what was formerly East Germany. Extending the Basic Law eastward poses difficult problems but as Rudolph Dolzer points out in his paper on German unity, »it is extremely questionable whether a [new] constituent assembly could . . . create a better or more just constitutional system.«

The other panelists, since they wrote about particular aspects of the Basic Law and the United States Constitution, devoted more attention to *comparative* analysis. Peter Lerche and Arthur B. Gunlicks described the varying functions and problems of federalism in the two countries. Their papers, as Frank Beytagh remarked, »illustrates *(sic)* the necessity for a constant rethinking of the changed (and changing) role of federalism in a vital democratic state.« The *democratic* state is the subject of detailed examination by Helmut Steinberger and Walter Murphy. What such a state requires in terms of meeting the demands of modern constitutionalism is their focus of inquiry. Here too, as with federalism, we notice crucial differences between the German and American perspectives, furnishing us with a basis for reexamining our sometimes conflicting and sometimes converging views on the limits of political tolerance, the role and status of political parties, and the nature of legislative representation.

The papers on basic rights illustrate the overriding importance our two countries attach to individual liberty and autonomy. But they also illustrate important contrasts between German and American conceptions of liberty, recalling Cole Durham's distinction between the American and German models of freedom. Kurt Sontheimer dealt generally with the influence of the Basic Law's human dignity clause while Fritz Ossenbühl described the vigor with which the Federal Constitutional Court has defended economic and occupational rights. John Attanasio ecamined standards of interpretation used by the American Supreme Court in the defense of personal freedoms and economic liberties. Mary Ann Glendon's commentary linked the concerns of this panel with the papers on political representation. »[A]ny attempt at comparative examination of the German and American welfare states and of the protection accorded to economic interests in each country,« she writes, »necessarily involves us in comparison of political processes.« She suggests that both political systems have yet to provide their citizens, particularly those persons who are most in need of the welfare state, with the means to acquire and practice the skills of self-government.

Our last panel was devoted to an assessment of Germany's economic system. We received the view of a German economist from Horst Siebert; the view of a German legal scholar from Rainer Schmidt; and the view of an American political scientist from Christopher Allen. As Ellen Kennedy notes, their papers »present different views of the development of liberal democracy in Germany after 1949, but their analyses focus on property rights as the central problematic of the Basic Law.« She characterizes the problem as stemming largely from the tension between liberal constitutionalism, with its emphasis on individual liberty, and the needs or demands of the *social* state. The principal question we are left with is whether the social market economy is *constitutionally* guaranteed or whether some other organization of the economy would be permissible within the framework of the Basic Law. This is a question likely to be vigorously debated in coming years in the light of German unity and the movement in Europe toward increasing economic and social integration.

Finally, we would like to return to the comparative observations made by Cole Durham at the outset of this conference. He reminds us that »constitutional traditions do not develop in hermetically sealed national compartments,« for »reciprocal influences between differing [legal] cultures are constantly felt« and »borrowings occur at numerous levels.« Several of our speakers have pointed to certain American influences on the growth and development of German constitutionalism just as Cole Durham has underscored the influence of German legal realist thought on the development of American constitutionalism. He also discerns in contemporary American constitutional thought some movement toward the German idea of an objective order of values. »[I]n view of the depth of commitment in both of our societies to certain key values, and the pervasiveness of our intellectual and economic ties,« he writes, »it seems clear that extensive mutual influence will continue« even as we »respond to concrete problems slightly differently.«

We are at one with Professor Durham in these remarks. But even at the level of everyday constitutional adjudication we think Germans and Americans have much to learn from each other. Professor Glendon remarks that »it would be interesting to explore further with our German colleagues the question of which regime in theory and in practice is in a better position to work out (and constantly reexamine) the optimal mix in each country's mixed economy as well as to establish priorities in the allocation of national

415

resources.« Professor Durham sees our differing models of personal freedom as a basis for deepening the conversation between German and American legal scholars. We know that Germany's Federal Constitutional Court often consults the opinions of the American Supreme Court in deciding constitutional issues and now we hear from Chief Justice William H. Rehnquist that »it is time that the United States courts begin looking to the decisions of other constitutional courts to aid in their own deliberative process.«

Clearly, something very important is taking place here. Just as the Basic law is at the threshold of a new era in German constitutionalism, our two countries are at the threshold of a new era in their political relationship, one now marked by full political equality. That political relationship, however, is reinforced by our common commitment to constitutionalism and democracy. Germany is now a stable and mature constitutional democracy, and like the United States the Federal Republic offers the world another compelling model of how to organize and maintain a constitutional state. We have been reminded in the last couple of days of our common values and common heritage as well as our differing perspectives and interests. We fondly hope that this conference marks the beginning of more exchanges of this kind as we continue to examine and rethink the premises of our two systems of constitutional government.

The Editors

Appendix

The Authors

Christopher Stevens Allen

born 1947; B.S., Boston College, 1969; trade representative, Exxon Corporation, 1969-72; M.A., Northeastern University (political science), 1975; guest lecturer, Northeastern University, 1977-78; guest lecturer, University of New Hampshire, 1980-81; lecturer, Brandeis University, 1981; guest lecturer, Colby College, 1982; Ph.D., Brandeis University (political science), 1983; Teaching and Research Fellow, Center for European Studies, Harvard University, 1983-86; Assistant Professor of Political Science and research fellow, Center for the Study of World Politics, University of Georgia, 1986 to present.

John B. Attanasio

born 1954; B.A., magna cum laude, University of Virginia, 1976; J.D., New York University School of Law, 1979; diploma in law, Oriel College, Oxford University, 1982; LL.M., Yale University, 1985; Associate Professor of Law, Law School, University of Pittsburgh, 1985-88; Professor of Law, Notre Dame Law School, 1988 to present; Fulbright Fellow and Lecturer on American constitutional law at the Moscow Pedagogical Institute, 1989.

Francis X. Beytagh

born 1935; 1956, B.A., University of Notre Dame; 1963, J.D., University of Michigan; 1964-66, private law practice in Cleveland, Ohio; 1966-70, Assistant to the Solicitor General, U.S. Department of Justice; 1968-70, Lecturer in Law, University of Virginia; 1970-76, Professor of Law, University of Notre Dame; 1972, Senior Law Clerk to Chief Justice Earl Warren, U.S. Supreme Court; 1976-83, Dean and Professor of Law, University of Toledo Law School; 1983-84, Visiting Professor of Law, Houston University; 1985 to present, Dean and Professor of Law, Ohio State University College of Law.

Warren E. Burger

born 1907; attended University of Minnesota, 1925-27; LL.B. (magna cum laude), St. Paul College of Law, 1931; Assistant U.S. Attorney General, Civil Division, Justice Department, 1953-56; Judge of the U.S. Court of Appeals for the District of Columbia, 1956-69; Chief Justice of the United States (appointed by President Nixon), 1969-86; currently chairman of the Commission on the U.S. Bicentennial of the Constitution.

Rudolf Dolzer

born 1944; 1963-65, Studied Sociology and Jurisprudence, Tübingen, Heidelberg; 1965-66, Recipient of Fulbright Award, Gonzaga University, B.A., 1971; 1971, Doctor of Law, Heidelberg; 1977, S.J.D., Harvard Law School; 1977-89, Lecturer, Max-Planck Institute, Heidelberg; 1977 to present, Member, Editorial Committee of the Encyclopedia of Public International Law; 1981-84, Chosen Representative, Research Assistance, Central Organ of the Max-Planck-Society; 1984, Lecturer, Law Faculty, Heidelberg University; 1984-86, Visiting Professor, University of Michigan Law School; 1987, Visiting Professor, Cornell Law School; 1988, Appointed Professor of Law, Heidelberg University; 1989 to present, Member of the Enquete Commission; 1989, Appointed Professor, Mannheim University.

W. Cole Durham, Jr.

1972, A. B., magna cum laude, Harvard University; 1975, J.D., cum laude, Harvard Law School; editor, Harvard International Law Journal; 1975-76, clerk for Judge Robert A. Ainsworth, Jr., U.S. Court of Appeals for the Fifth Circuit; 1979-80, Max Rheinstein Fellowship, Alexander von Humboldt Foundation; 1980 to present, Professor of Law, J. Reuben Clark Law School, Brigham Young University; 1986, Visiting Professor, Johann Gutenberg University, Mainz, Germany; 1985-87, chairperson, Law and Religion Section, American Association of Law Schools; Secretary, American Association for the Comparative Study of Law; Member, Board of Editors, American Journal of Comparative Law; and Member of Executive Board, Center for Church-State Studies, De Paul University.

Mary Ann Glendon

born 1938; 1959, B.A.; 1961, J.D.; 1963, LL.D., University of Chicago; Honarary degrees from Holy Cross College (1989) and Brigham Young University (1990); 1962-63, Foreign Law Fellow, Univ. Libre de Bruxelles; 1963, Legal Intern, EEC, Brussels; 1963-68, private law practice in Chicago; 1968-86, Professor of Law, Boston College; 1974-75, Visiting Professor of Law, Harvard University; 1975-76, Ford Foundation Fellow, Radcliffe Institute; 1983, Visiting Professor of Law, University of Chicago; 1986 to present, Professor of Law, Harvard University.

Arthur B. Gunlicks

born 1936; B.A., University of Denver, 1958; study at Freiburg University, 1958-59; study at Georgetown University, 1961-64; study at Göttingen University, 1964-65; Ph.D., Georgetown University, 1967; Assistant Professor, East Tennessee State University, 1966-68; Assistant Professor, University of Richmond, 1968-71; Associate Professor, University of Richmond, 1971–81; Professor of Political Science, University of Richmond, 1981 to present; Visiting Professorships: Göttingen University (1980); School of Public Administration, Speyer (1982-83 and 1989); Heidelberg University (1983); and University of Virginia (1988).

Roman Herzog

born 1934; 1958, Doctoral Degree, Munich; 1958-64, Research Assistant, Munich University; 1964-66, Senior Lecturer, Munich University; 1966-69, Professor of Public Law and Politics, Free University of West Berlin; 1967-68, Dean of Faculty of Law, Free University of West Berlin; 1969-73, Professor of Political Science and Politics, School of Public Berlin, Speyer; 1969 to present, Member of the Chamber of Public Responsibility of the West German Protestant Church; 1971-72, Director of the School of Public Administration Speyer; 1971-80, Chairman of the Chamber of Public Responsibility of the West German Protestant Church; 1973-78, Secretary and Delegate, Federal State of Rhineland-Palatinate in the Federal Government; 1976-78, Deputy Federal Chairman, Protestant Working Group of the CDU/CSU; 1978-83, Federal Chairman; 1978-80, Minister of Education and Sport, Baden-Württemberg; 1983-87, Vice President,

Constitutional Court; 1987 to present, President, Federal Constitutional Court; 1984, Honorary Professor, School of Public Administration, Speyer; 1986, Honorary Professor, Eberhard-Karls University, Tübingen.

Ellen Kennedy

born, 1946; 1968, B.A., Trinity College; 1970, M.A., Indiana University; 1977, Ph.D., The University of London; 1968-69, Management Intern, U.S. Department of the Treasury; 1970-73, Legislative Analyst, National Institutes of Health; 1975-77, Lecturer in Government, University of Manchester; 1977-87, Lecturer in Politics, The University of York; 1984-86, Visiting Lecturer in Political Science, University of Freiburg; 1987, Lecturer in Politics, Queen Mary College, University of London; 1989 to present, Associate Professor of Political Science, University of Pennsylvania.

Paul Kirchof

born 1943; studied law at the Universities of Freiburg and Munich, 1962-66; 1st state examination, Munich, 1966; doctorate in law, Munich, 1968; 2nd state examination, Stuttgart, 1969; research assistant in the Institute for German and International Tax Law, Heidelberg University, 1970-75; qualified as lecturer (constitutional and administrative law), Heidelberg University, 1974; Professor of Public Law and Director of Institute for Tax Law, Münster University, 1975-81; Vice-President of Münster University, 1976-78; Professor of Public Law and Director of the Institute for Finance and Tax Law, Heidelberg University, 1981 to present; Dean of the Law Faculty, Heidelberg University, 1984-85; since 1987 judge on the Second Senate of the Federal Constitutional Court.

Donald P. Kommers

born 1932; 1954, B.A., The Catholic University of America; 1959, M.A., University of Wisconsin-Madison; 1962, Ph.D., University of Wisconsin-Madison; 1954-56, Officer, U.S. Marine Corps; 1959-63, Assistant Professor, California State University; 1968-69, Ford Foundation Fellow, West German Federal Constitutional Court; 1971-72, Alexander von Humboldt Fellow, University of Cologne; 1975-81, Director, Center for the

Study of Civil and Human Rights, Notre Dame Law School; 1977-80, Advisor to President Carter's Commission on the Holocaust; 1981, Rockefeller Foundation Fellow; 1982, Visiting Scholar, Harvard Law School; 1987, Fulbright Lecturer, University of Tokyo; 1981 to present, editor, *The Review of Politics*; 1963 to present, Professor of Government and International Relations, University of Notre Dame; 1975 to present, Professor of Law, University of Notre Dame.

Peter Lerche

born 1928; 1951, Prize Awarded by Faculty of Law, Munich; 1958, Doctorate, Munich; 1960-65, Professor of Public Law, Free University of Berlin; 1965 to present, Professor of Public Law, Munich University, Deanships in Berlin and Munich; 1974 to present, Member of the Bavarian Academy of Science, Member of the founding committee for an Academy of Science in Berlin; 1982-83, Chairman of the Association of German Teachers of Constitutional Law; 1981-84, Member of the Science Council.

Walter F. Murphy

born, 1929; 1950, B.A., University of Notre Dame; 1954, M.A., George Washington University; 1957, Ph.D., University of Chicago; 1950-55, U.S. Marine Corps, 2nd Lt. to Capt.; 1952-55, Instructor in Political Science, U.S. Naval Academy; 1957-58, Brookings Institute Fellow; 1958-68, Professor of Political Science, Princeton University; 1955-74, U.S. Marine Corps Reserve, Capt. to Col.; 1958, Recipient of the Birkhead Award, American Political Science Association; 1963, Recipient of the Menjou Award, American Civil Liberties Union; 1964, Ford Professorship, Princeton University; 1968 to present, McCormick Professor of Jurisprudence, Princeton University; 1973, Guggenheim Fellow; 1979, Chicago Foundation for Literature Award.

Fritz Ossenbühl

born 1934; 1951-56, Civil Service Career, Communal Administration, Duisburg; 1962, Doctorate, University of Cologne; 1964-66, Assistant Lecturer, University of Cologne; 1968, Qualified as Lecturer at the Faculty of Jurisprudence, University of Cologne for Public Law; 1970, Full Professor, University of Bonn; 1978, Offered a Professorship, University of Tübingen; 1986, Offered a Professorship, Free University of Berlin;1972-73, Dean of the Faculty of Jurisprudence and Political Science, University of Bonn; 1974 to present, Member of the Selection Committee, Alexander von Humboldt Foundation; 1976-84, Adviser to the German Research Council; 1979 to present, Principal Lecturer, Bonn Academy of Management and Economics; 1984 to present, Member of the Permanent Deputation, German Conference of Lawyers.

William H. Rehnquist

born 1924; U.S. Army Air Force, 1943-46; B.A. (with great distinction) Stanford University, 1948; M.A., Harvard University, 1949; LL.B. (highest honors) Stanford University, 1952; Law Clerk for Justice Robert H. Jackson, U.S. Supreme Court, 1952-53; private law practice, 1953-69; Assistant Attorney General, U.S. Department of Justice, 1969-71; appointed Chief Justice of the United States in 1986 by President Reagan.

Annemarie Renger

born 1919; 1953 to present, Member of the German Bundestag; 1961-73, Member of the SPD Executive; 1969-72, Parliamentary Leader, SPD Budestag Group; 1970-73, Member, SPD Executive Committee; 1972-76, President of the Bundestag; 1976 to present, Vice President of the German Bundestag, Chairwoman of the German-Israeli Parliamentary Group; 1979, Candidate, German Social Democratic Party; 1976-86, Member of the SPD Supervisory Committee.

Reiner Schmidt

born 1936; 1963, Doctorate in Law, University of Würzburg; 1964, Engaged as an Attorney, Munich; 1965, Assistant Lecturer, Würzburg; 1971, Qualification as Lecturer, Würzburg; 1972 to present, Chair in Public Law, Political Science, Constitutional Law, University of Augsburg.

Horst Siebert

born 1938; 1965, Doctoral Degree, Münster University; 1967-68, Assistant Professor, A&M University of Texas, Department of Economics, Member of Graduate Faculty; 1969, Inception at the Faculty of Law and Political Science, Professor of Economics, Münster University; 1969-84, Professor of Economics and Foreign Policy, Mannheim University; 1980 to present, Scientific Coordinator, »Economics of Natural Resources« project of the German Research Association; 1984-89, Chair of International Economic Relations, Constance University.

Kurt Sontheimer

born 1928; 1953, PhD; 1960, Qualified as Lecturer of Political Science, University of Freiburg; 1960-62, Professor of Political Science, College of Education in Osnabrück; 1962-69; Professor of Politicial Science, Otto-Suhr-Institute, Free University of Berlin; 1969 to present, Professor of Political Science, Geschwister-Scholl-Institute, University of Munich; 1985, Ernst Robert Curtius Prize for Essayistics; 1988, Honorary Doctorate from Bradford University, United Kingdom.

Helmut Steinberger

born 1931; 1951-56, Studies of Economics and Law, Universities of Munich and Heidelberg; 1958-59, Research Assistant, Institute of International and Foreign Trade Law, Georgetown Law Center; 1961-71, Research Fellow, Max-Planck-Institute for Comparative and Public International Law, Heidelberg; 1972, Full Professor of German Public and International Law, University of Mannheim; 1975-87, Justice, Federal Constitutional Court, Karlsruhe; 1987, Co-director, Max-Planck-Institute for Comparative and Public International Law, Heidelberg, Full Professor, University of Heidelberg; 1990, President of Arbitral Court between the Federal Republic of Germany and the German Democratic Republic.

Klaus Stern

born 1932; 1956, Doctor of Law, University of Munich; 1961, Qualified Lecturer, Public Law, University of Munich; 1962-66, Full Professorship, Free University of Berlin; 1966, Chair for Constitutional and Administrative Law, University of Cologne; 1969-75, Dean of Law Faculty, University of Cologne; 1976 to present, Constitutional Court Judge of the State of North-Rhine Westphalia.

Index

A

Abortion, 22, 51-55, 66-67, 111, 236
Administration, 20-30, 38, 44,
    71-72, 75-80, 83, 92-93,
    102-103, 118, 136-137, 144, 189,
    218-219, 255, 271, 314, 327-328,
    382, 392, 403; functional, 93, 94;
    horizontal, 94; territorial, 93, 94;
    vertical, 93, 94, 101
Advisory Commission on Intergo-
    vernmental Relations, 103, 109
Allies of World War II, 17-20, 72,
    173, 346, 365-366, 369-370, 373,
    384-387
Amendments. See US Constitution
American Cill of Rights. See Consti-
    tutions, Bill of Rights
Application of federal law by Länder.
    See Implementation of . . .
Articels of Confederation, 91,
    174-175, 407-409
Associations, 26, 122-123, 129, 132,
    155, 157, 161, 181, 184-185, 209,
    252, 302, 304, 324, 400, 404
Atomic Energy Law, 144

B

Balancing, 42, 52, 54, 56, 285
Ban on an occupation, 258 et seq.
Banks, 303-304, 326, 341-346
Basic rights, 18, 21, 23, 29-31, 41,
    65-67, 122, 127, 148-149,
    154-155, 160, 163, 181, 213-287,
    311, 314-318, 332, 356, 358, 386,
    400-404, 413-414
Basic Treaty of 1972, 367, 369, 373-374
Berlin, 74, 327, 365, 367, 370, 376, 384,
    407

Berufsverbote. See Occupational prohibitions
Bill of attainder, 187
Broadcasting. See Media
Budget, 82, 103, 112, 136, 142-145,
    150, 153, 187, 264, 298, 314,
    319-325, 405
Bundesrat. See Federal Council
Bundestag, 20, 27, 65, 77, 108, 123,
    125-126, 129-146, 150-155,
    162-163, 182, 323, 381, 392, 398,
    404
Bundesverfassungsgericht. See Federal
    Constitutional Court

C

Case law, 38-40, 241, 285, 306, 395
CDU/CSU. See Political parties
Certitude, principle of, 122
Checks and balances, 132, 137-138,
    209
Chief Justices. See Presidents, Court
Church, 38-43, 48-49, 235
Citizens' initiatives, 158-161, 164
Citizenship, 97, 124, 378
Civil law, 75, 149, 224, 233, 235, 355
Civil rights, 79, 97, 108, 216, 222
Civil War, American, 92, 97-98, 183,
    225-226, 409
Codetermination, 124, 311, 340, 343,
    347-351, 357
Codetermination judgment, 263, 269,
    315-317, 358-359
Commerce Clause. See US Constitu-
    tion Art. I § 8
Committee of Inquiry into Constitu-
    tional Reform, 20, 27-28, 162-163
Committees of Inquiry, 130,
    151-155, 210

Common good, 109, 127-128, 132, 153, 156, 209, 297, 324
Communists, 181-189, 193, 207, 217, 348, 367, 376, 385, 399, 410
Communities, 92-94, 98-112, 124, 133-134, 184, 327, 372, 401
Concentration of wealth, 231, 239, 241, 299, 341
Concerted Action, 324
Concurrent legislation, 75
Confederates, 183
Confessional schools, 47, 55
Congress Acts, 96-107, 179, 183-188, 191, 207, 229
Constituent assembly, 17-19, 22, 29-30, 77, 85, 91, 131, 139, 174-179, 213-214, 225, 252, 291, 294, 312, 356, 358, 369-370, 386, 403, 408, 414
Constitutional change, 23, 38, 76, 127, 163, 183, 186, 207, 213, 294, 307, 332, 392, 413
Constitutional court. See Federal Constitutional Court; Supreme Court
Constitutionalism, 18, 21-24, 30, 32, 37-39, 45, 51-59, 65-67, 128, 173, 177-182, 190-194, 208-209, 287, 316, 414-416
Constitutionality, 23, 43, 47, 53, 55, 153, 158, 181, 194, 207, 226, 229, 236, 259-263, 266, 320, 325, 331, 360, 411
Constitutional state, 24-26, 30, 66, 214, 217-218, 334, 370, 400, 416
Constitutions
  of States or Länder, 26, 40, 118, 131, 139;
  of the first German Empire, 71;
Declaration of Independence 1776, 18, 174, 403;
Philadelphia Convention 1787/89, 18, 174, 176, 409;

Bill of Rights 1791, 18, 29-30, 41, 176-177, 229-230, 233; see also US Consitution, Amendments 1-10;
Bavarian of 1818, 148;
German Empire 1849/71, 29, 31, 71, 81, 393;
Weimar 1919, 18, 23, 26, 29, 72, 81, 138, 213, 397-398;
Basic Law of the Federal Republic of Germany 1949; See p. 433
Italy, 189;
France 1958 (5th Republic), 147;
Chile, 178, 189
Contestable markets, 295, 298, 304
Continental Congress, 174, 408
Coordination theory, 49
Councils, Soviet style, 161
Court packing, 49, 228
Criminal Law, 75, 152, 191, 236, 355, 405
Culture and education, 48, 75, 86, 111, 401-402

D
Democracy, 23, 27, 29, 66, 71, 117, 147, 217, 272, 358-359, 407, 416; direct 26, 28, 66, 121, 130, 403-404; liberal, 159, 161, 181, 366, 415; militant, 180-182, 191-193, 207-208; representative, 27, 65, 121-210, 284-286, 331. 394, 397, 403-406, 413
Democrats. See Political parties
Dissolution of parliament, 139-145, 163, 398
Doctrine of materiality, 149
Domestic security, 207, 217-218
Dred Scott v. Sandford, 97, 225-226
Drittwirkung. See Effect on third parties
Due process, 40, 226-233, 236

E

Economic system, 26, 239, 251, 269,
271, 274, 291-361, 369, 380, 413

Effect on third parties, basic rithts',
49-50, 255

Elections, 27, 78, 109, 122-146,
150-151, 155-164, 173-184,
188-191, 194, 200, 232, 239, 365,
394, 398-399, 403-406

Emergency decress, 397-398

Emergency laws, 136, 144

Employment, 99, 101, 104-105, 124,
187, 227, 231, 253, 261, 264-265,
293, 300-305, 320-321, 324, 328,
340, 343, 350, 401

Enlightenment, 37, 46, 49-50, 55,
225, 230-231, 371

Environment, 20, 24, 104, 109, 164,
218, 258, 265, 271, 287, 297,
303-308, 334, 366, 379, 382-385

Equality, 23, 39, 108, 138, 176, 184,
217, 224, 230-236, 266, 376

Europe, 18-19, 27, 31, 93, 118, 126,
147, 291, 297, 299, 307-308, 346,
351, 368, 371-376, 384-386, 399,
401, 403, 407, 409-410, 415

European Communities, 26, 32,
85-87, 159, 274, 296, 302-306,
327-333, 339, 342-344, 352, 357,
361, 468-369, 375-383, 387, 395,
407-408, 412

European Recovery Program, 17,
37, 327, 329

Exclusion of political parties,
180-181, 191, 194

Executive authority. See Administration; Government

Extra-parliamentary opposition, 160,
164

F

F.D.P. See Political parties

Federal Assembly, 133

Federal Bank, 298, 312, 324,
328-334, 346

Federal Chancellor, 132-134,
138-145, 150, 155, 397-399; competence for issuing guidelines, see
Art. 65 BL; vote of confidence,
139-143, 151, 153

Federal Constitutional Court, 21-23,
26, 30-31, 43, 47-48, 52-53, 58,
65, 74-76, 82, 87, 108-109, 123,
127, 130, 137-118, 142-158, 177,
181-183, 188, 192, 207-210,
215-217, 251-263, 266-274,
283-286, 311, 315-320, 331,
356-361, 370-371, 376-379,
392-394, 400, 411-416

Federal Council, 71, 77-79, 82, 86,
123, 132-137, 323, 332, 389, 393,
395, 404

Federal enforcement, loyalty, supervision, 74, 85, 136-137

Federal Government, 73-86, 92, 96,
98, 100, 103-104, 110, 123, 127,
132-136, 139-157, 177, 186-187,
227, 261, 314, 319-332, 348, 369,
374, 376, 393-398, 404

Federal grants, 100-103, 111

Federalism, 17, 40, 71, 118, 153,
174, 225-229, 306, 332, 386,
393-394, 400, 413-414; cooperative, 80-82, 92, 100-101; creative,
101; dual, 91-97, 100, 102, 107;
new, 92, 101-102, picket fence,
93-94

Federalist Papers, 391, 403

Federal President, 27, 132-141, 144,
162-163, 397-398

Financial reform of 1967/69, 79, 94

Founding Fathers. See Constituent
assembly

Free democratic basic system, 19,
181, 188

Freedom of contract, 223, 226-227,
  231-232, 252, 268, 295, 313/314
Freedom of the entrepreneur, 98,
  251-252, 257-264, 269, 314
Freiburg school, 346-347

G
German Customs Union, German
  Reich, 91
German Federation, 71, 91
German Treaty, 373
Glass-Steagall act, 341
Government, 29-31, 38, 40, 43, 46,
  50-51, 73-75, 91-99, 106-112,
  117-118, 122, 134-138, 142, 157,
  159, 175-178, 183-186, 191-194,
  209-210, 221, 223, 226, 230, 233,
  235-238, 253, 264-266, 274,
  283-284, 297-311, 318-319, 326,
  329, 333-334, 341, 350, 360,
  367-372, 392, 397, 402-403,
  406-409; see also Federal government
Government of judges, 22, 43
Great society programs, 92, 101
Greens. See Political parties
Groups. See Alliances

H
Hartford Convention, 96
Health protection, 101, 108, 110,
  227, 258, 260, 265, 267, 271, 303
Herrenchiemsee Committee, 18
Human dignity, 19, 30, 52-53, 65,
  127, 150, 192, 213-219, 283, 291,
  356, 367, 414
Human rights, 19, 30, 138, 177,
  214, 271, 292, 371, 403, 412

I
Ideal competition, 268
Implementation of federal law by Län-
  der, 77, 136-137
Independence of judges, 138, 396

Initiation of legislation, 136, 143
International Law, 146, 331, 366,
  368, 372-374, 379, 382-387
Interventionism, 291, 296-297, 302,
  306, 332, 347

J
Joint Committee, 138
Judicature, 30-31, 57
Judicialization of rights, 43-44
Judicial review, 22, 43-44, 51, 91,
  95, 106-107, 392-393, 411-412
Jurisdiction, 44, 66-67, 75-78, 91,
  95, 97, 122, 125-131, 134-135,
  138, 144-145, 152-153, 178, 180,
  182, 186-187, 193-194, 207-210,
  213-214, 217, 222, 231-232, 235,
  237, 253, 258-260, 264, 266, 269,
  273, 283, 294, 312, 358, 360,
  378-383, 392, 402

K
Keynesianism, 312, 321, 325

L
Laissez faire, 98, 240, 339-347, 351,
  357, 361
Land, 18, 22, 27, 47, 72-86, 92-93,
  108-111, 118, 124, 126, 130-139,
  154-157, 174, 188, 314, 319-327,
  331-334, 369, 381, 393-396, 404
Legal person, 252, 328, 359
Legal realism, 56-57
Legislation, 21-23, 26, 30-31,
  39-40, 44, 52-53, 72, 75, 77-78,
  81, 91-94, 97-98, 101, 109, 112,
  123, 125, 127, 133, 135, 139, 142,
  146-151, 158, 163, 174-177, 180,
  184, 187, 193-194, 207-210,
  213-214, 217-218, 229-232, 238,
  253, 255, 258-262, 265, 270-274,
  284-286, 294, 315-323, 329-332,
  356-359, 381-382, 394-396, 403,
  414

430

Legislative facts, 253, 259, 272
Legitimacy, democratic, 18-19, 27,
  51, 71-73, 78, 123-125, 133, 137,
  143, 145, 152, 157, 160-164,
  174-175, 190-193, 209, 358-360,
  367, 376
Lemon v. Kurtzman, 42, 235
Lex specialis, 330
Liberalism, 215, 306, 311, 313,
  356-358, 361
Liberty rights, 39-40, 43-44, 47, 49,
  55-56, 66, 232

M
Majority, 44, 52-53, 104-106,
  127-128, 134, 138-142, 150-156,
  164, 176, 185-187, 193, 209, 227,
  232, 238, 294, 367, 374, 379, 394,
  397, 404-406
Mandate, 157, 159; circumscribed,
  129; common political, 124, 161,
  174; excess, 126; free/imperative,
  27, 121, 126-129, 137, 143, 158
Marbury v. Madison, 106
Market place of ideas, 160, 164, 182,
  237-241
Media, 27-30, 54, 75, 84-86, 123,
  131, 151, 155, 158, 180, 240, 303,
  376, 379, 400-401
Mediation Committee, 77, 135
Mill case, 260, 262
Minister president. See Land
Monopoly, 129, 225, 256, 259-260,
  266, 297-298, 303, 311, 329

N
Nation, 300, 371-375, 385, 407
National emergency, 136, 144
National population, 157, 159, 164
National Socialism, 19, 24, 26, 52,
  55, 57, 59, 72, 181, 184-185, 188,
  214, 217, 291, 341, 345-348, 368,
  372, 385, 399, 407, 409
Nature conservation, 123

Neutralism, 369, 372, 375-376, 387
New Deal, 37, 39, 57, 92, 95,
  99-101, 228, 285
North German Federation, 71

O
Occupational prohibitions, 218
Office of Management and Budget,
  103
Opposition, 134, 136, 138, 142, 151,
  154, 156, 179-183, 189-192
Ordnungspolitik, 340-341, 345,
  351-352, 357
Organstreit, 178
Overall economic equilibrium, 82,
  314, 319-325, 328

P
Parliamentary Council. See Constituent assembly
Parliamentary prerogative, 144-146
Parliaments. See Bundestag, Congress acts, Land, Legislation
Party state, 23, 128, 158, 178, 180,
  190
Petitions, 12, 404. See also US Constitution, 1st Amendment
Pharmacy judgment, 253, 256, 260,
  273
Plebiscites, 20, 27-28, 65-66, 78,
  130-132, 162-163, 174, 381,
  403-406
Pluralism, 39, 41, 44, 59, 122, 159,
  186, 324, 331, 358
Police law, 75
Political parties, 18-23, 27-29, 66,
  78-79, 125-131, 134, 138-141,
  145, 150-151, 155-164, 173,
  178-183, 186, 193, 207, 210, 234,
  285-286, 307, 311, 340, 348-349,
  359, 394, 398-400, 403-406, 412,
  414
Popular sovereignty, 72, 123-125,
  138, 174, 359, 360, 407

Popular will, 126-127, 131-132,
177-178, 190-191, 209
Preservation of Historic Buildings and
Monuments, 123, 395
Presidents of Courts, 21, 91-92,
96-97, 99, 108, 214, 225, 230,
283-284, 393, 411, 413, 416
Presidents, US, 18, 47, 92, 96,
99-103, 112, 176, 179, 183, 189,
192, 228, 230, 339, 368, 373, 407,
409
Presidential regime, 138, 162
Press. See Media
Privacy of data, 54, 218
Procedural law, 75, 153-154
Property rights, 222-233, 237-241,
268-270, 283-285, 295, 304, 307,
355-356, 358, 382, 415
Proportionality of means, 122, 256,
258
Proviso of legality, 53, 148-149
Public law, 123, 131, 251, 328, 341,
405

Q

R
Reich President, 26, 138, 140, 397
Reichstag, 138, 140
Reimbursement of electorial costs to
political parties, 28, 158, 210, 412
Rendering account of the Federal Go-
vernment to the Bundestag, 151
Rent seeking, 298, 301-305, 308
Republicans. See Political parties
Responsible government, 405
Reunification of Germany, 18,
365-387, 414-415
Revenue equalization, 82, 111
Revolutions, 18th century, 29, 37,
126, 183, 403
Reynolds v. United States, 41-42
Right to resist. See Art. 20 Basic Law
Roe v. Wade, 51, 53, 236

S
School prayer, 42-43, 47-49, 67
Separation of powers, 23, 56, 73,
117, 135-138, 144-147, 150, 152,
177, 209-210, 221, 386, 391-402,
409, 413
Slavery, 97, 175, 183, 221, 225-226
Social market economy, 291-301,
306-308, 311-315, 356-357, 361,
415
Social state, 23-29, 38, 45-46, 50,
65-67, 73, 79, 83, 215-219, 256,
283-286, 293, 299, 312, 334, 340,
347, 359, 414-415
Sovereignty, 32, 72, 77, 81, 85,
95-97, 104-105, 128, 157, 161,
175, 191-192, 292, 306, 324,
331-332, 371-372, 376-381, 385,
387, 392, 408-409
SPD. See Political parties
Special districts, 93
SRP. See Exclusion of political parties
Stability and Growth Act, 311-314,
319-325, 328, 330
State, affirmative/regulative, 38,
45-46, 50-51, 54, 66-67
State monopoly of force, 25
State objectives, 20-21, 25, 156
Subjective rights, 30, 41
Supreme Court, 22, 39, 42, 47, 67,
95-99, 104-109, 127, 138, 179,
182-188, 209-210, 222-241,
283-286, 392-393, 411-416

T
Taxes, 24-25, 42, 49, 81-82, 98,
101-104, 107, 111-112, 216, 225,
230, 238-239, 263-264, 302-303,
323-326, 392, 405, 410
Television. See Media
Terrorism. See Domestic security
Three stage theory of freedom of occupation, 256-258, 270

432

Topoi, 55–59, 253, 272
Transition state, 20, 370

U
Ultra vires, 92
Unitary state, 71–79, 84, 91, 94, 117
United States v. Carolene Products, 222, 228–241

V
Virginia Bill of Rights. See Constitutions, Bill of Rights

W
Weimar Republic, 27, 37, 83, 121, 129, 139–140, 156, 193–194, 298, 346, 348, 358–359, 399, 406
Welfare. See Social state

X

Y
Youth protection, 266

Z
Zones of occupation. See Allies of World War II

Basic Law of the Federal Republic of Germany

Preamble: 19, 31–32, 164, 365, 370, 376–378
Art. 1: 21, 29–30, 46, 127, 150, 154, 177, 213–216, 262, 291–292, 314
2: 29, 51, 252, 262, 266–268, 292–293, 312–314, 318, 359
3: 29, 266–267
4: 29, 48
5: 29, 181, 292
6: 29, 47
7: 29, 48

9: 29, 122, 181, 252, 265, 314, 324
11: 29, 252, 292
12: 29, 252–253, 256–260, 263, 265–269, 273, 318, 326, 356–359
15: 29, 314, 326
18: 29, 181
19: 29–30, 252
20: 21, 23, 27, 122–127, 131–132, 135, 143–149, 157, 159, 162, 193, 210, 213, 215, 283–284, 293, 324
21: 23, 129, 155–158, 178, 181, 189, 193, 207, 412
23: 19, 366, 381–383, 386
24: 32, 85, 87, 331–332, 372, 378
25: 331, 372
26: 372
28: 23, 74, 81, 109, 124, 131
29: 27, 83, 130–131
30: 75–76, 108
33: 79
38: 125–129, 143, 155, 158, 175, 210
39: 126
40: 143
42/43: 136
44: 151–153
45a: 151–152
46: 129
50/51: 77
53a: 138
58: 144
59: 145–146, 331
63/64: 138–139
65: 143, 145, 398
67: 139, 141, 143
68: 140–145, 163
79/71/73/74/75: 75
72: 75, 108, 293, 326
74a: 76
77/78: 77
79: 20, 23, 76, 131, 213, 392
80: 147–149, 209
81: 144–145
83/84/87: 76, 78

88: 328-331
91a, b: 80, 108, 326-327
92: 135
93: 30, 320
101/102/103/104: 29
104a: 76, 81, 108, 326-327
105/106/107: 81-82
109: 81-82, 311, 314, 319-322
113/115: 321-322
114: 153, 320
115a-1: 138, 144
116: 19
146: 19, 366, 383

United States Constitution

Preamble: 177
I § 8: 95-96, 100, 104-105, 231, 410
§ 9: 187

§ 10: 225, 237
II: 176
V: 95
VI: 95

Amendments

1: 39-40, 179, 186-187, 224,
    230-235, 239, 241
4: 230
5: 98-99, 187, 223, 226-231,
    237-238, 284
6: 230
9: 177
10: 92, 95, 99-108
13: 97, 177
14: 39-40, 97-99, 177, 179,
    183-184, 225-238, 284
15: 97, 183
16: 225
17/19/24/26: 176

Paul Kirchhof/Donald P. Kommers (Hrsg.)

Deutschland und sein Grundgesetz

Themen einer deutsch-amerikanischen Konferenz

Die Verfassung des vereinten Deutschlands steht im Mittelpunkt einer öffentlichen Diskussion. Fragen des Asylrechts, der internationalen Rolle der Bundeswehr, des Umweltschutzes als Staatszielbestimmung oder die beabsichtigte Europäische Union stellen eine Bewährungsprobe dar. Die Identität des deutschen Verfassungsstaates muß dabei in seinen Grundstrukturen gewahrt werden; einige Einzelregelungen bedürfen jedoch der Überprüfung.

Es ist ein Anliegen der Dräger-Stiftung, das Verständnis des Grundgesetzes durch einen Vergleich zwischen deutschen und amerikanischen Verfassungserfahrungen zu fördern und so die aktuelle Diskussion zu begleiten.

Die aktualisierten Beiträge gehen auf eine von der Dräger-Stiftung aus Anlaß des 40jährigen Bestehens des Grundgesetzes und des 200jährigen Bestehens der amerikanischen Verfassung in Washington veranstaltete Konferenz zurück.

Im Mittelpunkt stehen vergleichende Erfahrensanalysen
– des Bundesstaatsprinzips, der repräsentativen Demokratie sowie der verfassungsrechtlichen Grundlagen der Wirtschaftssysteme,
– des gemeinsamen Fundaments der Grundrechte sowie
– die Frage nach der Bewährung des Grundgesetzes und seiner Offenheit für ein vereintes Deutschland.

Das Buch erscheint parallel auch als englischsprachige Ausgabe.

1993, 473 S., brosch., 48,– DM, ISBN 3-7890-2366-3
(Edition Dräger-Stiftung, Bd. 13)

 NOMOS VERLAGSGESELLSCHAFT
Postfach 610 • 7570 Baden-Baden

Christian Dräger/Lothar Späth (Hrsg.)

Internationales Währungssystem und weltwirtschaftliche Entwicklung

The International Monetary System and Economic Development

Das 7. Malenter Symposium fand im April 1988 unter dem Thema »Weltwährungsordnung und weltwirtschaftliche Entwicklung« statt.
Im Vorfeld der Jahrestagung des Internationalen Währungsfonds und der Weltbank im September 1988 in Berlin, diskutierten Entscheidungsträger aus Wirtschaft und Politik sowie namhafte Wissenschaftler und Medienvertreter aus dem In- und Ausland über die aktuellen Probleme und mögliche Lösungsansätze in diesem Bereich.

Von besonderer Bedeutung waren dabei
– die gegenwärtig erörterten Vorschläge zur Reform des Weltwährungssystems
– die Forderung nach deutlicheren Wachstumsimpulsen zum Abbau der weltweiten Handelsbilanz-Ungleichgewichte
– die Suche nach geeigneten Strategien zur Bewältigung der internationalen Verschuldungskrise
– die Rolle des Europäischen Währungssystems und Vorschläge zu einer europäischen Zentralbank
In Arbeitskreisen wurden diese Grundfragen vertieft und zum Teil provokativ und kontrovers diskutiert.
Den Schlußvortrag hielt Bundeskanzler a.D. Helmut Schmidt zur Rolle der Bundesrepublik Deutschland im Kontext der internationalen Wirtschafts- und Währungsbeziehungen.

1988, 415 S., brosch., 39,- DM, ISBN 3-7890-1651-9
(Edition Dräger-Stiftung ZUKUNFT Band 12)

 NOMOS VERLAGSGESELLSCHAFT
Postfach 610 · 7570 Baden-Baden

Edition Dräger-Stiftung
Zukunft 11
Die Europäische Gemeinschaft in der Weltwirtschaft

Die Europäische Gemeinschaft ist ein wichtiger Faktor in der Weltwirtschaft: Zusammen mit den USA und Japan erarbeitete sie 1985 fast die Hälfte der Weltproduktion. Das »Europa der Zwölf« mit 320 Mio Menschen erwirtschaftet mehr als 60 % des Bruttosozialproduktes der Freien Welt. Die EG ist damit eine der »drei Säulen« der Weltwirt schaft und trägt eine besondere Verantwortung für die Erhaltung und den Ausbau der internationalen Handelsordnung.

»Die Rolle der Europäischen Gemeinschaft in der Weltwirtschaft« war Gegenstand des 6. Malenter Symposions. Wissenschaftler, Politiker, Unternehmer sowie hohe Beamte aus Bonn und Brüssel behandelten und diskutierten dieses Thema unter zahlreichen Aspekten.

Besonders eingehend behandelt wurden

- die Bedeutung des freien Welthandels,
- die Beziehungen der EG zu anderen Industrienationen und
- die Zusammenarbeit der EG mit Ländern der Dritten Welt.

1988, 410 S., brosch., 45,- DM, ISBN 3-7890-1427-3
(Schriftenreihe Edition Dräger-Stiftung, Band 11)

 NOMOS VERLAGSGESELLSCHAFT
Postfach 610 · 7570 Baden-Baden

Edition Dräger Stiftung (Hrsg.)
ZUKUNFT10

Die internationale Verschuldungskrise

Ursachen, Auswirkungen, Lösungsperspektiven

Die internationale Verschuldungskrise ist multikausal. Wesentliche Ursachen sind die beiden Ölpreisschocks von Ende 1973 und 1979/80, zu ehrgeizige Industrialisierungspläne einiger Entwicklungs- und Schwellenländer und ein zu großes Angebot an Kapital auf den internationalen Finanzmärkten. Erstmals weltweit bemerkt wurde die Verschuldungskrise 1982, als Mexiko sich für zahlungsunfähig erklärte. Die gesamten Schulden der Entwicklungsländer (ohne Opec) sind zwischen Ende 1973 und Ende 1985 von 130 auf rund 660 Milliarden US-Dollar angewachsen. Welche Strategien müssen zur Vermeidung neuer Verschuldungskrisen entwickelt werden? Diesen Themenkreis behandelte das 5. Malenter Symposium der Dräger-Stiftung Ende 1985. In- und ausländische Fachleute aus Wissenschaft und Politik, Verwaltung und Wirtschaft haben über Ursachen und Auswirkungen der Verschuldungskrise referiert und Lösungsperspektiven aufgezeigt. Patentrezepte gibt es nicht. Erforderlich ist eine »Politik der kleinen Schritte«. Die internationale Verschuldungskrise mit ihrem Zentrum in Lateinamerika kann dauerhaft nur durch ein beispielhaftes Zusammenwwirken aller Betroffenen gelöst werden:
- Bereitschaft der Schuldnerländer zur Durchführung strenger Anpassungsmaßnahmen zur Stärkung ihres Wachstumspotentials und Schaffung stabiler politischer Verhältnisse sowie einer marktwirtschaftlich ausgerichteten Wirtschaftspolitik
- Bereitschaft der Gläubigerstaaten zur Unterstützung der Entwicklungsländer durch Schaffung günstiger weltwirtschaftlicher Rahmenbedingungen und Leistung weiterer Entwicklungshilfe
- Mittelaufstockung beim IWF
- Umschuldungen von öffentlichen Krediten im Rahmen des Pariser Clubs

1987, 411 S., brosch., 45.- DM, ISBN 3-7890-1426-5
(Edition Dräger-Stiftung - 10)

 NOMOS VERLAGSGESELLSCHAFT
Postfach 610 · 7570 Baden-Baden